1969

[

EDUCATIONAL ISSUES
IN A CHANGING SOCIETY

EDUCATIONAL ISSUES
IN A
CHANGING SOCIETY

Third Edition Revised and Enlarged

Edited by August Kerber
Associate Professor of Educational Sociology
Wayne State University

Wilfred R. Smith
Associate Professor, College of Education
Eastern Michigan University

Wayne State University Press   Detroit   1968

Waynebook No. 3

Preface

It is our hope that this book will be used seriously as a supplement to the main and practical efforts of the professional educator and the interested layman. The book is organized and presented in such a manner as to be encompassed in several readings. It is expected that its best use will be as an informative source book for the problems that the reader will encounter. The book is organized so that a segment may be studied as a fairly complete unit. We have not forgotten that social science is not made up of discrete parts. We therefore allude to implications that make the subjects under discussion relate to one another.

If the reader will do himself justice, he will carefully read the commentaries, transitional writings, and lists of related readings designed to supplement the body of the material. The person who is exploring a problem in depth, of course, will merely take this book as a point of departure. We can only help by making this process mechanically more feasible as space limits are an overriding consideration on a subject of such vast proportions.

We wish to acknowledge the work and helpful advice and criticism (negative and otherwise but always useful) of many colleagues and students. Especially valuable have been the careful perusing, editing, and critical comment of Miss Christine Colditz, staff editor

v

of Wayne State University Press and the thorough, time consuming research done by Joseph Starchler. Many students have done yeoman service as readers and critics.

A. K.

W. S.

Contents

Introduction

The outstanding feature of our modern age is change. Change is so pervasive that it touches the lives of each of us in ways that we are not quite aware, causing problems at all levels and in many directions. Even if we could agree at any particular moment about a policy or philosophy, the next moment would bring differences, because the new "lay of the land" would divide us into new contending camps. Since men find it difficult to agree at any time, change aggravates the general conditions of disagreement, and in fact creates a gigantic problem in itself.

Any of the commonly debated issues of education, for example—the curriculum, have roots in disturbances caused by change, and must take change into account in any forecast of purpose. All the popular and unpopular views, the striving factions, the powerful and the weak, the selfishly interested and the noble, and the various monopolists of truth and excellence make a common head-on struggle. For the school has the task of reconstituting society, and, while educators must listen to all sides and give a hearing to the most ignorant and most fanatic, the school is expected to *do* something.

How do we learn about democracy? We believe that this comes from living and doing. It is necessary, but not sufficient, that we read the Constitution, Declaration of Independence, the speeches of

1

great men, and the history of martyrs. We must learn democracy by living it, and we say this without "tongue-in-cheek," though some mighty and difficult concepts are required in this living. And how can we experience democracy when it is indefinable and, admittedly, has never been attained? We can approach achieving it by grappling with the real problems that smother its idealism and even rob us of the clear deed of heroism, since so much of dull work and cloying uncertainty enshroud it.

The Problem of Education

We do, then, have a purpose: To preserve our democratic society and foster its growth in time of change. To accomplish our purpose, it is needful first to identify the problems of our society. True enough, there are differences of opinion about the nature of the problems, their number, priorities, limitations, and emphases. But the problems are of such scope and inclusiveness that the reader will find meaty argument wherever he turns. If we can stimulate some intelligent concern about those issues, we are satisfied.

We have considered eight broad areas of problems in this book.

Part I: Education Amidst Technological and Social Change. This section explores some of the salient ramifications of the *leitmotif* of change. What is technology doing to us as a society? What can education do, or need to do, about the expanding population? What is mass culture? Does it really exist, to what extent, and what can education do about it? The overview attempted is to see change in its broadest perspective, and set up tenets of responsibility for educators and society to meet the challenge.

Part II: The Purpose of Education. Our schools have the mandate to preserve the democratic society. This is such a broad and elastic concept that most people will interpret it differently. Therein hangs a quarrel. The best we can offer in such a juncture is to open the forum to the most noteworthy, clear, and forceful interpretations. To be culturally literate, we should understand the essential arguments of such main issues and problems as: democracy as a philosophy to be explicated, the political and economic base of our society, the reevaluation of the place of religious doctrines, and the essentials of curriculum, to name a few. Education, as democracy, represents mostly potentiality, but it must encompass a certain broad base of experience to fulfill its promise.

Part III: Equalization of Educational Opportunity. True believers in democracy will agree in principle to the equality of opportunity in education. Variant interpretations then complicate the issue—as to such things as definition, responsibilities, and methods of attaining results.

Part IV: Freedom and Control in Education. Some people revere democracy so much that, like the colonel in *Teahouse of the August Moon*, they want to shoot everyone that will not accede to it. A constant question arises over the demarcation between liberty and license, free speech and incitement, free thought and sedition; and free expression and filth. It is pointed out that along with freedom we have *rights* —and parents can claim their right of protection against an instructor whose attitude is detrimental to their children. Cases where the traditional freedom of individuals is at stake should be judged carefully.

Part V: Financing Public Education. Bertrand Russell said that one of the best ways to determine the strength of a man's belief in something is to observe how much money he will put down on it. Americans show how much they want education in the amount and manner they pay for it. In the first chapter of the section we examine a controversy which is bound to become more heated—the amount, kind, and ramifications of federal aid as seen by authorities of divergent opinions. A second chapter is somewhat more informative and less disputatious. It covers financial needs and disbursements of public schools. In finance, however, there is always a battle, or at least one in the offing.

Part VI: The Assessment of Schools. Obviously, one way of assessing the schools is to get into the classroom, examine the facilities and the staff, the curriculum, school records and other matters as a professional accreditation group would do. In this section, we make a departure and attempt to assess our schools by examining the product, and by comparing our schools with others', particularly Russia's. The rationale is that we need to understand the system by its fruits, and by comparison, so that we can pass judgment on the criteria we have been using.

Our quest is not to level charges and fix blame. We need to examine our youth and judge the evidence as to whether the schools are making good their promise to produce literate, mature, responsible citizens. If we find that the schools operate in a cultural milieu that is dysfunctional, and they are stymied at the outset, we want to know. We want to find out exactly where the schools stand in all the advertised juvenile delinquency, and what can be done by both the schools and society to meliorate the conditions that can be meliorated.

The success of Russia in building its society must be due in part to its schools. The success need not be accepted as the final "proof of the pudding," but it should bring home that human problems in a complex society can be solved. If we flounder and fail to find direction, Russia will certainly overtake and pass us in many important lines. We must, therefore, consider its case and give intelligent heed.

Part VII: The Teaching Profession. If the licensing of teachers were the same as tavern licensing, or civil-service processing of clerks, we would not be unduly concerned about the teacher's professionalization. If, however, teachers stand at the crossroads of our culture, between a past of accelerating change and a future in which the democratic society hangs in the balance, the selection and processing of teachers is crucial. In any event, the recruitment of teachers is a high-level problem in our society and will continue to be. The enlightened professional educators know that the only long-run successful means of getting more teachers is to make their position a truly professional one. The implications of this whole problem touch every child and every parent in the land.

Part VIII: Organizing for Better Schools. Whatever the shape of things to come, it is most important that the school does not have its role imposed on it by society. It must take a position of leadership, making new values for a new age. Whatever the type and organization of the local unit in which the school has its setting, it will have to implement its effects on that level.

Another type of problem which must concern the schools in the future is the whole matter of teaching via mass media and automated devices. Technology introduces opportunities for change, as, for instance, travel, work in offices and laboratories, teaching machines, kits, demonstration devices, TV, tape, and novel buildings and accessories.

If the schools let others experiment and impose changes, as, for instance, canned courses for economy's sake, the schools will lose their chance for experimentalism. Intelligent, guided experimentalism—not galloping empiricism or experiment for the sake of experiment—gives the school opportunities for leadership. Once some leadership is established, the dynamism of the age will make it possible to attain more; success breeds success. Teachers, therefore, should be most interested in the potentialities lying in new information, methodology, and technology.

PART I

EDUCATION AMIDST TECHNOLOGICAL AND SOCIAL CHANGE

Our society is a changing one, and we are all forced to take a basic attitude toward change. It is common to find the point of view that alterations and modifications in the structure of education are not needed, while at the same time all kinds of new technological apparatus are welcomed.

We recognize the interdependence of all the parts of society. This means that education is implicated in technological change, in that the admission of any important invention sets up many different changes in society by cyclical causation. The folkways and mores, the functions of institutions, the demographic and ecological conditions, and the composition of social classes are all modified by the innovation. The invention of gunpowder, the cotton gin, or a new kind of safety pin illustrates this. We hold the belief that society must alter its mode of education to accommodate change. Nevertheless, since our purpose is to give the reader an acquaintance with the problems, we have to take into account the fact that many do not believe this. Their opinions are an essential feature of the whole picture.

Since a change in a man's limbs, so to speak, comes back and affects his head, the conclusion is obvious that we should plan with our head first. Unfortunately it is not that simple. Our society is very complex, and each part can never assess beforehand what its particular reaction is going to be to any change. Even if each man could see clearly how he stood on a certain increase of taxes, for example, he could not tell how his own thoughts and desires would affect the other man. So education cannot direct itself in change, and certainly education cannot direct society with specific programs.

Yet man cannot accept the fate of being helplessly trapped in his own productions and social structure, like Laocoön and his sons. The same thought which initiated the new conditions can shape these conditions, or at least make plans for adjusting to the new eventualities. This is not only a problem of quantities, but of qualities: how to preserve and amplify the values under which we operate.

Mass communication and the mass media have greatly altered the conditions of life. We cannot say whether the totality of these changes is good or bad, but we know that society is in a state of change as never before. We also know that the prime mover is the mass media or, to put it another way, the intended effects are brought about by them. It may be that we are becoming a nation of lotus eaters—bloated, materialistic, cultural Philistines; or it may be there is a steady upward progression of knowledge and taste of the average man. In any case, we know that no general head or purpose oversees the process of communication. Mass communication proceeds like a great monster of many tentacles and ganglia, engulfing everything with a blind force. A state of default exists in the general culture, providing a challenge to education.

The changes brought by technology have caused a bigger, healthier population, great migration and population shifts, and the restructuring and new development of cities. Alterations in our economy have been vast; family life has modified greatly; and schools have added to their functions, taking over many practices of the family and other institutions.

The task of education is to find a purpose for society that makes use of the means and power behind those changes. The culture must "add up" and get meaning from a set of values that all men can adhere to throughout these times of stress. Finally, we must completely face the truth that we cannot dodge the moral responsibility for changes; the making of a better can opener sets off a train of changes that act and react throughout the whole tissue of traditionally founded relations. That man, the individual, and man, in general, get increased power and meaning from these changes is the greatest challenge of education.

We follow in this section with three chapters on areas of cultural change we think significant: (1) the technological revolution, (2) the population explosion, and (3) mass media. These are all interrelated, and yet all three do not cover the whole subject fully. The reader will have to apply his imagination and life experience to draw a complete picture.

I

Education and the Technological Revolution

Editors' Comment

The modern teacher and the public are told over and over again that they must get used to change, be able to adjust, and attain the mental set toward living in the permanent crisis of a cold war. Apparently this means that they should be immediately adaptable to acceptance of new findings that outmode the methods of the moment past. The teachers are persuaded to think, "Wear your hat lightly—the style may be changed at a moment's notice."

The present rate of change has somewhat the effect of a war, in which education is put on a stand by basis, and continual and excessive demands are made on it without its having the privilege of determining the direction of action. The tragedy is not that of education, but of society, which has put itself in this posture of affairs. When society rings hollow, all its agencies become purposeless. The greatest oratory is lost on the ears of an individualistic mass. The appeal to purpose is like trying to substitute an edifice with words.

In such a society as this (which we describe but do not assert yet exists), the attempt to meliorate by means of the school is to push a lever from the wrong end. Society must be moved to define its purpose and crystallize its meanings. The school cannot autonomously initiate the action. To pretend to serve well by ladling out the old warmed-over soup in a time of confusion is only to aggravate the general deterioration.

This is not to say that change in itself is bad. We need mighty changes, and it would be desirable for these to be at a greater rate than now. These changes must be along lines that men can understand as satisfying the needs of the day and serving man in general for a greater tomorrow. Movement, "busy work," a mélange of stimuli, and an avalanche of things only serve to immobilize men in the indecision of thousands of meaningless alternatives. When a crowd is milling around, the good man may be trampled, and his voice is lost in the multitude.

It would be a disservice of education to pretend that it can provide a better life by piecemeal gratifications and enterprises in a whole society that does not add up. It would only be subserving selfish interests and at best could only prolong and deepen the decay of society.

This may seem an overly grim and pessimistic picture. We hope it is, and believe that it is exaggerated. But even so, we think that society in general and education in particular should be alerted to their real social responsibilities, and not stand helpless while the dysfunction of society proceeds with the onslaught of massive change. To this end, we would emphasize some general observations: 1) At all times society, not the schools, is responsible for its deepest problems. 2) If the schools are to serve society well at any time, and crucially in times of change, the schools should be given a clear mandate to inculcate values appropriate for continuing the growth of society. The schools can be the source of leadership and the resource of new values to apply to a new world.

The readings which follow explain some facets of the problems which technological change, expanding population, and mass culture bring to the schools. The reader will notice that despite many astute observations and suggestions, the school cannot do much about these things and prepare the children for such changes, because the school is in the changes like a ship in the gathering sea swell before the storm. To have the sailors scurry about with bits of tackle and rope, or to tell the passengers all about storms is not enough. The ship must be properly fitted for the kind of sea and weather it has to navigate. This it can do with the proper direction applied in time, and by the institutions properly intermeshing their functions.

11

Charles Frankel briefly recapitulates the rate and kinds of historic changes. The acceleration has been increasing of late with blinding speed. He warns that technology has imposed some irreversible emergents in the nature of war, population, and an undiscernible number of unknowns that "changing change" has brought in train. He makes a plea for purpose and control as part of our over-all design for living as delineated by the following excerpt.

THIRD GREAT REVOLUTION OF MANKIND
*Charles Frankel**

. . . Some 25,000 years ago an "Agricultural Revolution" took place which changed man from a nomadic hunter and berry picker into a deliberate cultivator of his food supply. In the latter half of the eighteenth century an "Industrial Revolution" began, with results which we have not yet fully absorbed. Both these revolutions began as changes in the ideas and tools men had used to adjust themselves to nature. They ended by changing men's relations to each other, their moral and political outlooks, and the very substance of the things they thought worth seeking in life. It is easy to overestimate the significance of events that happen in one's own day. But the revolution that has taken shape in the last fifteen years must be put in company like this to be seen in its proper perspective.

Indeed, in the natural energies it has released, and in the speed with which it has done so, the present shift in the relation of man to his environment dwarfs either of its predecessors. It is impossible to believe that its other consequences will not eventually be as great. Now that we have had a chance to absorb the first impact of the sputniks, it may be worth while to sit back and reflect on some of the long-range social issues of which the sputniks are a portent.

We can already see some of the more obvious issues. War, for example, has changed its character and has lost one of its traditional functions in international affairs. Leaving all issues of morality aside, large-scale war can no longer be used, as it has sometimes been used in the past, as an intelligent instrument even of national selfishness. While

* Charles Frankel, "Third Great Revolution of Mankind," *The New York Times Magazine* (February 9, 1958), pp. 11, 70-71, 78. Reprinted by permission.

the danger of all-out nuclear war has not substantially receded, such war can only be an instrument of utter desperation.

Similarly, the problem posed by the expansion of population in the world promises to become even more acute as a result of the advances in medicine and technology that are almost surely in prospect. Through most of its history the human race has had to struggle to keep its numbers from declining. But our very success in improving the basic conditions of human existence now threatens to turn back upon us and to lead to incalculable human suffering unless organized measures are taken to control the birth rate.

But war and the growth of the world's population are relatively familiar problems, even though the penalty for failing to solve them has suddenly become astronomically high. The present revolution in human affairs is likely to bring other changes, however, to which somewhat less attention has been paid. And not the least important is a possible change in the way in which human work will be organized with the advent of new industrial processes such as automation.

One possible consequence of automation, for example, is a sharp increase in the ratio of skilled workers to unskilled workers. This means a host of new issues for industrial unions, and new problems for both labor leaders and industrial managers. Of equal significance is the possible impact of the automatic factory on the way in which the working day may be arranged. As the British engineer Landon Goodman has pointed out, the cost of introducing automation may be so high in many cases that it will be uneconomical to operate a plant only eight hours a day. If many industrial plants are going to find it necessary to operate around the clock, obvious consequences will follow for everything from the nature of home life to the way in which cities are organized. Even the old phrase, "as different as night and day," is likely to lose some of its force.

The new way in which work may be organized also affects the attitudes that men may take toward other parts of life. Most of the work that men have had to do in history has been disagreeable; most of the leisure that men have had has been the prerogative of the few. This fact has colored much of our thinking about the way in which life ought to be lived. The democratically-minded have been suspicious of what is "useless"; the aristocratically-minded have regarded the use-

13

ful as just a bit vulgar. But if leisure becomes everybody's prerogative (and problem), and if automation can be used to make human work less routine and to give more workers the opportunity to exercise their individual skills and discretion, the sharp division between work and leisure will make even less sense than it makes today. The effects will be felt, to take only one example, in our ideals of "liberal" education, which are still primarily leisure-oriented, and in our conception of "vocational" education, which is already anachronistic in its views of what ordinary people need to be "prepared for life."

But the new processes of industrial production are parts of a larger trend which has even deeper implications of its own. During most of the past, developments in technology were largely independent of developments in pure scientific research. To some extent this remained true even in the nineteenth century. But technology has now become almost entirely the child of fundamental theoretical inquiry. This means that we can count in the future on a steady process of technological innovation, and at a steadily more rapid pace.

We come at this point to perhaps the profoundest consequence of the present revolution in human affairs. It is the simple change in the tempo of change. For nothing cuts more quickly or deeply into a society's way of doing things than changes in its technology.

This quickened tempo represents an unprecedented challenge to the human ability to adjust to social change. It took man roughly 475,000 years to arrive at the Agricultural Revolution. It required another 25,000 years to come to the Industrial Revolution. We have arrived at the "Space Age" in a hundred and fifty years—and while we do not know where we go from here, we can be sure that we shall go there fast. Our expectations of change, and the ability of our nervous systems or our social systems to withstand the shock of change, have been formed in the long experience of the race. And this experience, even in the nineteenth century, has not prepared us for the pace of events that lie ahead.

Such an extraordinary change in the basic tempo of human history means that new and deliberate efforts will be needed to control the processes of social change. As the last hundred years of Western history demonstrate, men can learn to change at a much quicker pace than before. But as these same years also suggest, there are limits, and it is

14

difficult to imagine a day when it will not take time for men to adjust to new conditions, to learn new skills and habits, and to get over the nostalgia and resentments that come when old and familiar things are destroyed. There is a conservative in every man and, in the world into which we are moving, he is going to get a harder workout than ever before.

Accordingly, if the things we cherish from the past are not going to be carelessly destroyed, and if the best possibilities of the future are going to be realized, it seems probable that we shall have to have institutions that have been deliberately set up to exercise long-range social forethought. A steady process of technological innovation, for example, can mean recurrent crises of technological unemployment. If this is not to happen, institutions will have to exist to envisage the new skills that will be needed, to undertake the continuing task of retraining workers, and to control the pace at which new techniques are introduced so that we can make a sensible adjustment to them. Given the pace and magnitude of the technical changes that are in prospect, we cannot count on the market place and the price system to do this job alone. Technological innovation means social change; and there is no more reason to introduce such innovations, letting the chips fall where they may, than there is to introduce a new and powerful drug on the market without first making it meet the test of medical examination and control. . . .

Fattu sees the broad picture of the future as one of desperation, with increasing mouths and diminishing resources, unless something is done to make society creative about change. To create the good society of the future, he declares, "a high quality of educational product" is the most indispensable necessity.

EDUCATION AND TECHNOLOGY
Nicholas Fattu*

Investment in the Nation's education is, of course, an investment in the future of its well-being. To those Americans disturbed by the "lag" in United States education it may be quite a surprise to realize that the country's educational accomplishments during the past decade already anticipated even the most liberally conceived tasks of the next. A pioneering effort, *America's Needs and Resources*, by the Twentieth Century Fund attempted to define some of America's potentials and shortages. Educational needs for 1950 were indicated as more students, more teachers and higher pay per teacher. The fund estimated that educational outlays were meeting only 70 percent of the needs of elementary and secondary schools and 50 percent of the needs of colleges. Since then primary and secondary school enrollments have risen 50 percent. The average schooling of the labor force rose from 10.6 years in 1948 to 12 years in 1958—a real investment in the future as the Nation faces the new age of research and automation.

The Country's outlays for education, not including school construction, were 3.1 percent of the gross national product, or 15.5 billion dollars in 1958. During the Sixties the big surge will come in advanced education, which is three times as costly per student as primary or secondary education. What is more, the population of college age will increase 50 per cent by 1970. On the other hand, the baby boom is leveling off. The elementary and secondary school enrollment during the 1960's will increase only 20 percent as against a 50 percent increase during the 1950's. However, as the decade ends, the children born during the baby boom of the 1940's will begin to have children of their

* Nicholas Fattu, "Education and Technology." Unpublished report, Institute of Educational Research, Indiana University (Bloomington, Ind.), pp. 1-3, 9. Reprinted by permission.

16

own, and the enrollment of elementary and secondary schools will begin to rise sharply again.

The problem of numbers is perhaps the least difficult of those facing American education in the years ahead. Much more significant and far more troublesome are the problems that arise out of the context of the direction of world social, economic, and political movements and their impact upon education.

Some of the realities that face all of us increasingly in the future are a world-wide expanding population, and a consequent accelerated diminution of the world's natural resources especially the energy fuels. At the same time more of the world's populations are demanding more of the world's goods. The time is past when people in under-developed countries are satisfied to live a sheer marginal existence. Their wants begin to approximate those of people in the more highly developed parts of the world, and as transportation continues to improve, these wants will tend to become more and more nearly congruent.

It becomes obvious that the solutions of the world's problems that were satisfactory during the past are obsolete for facing the future. An inevitable trend is the increasing technological complexity of our world since it has proved to be the only way that we could meet these problems. . . .

The message of this paper is simply that education for the future must be changed, in some spots, drastically if we are to meet the challenges of the times. During the Sixties we may expect to see emphasis on learning more in the given time; a lengthening of the schooling period for the population, or more higher education for more people; more emphasis in development of the higher mental processes and skills—originality, creativity, problem-solving proficiency, diagnostic skill, inventiveness; and, above all, a constant vigilance to maintain a high quality of educational product imposed by the requirements of our environment and by the competition from the Communist Bloc. . . .

Whatever the reason, the fact is that we hear a great deal about the low level of productivity of education and the need for introducing more tools and technology into the process. Various audio-visual devices such as television, motion pictures, slides, radio, recordings have been suggested as panaceas. Military, business and industrial groups have been developing the technology of teaching machines. These have been

17

suggested lately as means for improving the productivity of education. Educators cannot continue to ignore these complaints by complacently insisting that theirs is the "best of all possible worlds. . . ."

Textbooks on established research areas such as physics or chemistry deal with scientific method in only a cursory way. Their emphasis is on technics and tools. In the present book there is considerable emphasis on methods. This is because the way of approaching a problem is critical in a new area of research, more important than the technics or tools employed. Before OR began to develop its own technics and tools, it was useful because of the power of its approach to problems. As indicated earlier, the reader should always consider each new technic as an aspect of the entire problem, not as a device that is valuable in itself. In this way he will avoid becoming committed to one or a set of technics or tools. An openness of mind about technics together with a broad knowledge of their usefulness and an appreciation of the overall problem are essentials of sound method in science.

As knowledge increases, the difficulty of selecting items to learn increases geometrically. The possibility exists of becoming immobilized in neurotic indecision.

To what extent does the increase of knowledge, and the modern enterprise of building up masses of facts, mean a real increase in knowledge for us, the men in the street? Roger Leatherman poses this question for us in a paper aimed mostly at the question of resources for learning, but it can be applied to our society in general. What is all our knowledge for, and whither do we go?

THE EXPLOSION IN LEARNING AND ITS IMPACT ON INSTRUCTIONAL MATERIALS AND RESOURCES
Roger L. Leatherman*

Everyone is today highly conscious of a major explosion in learning. Before [we] can begin to consider the impact and consequences of this explosion, we must, as in the explosion of an atomic bomb, con-

* Roger L. Leatherman, "The Explosion in Learning and Its Impact on Instructional Materials and Resources." Mimeographed working paper for the ASCD Seminar on a Theory of Instructional Materials (Washington, 1959), 1-3. Reprinted by permission.

sider the nature of many parameters. As heat, radiation, shock waves, altitude of blast, even psychology become necessary fields of concern in studying an atom bomb, the explosion of learning must consider not only the gross quantitative increase in facts about our universe but also the negation of previous understandings and the consequent need for correcting these misunderstandings, while at the same time exploring the many newly uncovered fields of potential human productivity which have lain totally uncultivated throughout human time.

Questions about current subject matter, materials, resources and curriculum rarely take more into account than how to handle the quantitative increase in factual knowledge; yet this aspect is the smallest and least dangerous parameter of the learning explosion. As Peter Drucker has pointed out, it is probably a fallacy to equate this quantitative growth of factual knowledge with a growth in understanding, since it accomplishes, practically, the wholesale confusion of scientists, citizens, and teachers. Ignorance of many fields with their growing specializations, unique languages, etc., leads one rapidly to the understanding of none, for the mental organization of the mass of data from all these areas requires a superhuman ability. Even if we hold that quantitative increases in knowledge have some minor part in the education and we wish to promote growth of this sort, we run immediately into major problems of technique.

We know from simple arithmetic that if we attempt to add more items to an established course or curriculum that amount of time available per unit item decreases. We further know (or should know) that increases in the classroom in quantity of subject matter (beyond fairly small and well-defined limits) will decrease the student's interest and ability to interrelate into pattern these many items, and will definitely be measurable in lowered retention and consequently in both lowered understanding and use. Even should we develop techniques in curriculum planning or subject matter presentation (which we do not now possess) that would make it possible for the student to retain more knowledge from more fields of growing diversity, we may have provided further insurance of intellectual confusion to that student. So we return again from this practical concern with method to the knowledge that we dare not be terribly concerned with increasing the volumetric capacity of students but rather must concern ourselves with the human changes this revolution has brought about. For the real issue in this entire matter is not that an expansion of knowledge has occurred, but that a diminution of understanding has come about in our entire society.

The central hub of this issue is simply that multiplication of knowledge frequently multiplies the alternatives of possible human behavior, yet weakens the rationale for any one selection. A growing knowledge of our universe is therefore associated with a drop in the specific utility of (or necessary dependence upon) any one (or group of) fact(s), and heavier demands are necessarily placed upon means for arriving at social consensus independent of the facts. Said simply, the more facts we possess, the more relative they become in terms of employment—like the child with a penny to spend who unhesitantly spends it if but a single selection is possible but who may spend an hour in front of twenty varieties of penny candy and then leave dissatisfied because he is sure he made the wrong decision.

The consequences of this chronic dilemma are many; all are indexes of the rate of change in knowledge occurring in modern society. Rapid growth of decision-making groups, committees, etc., with diminishing abilities to provide objective reason for the decisions they arrive at, is one of the hallmarks of our time. Determination of human goals by such groups becomes increasingly characterized by a priority—be these goals research achievement, educational achievement, or whatever. No longer can future direction be extrapolated from past research results, for they are too numerous, and no group could finance further research in all areas. It also becomes difficult to say whether one line of endeavor will be more profitable than another. Increasing concern with the possible permutations and combinations of known data along wtih differing opinions of best human directions leaves less time for speculative work on unknown areas. Computer facilities and men alike cheat themselves more each year by spending larger amounts of time and money sorting previously collected data of progressively (through time since collection) questionable validity. This is done of course because of the felt need to find common denominator understanding from mountains of data, but the frequency with which this is in fact the product is very low, and more frequently even more data of a more questionable nature is spawned from the process—that which was intended to solve a human problem has actually intensified the crisis. . . .

In the next selection the author makes the point that the relationship between education and urbanization is "reciprocal and necessary." Urbanization is now preponderant, and the human enterprises of education and city living are conjoined.

URBANIZATION AND EDUCATION
Ranjit Bajwa*

Urban life is a way of living that has changed the values of man from the time when life ways were pre-civilized. Urban life is primarily distinguished from the primitive by greater control of the environment by man. In the words of Green and others,

> The city is a crucial area in which contemporary man is struggling to control his environment for his own improvement and benefit. Although the efforts of various groups in many cities give promise of a better future, too often they are dictated by expediency and seldom is a plan made in terms of the whole need.[1]

Even though it represents an evolution of progress in technology, ethics, and aesthetics, still there is a clear-cut need for "man to control his urban environment in a rational, imaginative, and radical way."[2] Urban life is, furthermore, characterized by greater population, more complex social structure, depersonalization and secondary social contacts, and a dynamic ecological set-up.

On the basic assumption that education is interdependent with all of man's works, the author holds that urbanization and education have many areas of common problems. The task of education is to define and create those qualities which are beneficial and constructive and to point out the factors which are damaging or limiting and impede the qualitative experiences. "Success depends on our ability to create through education an informed, enlightened and dedicated citizenry."[3]

* Ranjit Bajwa, "Urbanization and Education." Unpublished monograph based on a class lecture, Eastern Michigan University, Ypsilanti, Michigan, 1965.

[1] Elizabeth Green et al. (eds.), *Man and the Modern City* (Pittsburgh, Pennsylvania: University of Pittsburgh Press), 1963, p. 1.

[2] *Ibid.*, p. 1.

[3] *Ibid.*, p. 6.

The objective nature of the city consists of the intelligent construction of physical apparatus and transportation areas, engineering life to become more predictable, secure and rational. The basic cause of the city sprang from the development of effective technology and sound social organizations which should contribute to the good life of the common man. The ultimate development of the city will make the whole population city livers. Further development will be along lines of qualitative improvement.

Urban environment is man-made. It increases in complexity as human needs become manifest with increasing arts. The generalization of this development can be described in the increasing use of the natural resources through technology, increasing specialization of human occupation and knowledge, decreasing percentage of knowledge of each man related to the sum of knowledge, and increasing dependence of each man upon society. It can be noticed in the higher levels of needs, i.e. those needs which are less tied to biological fulfillments, however complex the means, and are devoted to *ars gloria artis*, ego aggrandizement and the gratification of ideational and esthetic purposes.

Historically, we can describe cities as mainly going through three phases of development. The first phase was a rationalization of the means of economic subsistence. In this phase human efforts and values were centered around the maximization of the production of wealth. This necessarily implies that work became distilled out as a rational product of man, and human beings themselves became means in a hierarchized value system epitomized by economic goods as the highest values.

The next phase of the city life can be called the ethical phase. It was achieved by historical man after much suffering. He had come to understand that he had sold his birthright for a mess of pottage. Man felt that the productivity of city life was not a sufficient end to justify human cruelty to man; there must, he decided, be certain minimal guarantees given to individual man, so that he would be able to avoid premature death and a body wracked with pain after fourteen hours in the "dark satanic mills." In other words, some statute of limitations guided by a concept of universal justice in the dealings of man-to-man was decided as a moral imperative. In the development of the ethical phase of city life more attention was paid to physical space, sanitation,

22

lighting, food supply, medical aid, housing, transportation, and laws related to working conditions.

Continued growth of civilization in the twentieth century led to the dream of the good life for the common man. This led to a new concept of the nature and ideal of urbanization. The new phase may be described as the aesthetic. Man said it is not enough to subsist and follow minimal laws of justice; each and every man deserves a beautiful life and, in the greater view, subsistence (the necessary physical means) and ethics (the general moral rules) were secondary and subsidiary to the primary purpose of achieving the highest qualities of experience.

Our thesis is that education is the avatar of urbanization. The relationship between education and urbanization is reciprocal and necessary. Man in making himself almost without use of brawn through knowledge and technology is on the threshold of living primarily for the purpose of gratifying his highest needs. These highest needs are dimensions of experience which have clarity and integrity of their separate highest nature, and are made possible by man's having solved the problems of subsistence and ethical human organization. Now man must make an environment which will develop each individual according to his ultimate capacities and in a way which is good both for himself and the society. The dimensions of the problems for education can be described in the differences between the kind of urbanization we have now and that which is technically feasible to provide for the needs of our aesthetic idealism.

The present city has many drawbacks. Some main drawbacks are: it is overcrowded and congested; it is unaesthetic—dirty, unsanitary, noisy, monotonous and lacking in style; it lacks identification and unique artistic constellations that please the aesthetic sense; it has, in an inversely proportional way, a population density and social complexity which accompanies social disorganization, misery, and repetitive monotony; it is economically wasteful and inefficient.

The task of education is to create values and understandings among men so that they will be able to implement urbanization to overcome the obstacles and make cities that are efficient, quiet and beautiful. The assumption that man must live in crowded, dirty cities is a false one. We have the capacity and know-how to make cities beautiful, where each moment of life brings a response of exhilaration and challenge.

An ideal city is no more a dream; it is reality. We need the will and the commitment to implement this reality.

The means for bringing this about can be described as made possible by advances in standardization, communication, transportation, ubiquitous energy resources, and democratization of planning and allocations aided by computer and feedback techniques.

Modern standardization practices make it possible for subassemblies of complicated products to be done in a decentralized organization. This means that large population is no longer necessary in one locale. Communication, becoming fast, universal and cheap, will make it possible for planning and implementation to be carried on according to the dictates of convenience and comfort. Efficiency in the area of transportation makes material and persons free from dictates of traditional time and distance rules. In the words of Lewis Mumford:

> The city in its complete sense, then, is a geographic plexus, an economic organization, and institutional process, a theater of social action, and an esthetic symbol of collective unity. On one hand it is a physical frame for the commonplace domestic and economic activities; on the other, it is a consciously dramatic setting for the more significant actions and the more sublimated urges of a human culture. The city fosters art and *is* art; the city creates the theater and *is* the theater. It is in the city, the city as theater that man's purposive activities are formulated and worked out, through conflicting and cooperating personalities, events, groups, into more significant culminations.[4]

[4] Lewis Mumford, *The Culture of Cities* (New York: Harcourt, Brace and Company), 1938, p. 480.

The ideal institution in our society or in any society is one which complements and supplements the other institutions in distinct, positive ways. Our society would therefore be best aided by one which promotes and achieves democratic values, such as freedom, individuality, responsibility, happiness and integrity of the individual. The family may furnish a means for achieving such values, but such elements as selfish interests, difference of outlook by generation and sex, different associational and habit patterns, and other influences in our complex age may make the family situation onerous. The following article makes a proposal about the modern family to apply to one area of high disorganization in our inner city. We would look upon this proposal not as an "either-or," but one of a variety of feasible social adaptations in a problematic area.

THE EMERGING AMERICAN FAMILY
Paul Sullivan*

The modern American family is best characterized by its diversity. Considering the diversity, it is still possible to describe trends exhibited to a greater or lesser degree in all American families. The pacesetter for the entire aggregation of American families would seem to be the white, urban, middle-class family. This family determines the direction while the greater numbers insure a broad range of subtypes and atypical forms embracing the general middle class family type. Thus, the diversity among American families viewed over time becomes more a diversity in degree rather than a differentiation in kind.

Settling upon the white, middle-class, urban family, it would appear that the salient feature of this family is change. Although this feature is evident, the type of change is difficult to determine. Is the change manifested in this family a structural disintegration, mutation, metamorphosis, or adaptation? Each of these possibilities will be treated.

Operating in a temporal frame of reference, and positing the traditional concept of the family, it would appear that the American family is disintegrating. However, this view depends on the family being abstracted from the conditions in which it exists. The view assumes that

* Paul Sullivan, teacher and graduate student. Unpublished manuscript, WSU, 1967.

25

family as it now exists and has existed, is an absolute of tradition. There would appear to be some disintegration of the traditional concept within the structure of the modern family, but nonetheless, there is extant today an operational structure readily identifiable as the family. (As much internal disintegration as there would appear to be in the family, the family institution shows no signs of disappearing). It does appear that the consanguineal nuclear family structure, is rapidly disappearing from American family patterns. The conjugal family structure however, is still very much in operation and thriving perhaps at the expense of the consanguineal nuclear structure. The view that the family structure is disintegrating is based on a particular definition of family.

That the modern American family is a mutation would seem to have some validity. This view is encouraged by the rapid appearance of the modern family structure. This is to be expected with the rapid advances that have been made in technology. One man's lifetime can easily encompass both Lindbergh's flight and a landing on the moon. The family structure caught up in the acceleration of technology could hardly escape a rapid modification of its structure since it is so directly influenced. Thus, to say the modern family structure is a mutation and imply that the condition is abnormal and undesirable would be to consider an absolute structure and ignore the influence of the present environment.

While a cursory examination of preceding generations will show more similarities than differences in the basic family formation, the differences will appear more in the operation of the family than in its mode of existence. That is, the family has become a consumer rather than a producer; a source of companionship for its members rather than the end toward which its members direct their activities; and part of a more expanded social scheme rather than the absolute core of our society. These are operational qualities. The formal qualities remain essentially unchanged in that marriage for the nurturing and care of children still describes the basic form of the family.

While there may be evidence to posit the argument of a metamorphic change in the family, it is too early to completely validate this since there is doubt as to the present structure being transitional or terminal. The social historian will be better able to view the theory and provide validity.

The last of the four possible types stated earlier is adaptability which is evident in the culture. Adaptability is listed by Ernest W. Burgess in an article published almost 20 years ago as one of six distinctive trends in the American family structure. In addition to adaptability, he enumerated the following trends: urbanization, secularization, instability, specialization, and the trend to companionship. Each of these will be viewed and evaluated in light of what has transpired over 20 years paying special attention to the role played by technology. It would be well to note that adaptability, especially in view of the impact of technology on our society could contain or at least account for all the other characteristics enumerated.

It is the adaptation to the influence of technology that has been responsible for much of change occurring in the American family. The adaptation of the family to the urban life is evident in our society. Urbanization by no means includes only the families living in the metropolitan areas but permeates those in every hamlet of the country. Factories which once clustered in metropolitan areas now are often found in rural areas where the people once isolated from the city now find city people living among them, exerting a cultural influence in the community. The decline of farming as an occupation (less than 9% of the present population) has uprooted many consanguineous nuclear family structures of rural America as employment is sought in industry and away from the farm. Various and efficient means of transportation have encouraged this phenomenon. The rural resident has been brought to the city and the urban resident has by means of the automobile moved to the suburbs which a generation ago was a rural area. Mass media, another product of technology, has served by means of its distinctively urban character to bring the urban values and family structure to the rural areas. It has sought to transform the rural resident who was once a productive consanguineous nuclear family unit into a consumptive conjugal family unit. Social mobility, which serves to foster the destruction of the consanguineous nuclear family unit, is also evident among the rural inhabitants as farms are abandoned along with the tradition of the transference of the farm from generation to generation within the family.

Closely incorporated with urbanization is the trend toward secularization. The control which religion once exercised over numbers of the population has to a large measure succumbed to the force exerted by material comfort (most of which are the products of technology). The "good life" is today defined by the number of laborsaving devices and mechanical contrivances found in the home. Thus relieved of most of the menial tasks necessary to sustain life, as it is understood by our culture, the members of the family are less bound by cooperative effort and are freer to explore their individual potentialities. Values as well as the structure of the modern family have been largely determined in adapting to a structure which can fully partake of the material comforts technology has to offer.

This adaptation considered in view of an advancing technology encourages a certain instability in the family structure. The mounting divorce rate is perhaps an indication of this instability. While this may be a valid assumption, it is reasonable to point out that the relatively small size of the American family (usually two children) leaves many husbands and wives still far from old after the children are raised, and, consequently, marriages entered into for the purpose of child rearing find little reason for continuing after the children have left the home. Furthermore, social mobility on the part of the husband often estranges him from his wife who has been trained only for child-rearing and homemaking. Perhaps, what is needed here is a fresh look at the motivations which prompted the marriage initially. Romantic love and the desire to rear children may no longer be the only valid reasons for a lasting marriage.

Another trend found in the American family is specialization. In the family as in industry, specialization is becoming more evident. Historically, the consanguineous nuclear family supplied housing for the young married couple, lent money to its members, cared for the ill and aged of the family, transmitted cultural heritage, and provided for the socialization of its members. Social services and agencies have largely undertaken these services to the point where the conjugal family is no longer in these ways dependent upon the consanguineous nuclear family. Even within the conjugal family, functions such as education, socialization, and acculturation of the children are performed outside of the family structure to a significant degree. With many of the functions which call for positions of authority among some of the family members being relegated to outside agencies, there has been a relaxing of authority in the family in lieu of a trend to companionship.

A spirit of independence pervades the contemporary conjugal family

28

which often places individual goals and desires over family goals and desires. Economic independence available now to the wife to a significant degree, and to the children to a lesser degree, has a leveling influence upon the authority structure in the family. Individual achievement, independence, and happiness, democratic decisions, and an emphasis on the equality of the individual members of the family have served to loosen rather than tighten the bonds which have traditionally held the family together. The individual lives the members of the family lead away from the home are taking on more importance. Consequently, the brief time during a given day which the family is spacially united functions little to promote group interests.

While what has been described here would seem to be the antithesis of family, the reverse may be true. The contemporary family must be evaluated in light of its ability to function effectively in the society, rather than its ability to conform to the traditional concept of family. From the viewpoint of effective functioning in contemporary American society, the white, urban, middle-class family described here is much more successful than the Appalachian, consanguineous nuclear family. A family does not exist in a vacuum but in a constantly evolving social structure which demands not dissolution of institutions such as the family but modification and adaptation of institutions to the conditions present.

Perhaps this can best be seen in interpreting the child rearing characteristics of the emerging American Family. As was pointed out, emphasis was placed on individual achievement through a relaxation of parental authority. The child is encouraged to realize at least his fullest potential. He is further encouraged to socialize outside of the family, and to seek approval for his actions in the peer group.

In our rapidly changing society which is oriented more toward the future than the present, there is significant danger in dependency. The present is transient and the future unpredictable. For example, the United States Department of Labor states that today's school children will be retrained for jobs three times in their work life. Many of these occupations are unknown today and are yet to emerge in the future, making it impossible to provide now for all the educational requirements. Consequently, preparing a child for independent action is desirable. He alone must cope with the future.

Another characteristic of the society is the present rapid rate of social change which will continue and probably increase in tempo in the future. Such changes serve to alienate one generation from another through a breakdown in communication between the generations. In such rapid advancement, the peer group's approval of actions will better serve the younger generation than that of his family. Finally, social mobility, as well as job mobility and geographic mobility are best weathered by one who from childhood has sought independent action.

The contemporary American family, then, is neither necessarily suitable for all times and all cultures, nor is it a corruption of the traditional family structure; rather it is an institution suited to the particular culture. The emerging American culture places a high premium on technology and the future which in turn demands independent people who are future-oriented toward personal achievement. The emerging American family structure would appear to be answering this need.

Editors' Summary

All the authorities agree in general that change has been of unprecedented magnitude, although undirected and disorganized. The extent and kinds of damage to our society are seen somewhat differently, but there is agreement on a generally negative impression. Still the reader may notice that the tone is one of a complaint about the waste of potentiality, not a pointing to inevitable decline. There is a scarcity of constructive proposals   ·

Change is a cosmic term which can include the switch from sleeves to sleeveless gowns or a movement toward a moral order in the nations of the world. We are unable to evaluate much of the change for lack of information, nor is it of a level of concern. Some changes, however, are of very subtle, complex kinds, in values, folkways, structures, and other high-level abstractions of millions of concrete events and kinds of relationships, and we desperately need more information in order to achieve control.

Control, purpose, and the expansion of the role of intelligence are our goals. Our position is founded on the belief in the power of creative intelligence—that man can create a better life for himself out of confusion and the adamantine clay clinging to his feet. For whether society is relatively stable or agog with movement the basic question remains: Can we change "this sorry world entire," or is it beyond the puny efforts of man to "shape it closer to our hearts desire"?

We have two basic alternatives in metaphysics: 1) the static and 2) the dynamic cosmos. Man has risen above the animals because of his constellations of thought, but at the same time he has most suffered from the tyranny of his order, once established. All social systems, all thought, have an inertia. The most vicious application of thought was the establishment of the conception of the static cosmos. In past times, man has revered his past productions as ultimate perfections, when really they were only parts of a process toward the future. The acceleration of change in many departments of modern life is not, we believe, getting man to see a new truth, or learning a new facet to conjure with. We believe that men are beginning to understand that change is a fundamental condition, an essence which was always here. The modern world of change, therefore, is not one of horrendous free-floating anxiety adrift from all security, but one of bright and happy wakefulness. We are now on the way to using creative intelligence as a tool in a world of flux, but a flux which is alive with potentiality, rising as a paean of progress in the voice of the race.

RELATED READINGS

Allen, Francis R. and others. *Technology and Social Change*. New York: Appleton-Century-Crofts Inc., 1957.

Ball, Daniel. *The End of Ideology*. New York: The Crowell-Collier Publishing Co., Collier Books Edition, 1961.

Berrill, Norman John. *Man's Emerging Mind: Man's Progress Through Time—Trees, Ice, Flood, Atoms and the Universe*. New York: Dodd, Mead, & Co., 1955.

Bloom, Benjamin S. *Stability and Change in Human Characteristics*. New York: John Wiley and Sons, 1964.

Brameld, Theodore. *Cultural Foundations of Education: An Interdisciplinary Exploration*. New York: Harper & Brothers, 1957.

Brookover, Wilbur B., and David Gottlieb. *A Sociology of Education*, Second Ed. New York: American Book Co., 1964.

Burnham, James. *The Managerial Revolution*. New York: The John Day Co., 1949.

Carskadon, Thomas R., and George Soule. *USA in New Dimensions: The Measure and Promise of America's Resources*. New York: The Macmillan Co., 1957.

Clark, Burton. *Educating the Expert Society*. San Francisco: Chandler Publishing Co., 1962.

Fortune Editors in Collaboration with Russell W. Davenport. *USA: The Permanent Revolution*. New York: Prentice-Hall, Inc., 1951.

Goodlad, John L. "Meeting Children Where They Are," *Saturday Review*, Vol. XLVIII, No. 12, March 20, 1965.

Holbrook, Stewart H. *Dreamers of the American Dream*. New York: Doubleday & Co., Inc., 1957.

Shumsky, Abraham, and Rose Mukerji. "From Research Idea to Classroom Practice," *The Elementary School Journal*, Vol. 63, No. 2, November, 1962.

Smith, Adam. *The Wealth of Nations*. New York: Modern Library, Inc., 1937.

Spindler, George D. *The Transmission of American Culture*. Cambridge, Mass.: Harvard University Press, 1960.

United States National Resources Committee, Science Committee. *Technological Trends and National Policy*. Washington, 1937.

Weintraub, David. "Effects of Current and Prospective Technical Developments Upon Capital Formation." Philadelphia: Works Progress Administration, National Research Project, 1939.

White, Lynn, Jr. (ed.). *Frontiers of Knowledge in the Study of Man*. New York: Harper & Brothers, 1956.

II

The Population Explosion

Editors' Comment

The rise of population is commonly considered among laymen to be an indication of progress. The human being is a wonderful entity whose existence is assured both by Eros and the Biblical injunction to be fruitful and multiply. To deprive a human being of his existence (except in an instance such as war) is a universal crime. Why, then, is not the forestalling him of his creation a heinous offense everywhere? It is often considered so, but there is a rising belief that such a measure is good. The reason is that overpopulation has become one of man's big problems.

Population can be treated as a dependent or independent variable. In either case there are drawbacks if we wish to assess the tangled net of cause and effect in education. Inevitably, the way one looks at population, or population and education, is a matter of his value system.

One way to treat the subject of population is to extrapolate the information and forecast the situation sometime in the future. The forecasts can be made either general, applying to the total world population, or precise and apply to only the 25-year-old age group in New England. A number of predictions can be made on an "if-then" basis, that is, first specifying conditions or presumptions and then extrapolating accordingly. This kind of population study, though necessary, will not solve the problem.

The proposals or solutions for population problems depend on the degree of social action the person is willing to take and on the kind of rationale of solution. Some will say that "Nothing can be done, but if it were done, the best course is as follows—." Others will say, "The following measures are essential and must be done!" There are logically several other positions and degrees of concern, of course.

A number of problem areas in education have arisen because of population pressures. Financing has become more critical, because more pupils are attending school longer. The kind of curriculum suitable for a mobile, changing population is subject to much debate. The whole social structure, its classes and themes of success and status, becomes subject to stress, and the school has to take a stand on how the new generation should face its new society. Stresses are created by population pressures which create conditions requiring a reconstitution or transvaluation of values.

Population may not be understood as a single problem, isolated from other problems of society. The desire for more sons and daughters may stand as a very high goal, but that goal is tied to effects which would happen in the society if people have these sons and daughters. The standard of living, the housing situation, the educational institution, industry, recreation, and many more aspects of life would be affected in subtle and unpredictable ways by a great increase of sections of our population. Population has multiple effects on the value system of any society by the principle of cyclical causation. A greater proportion of old people means a larger sale of wheelchairs and fewer baseball bats. Older people will be more conservative in some respects, but will want more pensions and social legislation favoring the old. They will be against increases of school taxes, as compared with younger people who are concerned with their children's education.

A larger population will mean crowding, wastage, erosion, pollution, tangles of utility lines and snarled traffic; more associations, movements, and pluralism will be generated in the culture. More cities will mean cultural lags in development, political structures, boundary lines, and services.

34

In all this the school will be torn and buffeted in many ways, some predictable and some unpredictable. It is most critical that the educational institution does not merely react to effects after they have happened, but act upon the society in ways that are mutually beneficial for the society and the school.

The general problem of overpopulation in the world today, its historical background, causes, characteristics and, most of all its seriousness, is delineated in the following excerpt by Clifford Earle.

In a section not included here, the author opines that voluntary family limitation is the best solution for the immediate future, but he offers little hope that this will do much more than slow down the rate of increase of population. America faces the same general problems of overpopulation with the rest of the world and is also especially concerned with such things as the "color shift" which may alter the position of Western man.

OVERPOPULATION: NEW THREAT TO SURVIVAL
Clifford Earle*

This is a pessimistic report about people. People in the aggregate, that is. There are too many of them, and they are far too enthusiastically obeying God's command to be fruitful and multiply.

A great deal has been said recently about the fantastic rate of population growth in the last generation or so and the incredible increases to come. The seriousness of the situation cannot be overstated.

At the time of the birth of Christ there were probably 350 million people on this planet. In the centuries before Christ the annual rate of population increase was about four per 100,000, and the rate did not rise much for several centuries following his coming. The world's population was in the neighborhood of 500 million in 1700 .

Then the rate began to go up, and population zoomed, thanks largely to the rise of modern medicine. The number reached the 1 bil-

* Clifford Earle, "Overpopulation: New Threat to Survival," *Presbyterian Life* (May 1, 1959), pp. 6-8. Reprinted by permission.

lion mark around 1820, rose to 2 billion in the late 1920's, and will pass 3 billion in 1962. The figure at the present moment is about 2.8 billion.

Dr. Pascal K. Whelpton, dean of America's demographers, shows that if the annual increment of the last century had been the rate of population rise from the time of the birth of Christ until now, there would be a million persons on this planet for every one now living. Indeed, if the rate of growth during the first thirty years of this century—which was only eight per thousand and per year—had been the prevailing rate since the beginning of the Christian era, there would be 8 million persons for every one person now alive.

Now take a deep breath and read on. If the present rate of world population growth—over 1.5 percent per year—continues unabated for the next six or seven hundred years, there will be standing room only—about ten square feet of land area for every living person.

Let us look at what will happen in the next decade or two or three. These are the years of accountability for us and our children.

The best sources of information are the population reports and estimates issued annually by the United Nations. According to the UN experts, the population of the planet will grow to 4 billion in less than twenty years, to 5 billion in about thirty years, and to well over 6 billion by the end of the century. These are medium estimates which assume a general decline in birth rates around the world after 1975.

The earth's population increased by 90 million in 1957 and 1958—a number equivalent to the population of Japan. In the next two years, the increase will be 100 million. Every two seconds there is a net gain of three persons in world population. In the brief time (about a minute and a half) you have so far devoted to reading this article, some 360 babies have been born and nearly 240 persons have died with a resulting increase of about 120 in the number of people living on our planet.

The experts remind us that the rate of increase is not the same in all parts of the world. It is much higher in the relatively underdeveloped areas than in the industrialized countries of the West. The Latin Americas are growing four times as fast, and East Asia more than three times as fast, as the countries of Northwest Europe. Ceylon,

Taiwan, and Malaya; Paraguay, Costa Rica, Colombia, and Mexico; Turkey and Syria—these countries have reached or are approaching a rate of growth which means a doubling of population in less than 25 years. This rate is nearly twice that of the fastest growing countries of the industrialized West.

To get the whole picture, it is important to realize that the "color ratio" is undergoing a dramatic shift. Right now the proportion of white to nonwhite in the world's population is one to two (one third white; two thirds nonwhite). At the end of this century, only forty-one years from now, the ratio will be 1 to 4 (one fifth white; four fifths nonwhite). Perhaps by that time, men everywhere will accept the idea that "color" is an irrelevant category in measuring the worth of persons.

At first glance it would seem that the population explosion is related somehow to a sudden increase in human fertility, but this is not the case at all. It is due to a dramatic decline in death rates. The population curve turned sharply upward with the development of medical science and public health, especially since 1850. Babies lived where their predecessors had died, and people generally lived longer and longer. When this happens without a corresponding decrease in birth rates, the population mushrooms.

The former high death rates were largely the result of diseases and epidemics which have now been brought under control. War has been a factor—an important one in countries overrun by prolonged bloodshed. Several million persons lost their lives in the Thirty Years' War in Central Europe in the 17th century. The Taiping Rebellion in China a century ago brought about the death of between 25 and 50 million people in a span of fifteen years or so. But on the whole, the great deterrent in generations past has been disease. Now this scourge has been reduced, and boom goes the population.

The reduction in death rates has been most revolutionary in the less developed parts of the world, especially in the last twenty years. In Ceylon, for example, the rate fell 34 percent in a single notable year and 70 percent in ten years. In a single decade, Puerto Rico showed a decline of 82 percent, Mexico a drop of 43 percent. New lows in death rates were achieved in 1957 and 1958 in several areas with previously high mortality. And all the time fertility continues at a high rate in those parts of the world where most of the people live and where economic development is least advanced.

It should be noted that the miraculous modern means for reducing death rates (antibiotics, new insecticides, public health programs) did not originate in the less developed countries where they have produced such startling results. Christian missionaries from the West were among the first to spread the new knowledge. Private programs such as those sponsored by the Rockefeller Foundation in the field of public health have had far-reaching effects. And now a variety of international and governmental organizations bring medical services to the remotest villages of Asia, Africa, and Latin America.

World-wide campaigns to eliminate malaria and to reduce to a minimum the incidence of yaws, two rampant debilitating diseases of the tropics, are having their repercussions. Another factor of vast importance is the continuing improvement of maternal and child care facilities, with resulting reductions in infant mortality.

Here, in these mounting assaults upon disease, is the key to the population explosion. It is ironic that man's efforts to conquer pain and death should give rise to some of the most serious and dangerous problems the human race has ever faced.

One of the problems raised by the population explosion is the question of food. Can the earth nourish a much greater number of people than are now living?

A few years ago many of the experts were considerably worried about the immediate future. The issue of the earth's ability to feed even the people then living was ably discussed in *Road to Survival,* by William Vogt (an authority on conservation and land usage), published in 1948. The problem is still regarded as serious, but today's agronomists believe that this old planet has capacity to take care of a population several times the number of people now living—if only we treat it kindly and use its resources wisely.

. . . .

Another problem raised by the population explosion is the effect upon living standards in the less developed parts of the world.

In many countries of Asia, Africa, and Latin America, population increases are so high that economic development can hardly keep pace. In spite of prodigious advances, the gap between living standards in these areas and living standards in the industrialized West is widening rather than diminishing. This is particularly true when the comparison is between the United States and almost any one of the newly developing nations.

. . . .

What is the solution? Such approaches as economic aid, food production, and education deal only with the side issues. The main problem is how to control this upsurge of population.

An answer has to be found—and soon—but at present no solution has been offered by anybody that is at once reasonable and acceptable.

Simply because there are more people in the world than ever we probably have more misery than ever in human history, because most of the people are "have nots" and they are outbreeding the "haves." The authors of the following article suggest that a new approach to education and technology can swiftly bring a quantum change in the lives of the "have nots," and without sacrifice on the part of the "haves." The argument is that human knowledge and power has achieved a breakthrough, and it is not only scientifically feasible but morally imperative that we implement this breakthrough in the greatest of human problems.

OPERATION BREAKTHROUGH: A PLAN FOR AUTOMATING HUMAN PROGRESS
Ranjit S. Bajwa and Wilfred R. Smith

Since World War II the world has moved swiftly in many ways toward implementing a dream of mankind several thousand years old—the unity of man. This is seen in the rising levels of aspiration of the common man in the undeveloped areas of the world, the pervasion of mass media, the explosion of knowledge with all sharing in it, the breaking off of colonial and other forms of exploitation with the emergence of new nations, and the evolution of qualitatively rather than quantitatively based concepts in judging fellow man. In this present phase, the U.S. has been forced to take, or is taking, willy nilly, a crucial role.

The history of man hitherto has largely been one of the development of groups in two dimensional space, with limited, slow-moving technology and population. The dialectic of communication in those two most basic areas—man in relation to man, and man in relation to nature —was settled by slow, traditional conflicts within the in-group, and occasional, relatively light wars with the out-group.

The communication of man has burst the bonds of this ancient dialectic, in which each man hoed his two-by-four garden and repeated rituals of greetings with his neighbors. He has no ground of his own in the ancient sense and, in terms of greeting neighbors, even the definition of neighbor suffers a change in the very process of action and reaction. He has finally come to realize that his fate as man is not tied to ancient formula and outworn form, but in the dialectic, or act of communication itself. "Each man writes his name before God" the old theologian said. This expresses the idea. We are all in the act of communicating at all times, insofar as we are human. (Disregarding, of course, sleep, infancy, sickness, etc.) Whether we dig in the ground, wear a feather in our hat, or sell a thousand shares of A.T. and T., we are "writing our name." We live in the acting; acting has supplanted Being. Our acting has an inescapable moral component, because it affects the lives of others, in that it affects their communication. We communicate with sticks and stones we put together, with noises from our faces, with budgets in Washington and Moscow, with symbols on paper we place in front of natives in Africa; and with locked doors, Berlin walls, our art, our lives, and the purposes we emblazon in summit meetings.

This communication can be noticed in the movements of words and symbols, in the observations of each other's arsenals and laboratories, and in the movement of men and materials. The irreversible forces, and things, and ideas that men have achieved are pushing us forward into a New world, and evidently man is not quite ready. We have let the genie out of the bottle, and we are not sure whether he will be our servant or destroy us.

We hope to suggest some ways that man can bring to a head this enormous accession of power. It is our belief that it can be done with existing frameworks, and existing human resources and knowledge, intelligently directed upon our major human problems.

The world can roughly be divided into the "haves" and the "have nots": those who have at least a minimum of the necessary goods for subsistence, and those who do not. A more precise gradation is in terms of the horsepower that various countries utilize. Norway, Canada and the U.S.A. utilize about 20,000 mechanical horsepower per capita per year in producing their goods and services. The U.S.S.R., Japan, Denmark, and Puerto Rico use about half as much. Angola, India, Thailand, Nigeria, and Sierra Leone utilize about 250 mechanical horsepower per year in economic production.*

The production of the United States is an often told story. With 5 percent of the population, we produce half the world's factory production. We have 40 percent of the world's income. We can produce a pound of wheat, flour, bread, butter, cheese, potatoes, lard, sugar, and one dozen eggs in less than an eighth the time it takes in the Soviet Union. The rate of increase of our production is so great that, if the present rate continues, by about year 2000 we shall produce in a 7-hour day what now takes us a 40-hour week.

We therefore understandably talk about "our" production, "our" wealth and technology, and not illogically follow it at times with talk of the "white man's burden" and "sharing the wealth" with our more unfortunate "little brown brothers." This is a great misconception.

We do not have a proprietorship, a God-given and exclusive right to getting things out of the ground and fabricating them, any more than we own our bodies, our children's bodies, the sunlight or morning dew. We act in certain effective, publicly replicable, and teachable ways upon nature, and nature gives us back our deserts in an inexorably measured way—and plays no favorites to any who use the same ways.

The technological genie is not peculiarly our slave. Technological progress is possible for all people who use this system. A great and obvious human mission is that we teach those who have poor technologies, who use animals and human brawn, to use solar, nuclear, hydro, thermal, wind, wave, and other kinds of power. It is a mission because

* Faculty of Engineering, Brace Research Institute, "Energy as a Major Factor in Man's Development," Technical Report No. T 11, March, 1964, McGill University, Montreal.

41

we can clearly comprehend how much human suffering we can over-come, and how much progress we can make in the world by spending our energy along these lines. We do not have to be taught the human sympathy which generates the mission, but it may take some reflection to see that teaching the technology is a national good.

The teaching of technology to build a higher standard of living need entail no sacrifice. Sacrifice means that the world would somehow lose in production if we take time off to teach the Indians how to make a hydroelectric plant. An initial dip in total world resources possibly could occur if our technicians moved en masse to India. This would not need to affect the income of technicians involved with the project: they would continue to get a commensurate salary. But after a plant is established, where none has been before, it could add to the world's output of power probably at a cheaper capital outlay than in developed countries. The old factory which technicians had left could soon be put back into full swing. And, as it could be funded on a credit system, those who put out the capital could receive it back with interest. In other words, by a modern magic far exceeding the legerdemain of me-dieval wizards, we would get something for nothing. Better still, the something could go on to increase as long as we all used the cornu-copia of science. With the institution of the requisite system, capital could quickly be reproduced ten times over, and would never be lost. The key to the new magic is education. The new technicians in India who would run the factories, who had once used animals and hand tools, would now be prepared to continue to run a factory.

A little imagination could suggest how plans and projects of teach-ing the technology could increase in variety and efficiency after the initial stages. With programmed-learning devices and computer sys-tems which set up the kinds of research most profitable for given so-cieties, the underdeveloped countries could rapidly move to a level of technological proficiency competitive with ours—with mutual benefit in the course of development. Again, the key to progress would be edu-cation—but we suggest an automated education. This would be pos-sible because a large proportion of the intelligent adults of the world in the "have not" nations could learn techniques in a relatively short time.

The argument that this would be too big a job is based on some misunderstandings related to past experience, and to certain axioms in social science. Past experience relates to piddling projects in which man attempts almost single-handedly to bring medicine to a whole region, or campaigns toward getting the natives to wear trousers and go through the Christian liturgy. Imagine a well-equipped team that goes into a tropical region where malaria, internecine strife, and a stone-age technology is keeping the natives in low population and poor health. The general relativistic concept that each culture is a "unique, equally rational, coeval phenomenon" and we therefore have no "right" to impose our values onto these wretched natives is largely a rationalization and a misinterpretation. Wiping out malaria we might say, is wrong, because it is "part of their culture." But if we did wipe out malaria, few of the natives would care to go back to the old conditions. There would be nevertheless, many valuable parts of such a culture which would be good for them and us to preserve. In other words, we cannot evade our mission to bring technology to the rest of the world by rationalizing a lack of responsibility with the shibboleth of cultural relativism. We could agree, perhaps, that an adult has a perfect right to his low standard of living. Can we therefore accept congenital blindness and ten times our mortality rate for the children? The new world of united mankind cannot go along with such barbarous notions.

When we look at the state of the world today and assess the various liabilities, the most obvious charge to be made for *cause* is the lack of education. The overpopulation, sickness, exploitation, the superstition, ignorance, and inhumanity of man-to-man would be eradicated if all men were educated upward to a sufficiently high level. This statement would be naive and tautological if it were left there. Everyone would agree, and say the statement is therefore meaningless. A sophisticated communist would point out that the two of us have different views of education, and he would say that therefore all plans we make would come into ideological clash, or would at best peter out in academic contention.

But things have been changing so much that this position is no longer valid. The axiom that "human nature" or "history" or some other semantic bug-a-boo will obviate our best-laid plans is incorrect because it is obsolete. It is based on a wisdom relevant to the past. The great truth is that the dynamisms of the age have swept away the truths of yesterday. We are not in an age of change—*we are in an age of changing change.* We have a reservoir of ideas and a horsepower actually at hand that are indeed working on the hearts and minds of man, but the "cliché curtain" of outworn shibboleths has made us unable to see the reality which is here.

Right now, man is changing fast in his norms and immaterial culture. The reason for this in its simplest statement is that the material and immaterial aspects of culture are inextricably tied together and, whether any one man jack or all fully knows it, the cornucopia of plenty has transmuted him ineluctably in the direction of the rising level of aspirations.

Let us then set up a program of international education according to a priority of needs. Those countries which are most in need and most undeveloped—*have the greatest need for education*—we would plan most to help. The structures, associations, personnel, and budgets that would go into this could be safely left to on-going planning by developed countries and interested bodies as long as the general principles were accepted.

By utilizing intelligence in dealing with this thorny nest of problems we could do much with an educational program.

We could give subsidies and scholarships in many ways and for many people, but in every case what we would do would be aimed at some aspect of the life of Indians to make them more educated. We assume that this term "education" means non-acceptance of the need for, or belief in, the depriving and dehumanizing aspects of Indian life which have been afflicting hundreds of millions for thousands of years. Several lines of approach we could utilize are:

1. Health and medical education. Corps of medical, sanitation, physical fitness and recreational guidance people would be needed. Doctors would learn medicine in the U.S. and elsewhere, and would contract to spend a minimum number of years in a project in India, but at a good salary. The doctor, nurse, nutritionist, teacher, employer, and mother and father would be working together in a planned program, with feedback, continuity, and integration.

2. Home arts, avocations, and self-help activities. The level of proficiency and usefulness of a person depends to a large extent on how he can utilize and enjoy the many arts and traits that man has invented to make life more worthwhile.

44

3. The meaning of plants made by investment capital requires technicians and engineers who can train the laborers, upgrade them, provide maintenance, and build in future investment in a step-by-step program of planned progress.

4. Intergroup and community planning.

5. Teachers and educators in formal education.

These five mentioned programs are suggestive. Any one or all, or a project much different in detail, could be instituted. But the important point to be kept in view is that it is now morally necessary and technically feasible to spread education—true education—to the whole human race. It is not only possible to provide this technically feasible education, but we think it can be done with unbelievable swiftness, and without sacrifice to the individuals involved.

Editors' Summary

The purpose of this chapter, which guided our selection of articles, is to show the causal relationship among culture, population, and school problems. The relationship is a far-reaching, pervasive, and cyclical one, and few solutions have been proposed at the school or governmental level. Nevertheless, the widest amount of information on the extent of the problem, especially among teachers, school administrators, government officers, and people in authority, is desirable so that implementations can be stimulated at every level.

The Bible says: "The poor ye shall ever have with you." This is often used to argue that blind, impersonal, and uncontrollable forces dictate the ways of man and nations. If this were so, there would seem to be an incubus of futility weighing upon all human planning. Why plan in America when the cosmic crystal ball ordains the inundation of the teeming millions of Asia? Why design a school in District 26 when we do not know what children or the district are going to be like ten years hence? Why deal with automation, interest rates, career counseling, farming problems, the International Geophysical Year, and nuclear fission when the pressure of population alters the situation and shifts the areas of real problems and concern with an inexorable mandate? The conclusion is obvious: Man must bring population under control if he is to master his destiny.

What can education do? The answer lies in the study and creation of values. No blueprint can be given, because the nature of this kind of direction is the conscious commitment to obsolescence of blueprints. The significant factor is one of attitude.

Although no determinative solution can be given, education can take a definite position because our democratic values dictate certain lines of attack.

1) More information is needed by all members and organizations of our society. Some problems can be solved by information alone. Some become illuminated, a necessary first step to solution.

2) Implementation of solution must be attempted at all levels and by democratic procedures.

3) The educational institution can furnish guidance by informing, deriving, selecting, and creating those values which truly serve greater social progress.

RELATED READINGS

Bagdikian, B. H. *In the Midst of Plenty: The Poor in America.* Boston: Beacon Press, 1964.

Bartky, John A. *Social Issues in Public Education.* Boston: Houghton Mifflin Co., 1963.

Brownell, Samuel M. "Pressing Problems in American Education—A Graphic Presentation," *School Life,* XXXVI (May, 1954), 120-22, 126-27.

Burns, E. M. *The American Social Security System.* Boston: Houghton Mifflin Co., 1949.

Drophin, Stan, Harold Full, and Ernest Schwarcz, *Contemporary American Education: An Anthology of Issues, Problems, Challenges.* New York: Macmillan Co., 1965.

Drucker, Peter F. *America's Next Twenty Years.* New York: Harper & Brothers, 1955.

Dublin, Louis X., and Mortimer Spiegelman. *The Facts of Life.* New York: The Macmillan Co., 1951.

Ehlers and Lee. *Crucial Issues in Education* (3rd Ed.) New York: Holt, Rinehart and Winston.

Fund for the Advancement of Education. *Teachers for Tomorrow.* Bulletin No. 2. New York: The Fund for the Advancement of Education, 1955.

Ginzberg, Eli (ed.). The Nation's Children. 4 Vols. New York: Columbia University Press, 1960.

Halsey, A. H., Jean Floud, and C. Arnold Anderson (eds.). *Education, Economy, and Society.* Glencoe, Illinois: Free Press, 1961.

Hertzler, Joyce Oramel. *The Crisis in World Population: A Sociological Examination with Special Reference to the Underdeveloped Areas.* Lincoln, Neb.: The University of Nebraska Press, 1956.

Herzog, Elizabeth. Children of Working Mothers, U.S. Children's Bureau. Washington, D.C.: USGPO 254.

Landis, Paul H. *Population Problems: A Cultural Interpretation.* 2nd Edition. New York: American Book Company, 1954.

Miller, Henry. "New York City's Puerto Rican Pupils: A Problem in Acculturation," *School and Society,* LXXVI (1952), 129-32.

Ruml, Beardsley, and Sidney G. Tickton. *Teaching Salaries Then and Now: A 50 Year Comparison with Other Occupations and Industries.* Bulletin No. 1. New York: The Fund for the Advancement of Education, 1955.

Seeley, John R., R. A. Sim, and E. W. Loosley. *Crestwood Heights: A Study of the Culture of Suburban Life.* New York: John Wiley and Sons, 1963.

Simpson, Hoke S. (ed.). *The Changing American Population.* New York: Institute of Life Insurance, 1962.

Snow, C. P. *The Two Cultures and the Scientific Revolution.* Cambridge University, 1960.

Thompson, Ronald B. *Estimating College Age Population Trends 1940-1970.* Columbus, Ohio: American Association of College Registrars and Admissions Officers, 1953.

Thompson, Warren S. *Population Problems.* New York: McGraw-Hill Book Co., 1953.

Woytinsky, W. S., and E. S. Woytinsky. *World Commerce and Government: Trends and Outlook.* New York: Twentieth Century Fund, 1955.

47

III

Mass Culture and Education:
The Communication Explosion

I HAVE A SPLENDOR IN MY EYE

There's a little story that I've wanted to share with you since the first day of class, but I just didn't know if anyone would be as moved by it as I was.

It happened two years ago in Peninsula. I was coming home from College one day, it was during early October when Indian Summer set every living thing aflame with color and vitality that almost becomes unbearable. The time was about 5:45 P.M. and most of the children had disappeared from the streets to their warm homes and warm suppers and warm beds. I was feeling peaceful and pleasantly tired and then I saw him. A little boy, about five years old with dungarees and little brown shoes and a t-shirt on, all alone, walking slowly and kicking leaves from his path. He had one arm half up-in-the-air and some green paper play money, in his hand and he was chanting softly "Money for sale, money for sale." The sight of that solemn little boy trying to *sell* money, with no conception of its bloated values or the struggles of his parents for it, or the fact that so many people today can think of nothing that could be exchanged for it, reasonably, just hit me with a load of loneliness and longing for the days when anything—a frog or a pretty stone or a cracked marble or a rusty jackknife—was more important than a picture of an old dead president on green paper.

—Dianne Tyrrell

Editors' Comment

Man becomes human by communication, by using the symbol in exchange with his fellows. All thinking, all motivation in man is possible through socialization, or the humanizing process. All normal human beings—excluding brain-damaged individuals—can be socialized. It follows that means which enable man to communicate more rapidly and with greater variety of content would make man more human. This general assumption cannot be granted without qualification. Many empires have fallen when communication has been much extended. There is no assurance that rubbing elbows in the pit with other groundlings will make us wittier, wiser, or more charming.

Mass media—printing, signs, radio, TV, and other mechanical devices for broadcasting symbols to humanity—have been enormously extended in the past hundred years in America. Television, becoming popular in the early fifties, is virtually a universal experience with our children. Most of the modern generation cannot imagine what society would be like without mass media and other modern means of mobility. It would be worthwhile for them to imagine such a primitive society. In such a life without mass media, people would become captives of local interest, and their sphere of experience would minify to people and things within a day's walk. They would become ignorant of the outside world and inclined to suspicion and hostility in relation to it. Language, folkways, and mores would be fixed into provincial patterns. Potentially at least, mass media offer advantages: they can offer unification, by which the group solidifies and strengthens its "we-ness" or social cohesion; they can standardize the practice and understanding of the same social pattern; they can provide the means of communication to facilitate this basic social process, giving advantage to the individual in citizenship, economics, and personal satisfaction; they can provide educational mobility, giving all men "windows on the world" so that all the ideas, events, and trends of men are brought to our awareness; and, finally, they can aid in education by extending in chronological length and breadth the process of cultural transmission to each of us. These advantages may be offset by threats. Social control may be usurped by monolithic states or selfish groups within the larger group. Propaganda and other methods of persuasion may monopolize the channels of mass media so that the people fail to achieve the five potentialities aforementioned. Lastly, a softening, lowering, cheapening, and basically dehumanizing effect may result from the dependence upon the means as ends in themselves. For example, instead of using TV as a means of information, a useful extension of our senses, we can give up all creative activity and useful purpose in the evening, and devote ourselves to watching the "Evil Eye" of our living room in a state of semitrance.

Sociologists like Herbert Blumer have pointed out that the mass media, in our American society at least, have created a new culture. This is the culture of the anonymous street-corner man, removed from his traditional bonds of patterns and institutions, and seeking his cultural directions in the neon signs, the store windows, the TV programs, and the "news" transmitted minute by minute to the detached mass of individuals in the passing parade of the street. By watching each other and the newest ads, these individuals know what the "latest" is, what names, jargon, mannerisms, consumer products, and belief systems are most valued. It is a synthetic, parasitic culture, but a nevertheless existent one which has the latent power to take over completely.

A momentous question is the stand of education on mass culture. All are agreed that we must use modern technology and the mass media to provide for better learning experiences for our children. Unfortunately, there is little of constructive planning, or even awareness of the role education may take in using mass media to improve our society.

50

BERNARD ROSENBERG

In the selection below, although Bernard Rosenberg fails to delineate clearly what mass culture is, he is quite explicit about what it is not. It is not an American innovation, not inspired by capitalism, and not a new democracy. Rosenberg thinks that mass culture is a definite reality on our modern scene, and he feels it is a negative influence. "Kitsch [a German term for cheapened culture] is institutionalized, and we are robbed of our spontaneity," he pronounces.

MASS CULTURE IN AMERICA
Bernard Rosenberg*

. . . Quite often the most "popular" teachers in our universities are those who simplify their material, make it look simple, and thereby foster the illusion that a challenging body of knowledge can be easily assimilated. This is catch-phrase pedagogy: Plato was an Idealist, Aristotle a Realist, Kant a Dialectician. All you need is a label, and every field has its Will Durant who will retail it for you. No discipline, however exacting, is insusceptible to this treatment. So, though we never really come to grips with philosophy this way, the dangerous belief that we have fully embraced it nevertheless persists. A true teacher will say, "No, there is so much more within your reach—only you must stretch yourself to find it." Such an attitude is frequently dismissed as snobbery, an egghead affectation, an expression of contempt for the ordinary man. It may be just the opposite, if we say to the *l'homme moyen sensuel*, "Here is what many of you could do. Why settle for so much less? What you consume now may please you for the moment; sub-art and pseudo-knowledge is shoveled down your open mouth; in another moment it will leave you ravenous and restless once again." As *kitsch* is institutionalized and we are robbed of our spontaneity, the likelihood of satisfaction, of tension followed by distension, gets to be more and more remote. Culturally, we become hungrier than ever—and our diet, though habit-forming, contains less nourishment than ever.

Success is still the bitch-goddess of American society. The purveyors of mass culture allege that it too can be achieved by passive absorption.

* Bernard Rosenberg and David Manning White (eds.), *Mass Cultures: The Popular Arts in America* (Glencoe, Ill., 1957), pp. 9-10, 11-12. Reprinted by permission of the Free Press, Glencoe, Illinois.

Simple rules are set forth in every sphere of activity. This is the significance of what Dwight Macdonald has called "how-to-ism." Surely any of our ancestors would have been bewildered by the library of contemporary books devoted to telling people how they should consummate the sex act—successfully.

. . . .

No effort to comprehend and evaluate mass culture can start anywhere else than in a large sociocultural context. From such a standpoint we may clear the air of certain obviously erroneous assumptions:

1. *Capitalism is responsible for mass culture*. Not at all. It flourishes wherever the appropriate technological apparatus emerges, whether slowly or suddenly, and nowhere more so than in Soviet Russia which, whatever else it is, cannot be considered capitalist. A strong case could be made for pinpointing the most malignant features of mass culture where music, art, and ideas are publicly expressed only if they conform with a dictator's infantile conception of music, art, and ideas. In this realm, capitalist America has lost its leadership to the communist world. We are no longer the pacesetters. The view that we are is parochial. A cross-mass-cultural survey would dispel it.

2. *America is responsible for mass culture*. Hardly, and for the same reason. There is nothing in our national character that makes us peculiarly vulnerable to a condition that is sweeping the earth.

3. *Democracy is responsible for mass culture*. Tocqueville was perhaps the first to make this common mistake. It was shared by democrats who thought that vulgarity through leveling was the price that had to be paid for an otherwise beneficial system, and antidemocrats who thought the price too high.

If one can hazard a single positive formulation (in the form of a hypothesis) it would be that modern technology is the necessary and sufficient cause of mass culture. Neither national character nor the economic arrangement nor the political system has any final bearing on this question. All that really matters is the most recent industrial revolution.

The tentative technological determinism implicit in this formulation may be valid only for the present. *Today*, wherever modern tools are introduced and superimposed on any culture, the mixture seems to be deadly. Differences between backward and advanced countries become attenuated. They meet at the same low level. Maybe at a higher stage of development, society will be "ready" for industrialization, with consequences very different from those we see all around us in the here and now. Meanwhile, change, followed by barbarous accommodation, proceeds at an accelerated tempo.

The author of the next selection agrees with the Spaniard, Ortega y Gasset, whom he quotes elsewhere in the same article: "The characteristic of the hour is that the commonplace mind, knowing itself to be commonplace, has the assurance to proclaim the rights of the commonplace and impose them wherever it will." The fine arts and the atmosphere of free thinking, says Alan Valentine, are not a separated and specialized product of a few elite. According to him, these come from some "deep common inspiration" which is general throughout the culture. He sees our current culture suffering from "spiritual myopia" which touches all parts. Conformity is something akin to religion; and the threat is the extinction of the great values of our culture.

THE AGE OF CONFORMITY
*Alan Valentine**

. . . It is probably the atmosphere and values of a society, more than its standard of material living, that lift or degrade its culture and inspire or discourage its artists. The Elizabethan Age in England, the Renaissance in Italy, the rise of the Republic in the Netherlands were all periods when their societies had a vitality of spirit and a clarity of aim—an atmosphere of values—which found dual expression in material prosperity and in cultural achievement. Artists, thinkers, adventurers, artisans, men of commerce and princes all felt the stimulus of that atmosphere and rose to new heights in their respective spheres. Art and thought may not then have flourished because wealth flourished; they may all have been the equal fruits of some deep common inspiration. The man of rare creative talent is more stimulated by the

* Alan Valentine, *The Age of Conformity* (Chicago, 1954), pp. 98-99, 102-103. Reprinted by permission of Henry Regnery Company, Chicago, Illinois. Copyright, 1954.

sense that society values him and his work than by a high standard of living. Conversely, a society that prefers mechanical perfection to great art, or that cannot distinguish the superior from the mediocre in thought and ethics, is a greater enemy to creative genius than poverty can be. Talented scientists are stimulated today by the knowledge that society esteems them, but talented humanists are less creative because they feel less appreciated.

.   .   .   .

In private social life informality has paradoxically become conventional, and carelessness of manners has been elevated to a social ritual. The wisecrack, the genial insult, the loud laugh and the peddling of minor emotions are substitutes for conversations. Good taste is no longer an expression of individual value-perceptions. It is determined by external professionals: editors of women's pages and etiquette columns, interior decorators, book clubs and home fashion magazines. One need only follow their mandates to win acceptance in most circles. The fervor to do whatever is being done has turned personal taste into imitative uniformity largely determined by commercial interests and popular vulgarians.

This kind of social uniformity threatens to create mental uniformity, for those who live in identical houses with identical furnishings, identical manners and identical clothes are in danger of adopting ideas equally identical and ready-made. To progress, free society must encourage variety, and those who take nonconformist positions should not be put on the defensive. Yet those few Americans who make occasional deviations from accepted opinion in even minor matters now feel constrained to be unduly defiant or unnecessarily apologetic. Even the current phrases with which an erring nonconformist explains his social aberration reveal his sense of sin. He "opened his big mouth" or "stuck out his neck" or "talked out of turn" or "went out on a limb." These are not attitudes that encourage or dignify independent opinion. The editors of *Fortune* magazine recently published the results of their own study of American conformity. They found the scene "a little frightening. . . . Conformity, it would appear, is being elevated into something akin to a religion. Perhaps Americans will arrive at an ant society . . . through unbridled desire to get along with one another.". . .

One of the few authorities who has anything good to say about mass culture is David Manning White, as the reader will see in the next selection. We would also make the argument that the standard of living of the common man has risen spectacularly in America in this century, and the indications point toward this becoming a world movement. As Arnold Toynbee says, "The Twentieth Century will be known as the century of the common man."

WHAT'S HAPPENING TO MASS CULTURE?
David Manning White*

. . . There is such a voluble hue and cry about the abysmal state of culture in the United States by well-meaning, sincere critics that I would like to present some evidence to the contrary. One is tempted to remind these critics that no country has ever achieved the complete integration of *haute culture* into the warp and woof of its everyday life. In the wishful memories of those who moon over the passed glories of Shakespeare's England it is seldom called to mind that bear-baiting was far more popular than any of Master Shakespeare's offerings. Who cares to remember that the same Rome that found a Juvenal proclaiming *mens sana in corpore sano* could also watch an Emperor Trajan celebrate his victory over Decebalus of Dacia in 106 A.D. with no fewer than 5,000 pairs of gladiators matched to the death? And this in the name of amusement!

My purpose, however, is not to argue with my friends who refuse to allow a television set in their homes for fear they may be contaminated. With no equivocation I'll state my thesis: The mass media hold out the promise to the "average" man that a cultural richness no previous age could give him is at hand. . . .

Television is capable of contributing its share to the best in our popular arts, as seen clearly in the Academy Award-winning movie "Marty," originally a television play. That its author, Paddy Chayevsky, should go from television to the legitimate theatre of New York, where his successful drama was staged by Joshua Logan, is [an] ex-

* David Manning White, "What's Happening to Mass Culture?", *The Saturday Review*, XXXI, No. 44 (November 3, 1956), 11-13. Reprinted by permission.

ample of the mobility of an artist who has something worthwhile to say.

To be sure, there is a great deal that is mediocre, repetitious, and patronizing in television, the movies, or any of our popular arts. Yet if we close our eyes to the significant contributions of the mass media, do we not encourage the very banality we purport to despise? For example, it is not difficult to look down our noses at the phenomenally successful *Life*, with its emphasis on photo-journalism. But not to take heed when *Life* presents a superb series, such as "The World We Live In," or when it gives its several million readers the initial publication of Hemingway's "Old Man and the Sea," is to invite the mass media to lose respect for the good things they themselves try to do. . . .

Certain critics of mass culture fear the influence of the majority taste on television offerings, since they believe the people will invariably choose the mediocre and the meretricious. If television (or the other media) provided only a diet of the tried and true stereotyped programs, that is, allowed the majority taste to mandate *every* choice, then I would agree with those who fear for the future. But the variety and quality of what is available to *national* audiences show this is not the case. . . .

There are dedicated groups of people in this country who instead of damning the media blanketly do something about improving what they dislike. Typical of such groups is the National Citizens' Committee for Educational Television, who have done more than cry about the low level of American culture. It is significant to note that by the end of 1956 there will be twenty-six educational television stations on the air. The eighteen stations now in operation are programming 340 hours weekly to a potential audience of 40 million. The new stations will bring an additional 7 million viewers within the TV orbit. According to a recent survey by the National Citizens' Committee for Educational TV, 57 percent of the programs were live and locally produced, the remainder were kinescopes and film. . . .

. . . Clifton Fadiman pointed out recently [that] we are in the midst of a reprint revolution that may be the greatest boon since Gutenberg. This revolution, which started in 1939 when Pocket Books experimented with 25-cent reprints, saw 300 million paperbound books printed last year! Since 1939 we've consumed about 2 billion copies.

The encouraging aspect of the paperbound books is that the quality of the titles is constantly improving. Whereas a few years ago the first association that came to one's mind was Mickey Spillane, today one thinks of the very successful Anchor books published by Doubleday, Harcourt Brace's Harvest books, Knopf's Vintage books, the Beacon Press paperbacks, Penguin books, to mention only a few. . . .

One further area which should give us reason for optimism is serious music. In the special fiftieth anniversary edition of *Variety*, which might appear to some as a most unlikely publication to present facts and figures about "longhair" art, Arthur Bronson has compiled some extremely significant data. In the fifty-year period covered by *Variety*'s life, serious musical expression has made extraordinary progress. Where in 1905 opera was the province of the few, today the listening audience of the Metropolitan Opera's Saturday afternoon broadcast alone is 15 million. To contrast with the half-dozen major symphony orchestras of a half-century ago, today we have thirty-two major American symphonies. Ballet, which virtually was unknown in this country fifty years ago, now has three major American companies. . . .

It has been observed that the general progress of human ideas has moved in leaps, in which relatively few facts have served as the basis for grand schemes. Today we have a reversal of that rhythm, in that we have a pile-up of facts, and have not achieved the universal theory wherewith to classify them. The computer, as seen in the "IBM 1500 instructional system" seems to offer potential for a breakthrough in instruction, to bring education abreast of the knowledge explosion and solve many thorny problems of poor teaching, failure of ghetto and suburban education, and the goal of humane, individualized instruction. In previous ages—as for instance in the advent of the book—time was available for communication and casuistical debate. But now the tyranny of conditions presses upon us in education. The federal monies released have brought about unforeseen bedfellows. A quantum change in atmosphere is taking place while we deliberate. But we cannot sit. We must move now. Otherwise others with more courage or selfish interest will move for us, to the detriment of school and society.

We find professional educators fumbling and indecisive about how to use the new technology at their disposal. Instead of their rushing to use what should seem clearly advantageous, the picture is one of unwilling, chary movements toward implementation. The case of television is typical. The following review tells how education has been underwhelmed by an instrument about which a few years ago many sanguine predictions were made.

THE ELECTRONIC EYE IN EDUCATION
Marie Olszewski [*]

Rapid and far reaching changes have occurred in many areas of communication, and we as teachers have far too little understanding of that significance. Stresses and strains are causing countless pressures in American civilization. There is evidence of unrest in the areas of government, capital and labor relations, economic control, personal relations, and exploitation. We are living during a rapid, social, economic and technological change. In education we must be conscious of these changes. Each year more and more students arrive at the school doors and at the same time there are fewer teachers and facilities available to handle them. How can a school system proceed to improve its program under these circumstances? That is not an easy question to answer. One effective way to accomplish this might be to direct boys and girls to make the best use of available resources at hand.

Children should be made aware of happenings in the world today. But there again, what are the most important concepts and generalizations to be developed with children? The answer is not easily arrived at. Which ones do children learn in their out-of-school activities? Television has resulted in tremendous learnings for children. Yet we actually know very little about these learnings. Television has dramatically extended the walls of the classroom so they encompass the world. Vital learnings are within the reach of the dial. The same experience can reach the child in a remote school as it does the pupils in a large city. Children have been able to look into the same microscope at the same time without leaving their desks—enthralled by a teacher many miles away.

[*] Marie Olszewski, Graduate Student, Wayne State University. Unpublished monograph, 1967.

The growth of classroom or instructional television has been enormous. About one of every five students has been exposed to the hypnotic fascination of the electronic eye. Still some feel television is a gimmick and has no place in the serious business of training young minds. The union of electronics and education occurred at a time when education was faced with an acute teacher shortage . . . which still exists. Television provides the opportunity for educators to reach several classrooms simultaneously and offer students new materials and techniques.

The California Department of Education—one of the 25 states with statewide systems of educational television already established—sums up benefits thusly: to improve instruction; to present subjects otherwise difficult to teach; to provide greater economy of teacher time in preparation and presentation; and to make more economical use of student learning time.

Teaching by electronics has been going on since 1953 when station KUHT was licensed for the University of Houston and the Houston public schools to broadcast instructions to Texans of all ages. As far back as the '30s minor experiments by such institutions as the University of Iowa, Purdue and Kansas City College and New York University have been taking place. In 1953 there were only two educational stations on the air. Today there are 104 offering educational TV.

The broadcasting of instructional television by the Detroit Public Schools began experimentally in 1957-58 with 2,683 viewing students in nine schools. This year, there are 285 schools with 65,000 regularly scheduled viewers. In addition, about 62,000 students in suburban areas now see programs that originate from the Detroit Public Schools.

Only six courses were offered in 1957-58. There are now 30 courses. Seven in-service programs for teachers are broadcast each week. Last year teachers received from the department 400,000 copies of various guides and student materials.

In 1961 a program of airborne television teaching was introduced in some Detroit schools in an experiment to test airborne television instruction. Lessons are broadcast to schools in Michigan, Indiana, Kentucky, and Illinois from a plane flying high above Purdue University. The instructional staff has been recruited from the very best in the nation. Each teacher is a specialist and a recognized authority in his field.

The on-camera teacher spends fulltime on one lesson per day. This permits unusually intensive preparation; besides, the camera permits close-up studies of exhibits. By using one or two television lessons a day, the classroom teacher is able to devote more time to preparation of those lessons which he teaches himself. He is able to view the equivalent of a demonstration lesson every time he watches.

A controlling concept of the Department of Educational Broadcasting is that teaching by television is part of a team-teaching effort. The team consists of the classroom teacher, the on-camera teacher, classroom teachers and supervisors who plan the course, the producer-director, the technical staff, and the students who receive the lesson.

By careful scheduling of television lessons, more children who have special needs are offered enrichment and remediation with quality teaching using the latest effective methods.

Obviously education extends far beyond what is offered in the classroom. Church, home and society have their influence on the development of boys and girls. And so does television outside the classroom. Commercial television educates indirectly by its public service shows, news and specials. Such programs as CBS Reports, the Twentieth Century, Face the Nation, Captain Kangaroo and The Hallmark Hall of Fame offer material of high informational, cultural and entertainment value. In addition some instructional programs are offered as CBS network's Sunrise Semester.

Educational stations can be on closed circuit and offering the school complete control of the subject matter. Seven Catholic diocesan school systems have applied for and received construction permits for ITV networks. Some 20 dioceses are now involved in developing such systems.

The New York archdiocesan system, according to Robert W. Sarnoff, president of the Radio Corporation of America, "is the largest ever devised to operate in the 2,500 megacycle band as an educational TV service and the first of its kind created for color programming. With facilities for originating live, film, tape and slide programs, this modern system should provide a new teaching tool of great versatility and flexibility.

So far ITV has made its greatest impact in the lower grades—kindergarten through elementary school—with courses in science and foreign languages predominating. The college level is also growing:

some 40 university owned educational TV stations are operating. There are over 400 closed-circuit installations on campuses. But whether by open or closed circuit, rented cable lines or by low-power microwave relay, the important thing is what is communicated and how well it is done.

The linking of electronics and education has already changed the basic procedures of teaching. Material can be brought into the classroom which might never get there otherwise. Photos, clippings, original documents, maps, charts and sketches which the ordinary teacher does not have access to can reach the students by way of the classroom screen. Newly developed mobile units now can visit places and tape material for future classroom use. Traditional audio-visual material can be used in conjunction with the TV camera.

ITV systems can be an aid to the teacher as well as to the pupils. "TV enables us," one teacher said, "to bring animals into the room or to conduct potentially dangerous experiments with electricity or chemistry." As another teacher phrased it: "TV broadens the total content of education." More than that the talents of exceptional teachers are multiplied.

Classroom TV stirs up a sense of immediacy about such things as history, political science and current events. Students can watch a team of astronauts soar into orbit or view a UN session. Teachers and parents are concerned with the results and effects of teaching with and by television.

Dr. George N. Gordon of New York University observes in his book, *Educational Television:* "The news was simply that in most cases under controlled experiments students taught by television did about as well—sometimes worse, frequently better—as students taught under normal conditions. In other words there was for the most part no appreciable difference noted between live classes and television classes."

"This piece of iconoclastic information," Dr. Gordon continues, "appeared to hold true under an enormously wide range of conditions: whether the subject matter was abstract or concrete, whether the teaching was of concepts or of skills. It held true of students in grade schools, in high schools, in colleges or in universities. And in most cases it held true whether television was used for enrichment, for cooperative teaching or—where it could be tested—for total teaching."

When Wilbur Schramm, noted mass media scholar, considered the sum total of research done on ITV's effectiveness and digested the findings for Stanford University's Institute for Communication Research, he came to the general conclusion that of 393 comparisons between instructional television and live instruction "in 65% . . . there was no significant difference. In 21% students learned significantly more (by television); in 14% they learned significantly less from television."

Not everyone is enthusiastic about classroom television. ITV is criticized for overemphasizing the importance of a teacher's showmanship and entertainment abilities. Teachers and critics say, there should be more stress on solid teaching values and approaches rather than charm and personality. Some raise questions about the differences among students. The TV teacher cannot properly gauge the students' response or non-response. Some maintain a needed teacher student contact is missing. The TV teacher cannot stop to review, repeat or explain more fully; or to answer questions.

The TV screen is impersonal and could reflect a mediocre program as well as a magnificent one. The same apparatus can bring great teaching into the classroom or lax and trite teaching. The media are but funnels, conductors or carriers. The value starts only when a teacher steps before the camera and adds to or subtracts from the child by good or bad teaching.

One of those to emphasize this is United States Commissioner of Education Harold Howe II. At a recent symposium he pointed out that our schools are spending hundreds of millions of federal dollars for new electronic educational equipment, yet they lack educational programs of sufficient high quality to feed into the machinery. Noting that about $200 million had been spent on the purchase of such aids (known as "hardware" in educational technology's new jargon), he said:

"We are quite uncertain that there is available the associated 'software'—the curricula and related materials—to make this equipment an effective tool for attacking the educational problems of the disadvantaged."

And so the debate continues among educators although facts seem fairly clear. One need only consider the steady growth of classroom television and the increasing recognition given by teachers to out-of-class commercial television for homework, classroom discussion and analysis of shows to stimulate minds. Today 1,223 primary and high school systems are equipped for TV and another 75 are planning to use it soon.

According to the latest National Compendium of Television (edited by Dr. Lawrence E. McKune of Michigan State University's Continuing Educational Service), the figures tell us that in the 1964-65 school year there were nearly 37 million TV course enrollments—up 232% from the preceding year.

The coming of television to the classroom should be viewed as a tool to aid the teacher not to replace him. TV and education must work together and not merely coexist. Initial effort is not enough. Sustained effort is necessary to master and use the gift profitably.

The National Committee for the Project on Instruction has delved into how the quality of instructional materials can be improved and how the products of modern technology can be used more effectively and came up with the following recommendation: "The use of educational television (ETV) and radio to broaden and deepen learning should be encouraged. Such use should be accompanied by a vigorous program of research and experimentation."

All that we have said about ETV in pro's and con's is an amazing reiteration of a series of remarks by educators at the time THE BOOK was substituted for THE WORD in instruction. The technological device of the book was so immensely superior to the word that it took over most of the functions of the pedagog intoning in front of the room. But classroom practice then (post book) and now (post TV) has retained much of its protean form. The reason is that irrational factors are in much better position to impede change than in grossly utilitarian practice. The combine will take over cardling, binding, threshing quickly when introduced. The gain in brain over brawn is clear. One teacher can lecture 10 million students an hour on TV, but many will argue that undemonstrable but real losses will occur if this is substituted for 500,000 teachers lecturing these 10 million.

The problem is not an either-or none, in which at one end, school becomes viewing of TV and at the other end of it is no TV schooling. The answer for the total educational effort is one in which TV is admixed and utilized in many more varieties and functions, along with many other technological aids where brain demonstrably replaces brawn more efficiently in education.

THE FUNCTIONS OF MASS CULTURE
August Kerber and Wilfred Smith*

The existence of mass culture has been questioned by some social scientists. They point out that the application of the term "culture" to the superficial trivialities of fashion and mode is a serious misuse of the word. They identify culture as patterns of family life, the government, religion, and the accumulated minutiae of human relations brought from the past. They consider the details of fashion and social ritual inconsequential and easily replaceable. The phenomena of mass culture may, indeed, seem superficial—they must, nevertheless, be considered integral components of our culture since they are vital to its continued functioning. Mass culture is a culture because it has the full complement of culture. Our de facto recognition of mass culture does not mean the exclusion of traditional culture: just as a person can function in two languages, he can live in two or more cultures. Mass culture can and to a large extent does co-exist with traditional culture. The very fact that mass culture came into being could support the contention that it has served a useful purpose, on the premise of functionalism. An examination of the current social scene would indicate that mass culture continues to perform the following useful educational purposes.

Interprets the Mores and Folkways of General Culture

The family, peer groups and school are still the primary sources of the individual's education in human relations. Industrialization and urbanization have resulted, however, in so many fragmented groups and new types of associations that, in the words of W. I. Thomas, the "situation lacks definition." Individual mobility results in frequent changes of society and conceives the notion of social responsibility toward all people in it. To understand what is happening outside of

---

* From a forthcoming book, *Culture and Education*.

one's immediate experience, and internalize transcultural values, mass media are necessary.

Induces Standardization of Values

The high degree of standardization and the resulting loss of individuality have been touted as weaknesses of mass culture. A certain amount of agreement on common goals and objectives is absolutely essential to social development—without it society would fragmentize into many conflicting groups as soon as it grew too large for primary associations. Society must have the structure and means of instilling in the individual a sense of social totality, a sense of belonging to a common society. Mass media, promulgating common values, are instrumental in instilling in the individual the concept of society and the sense of belonging to it.

The idealized values of our society are constantly headlined, featured, or implied by our mass media. They are presented in an effective, though frequently idealized, form predigested to be understandable to all. The "American way" is the thread of consistency running through all our television, radio and motion picture programs. The child who studies the stated values of the Declaration of Independence and the Constitution is further saturated with these values through television.

The child has a continuous exposure to an immediate environment which conflicts with these idealized values, and he could grow up in a world of make-believe, unprepared for the realities of life. In his process of maturation the youngster must reconcile the stated value of brotherly love with the actual dog-eat-dog practices of the business world. He must reconcile the stated value of concern for his fellow man with a national promotion which admonishes him to drive carefully because "the life he saves may be his own." The clear implication is that if he believes that his own life is in danger, he will drive carefully. He must reconcile the stated value of civic responsibility in democracy with the national pastime of income tax cheating. The conflicts between stated values and actual practices are seldom pointed out by design; nevertheless, the individual who is aware of his surrounding society surely must be cognizant of the contrasts. The realization of these conflicts is tantamount to a recognition of the desirable direction of our social development. The individual may not be able to change society —he may be able to modify his own behavior in the direction of reducing the gap between actual practices and stated values. The direction of our society will, of course, depend on the number of individuals who will so modify their individual codes of behavior.

Mass media are admittedly heavily controlled by interest groups which represent accumulations of wealth. There is, nevertheless, considerable opportunity for the complaints of the "underdog" to be heard by mass media. Even a minimal regard for news values must air some of the social conflicts and problems we face. An individual Negro applying for admission to a previously all-white school in the South is promptly catapulted into the national limelight, focusing attention on the entire issue of equality versus segregation. The Indian tribe that attempts to renegotiate the value of property it sold to the invading white man centuries ago rapidly finds its way into the headlines. The unpopular movement, the minority group, the victim of circumstances have little difficulty in gaining the ear of a society attuned to favor the "underdog." He who has access to mass media today is in a far stronger position than his predecessor who had gained the confidence of royalty. The crystallization of values usually speed up the process by which consistency and harmony are attained. The ambiguity of our system is polarized as clear-cut conflicts between actual practices and stated values. The existence of unresolved conflicts produces social sensitivity, and a certain degree of unrest and energy is exerted in the direction of the resolution of these conflicts.

Mass Communication Creates Unity and a Common Culture

The pamphleteering of Thomas Paine was instrumental in fending off mounting defeatism during the American Revolution. The printed word in that instance was far more effective than speech. The pamphlet was handed down from hand to hand. It reached a large group, and its effect was not limited as is a speech. Thomas Paine dramatically convinced Americans that they had a common cause, that their cause was just, and that it was worth fighting for. Paine's pamphlets unified Americans, and since his days the same feat has been repeated many times—though, perhaps, in less dramatic dimensions—by the media of newspapers, magazines, radio, and television.

The outcome of an issue today is determined frequently by one's ability to capture the minds of men. The fighting has been transferred from Yorktown to Madison Avenue. Instead of shedding lives we now shed integrities. Democracy has been vindicated by its consistent triumph in a system which permits free and equitable access to mass communications, and to points of view which frequently contradict its very essence.

The man in the street has little opportunity to actually participate in significant developments wherever they may occur. Through mass media, however, he can identify himself with such developments. There is always the potentiality that he may act swiftly for a popular cause or protest an injustice that comes to his attention. An axiom of public communication is that the language must be couched so those of the lower quartile can understand it, with the implication that shrewd operators and demagogues can manipulate them. But there is a solid structure to truth, and those who manipulate the public must remember they "can't fool all the people all the time." Mass communication makes everybody live in a goldfish bowl, and there is always the possibility of an informed public acting against organized schemes of exploitation. This applies to ideologies, cults, vested interest, nostrums, facts, and fancies.

The influx of large numbers of immigrants in a relatively short period of time during the formative years of mass communications endowed mass media with added meaning and effect. Hosts of people who were anxious to accelerate their process of Americanization found mass media an excellent avenue for the observation of "the American way" in the privacy of their homes without exposing their own patterns to possible ridicule. New Americans accepted to a considerable extent the folkways portrayed by radio, television, and the printed word as the standard to emulate. They were eager to imitate the language used, the mannerisms and conventions, the values and patterns. Mass media thus forged a common language, a common stock of gestures and social patterns and a host of identifiable and recognizable symbols. It was the broad avenue of acculturation.

This common language and common set of social patterns is gradually supplanting the variety of dialects of our many subgroups. School boys and school girls are beginning to talk more and more alike and to act in increasingly similar patterns regardless of whether we observe them in Portland, Oregon, or Jacksonville, Florida. Their habits, be they food preferences or fads in attire, acquire national dimensions rather than regional as they did prior to the advent of mass communications.

Editors' Summary

We do not here propose to settle the questions of whether mass culture exists and whether it is a great threat, nor offer our pros and cons on the subject. Such arguments, we feel, are likely to be settled by history when we can luxuriate in hindsight. We are most concerned with the general quality of culture now. Some think that the advantages of mass culture are as apparent as the hooks and handles of modern gadgets, and that all we need is more of them. Others, however, feel that we are losing something through mass culture, but are vague about schemes of improvement. Where the suggestions amount to the cosmic prescriptions that "we are all doing wrong," or "we must all do better," we have very little hope of formulating strategy or tactics. Even when we are clearly convinced that an epic campaign is necessary, we shall press for specifications.

Some things, however, are possible now, and will continue to press with greater urgency and crisis. We can strengthen our institutions that furnish the steel beams and rods of support of the democratic edifice. We here repeat a leitmotif of this volume. Through a strengthening of the school—the serious, contemplative, resourceful, and creative center of the culture—we can build individuals who will use mass media as they should be used as tools to enrich our living, and all living in the final analysis, said Alfred North Whitehead, is "the illumination of the present moment." When each of us lives our present moments with the full illumination of the dimensions of experience that enriched living brings us, we shall have overcome the threat of mass culture. Most of the authorities we quote in this chapter see mass culture as a threat, a lowering and debasing influence, an overspreading and oozing middlebrow culture. In the selections we have presented, only the last one deals directly with education and mass culture. The reader should

68

be able to discern, however, that the school, as part of society, is affected by this social phenomenon as are all segments of society.

Since the selections we present are generally negative about mass culture, we feel it behooves us to make some positive remarks about this modern movement.

The critics lump together many things under the term mass culture that could bear more careful screening. Wallpaper, china, paperweights, and clothing are mass-produced, and it is hard to see how human happiness is diminished by having more people enjoy these things than only the fortunate few who can afford to patronize artisans. The telephone, railroad, steamship, and airplane are now used by everyone, but it would be difficult to defend the thesis that proper screening and content analysis must accompany human utilization of these things lest we become sloths and Sybarites. Much of the supposed mass culture is simply a reduction of daily work hours, and an increase of beef over grits in diet.

Next, much of the presumed denigration of culture from mass media are simply structural and quantitative changes, and to presume ipso facto that these are bad is irrational. It does not give the accused his day in court. More people are able to communicate with each other, and each man comes in contact with an infinitely greater variety of things than ever before. If any presumption is to be made, we would think that the opposite of the one of threat and destruction would be more likely. A most common measure of progress is the increase of men, material, ideas, and communication. The burden of proof, then, should be on the detractors, those who maintain that general conditions would be better without mass media.

Education of the general mass is achieved by the abstractions, vicarious experiences, and formulated contents that are presented. The average urban dweller today lives a very humdrum life from the standpoint of his experience with people. He works according to habit and routine, and though the background of the city is full of movement, he has a very dull, repetitive task, and he meets few people who are personally interested in him. He feels disassociated from life—in it but not of it. Mass media have the potential of bringing meaning to this world. They tell him that other people have hearts and feelings, that they lie, steal, cheat, and run off with each other's wives. Reading about them, he can *understand them better than merely watching them swarm in and out of downtown caves. He can see how the city is constructed, and how other cities make the nation and the world. Through TV and radio, he enters the intimate lives of heroes, and ponders the fate of nations with the delegates at the UN.*

We, of course, make the reservation that mass media, though having this potential to help Joe Doakes understand why *everything is as it is, can no more be assumed to obey its optimum than it should be condemned out of hand by those who profess to uphold "culture."*

RELATED READINGS

Bogart, Leo. *The Age of Television*. New York: Frederick Ungar Publishing Co., 1936.

Callahan, Raymond E. *Education and the Cult of Efficiency*. Chicago: The University of Chicago Press, 1962.

Coleman, James S. *The Adolescent Society*. New York: The Free Press of Glencoe, 1962.

Coleman, James S. "The Competition for Adolescent Energies," *Teaching in America*, Anthony C. Ricco and Frederick R. Cyphert, Editors. Columbus, Ohio: Charles E. Merrill Books, 1962.

Erikson, Erik H., Editor. *Youth: Change and Challenge*. New York: Basic Books, 1963.

Farnsworth, Paul R. *The Social Psychology of Music*. New York: The Dryden Press, Inc., 1958.

Henry, Jules. *Culture Against Man*. New York: Random House, 1963.

Himmelweik, Hiede T. *Television and the Child*. New York: Oxford University Press, 1958.

Hofstadter, Richard. *Anti-Intellectualism in American Life*. New York: Knopf, 1963.

Johnstone, J., and E. Katz. "Youth and Popular Music: A Study in the Sociology of Taste," *American Journal of Sociology*, LXII (May, 1957), 563-68.

Katz, Eli, and Paul Lazarsfeld. *Personal Influence: The Part Played by the People in the Flow of Communications*. Glencoe, Ill.: The Free Press, 1955.

Kelley, L. L., and Volkart. "The Resistence to Change of Group Anchored Attitudes," *American Sociological Review*, XVII (1952), 453-65.

Larrabee, Eric, and Rolf Meyersohn (eds.). *Mass Leisure*. Glencoe, Ill.: The Free Press, 1959.

Mayer, Martin. *Madison Avenue, U.S.A.* New York: Harper & Brothers, 1958.

Michael, Donald N. *Cybernation: The Silent Conquest*. Santa Barbara, California: Center for the Study of Democratic Institutions, 1962.

Riley, John W., and Matilda W. "Mass Communication and the Social System." In R. K. Merton, *et al.* (eds.). *Sociology Today*. New York: Basic Books, Inc., 1959.

Rosenberg, B., and D. M. White (eds.). *Mass Culture*. Glencoe, Ill.: The Free Press, 1958.

Schramm, Wilber. *Responsibility in Mass Communication*. New York: Harper & Brothers, 1957.

Seldes, Gilbert. *The 7 Lively Arts*. New York: Sagamore Press, Inc., 1957.

Steinberg, C. S. *The Mass Communicators*. New York: Harper & Brothers, 1958.

Turner, Ralph H. *The Social Context of Ambition*. San Francisco: Chandler Publishing Co., 1964.

PART II

THE PURPOSE OF EDUCATION

For the most part, men have been sure of their way of life and where they were heading. In most primitive cultures, gods and myths explain the nature of the ideal, and men follow it as best they can. They have rituals and talismans to combat the deviations from the ideal. These cultures lack articulated prescriptions, but the members know their way of life from constantly watching each other. More complex cultures have codes, expressed bodies of belief, and organized bodies determining issues of doubt. The common man in most cultures lives in the culture to such an extent that he is not conscious of, or at least not speculative about, major alternatives to his way of life.

In such cases the problem of transmitting the culture to the new generation has no serious obstacles. The job may be frustrating and difficult, like skinning a large animal, or plowing on rocky ground, but the mandate is unavoidable. Where a different culture or society becomes infused with the old one, men simply have to battle their way out, through a period of suffering and indecision, until things become stabilized. The task of the transmission of culture has to wait until the new society is formed. (Education does not cease, however, simply because a society may be engaged in contentious communication.) The educational institution by itself does not make decisive interpretations and decisions about the direction of the society in times of change.

Our society is changing rapidly, and no voice of authority can tell us which way we are going, although many give us various ideas and imperatives. In some predictions or prescriptions the authorities deal with matters of great consequence: the population increase, the price index, the standard of living, the number attending school. They also concern themselves with immigration, foreign aid, insurance rates, public utility rates, liquor and narcotics, anti- and un-Americanism, psychiatry, subliminal advertising, reading level of school children, game and fishing laws, and protection of American property abroad. No doubt all of these are important in varying degrees. But virtually everybody differs on how important any policy is and how to implement it, unless he belongs to an organization which formulates a blanket policy for them. The result of all these voices crying their respective "shoulds" and "oughts" is not predictable in the same way the ebb and flow of tides are charted.

If the general society is in flux, the schools can traditionally do nothing but reflect the general temper of the times. The greatest criticism of our schools is that they have tried to be all things to all men; and since the society is pluralistic and changing, this cannot fail but to create some dissatisfactions for almost everybody.

One alternative which has been allowed is to permit groups to have their own educational system when they strongly feel the need of one, providing certain necessary conditions are fulfilled. Yet these people still may not like double taxation. To give the government of the schools to local bodies may seem to be the most democratic procedure, but with the rise of larger congeries and the increase of knowledge requiring professional understanding, local amateurs may lack vital information and training to give requisite leadership in their district.

Even if the professional educators were given free rein in organizing the school, the curriculum, administration, and teaching methods, there would be no less divergence of aims and methods. One point of view would be to have an eclectic approach, in which all philosophies and methods would be given a proportionate emphasis. The difficulty of having methods which are very free, moderately free, and strict, *all at the same time*, is obvious. Others would hold for the eternal verities and teaching children to *think*, with the belief that a mind trained in logic, rhetoric, and grammar can transpose the form and ignore the content of the Space Age. Still others would hold for experimentalism, but be so open to the acceptance of any novelty as to be guilty of the charge of "galloping eclecticism."

Whether our society can or will fail is speculative, but the dangers are great. We are faced with competing ideologies, with gigantic focuses of power that function for their special interests, with technological advances, and with a mass communication that dilutes social cohesion. In the modern crisis, if the society is to remain strong, it must take new strength from the new forces we have generated. There must be a synthesis, a "transvaluation of values" from the older themes that brought success up to this point. We need to understand a purpose, to experience this purpose in all the sinews of our daily life, as we work with the new apparatus we have created.

To do this we need a central agency which is purely devoted to the welfare of the whole. Of all of our institutions, that of education is pre-eminently fitted to the task. Of course all parts need to be supportive. When we know that the school is devoted to creating new values for a new society, all the lesser problems concerning Johnny and what he will be taught will fall into place. Philosophies, curricula, organization, and media will not gibe stridently at each other, but will be exploited for their value and productivity in making the society greater.

In this section we have two chapters. The first, "Moral Values in Education," discusses and debates the broad question of *purpose*— what education is finally and importantly to mean in our culture. As always, many hold different opinions on this. The second chapter deals more with what should be taught. When we discuss *what*, we find that the *why* is inseparable. Therefore the emphasis of this chapter is not on cataloging courses which have their enthusiastic adherents. Nevertheless we believe the reader will be able to look at such a catalog with a more discerning eye after reading the chapter.

IV

Moral Values in Education

Editors' Comment

We live in an age of foment, with giant forces in contention, with movements of all kinds able to burst forth into full form at any time. The present century has seen two world wars, world-wide economic depressions, and now the "permanent crisis" of an ideological struggle between the East and West, with the H-bomb hanging over the head of civilization like the sword over Damocles. Leaders and movements to set all straight exist, but none has been universally accepted.

One great danger, aside from the lack of agreement, is that of not caring at all. A great apathy about the momentous issues, a lack of feeling for man in general is the ground swell of our time. Various explanations are given for this: too many great crises have worn down man's ability to carry the emotional responsibility any more; so many changes, improvements, and additions to the conscious horizons have smothered the particulars and the gross in a low-level threshold of affect; the mass stimuli channeled by the Pied Pipers of our affluent markets have persuaded us to assume a homogenized middlebrow culture which flees real social sensitivity like the plague. Whatever the truths of these observations, certainly our modern civilization is one of mixed neurosis and apathy.

A common cry is one of return, of seeking the security of familiar patterns and traditional values. A neurotic dread of change in toto besets us, but we will accept many particular kinds of change. The result is a curious mélange of confrontism and a drive for "the latest" in glitter and hormone pills. It is a civilization of Cadillacs, TV, shaggy dogs, and socially-homogenized suburbias. Rock of Ages sung with self-conscious ardor mingles with the alcoholic clangor of the office party.

One of the more unfortunate aspects of this modern phenomenon is the pressure being put upon the schools. On the one hand, they are being scapegoated for the low moral tone of the age, the social disorganization, and delinquency. On the other hand, they are made responsible for acculturating the young with the core values of our civilization. Since the older generation has brought on itself wars, depressions, futility, and folly, the schools are charged with the task of doing better with the new generation.

We hear so much today about the amorality of science and the necessity of being objective in order to be truly educated. Because of this the intelligent layman would probably agree that the public schools should not teach moral values. His argument would be that the school cannot and should not do this: cannot because morals are not of the quality of things teachable in the teaching-learning framework of school lessons; should not because, if moral values are inculcated, by whatever means the school promulgates, the child is indoctrinated, rather than taught.

A deadly affirmation of bankruptcy of moral purpose lurks in this specious reasoning. We cannot escape teaching morals or moral values any more than we can escape breathing. The whole culture, the individual, and the school are all fully responsible for what moral values they have, and how they are applied. We accept values everyday in the shape of our houses and buildings, the allocation of land use, and the greeting we give people on the street. The question is not, therefore, whether or not we shall teach values, but what values we shall teach. This issue may have become clouded in the minds of many well-meaning people because of the notion that so much that has been taught in classrooms is not morally acceptable.

People must live, and they must live in happiness and purpose. To this end, we are bound to promote the following values:

1) *The existence of the individual in the full power of his potential in years, intelligence, and talents must be secured. The killing of a man by an individual or the state cuts off not only the individual from his right to full existence, but the opportunity of society to enrich itself from that existence.*

2) *Kindness, love, or acceptance is necessary for each individual to find a purpose in society. We need to understand the important effect love has on the behavior of the individual and proceed accordingly.*

3) *Each person has a right to individualism. He must be allowed to cultivate his unique capabilities, philosophy, demeanor, or way of life that distinguishes him from the group. The values of responsibility, dedication to society, and social sensitivity must be cultivated in the individual so that he can be intelligently motivated to fulfill himself and society.*

4) *The greatest possible competence and knowledge is necessary for the individual to be fully moral and responsible.* Knowledge is a moral value. *By knowledge, the individual can perform moral acts which he could not otherwise perform. To withhold this knowledge, or to refuse to seek it, are alike immoral.*

The public school, under whatever political climate, or constitutional interpretation, will have to teach the above values in the classroom if our society is to continue strong and dynamic.

What is needed is a set of values that can be taught and will stand up in this modern world. The following excerpts give some significant and important views that should serve as stimulators in helping the reader infer some values of this sort.

John Dewey did more than any other man to formulate the main ideas of the American philosophy of education. But he was misunderstood in his own time, and a considerable revisimist literature has developed which tells how his ideas "just don't work". In general, the non-function comes from a lack of understanding and misapplication. In the following article, the author tells how the ideas of Dewey are just as appropriate as ever, and the stakes in the game are higher.

THE LEGACY OF JOHN DEWEY
*Wilfred Smith**

John Dewey died at 93, in 1952, after a long and useful life dedicated to philosophy. During his lifetime he had seen great changes in the human scene, particularly in technology. The views he had of whirring machinery and atomic explosions excited him, but did not unduly amaze him. What he was most concerned about was education of man, from the specific lessons of real children in classes in Peoria, to the pronouncements of savants on "whither mankind" after World War II.

The educational enterprise changed greatly in his own time, partly because of his influence but chiefly through the dynamism of the age— in force of numbers and material production. It is a tragedy of life that inexorable death should take away such a man, when Purpose is the greatest need. Although everybody agrees in the cosmic sense about the importance of education for directing human purpose, the complexities of modern life have well nigh obliterated Purpose in inconsistency, conflict, and apathy. While directions are quite clear at the level of inventory of tomato cans, millage formulae, curriculum at Northwestern and the cut of naval uniforms, the directions of general society fade into universal neurosis of indecision.

Dewey envisaged the potentials of the age for the realization of the ideal of the Common Man. He believed the ideal to become possible through equalitarian, democratic, lifelong, and superior education. He considered the classic and European educational systems to be dead ends because of philosophic misapprehensions which could serve only

---

* Author's unpublished monograph.

as rationalizations for preserving the dominant social orders. He saw pragmatism, the philosophy of experience containing scientific method and democracy, as the general theory of modern democratic education, and education as the great, everwelling source of new opportunity and dissolver of ancient ills.

In his own time he developed cultist and slogan-serving followers, and also strong reaction movements of critics of various kinds. The particular terms "progressive education," "project method," "teach the whole child," "permissivism," and many others have been attributed to Dewey as at least the benign godfather, and frequently, nowadays, with adverse criticism.

The general criticisms of Dewey can be classified under three headings:

1) Too general. Dewey talked about the social nature of man and education, of education as being life and vice versa, of democracy as being necessary for art and chemistry, and of the mistakes of Plato and Erasmus. There was little in this that the average schoolman felt he could use. He did not feel that any specific changes in subjects, methods, or administration that he could implement were advocated by Dewey.

2) Too impractical. It is all very well to philosophize among the philosophers, and to eulogize the ends of man, of democracy, science, logic, ethics, and art, but school has to keep. As a warden said to a sweet young co-ed who suggested a series of reforms, developed from one of her courses, to apply to the penitentiary, "But ma'am—you have to have the prisoners!" Most teachers on the firing line quickly tell you that "Permissivism will not work" and "You can't have the kids running around on the walls." The social disorganization after World War II, with all its broken families and juvenile delinquency, has created reactionary movements and retrenchment into authoritarianism in the school.

3) Too vague. Dewey has often been accused of writing in a difficult prose, with many qualifications and knotty turns of thought as he spun away in his ivory tower, far removed from the teacher as he faced his last class in the afternoon. This is truly ironical when we remember that Dewey considered that one of his main tasks was to bring philosophy down from the clouds and make it work in the mundane hurly

burly of the contesting moment. Nevertheless, a common aspersion hurled at Dewey is that he well fitted the stereotype of the professor with his head wreathed in blue smoke.

Now that the sycophantic claques and the carping critics have had some time to air their views, and the movements of the times have even brought into question the relevancy or usefulness of a postlude interpretation, it seems useful to us to reinterpret Dewey in the light of the times. He would know best the hazards of interpretations twice or thrice removed. But, shades of American Pragmatism! The value of thy word lies in its universality and timelessness. We would rehear your counsel in this age of mighty portent.

First, a minimal recapitulation of some basic concepts in Dewey's philosophy is in order. We shall consider these in the following order: (1) social environment; (2) method; (3) subject matter; (4) intelligence, mind, and thinking; (5) morals; (6) discipline; (7) meaning and purpose; and (8) educational philosophy.

1) The social environment. We are concerned as live, sentient, beings, with our most important surroundings, which we react to and act upon. Man has a vastly and qualitatively expanded environment compared with animals, because he is intrinsically and morally a part of the social environment. His essence is a set of relationships; his motivation is social *and cannot be amoral or asocial*. "He cannot perform his activities without taking others into account."

Dewey spent little time in more technical, metaphysical, or cosmological expositions of his philosophy, and what concern he showed for other philosophies in this area was largely to recriminate these philosophies for misspent time.

2) Method. Scientific method, logic, mathematics, and other symbolic systems which man has developed in the search for truth and reality, Dewey constantly thought about pragmatically in terms of application to the problems of man. He was the stoutest upholder of new departures, styles, and experiments, but loathed idle mental choreography and pride in sterile occultism, almost as much as those systems which avowedly sought to rationalize institutionalized evil. The scientific method, thought Dewey, while being a stern task master, was the great humanizer and ennobler of the individual, because it enabled all to perceive impartially and move along with reality without fear of ir-

rational discrimination. The scientific method requires a commitment and grants no favors, but it is the only workable, public, communicable, teachable, and efficient way to solve man's problems and assault the adverse conditions. Logical systems are built to solve real problems; they are not viable human ends or meanings in themselves.

3) Subject matter. Ever since man has been speaking, he has been in danger of becoming captive to his words, rather than to deal with reality. (Admittedly, words are also part of reality, but not a privileged part.) With words, philosophers have built spurious, fictive systems and terminological problems. They have failed to define Truth, which it is the task of Mind to digest. To Dewey, this is a meaningless separation. What the mind learns and what the mind is blended into is an ongoing process. The nature of this process is open to increased learning power, by utilizing better method, integrated intelligence, and more extensive social cooperation. Subject matter—what one learns—and mind—the activity of learning—are really so bound together in the ongoing process of man's making himself that subject matter can only conceptually be separated from learning. When great emphasis is placed upon this separation, a deprivation of real learning occurs.

4) Intelligence, mind, and thinking. A common perception of what an individual with a brain does is to apply himself as a distinct entity with a rational set of rules to eternal truths and emerge with individually possessed ideas that are now his. This Platonic view is opposed by Dewey and the pragmatists, who see a world of ongoing process or change, in which entities are groups of interrelations whose nature is defined in the crucibles of change. Such factors as immediate condition, the apprehension of the problem, the reactions in process, determine the mental activity. Mind is a convenient label for all mental activity having social purpose. Thinking is the subjectively experienced part of dealing with problematic areas. Intelligence is a measurable aspect of the efficiency, quality, and quantity of the mental activity, which basically aims at responding with best results in the environment. In all this it is better to think of a social being who is a relative, cooperating being, making his way among other relative, cooperative beings, in a totality of continual flux.

5) The moral. "Morals are as broad as relationships which concern

our relationships with others," said Dewey.[1] Morality concerns our sense of rightness in our human relations. Every social relation includes a moral aspect. Morality is not therefore a separate subject, or something which is taught specifically, in most cases. It is an essential aspect of being human. Education must be moral, i.e., have a purpose of producing morality as an integral, indispensable part of its mission. Education is not primarily individualistic, amoral, objective, neutral, or any other rationale as against morality. The primariness of morality in education cannot be evaded or equivocated.

Even though the problems of morality are as deep as any in philosophy, education cannot evade its mission of inculcating morality. This does not, of course, mean that it must espouse certain moralistic, sectarian, or dogmatic views. It must produce the moral man as an integral part of the educated man.

6) Discipline. To produce results all behavior must be coordinated. Some give-and-take, some inhibition of motives, some continuity of action and concentration of purpose with a moral sensitivity must take place in the social person. All human action is moral; i.e., each partner to an act must feel that he is fulfilling a purpose that he ought to fulfill. He may wish to change the act, the partner, the conditions or the goals, but he wants most of all to uphold and promote the grounds of his behavior. Discipline is a result of a meeting of minds on what the social cooperative action ought to be; it is not an end in itself, but a product of intelligence and morality.

7) Meaning and purpose. When men work together for common ends, they develop understandings about their environment, and have basic attitudes or values about them. The experience of these understandings subjectively in the individual amounts to meaning. These meanings are usually expressed in language, but language does not include all of meaning, and the expression in itself is not meaning. Language is one way of signalling meaning. The understandings of men also include goals. The individual is challenged in his highest capability to produce new goals. To be able to produce individually, each must be stimulated by, and communicate in, an environment of

---

[1] John Dewey, *Democracy and Education*, New York: Macmillan, 1916, p. 414.

83

freedom and democracy. The individual striving to produce ends which amplify, make more secure and richer these goals is purpose.

8) Educational philosophy *is* philosophy. To say that it is a particular kind of philosophy is reductionist for Dewey, because education and human life are virtually synonymous. The accent here is on the *human*, because those aspects of life which are not distinctively human we can dismiss as irrelevant. Necessary, yes, for physiology, and non-symbolic existence, but not meaningful in what we do as human beings. Philosophy has the task of selecting, classifying, and resolving human experience. Experience is the basis of all knowledge and purpose. Philosophy aims "to attain as unified, consistent, and complete an outlook upon experience as possible."

With the above interpretations of Dewey's philosophy, let us attempt to answer some of the critics of his own and recent days, and sketch the stand Dewey would take on education today.

To say that Dewey is too general, impractical, and vague is to indicate a lack of good readership of any of his major works on philosophy and education.

The focus of Dewey's philosophy can be sharpened and delimited by first ascertaining what it denies, and then what it affirms.

It does not admit of any method for knowledge, except the scientific. It will not accept pleasant words or psychological satisfaction as a basis for knowledge. It negates inconsistency, incoherence, incompleteness, and incomprehensiveness. It rejects fixed knowledge of any kind. The charge that pragmatism does have something fixed—its own outlook—is a play on words.

What has been said about Dewey here rejects the bulk of all that the human race has said, and all the "isms" and "ologies" based on dogma, mysticism, intuition, tradition, and irrational appeal. Most importantly, Dewey rejects any system purporting to be "the way" which does not have change as a postulate, and acceptance of freedom, open inquiry, scientific method, and democratic procedure as main parts.

Before mentioning what Dewey positively affirmed we should assess the main changes that have occurred in society and education since his time or, more precisely, describe the increase of the "un-reality gap" between education and modern society.

Dewey noticed that society had undergone major changes in industrialization, knowledge, and democratization. He urged that education become the reconstructionist force to direct human society with principles that could lead to further growth. Education would also serve as a conservator of the important values of the past, but this is less important than reconstructionism. In his time the formal school grew along with general society, and in raw numbers reflected a general agreement about the value of education.

Since Dewey's time the technological and knowledge rate of increase has accelerated, and a matrix of urbanization, population increase, and international communications has moved toward a "moment of truth" crisis, all overhung by the doomsday bomb threat of total annihilation by the contesting camps of capitalism and communism.

What, positively, could Dewey have to say about "whither mankind" in the present state?

He would say that it is the moral duty of mankind to educate all men to the ultimate of their capacities, and the full achievement of this will take place within the framework of democratic ideology. The directions of man are given by philosophy; educational philosophy includes all that is relevant for human concern in philosophic problems; the end of educational philosophy comes about when man is able to attain a unified, consistent and complete, self-actualizing growth as is attainable only in the democratic ideology.

Instead of becoming more nebulous and meaningless in modern times, the philosophy of Dewey, or pragmatism, has intensified in meaning with the numbers, knowledge, and horsepower available to modern man. Those forces which would militate against democracy are magnified by the titanizing forces of today, and the crisis between growth and all forms of tyranny is deepened by the polarizing effects of modern life. Traditional balances in long-established societies, the internecine battles among relatively small groups, and the conflicts of a variety of small warring camps have hitherto hampered progress but have also prevented annihilation. Now we are moving into an age when a smaller number of men can make a "yes" or "no" decision about our existence or, what is more likely, our type of ideology.

In this dynamic disequilibrium, the gamesmanship advantage rests with the cunning and ruthless, who want a monolithic state.

Hence the word and mission of Dewey need updating. The democratic ideology requires thought control. Democracy is *not* all things to all people. It is a mode of human communication that requires truly educated people to act and interact at all levels, responsibly, and involves all human qualities. The democracy and communication are not embodied forms and ideas; they are the processes by which all great human meanings are attained. These meanings in Knowledge, subjective experience in human relations and art, and relationships to the physical universe are expressible only by means of and through the end of democracy.

This means that democracy must be inculcated, that it has constant battles in the psyche of the learner and in international relations. It admits of many choices and varieties of procedure, many styles, personalities, curricula, organization and activities, but it requires clearly, steadfastly, and coercively its ideological commitment. This ideology is certainly more difficult to understand and implement than those based on fixed knowledge or special interest, but the commitment is nevertheless more rigorous, complete, and warrantable.

This then, is Dewey's importance, brought up to date. What in his time was an intelligent choice with the either-or threat as one of living at a lower level of existence is now one of survival with the threat of an either-or of life or anti-life. In this case, the views of education that mis-educate by inculcating anti-democratic dogma, and those that assume education has a "neutral" mission of informing learners about knowledge, are alike viciously dysfunctional, seen in the light of the requirements of democracy and education. The tragedy of the age is that man may be done in by partial truths, half truths, stereotypes, and shibboleths of democratic education. In taking the shards of tablets written by epigones, or in accepting "proofs" of three times interpreted pronouncements, we may find ourselves in the formal school lint-picking in the anteroom while the battle of Armageddon flares up without.

The following selection is frankly secular in tone, at least in the sense of being opposed to the most sectarian and dogmatic forms of religious practice. Frederick Neff argues that secularism has risen to the stature of a truly moral force in the modern era, suited to grapple with problems that the dualistic theisms of orthodoxy are not aware of, or are incapable of handling.

HOW MORAL IS SECULAR EDUCATION?
*Frederick C. Neff**

The last decade has seen an outcropping of critics of American education unparalleled in recent times. Books and articles dealing with some variation of the theme "What's wrong with our schools?" are as much in demand as hot dogs at Coney Island. It is encouraging to note that the American public seems never before to have been so much interested in what goes on in its schools. The disheartening thing about it all is that so many of the critics have been of the self-styled or "wildhaired" variety. Educators themselves are partly to blame. They have a habit of talking to themselves instead of communicating to parents the temper of their thinking. In their professional journals and at their conferences they write and talk to each other, and little of what they say sifts through to the general public. As a result the professional educator is seldom heard from, while those less qualified to assess the philosophy, the curriculum and the administration of public education enjoy a field day whenever they decide to play critic.

Of the many confused areas in modern education one of the most benighted is the problem of moral values and how to teach them. What is said here is not for the tender-minded, nor is it for those to whom morality is simply "blind obedience to words of command." It is intended for those who have both an honest concern in clarifying a crucial issue in the education of our nation's youth and the courage to loosen some ancient shackles in the process. . . .

[In the historical tradition] the metaphysical dualisms which separated the physical from the mental, or the natural from the supernatural, lent philosophic respectability to the doctrine that spiritual education was one thing and secular training quite another. The question of morality was easily disposed of. It pertained to "true" education for

* Frederick C. Neff, "How Moral Is Secular Education?", *Christian Century*, LXXIII (November 14, 1956), pp. 1323-25. Copyright, 1956, *Christian Century Foundation*. Reprinted by permission.

spiritual or mental life and had nothing to do with secular pursuits. Or, stated philosophically, mind is mind and matter is matter, and never the twain shall meet. Why can we not continue under the earlier philosophic system? What has happened to unseat the old dualisms? More specifically, why has it become necessary to align the moral with the secular?

. . . .

If we have been taught to be secure in the conviction that mind is a kind of spiritual endowment peculiar to man and to no other living creature, that it is reason that sets man apart from other animals, we become confused when the psychologist tells us that "mind" is descriptive of the problem-solving process in which man engages along with many other animals, and that even abstraction has on occasion been demonstrated by rats and the higher primates. If, in good Platonic fashion, we have been taught to be secure in the notion that matter exists but to subserve mind, that matter is different and separable from its qualities, we become uneasy when the modern physicist reports that the qualities of matter simply denote ways in which matter functions, and that no function has ever been observed in the absence of matter, just as no matter has ever been observed that fails to function.

All this is but another way of saying that early conditioning in notions of the fixity of truth is one of the surest ways of guaranteeing later disillusionment, insecurity and frustration. While the evidence does not support any such absolutist approach, many well-intentioned educators perpetuate the old dualisms in the rather pathetic belief that progress consists in retreating to the "security" of some bygone age.

Another factor that has made dualism more and more tenuous and has thus induced the rise of secularism is the increasingly global approach to a solution of human problems. In solving problems at the international level it often becomes necessary to cut across some of the most ingrained habits of thinking of particular people in the name of a common humanity for all people. The only area where there can be a meeting of minds is at the level of the practical, the nonmystical and the demonstrable. The differing moral codes of various peoples can be pooled and assessed only in terms of a demonstrated conduct upon which judgment may be passed. There is no way of evaluating a belief on any other basis than that of its observable consequences in behavior. This is to say that the nonmystical, or the secular, insofar as it represents the common practices and basic ideals of various peoples, is the only framework from which a common criterion of what constitutes the just, the right and the moral can emerge.

These two factors—the impact of science and the emergence of international-mindedness—are largely responsible for the "educational crisis" about which so much is spoken and written these days. More than just an educational crisis, however, it is a cultural crisis. If education is presently confused, it is because it reflects a turning point in the affairs of men, a crisis in moral codes and ways of human association that all civilized peoples are at the moment facing. When education ignores the changing world which it is supposed to be preparing young people to live in, then it is guilty of being unrealistic and impractical. When it undertakes to foster a scientific outlook and a world view, it is accused of being "godless" and unpatriotic. And when it attempts to embrace both the cultural and the scientific, both the indigenously patriotic and the broadly international, it is blamed for its neutrality and for its failure to take a stand that will promote any point of view with conviction.

Two further points need to be made in order that the secular position may be more clearly understood. The first is that secularism arose primarily not as an antireligious or even nonreligious movement but rather emerged in response to a recognized need for operating free from dogmas and absolutes. The fact that certain religions represented fixed principles from which deviation was impossible was only incidental. The schism that arose between religion and secularism was due chiefly not to the ancient differences between idealism and materialism but, actually, to differing conceptions of the moral life. With a religion emancipated from dogma and static principles, secularism could have little quarrel. It is the notion of fixity, finality and absolutism—and the inevitable authoritarianism which it breeds —that caused men to counter with a flexible, more enlightened and more humane way of conducting their affairs.

Protestantism in this sense may be considered a step in the direction of secularism, for it staunchly opposed much of the absolutism of earlier ecclesiastical dogma. While it has in principle maintained the essence of a fighting doctrine of freedom and individualism, yet on occasion, as in its recent heresy trials, it appears to yield to the old temptation to exorcise and ostracize the nonconformist. If there is tragedy in Protestantism, it is that the heresy that gave spirit to its inception is in serious danger of becoming simply another orthodoxy. It might be well to ponder the fact that, whatever else Jesus may or may not have been, he certainly was not orthodox. Of all the great heretics of history, he was probably much the most radical.

A second characteristic of secularism is that it appears to have outgrown its negative role of antagonist and is more and more assuming the role of protagonist. Instead of being merely a makeshift or compromise measure, it is becoming a virile movement representative of the only feasible way for resolving human differences. In so doing it is beginning to accumulate a moral content and a moral outlook that are fairly distinctive. Insofar as democracy is basically a secular ideology, secularism bids fair to represent the moral precepts of the free way of life. Lest this seem too easy a conclusion, several considerations may be in order.

The democratic community is made up of countless numbers of diverse elements, so much so that one wonders sometimes just what it is that holds them together in any semblance of harmony or order. In structuring his moral outlook the theist may look to revelation, the rationalist to reason, the empiricist to experience, the philosopher to reflection and metaphysics, the humanist to the human family itself. The scientist, moreover, may hold that a free unfettered inquiry into verifiable truth is the most moral occupation man can engage in.

It would be as futile to attempt to move these men from their dedicated commitments as it would be to try to establish the kingdom of heaven on earth merely by wishing it were so. Yet, ideally, the democratic way of life condemns or persecutes none of them, and they somehow get along with one another. What is it that guarantees an ordered survival of differences? How can such differences be permitted if we are at the same time concerned with perpetuating a way of life?

The answer lies in the fact that differences could not harmoniously persist without a basic principle to which there is common dedication. While theists, intellectualists, empiricists, philosophers, humanists and scientists may disagree *ad infinitum* on any number of questions, the fact remains that they do reach a significant degree of unanimity at the nonpartisan level. The reason is that there is a common, basic principle to which all democratic citizens are morally committed; namely, a mutual respect for human differences. And this appears to be a secular principle.

. . . .

The problem of choice between secular and other kinds of education is not a matter of choosing between the moral and the nonmoral. Rather, it involves a choice between two competing standards of the good life. In precise terms, the choice is between intelligence and dogma, between·experience and speculation, between the demonstrable and the mystical, between diversity and uniformity; it is a choice between standards that are flexible and standards that are rigid, between methods that are critical and methods that are premised. A basic issue confronting the free, public, secular school of our time has to do with the moral struggle between freedom and the hostile remnants of a prescientific and predemocratic past. It is the issue of democracy versus absolutism.

The following summary on the "Communist morality" trained into Russian youth is interesting in many ways. The reader might consider these questions: How much did you know about this subject? Is this line of argument, or program, unfamiliar to our ears in America? Is modern Russia heedless of all morality?

BOLSHEVIK CHARACTER
*B. P. Yesipov and N. K. Goncharov**

Essential elements of education in communist morality. Communist morality serves our general purposes and is wholly linked with the building of a new communist society.

The Stalin Constitution declares the defense of the fatherland to be the duty of every Soviet citizen. It speaks of the obligation to guard public property, and of the obligation to observe the rules of socialist life.

A morally educated individual, according to our understanding, is one who in his conduct subordinates his own interests to the service of his Motherland and his people. Such service presupposes wrath and hatred toward the enemies of the Motherland who imperil the battle-won rights of the people and all that has been created in the realm of material and cultural life by both the older and the younger generation. Communist morality presupposes action and makes struggle obligatory. . . .

The entire work of the school must be directed toward the education of children in communist morality. In giving knowledge to pupils and in formulating their world outlook, the school must cultivate in them the habits of communist conduct. . . .

Consciousness of the learner. Moral conduct does not have great value if the individual complies with regulations merely because "he is told," or because he is threatened with some unpleasant consequence in the event of their violation. . . . It is important that he

---

* B. P. Yesipov and N. K. Goncharov, *I Want To Be Like Stalin*, translated by George S. Counts and Nucia P. Lodge (New York, 1947), pp. 42, 43, 45, 94, 95, 141, 142. Reprinted by permission of The John Day Company, Inc., publisher. Copyright, 1947, by The John Day Company.

behave in accordance with the canons of communist morality because of inner *conviction*. . . .

While giving foremost place to methods of persuasion, Soviet pedagogy does not repudiate methods of coercion. In our socialist society there are no requirements governing the conduct of adults and children which would do injury to the dignity and the rights of personality. The young are confronted with rules which are unreasonable. If the learner grasps the essence of a given rule, he will understand why it should be obeyed; but if he still fails to conform and violates the established procedures, he must be forced to observe them. Indulgence of and indifference to violations of moral requirements will bring harm to society and to the learner himself. If the teacher overlooks such violations, the child will permit himself to disregard moral rules and standards in the future. . . .

. . . .

Basic traits of discipline required of the Soviet pupil. . . . The discipline which we cultivate in our children under socialist conditions is characterized by the following qualities: In the first place it is *conscious*, that is, it is founded on an inner conviction of the necessity of following definite rules and regulations in conduct which in turn are based on an understanding of their meaning and significance. In the second place, discipline is *self-initiated*, that is, it is not a discipline of simple obedience but rather a discipline which is linked with the desire to fulfill in the best possible manner a given assignment, order, or commission. More than this, it is linked with a readiness always to do one's duty, not waiting for an order or a reminder, but displaying initiative. In the third place, discipline is *firm*, that is, it is unquestioned obedience and submission to the leader, the teacher, or the organizer. Without this there is no discipline; submission to the will of the leader is a necessary and essential mark of discipline. In the fourth place, discipline is *organizational*, that is, it is a discipline which prompts and habituates the pupil to the precise organization of individual and collective work, to organization in games and life. In the fifth place, discipline is *comradely*, that is, it is founded on mutual respect of the members of the collective. In the sixth place, discipline is *resolute*, that is, it surmounts difficulties, prompts the completion of every task, subjects conduct to high purposes, and conquers motives of low degree.

. . . .

The overruling purpose of the school, according to Lenin, must be the cultivation of communist morality in the pupils. The entire business of the education of contemporary youth must be the development in them of communist morality.

Lenin showed that eternal and unchanging ethical standards do not exist. Ethical standards are determined by the development of society and by social relations. Also for every concrete social form there are corresponding ethical standards. The conduct of the individual is determined by social relations and by social position. The ruling ethics in society is the ethics of the ruling class. Wealthy classes, as Lenin says, regard their morality as the morality of all mankind and founded on "the commandments of god." "We reject any such morality which is derived from extra-human or extra-class conceptions. We say that it is a fraud, that it is a deception designed to dull the minds of workers and peasants in the interest of landlords and capitalists."

In place of such ethics, created in the interests of exploiters, the working class creates a new ethics, which develops out of the interests of the struggle for a new society in which there will be no exploitation of man by man. The new ethics, the ethics of the forward-looking class, serves the cause of the reconstruction of society. Communist ethics unites the workers for the struggle for the welfare of all mankind, for deliverance from oppression and violence. Communist ethics therefore is the most advanced, the most human, and the most noble; and it is devoted to the purpose of creating a communist society. . . .

All his life Dewey was concerned with education. His philosophy was pragmatic and democratic; he had the belief that everything important in philosophy was implicated in educational philosophy. All the perennial problems of philosophy he found meaningful only insofar as they aided the solution of human problems. A central concept of

94

Dewey's was the democratic ethic. This ethic, carried on in human life, was a means and an end, the structure and the process, the result of intelligence and the working of intelligence: it was goal of goals, principles, the how, what, and why of curriculum; the encompassing absolute that denied all absolutes; the great human ideal that implicated change, scientific method, intelligence, sociality, human purpose and growth in one simple yet infinitely variable and uniquely applicable human endeavor.

THE DEMOCRATIC CONCEPTION IN EDUCATION
*John Dewey**

I. *The Implications of Human Association.*—Society is one word, but many things. Men associate together in all kinds of ways and for all kinds of purposes. One man is concerned in a multitude of diverse groups, in which his associates may be quite different. It often seems as if they had nothing in common except that they are modes of associated life. Within every larger social organization there are numerous minor groups: not only political subdivisions, but also industrial, scientific, religious, associations. There are political parties with differing aims, social sets, cliques, gangs, corporations, partnerships, groups bound closely together by ties of blood, and so on in endless variety. In many modern states, and in some ancient, there is great diversity of populations, of varying languages, religions, moral codes, and traditions. From this standpoint many a minor political unit, one of our large cities for example, is a congeries of loosely associated societies, rather than an inclusive and permeating community of action and thought.[1]

The terms society, community, are thus ambiguous. They have both a *eulogistic* or *normative* sense, and a descriptive sense; a meaning *de jure* and a meaning *de facto*. In social philosophy the former connotation is almost always uppermost. Society is conceived as one by its very nature. The qualities which accompany this unity, praiseworthy community of purpose and welfare, loyalty to public ends, mutuality of sympathy, are emphasized. But when we look at the facts

* John Dewey, op. cit., pp. 111-118.
[1] See *ante*, p. 24.

which the term *denotes* instead of confining our attention to its intrinsic *connotation*, we find not unity, but a plurality of societies, good and bad. Men banded together in a criminal conspiracy, business aggregations that prey upon the public while serving it, political machines held together by the interest of plunder, are included. If it is said that such organizations are not societies because they do not meet the ideal requirements of the notion of society, the answer, in part, is that the conception of society is then made so "ideal" as to be of no use, having no reference to facts; and in part, that each of these organizations, no matter how opposed to the interests of other groups, has something of the praiseworthy qualities of "society" which hold it together. There is honor among thieves, and a band of robbers has a common interest as respects its members. Gangs are marked by fraternal feeling, and narrow cliques by intense loyalty to their own codes. Family life may be marked by exclusiveness, suspicion, and jealousy as to those without, and yet be a model of amity and mutual aid within. Any education given by a group tends to socialize its members, but the quality and value of the socialization depends upon the habits and aims of the group.

Hence, once more, the need of a measure for the worth of any given mode of social life. In seeking this measure we have to avoid two extremes. We cannot set up, out of our heads, something we regard as an ideal society. We must base our conception upon societies that actually exist, in order to have any assurance that our ideal is a practicable one. But, as we have just seen, the ideal cannot simply repeat the traits which are actually found. The problem is to extract the desirable traits of forms of community life which actually exist, and employ them to criticize undesirable features and suggest improvement. Now in any social group whatever, even in a gang of thieves, we find some interest held in common, and we find a certain amount of interaction and cooperative intercourse with other groups. From these two traits we derive our standard. How numerous and varied are the interests which are consciously shared? How full and free is the interplay with other forms of association? If we apply these considerations to, say, a criminal band, we find that the ties which consciously hold the members together are few in number, reducible almost to a common interest in plunder; and that they are of such a nature as to isolate the group from other groups with respect to give and take of the values of life. Hence, the education such a society gives is partial and distorted. If we take, on the other hand, the kind of family life which illustrates the standard, we find that there are material, intellectual, aesthetic interests in which all participate and that the progress of one member has worth for the experience of other members—it is readily communicable—and that the family is not an isolated whole, but enters intimately into relationships with business groups, with schools, with all the agencies of culture, as well as with other similar groups, and that it plays a due part in the political organization and in return receives support from it. In short, there are many interests consciously communicated and shared; and there are varied and free points of contact with other modes of association.

1. Let us apply the first element in the criterion to a despotically governed state. It is not true there is no common interest in such an organization between governed and governors. The authorities in command must make some appeal to the native activities of the subjects, must call some of their powers into play. Talleyrand said that a government could do everything with bayonets except sit on them. This cynical declaration is at least a recognition that the bond of union is not merely one of coercive force. It may be said, however, that the activities appealed to are themselves unworthy and degrading—that such a government calls into functioning activity simply capacity for fear. In a way, this statement is true. But it overlooks the fact that fear need not be an undesirable factor in experience. Caution, circumspection, prudence, desire to foresee future events so as to avert what is harmful—these desirable traits are as much a product of calling the impulse of fear into play as is cowardice and abject submission. The real difficulty is that the appeal to fear is *isolated*. In evoking dread and hope of specific tangible reward—say comfort and ease—many other capacities are left untouched. Or rather, they are affected, but in such a way as to pervert them. Instead of operating on their own account they are reduced to mere servants of attaining pleasure and avoiding pain.

This is equivalent to saying that there is no extensive number of common interests; there is no free play back and forth among the members of the social group. Stimulation and response are exceedingly one-sided. In order to have a large number of values in common all the members of the group must have an equable opportunity to receive and to take from others. There must be a large variety of shared undertakings and experiences. Otherwise, the influences which educate some into masters educate others into slaves. And the experience of each party loses in meaning, when the free interchange of varying modes of life-experience is arrested. A separation into a privileged and a subject class prevents social endosmosis. The evils thereby affecting the superior class are less material and less perceptible, but equally real. Their culture tends to be sterile, to be turned back to feed on itself; their art becomes a showy display and artificial; their wealth luxurious; their knowledge over-specialized; their manners fastidious rather than humane.

Lack of the free and equitable intercourse which springs from a variety of shared interests makes intellectual stimulation unbalanced. Diversity of stimulation means novelty, and novelty means challenge to thought. The more activity is restricted to a few definite lines—as it is when there are rigid class lines preventing adequate interplay of experiences—the more action tends to become routine on the part of the class at a disadvantage, and capricious, aimless, and explosive on the part of the class having the materially fortunate position. Plato defined a slave as one who accepts from another the purposes which control his conduct. This condition obtains even where there is no slavery in the legal sense. It is found wherever men are engaged in activity which is socially serviceable, but whose service they do not understand and have no personal interest in. Much is said about scientific management of work. It is a narrow view which restricts the science which secures efficiency of operation to movements of the muscles. The chief opportunity for science is the discovery of the relations of a man to his work —including his relations to others who take part—which will enlist his intelligent interest in what he is doing. Efficiency in production often demands division of labor. But it is reduced to a mechanical routine unless workers see the technical, intellectual, and social relationships involved in what they do, and engage in their work because of the motivation furnished by such perceptions. The tendency to reduce such things as efficiency of activity and scientific management to purely technical externals is evidence of the one-sided stimulation of thought given to those in control of industry—those who supply its aims. Because of their lack of all-round and well-balanced social interest, there is not sufficient stimulus for attention to the human factors and relationships in industry. Intelligence is narrowed to the factors concerned with technical production and marketing of goods. No doubt a very acute and intense intelligence in these narrow lines can be developed, but the failure to take into account the significant social factors means none the less an absence of mind, and a corresponding distortion of emotional life.

2. This illustration (whose point is to be extended to all associations lacking reciprocity of interest) brings us to our second point. The isolation and exclusiveness of a gang or clique brings its antisocial spirit into relief. But this same spirit is found wherever one group has interests "of its own" which shut it out from full interaction with other groups, so that its prevailing purpose is the protection of what it has got, instead of reorganization and progress through wider relationships. It marks nations in their isolation from one another; families which seclude their domestic concerns as if they had no connection with a larger life; schools when separated from the interest of home and community; the divisions of rich and poor; learned and unlearned. The essential point is that isolation makes for rigidity and formal institutionalizing of life, for static and selfish ideals within the group. That savage tribes regard aliens and enemies as synonymous is not accidental. It springs from the fact that they have identified their experience with rigid adherence to their past customs. On such a basis it is wholly logical to fear intercourse with others, for such contact might dissolve custom. It would certainly occasion reconstruction. It is a commonplace that an alert and expanding mental life depends on an enlarging range of contact with the physical environment. But the principle applies even more significantly to the field where we are apt to ignore it—the sphere of social contacts.

Every expansive era in the history of mankind has coincided with the operation of factors which have tended to eliminate distance between peoples and classes previously hemmed off from one another. Even the alleged benefits of war, so far as more than alleged, spring from the fact that conflict of peoples at least enforces intercourse between them and thus accidentally enables them to learn from one another, and thereby to expand their horizons. Travel, economic and commercial tendencies, have at present gone far to break down external barriers; to bring peoples and classes into closer and more perceptible connection with one another. It remains for the most part to secure the intellectual and emotional significance of this physical annihilation of space.

II. *The Democratic Ideal.*—The two elements in our criterion point to democracy. The first signifies not only more numerous and more varied points of shared common interest, but also greater reliance upon the recognition of mutual interests as a factor in social control. The second means not only freer interaction between social groups (once isolated so far as intention could keep up a separation) but change in social habit—its continuous readjustment through meeting the new situations produced by varied intercourse. And these two traits are precisely what characterize the democratically constituted society.

Upon the educational side we note first that the realization of a form of social life in which interests are mutually interpenetrating, and where progress, or readjustment, is an important consideration, makes a democratic community more interested than other communities have cause to be in deliberate and systematic education. The devotion of democracy to education is a familiar fact. The superficial explanation is that a government resting upon popular suffrage cannot be successful unless those who elect and who obey their governors are educated. Since a democratic society repudiates the principle of external authority, it must find a substitute in voluntary disposition and interest; these can be created only by education. But there is a deeper explanation. A democracy is more than a form of government; it is primarily a mode of associated living, of conjoint communicated experience. The extension in space of the number of individuals who participate in an interest so that each has to refer his own action to that of others, and to consider the action of others to give point and direction to his own, is equivalent to the breaking down of those barriers of class, race, and national territory which kept men from perceiving the full import of their activity. These more numerous and more varied points of contact denote a greater diversity of stimuli to which an individual has to respond; they consequently put a premium on variation in his action. They secure a liberation of powers which remain suppressed as long as the incitations to action are partial, as they must be in a group which in its exclusiveness shuts out many interests.

The widening of the area of shared concerns, and the liberation of a greater diversity of personal capacities which characterize a democracy, are not of course the product of deliberation and conscious effort. On the contrary, they were caused by the development of modes of manufacture and commerce, travel, migration, and intercommunication which flowed from the command of science over natural energy. But after greater individualization on one hand, and a broader community of interest on the other have come into existence, it is a matter of deliberate effort to sustain and extend them. Obviously a society to which stratification into separate classes would be fatal must see to it that intellectual opportunities are accessible to all on equable and easy terms. A society marked off into classes need be specially attentive only to the education of its ruling elements. A society which is mobile, which is full of channels for the distribution of a change occurring anywhere, must see to it that its members are educated to personal initiative and adaptability. Otherwise, they will be overwhelmed by the changes in which they are caught and whose significance or connections they do not perceive. The result will be a confusion in which a few will appropriate to themselves the results of the blind and externally directed activities of others.

RELATED READINGS

Anderson, V. E., and others. "Lay Participation in Curriculum Development," *Educational Leadership*, XV (April, 1957), 398-431.

Barnett, Homer G. *Innovation: The Basis of Cultural Change*. McGraw-Hill, New York: 1963.

Bode, Boyd H. *Progressive Education at the Crossroads*. New York: Newson & Co., 1938.

Champlin, Nathaniel L. "The Attacks Upon Public Education: Their Significance for Philosophy of Education," *Educational Theory*, VIII (July, 1958), 157-61.

Cremin, Lawrence A. *The Transformation of the School: Progressivism in American Education, 1876-1957*. New York: Knopf, 1961.

Dewey, John. *Experience and Education*. New York: The Macmillan Co., 1939.

Edwards, G. W. *The Evolution of Finance Capitalism*. Longmans, New York: 1938.

Gross, Richard E. & Zeleny, Leslie D. *Educating Citizens for Democracy Curriculum and Instruction in Secondary Social Studies.* Oxford University Press, New York: 1958.

Hoselitz, Burt F. *The Sociological Aspects of Economic Growth.* The Free Press, Glencoe, Ill., 1960.

Justman, Joseph. "Wanted: A Philosophy of American Education," *School and Society,* LXXXIII (May 12, 1956), 159-61.

Krathwohl, David R., Benjamin S. Blooman, and Bertam B. Masia. *Taxonomy of Educational Objectives.* New York: David McKay Company, Inc., 1964.

Kyte, George C. "A Core Vocabulary in the Language Arts," *Phi Delta Kappan,* XXXIV (1953), 231-34.

McGrath, Earl J. "Language Study and World Affairs," *Phi Delta Kappan,* XXXIV (1953), 144-48.

Melby, E. O. "Where and What Are the Educational Wastelands?" *School and Society,* LXXXIII (March 3, 1956), 71-75.

Morphet, Edgar L. "Answering the Critics of Education." Address to the NEA Convention held in Los Angeles, California, June 30, 1960.

Neff, Frederic C. *Education for American Society.* 1962.

Riesman, David. *Constraint and Variety in American Education.* Lincoln: University of Nebraska Press, 1956.

Sheviakov, George V., and Fritz Redl. *Discipline for Today's Children and Youth.* Washington, D.C.: National Education Association, 1958.

Smith, Mortimer. *Public Schools in Crisis: Some Critical Essays.* Chicago: Henry Regnery Co., 1956.

Werth, Alexander. *Russia Under Khrushchev.* Crest, New York: 1962.

Woodring, Paul. *A Fourth of a Nation.* New York: McGraw-Hill Book Co., 1957.

V

The Perennial Debate Over Curricular Goals

Editors' Comment

The discussions of curriculum in this chapter may seem to some to be too general, or perhaps even unrelated to curriculum. Curriculum is usually described as the program of academic studies, or the articulated list of studies pursued in school. Obviously an extended study of types, trends, and statistical analyses could be done of such lists used in the United States, with perhaps some broad comparisons with other countries.

Because of the relatedness of things and ideas, however, many of the authorities who look at curriculum think of it in terms of what it is for. They see content as a means to an end, and the school as a learning situation using the curriculum as a tool. They see curriculum as a middle-sized idea to be studied in terms of big ideas. The reader will notice that all the selections stress a common theme—that learning in school should make the child more competent and happy in fulfilling his role in a democracy.

It is becoming more patent to all thinking people on the modern scene; education is more important than ever, and the lack of it deprives the individual and society; education is a lifelong process, in which the individual is constantly being educated insofar as he is a *viable citizen in the modern world able to do his part in the stream of human communication; education is most vital and irretrievable at the access level, in the years before kindergarten; that the most important part of education is in learning to speak. Those who do not learn to speak like middle classers in their first years suffer the rest of their lives from the symbolic gap. As we speak, so we symbol; as we symbol, so we are human beings. The modern goal of democratic culture is enabling all of us to participate at our full potential in this play of mankind. Now, cultural accidents decide our fate. In the enlightened future, human intelligence and responsibility must supplant the accidents of tradition.*

We are learning today that the early education of the child is determinative of his later progress through school and in life. Studies of animals, of isolates and institutionalized children, of masses of children in the public school point to a portentous fact: The first three years of life set the basic foundation of personality, and lack of a good socialization in this period causes irretrievable and irremediable damage. Despite the diversified nature of our culture, a rather clear picture emerges of the difference between lower-class and middle-class children. The difference is principally seen and chiefly important in language usage. The lower class do not learn language usage as well as the middle class, and this condition, embodied in the neural system and never fully remediable for the lower class child, we call "the symbolic gap."

THE SYMBOLIC GAP
Edith King*

In an article, "The Social Context of Language Acquisition," John and Goldstein discuss the implications of their research of language acquisition in the socially disadvantaged child. Drawing from the

* Assistant Professor, University of Denver, Dept. of Education and Social Science. The article is adapted from the author's Ed. D. dissertation, "A Sociological Approach to Early Childhood Learning."

findings of previous investigations, the author selected the observation that children from high income, high status families were found to speak in longer sentences, more articulately, and with a more varied vocabulary than do children from lower class families. This finding indicated a *qualitative* difference in children's abilities to use language as well as a quantitative one.

Using 40 lower class Negro children of four years of age enrolled in a pre-school enrichment program in Manhattan, New York elementary schools, the investigators administered the Peabody Picture Vocabulary Test (PPVT) to the children at the beginning of their experience in the enrichment program. The PPVT consists of a series of increasingly difficult items which require the child to display his comprehension of labels, when confronted with four drawings, by pointing to the correct picture-referent. In analyzing the results of the test, three clusters of words were found to be particularly difficult: action words (digging, tying, pouring) words related to rural living (leaf, bush, nest), and words whose referents may be rare in low-income homes (kangaroo, caboose, accident).

John and Goldstein contend as a result of these findings that:

> . . . It is our contention, therefore, partially supported by Bernstein's research that the crucial difference between middle class and lower class individuals is not in the quality of language, but in its *use*. The functional diversity in language may be a direct result of the occupational and educational experiences of the speaker. . . . The middle class child learns by feedback; by being heard, corrected, and modified— by gaining "operant control" over his social environment by using words that he hears. The child learns by interacting with an adult teacher who plays an active role in simplifying the various components of word-referent relationships.[1]

Further investigations by these researchers uncovered that the child's acquisition of words with shifting and complex referents will be impeded if the required adult-child verbal interaction is insufficient or lacking. From the PPVT data of the lower class, four-year-old Negro

[1] Vera John and L. S. Goldstein, "The Social Context of Language Acquisition," *Merrill-Palmer Quarterly of Behavior and Development*, Vol. 10, No. 3 (July, 1964), p. 269.

children, was derived evidence that indicated that these children were having difficulty in acquiring words which appear in a number of different contexts.

Included in a larger study designed to gather information about the verbal skills, intellectual performance and motivational approaches of white and Negro, first and fifth grade, lower and middle class children in New York City, a test to investigate category formation in young children was devised. Named the Concept Sorting Test, the instrument, consisting of 16 simple drawings to be grouped into functional pairs (sailor—boat) or into logically consistent piles, was administered to lower class and middle class Negro first-graders. The results indicate that the middle class Negro children tended to produce category labels more often than their lower class peers who instead were inclined to focus on non-essential attributes.

> Language is seen as functional behavior for the young child. While he uses his slowly developing communicative skills to inform those who care for him about his needs, he is also organizing his perceptual and social worlds through language. . . . In our analysis, the child from a lower socio-economic background may experience a deficient amount of verbal interaction. He learns most of his language by means of receptive exposure—by hearing, rather than by the correction of his own active speech.[2]

These researchers see implications from their work by stressing an emphasis on vocabulary expansion for socially disadvantaged children. They describe the activity of having these children tell stories, "made up" and also "old favorites" for retelling, before a tape recorder. The children often spoke with poor articulation but did demonstrate forcefulness and were able to communicate their thoughts to others. John and Goldstein advise that "the teaching of words needs to be carried out with originality, flexibility, and restraint."

Bernstein's work has stimulated research on the socialization of the young child by sociologists as well as educators and psychologists. At the University of Chicago's Urban Child Center, Hess and Shipman are conducting a longitudinal study attempting to ascertain what *is* cultural deprivation and how does cultural disadvantage affect the mind of the young child. Derived from his theories that there exist two

[2] *Ibid.*, p. 273.

modes or styles of linguistic expression, the restricted and elaborated modes, Bernstein further contends that social interaction and language will set a precedent in the child's family as to the type he will be socialized with. Bernstein has further explicated his theories to describe two types of families—those oriented toward control by status appeal or those families whose language falls in the restricted mode; and those oriented towards persons whose language falls in the elaborated mode as they take cognizance of the unique characteristics of the child and modify their status demands. "It is our argument that person-oriented families tend to modify behavior and emphasize its consequences; and that status-oriented families ask for rote learning and acceptance of the status quo—that is, they use a more rigid learning and teaching model, in which compliance, rather than rationale, is stressed."[3]

The research involves 160 Negro mothers and their four-year-old children selected from four different socio-economic levels: (1) college educated, professional, executive and managerial occupational level, (2) skilled blue collar occupational level, (3) unskilled and semi-skilled levels, (4) families on public assistance. All subjects were from the Metropolitan Chicago area. The subjects were brought to the University to participate in a series of sessions where mother and child interacted in task teaching activities. The tasks consisted of sorting blocks by two characteristics simultaneously, and copying five designs on a toy called "Etch-a-Sketch." The researchers, observing the mothers and their children, are attempting to relate the behavior and performance of individual mothers to the cognitive and scholastic behavior of their own children.

Results indicate marked social class differences in the ability of the children to learn from their mothers in the teaching sessions. Children from middle class homes ranked above children from the lower socio-economic levels in performance on these sorting tasks, particularly in offering verbal explanations as to the basis for sorting. Children from the lower socio-economic groups were, on the whole, less able to explain the sorting principle. Hess and Shipman state:

> The significance of the maternal environment lies not only in the lack of verbal exchange but also in the kind of interaction that de-

[3] Robert Hess and Virginia Shipman, "Early Blocks to Children's Learning," *Children*, Vol. 12, No. 5 (Sept.-Oct., 1965), p. 19.

velops between learner and teacher. Mothers of blue-collar classes appear to be socializing passive learning styles on the part of the child, teaching him to be docile in such learning situations—in contrast to more active, initiatory behavior of the child from a middle class home. . . . One of the features of the behavior of mothers and children of lower socio-economic class is a tendency to act without taking sufficient time for reflection and planning. . . . The picture that is beginning to emerge is that the *meaning of deprivation* is a *deprivation of meaning* (emphasis is author's)—a cognitive environment in which behavior is controlled by status rules, rather than by attention to the individual characteristics of a specific situation, and one in which behavior is not mediated by verbal cues or by teaching which relates events to one another and the present to the future.[4]

It is evident that we are on the verge of a breakthrough in educational theory. Education will be lifelong, individualized, universal, and varietal. More and more evidence is coming in that the pivotal, determinative years of learning are in the years before formal schooling—and most importantly, from birth to three years of age. It is in this period that the child begins to live the symbolic existence. We are learning that the deprivation of meaning previously referred to is probably irretrievable for millions of our children. This lack is a primary problem and a responsibility in our society. The gap between what Susan Archer is able to do symbolically as a lower class child, and what she is able to do as a middle class child is a tragic one. Multiplied several million times, it amounts to an awesome obstacle to education —to the quality of existence of each person affected. We call it the symbolic gap.

In our culture there are selective processes about cultural change. In general, we accept change, but in some areas change comes slowly and with great resistance. Education is generally behind times. Most of the classrooms of our country have a single teacher in front of about thirty students, most of the time making noises from her face about eternal verities. Technology can quickly change this, but how can we get people to accept technology? One powerful argument we can use

[4] *Ibid.*, pp. 93-94.

is that we can get more quality education per dollar that way. That is Paul Sullivan's argument.

A few years ago the planning of education, or determining the curriculum, was easy because no changes were contemplated. Students ten years removed could be expected to go through the same repetitive process. Therefore not much planning was done. A principal could verbally give next year's curriculum in a moment. Now a crisis has developed: we are in the throes of great change which make the future indeterminable for us. Yet planning has become a way of life. Social security, space programs, systems' approaches require planning over a longer time than ever. How, then, can we make long-range plans in education to include what will be taught in 1984? We cannot say what will be taught, *but we can plan now so that the educational system will be much more effective in fulfilling its demands than it is now. The following article tells how.*

The anthropologist Titiev describes four laws of cultural growth, one of which is the decreasing use of time and HME (human muscular energy). The simpler way to put it is that man is gradually substituting brain for brawn to do his work. We may assume a long-term inevitability about this—rocket planes instead of feet, or ships instead of coracles, etc. But education is full of cultural lags, and many teachers are not convinced, are afraid of, or do not want to know about computers. The following article is a good introduction to the subject.

THE CHOICE FOR EDUCATIONAL PROGRESS: THE COMPUTER*
Paul Sullivan

The dilemma of American education has been how to achieve the ideal of universal education without sacrificing quality education. The rapid technological advances of the past decades have shown the need for quality education to perpetuate these advances in our society. The resultant disappearance of the need for certain skills in operations which are now automated and the need for new skills for operations which did not exist a decade ago serve to point out the critical demand

---

* Unpublished monograph, Wayne State University.

for quantity placed upon our educational system to conform to the "Age of Technology." In practice, the educational system has been found to be amiss in producing quality to a degree sufficient to enable this country to enjoy an early participation in the exploration of space. The launching of the first Sputnik made this all too evident. Conversely, the goal of universal education is far from being achieved to a meaningful extent when the United States Department of Labor reveals that out of a labor force of 30,000,000 in the next decade, 7,000,000 will not finish high school and 2,000,000 will never attend high school under the present educational policies. Essentially the problem remains. How can we increase quality in education to keep our society dynamic, and yet educate the great masses of our population to partake in this dynamism?

The resolution of the dilemma lies in that which has most complicated the dilemma. Technology, which has forced the dilemma to crucial proportions, can also be applied in such a way as to resolve the dilemma. The necessary technology already exists; its application to the problem must be sought. The techniques already used successfully in business and industry must be modified and adopted by the educational system. The "systems approach" that has been responsible for the closing of the "space gap" under some modification could be applied to the educational lag and achieve a closing of the "educational gap" that exists today. Basically, the "systems approach" seeks an orderly, rational, logical approach toward fulfilling carefully specified goals. It is a total approach which shows promise of accomplishing for our schools similar rapid advancements as evidenced in the space program. It must be emphasized though, that technology must not be added on to the present educational system, but meaningfully assimilated by the present system and the system modified in such a way as to take full advantage of the technology. If this is not done, the risk is that technology will become an operation in itself and even possibly an encumbrance to its inherent potentiality for efficiency.

Accepting electronics technology as the means to the goal of quality education in quantity, two questions present themselves: (1) How can electronics technology be integrated in the educational system? (2) How much will it cost? Succinctly stated, electronics technology will cost more than what we are paying for the present techniques, but if we were to produce the same *quality* of instruction and the increased quantity of instruction through the use of our present techniques which the incorporation of electronics technology promises, the cost would be prohibitive. Thus, our ultimate goal becomes, highest quality of instruction to the greatest quantity at the lowest *possible* cost. Before a full discussion of cost however, it would be only fair to view what needs to be purchased.

Electronics technology can be applied to four areas of our schools: (1) Administration, (2) Research, (3) Information Storage, (4) Enhancement of the Learning Process. The principal value of electronics technology in these areas lies in the ability of technology to perform tasks which will free people to undertake the more creative and substantive aspects of their work. The computer is especially well suited for this function.

In the administration of the educational process the computer can assume a vital role. The processing of conventional business data is only one function. The preparation of examinations, grading, and reporting can be accomplished with speed and objectivity. Scheduling, involving classrooms, teachers, students, and flexibility to suit individual student needs and interests, can be accomplished within the capabilities of the computer. Ready reproduction of student records (diagnostic test scores, achievement profiles, etc.) and a constant evaluation of student progress through high-speed data gathering and storage will enable curriculum specialists, guidance counselors, and teachers to alter their techniques as the evaluation dictates.

In coping with the dynamism of the society, the educational experimentalist could employ the new direct access computers and thereby conduct and evaluate a project without the need of technicians operating between the raw data and the computer. Time and the rapid problem solving capability of the computer would encourage innovation in education since one man could conduct a research project which now takes a staff and cumbersome, slow procedures.

The third area in which the computer and electronics technology can serve to improve the quality of education is in information storage. The advantage of computer and electronics technology over other methods of information storage are multifold. First, the space needed is minimal. Second, the information retrieval time is almost instanta-

111

neous; third, is the ability to store several different media. Fourth, the eventual possibility of interconnecting one storage area with many schools through the use of high-speed data transmission lines which would enable the smallest and remotest to have a multi-media "library" unattainable by any other means. Such "libraries" could contain bibliographies, audio reproductions of music, speeches, and plays, visual reproduction of film strips, movies, closed circuit telecasts, and kinescopes. Two such "libraries" are being planned for the Big Ten and Middle Atlantic schools.

Technology offers the greatest contribution, however, in the learning process itself. Two principal contributions can be seen: (1) individualized learning suited to the rate of learning of the pupil and (2) maximum utilization of the most effective teachers as well as the utilization of all teachers in a manner in which they are most effective.

Through the use of electronic teaching machines, used successfully in language instruction, and programmed learning, the student can advance according to his individual capacity. The slow learners can, through extra work at the machines, raise their level of proficiency in a subject, while the rapid learner can be challenged to fulfill his greatest potential for the subject. Time consuming drills in spelling and mathematics, for example, can be readily handled by machines, relieving the teacher for more meaningful activities. The dropout rate could be decreased since those who become dropouts because they are not challenged and those who become dropouts because they consistently fail to achieve would be encouraged to stay and advance at their own rate. Teachers could devote more time to developing techniques to rescue potential dropouts, if they were relieved of their repetitive tasks. Further individualization of the learning process could be accomplished through the employment of tutorial and dialogue techniques using electronic teaching machines. The superior teacher, through taped video presentations could reach hundreds of students enabling them to have the best possible instruction.

Consequently, the teacher's role will be altered with the introduction of electronic technology in the classroom. He will become a manager of a system of techniques and resources which he will deploy in a manner suitable to the individual needs of his students. His time will be spent in personal counseling and encouraging students to inquire and seek knowledge through their own motivations, rather than serve as a repository of factual information. It is possible to envision the day when a teacher may be handling subject matter in which he is not thoroughly conversant through electronic teaching machines. The gap between the discovery of knowledge, its assimilation, and presentation to the student could be closed through the use of electronic teaching machines.

In essence, the introduction of electronics technology in the schools and its judicious application promises to resolve the dilemma of quantity or quality through the individualization of the learning process. However, if this cannot be accomplished within the present or foreseeable financial potentialities of the schools, then it will remain only a textbook method.

Electronics technology promises to revolutionize education in the future but what has it contributed to the present status of education? Two applications of technology have been made in two different areas which will serve to give a preliminary evaluation of the effectiveness of the introduction of technology in education as well as some indication of the future applications and their costs. The two applications of technology dealt with here are: Patrick Suppes' use of the computer in a program seeking to achieve learning in mathematics among grade school children at an accelerated rate while seeking to appeal to, rather than ignore, individual differences among the pupils; and the use of television by the National Association of Education Broadcasters as the nucleus of an emergency revamping of the American Samoa school system. Within the limits of space some idea of the breadth of electronics technology should be seen.

Suppes' use of the computer in teaching grade school mathematics assumes two premises fairly well documented in educational research. They are: (1) Individual differences exist in the rate of learning among students even when they are homogeneously grouped according to I.Q., and (2) repetitive drills in mathematics learning are desirable, especially in arithmetic. The curriculum for grades three through six was structured in such a manner as to appeal to both of these premises.

The curriculum for each of the grades was divided into concept blocks which were presented over a period of four to ten days. In turn each of the concept blocks was divided into five levels of difficulty with

113

the student entering the concept block at the middle level of difficulty, then moving up or down depending on his ability to perform. Furthermore, five levels of difficulty were used for a group of drills which accompanied each concept block. The student was not only free to move up or down in level of difficulty for each concept block but he could also move within the concept block itself depending on his daily performance. A preliminary evaluation of the system bore out Suppes' expectations as specific improvements in performance on arithmetic-achievement tests were exhibited by the experimental group when tested against a control group.

Of course, it would be possible for the same technique to be conducted by teachers, not computers. But the teacher would have to assign daily a level of difficulty to each of his pupils based on the previous day's performance and after the work was completed immediately grade it so that a new level could be assigned the next day. This is almost impossible under the present teaching load of the elementary teacher.

The value of such a system is evident. However, how much will it cost to take advantage of computer-assisted teaching? Suppes supplies some data in this area based on the equipment now available. Using a central computer and individual consoles in classrooms, linked to the computer through telephone lines, the cost per console now would be $2,000. Mass production of this equipment should halve this cost. Operating within a ten-year period in equipping all 1,000,000 elementary classrooms in the country would bring the expenditure to $1 billion. During this same ten-year period we will be spending only five per cent of our gross national product on education, or $500 billion. Providing reasonable numbers of our classrooms with equipment currently available would provide machine tutoring in spelling and arithmetic at a cost of about $40 to $50 per student per year or an increase of 1/12 more than we are currently providing. Future technology promises to lower this cost to perhaps 30 cents per student per hour. A teacher performing the same tutoring function, assuming there were enough teachers, would cost from $3 to $5. It would appear that the cost of excellence is within the means of our economy.

There is another way to assessing the cost of education and that is in what the dollar spent for education will buy. In the case of American

Samoa, the increased cost of using technology bought time, to evolve the school system rapidly into a modern one; educational services, previously considered too expensive; and quality, through the application of existing resources in a broader scope. In this case the application of television helps to alleviate the inadequacy of a school system to improve the general welfare of the community. An outline of the school system conditions before the advent of technology will point this out.

When Governor Lee was appointed in 1961, he found the school system to be inadequate in the following areas. The curriculum was poorly defined; fundamental skills were not being taught effectively; school plants were substandard and overcrowded; textbooks were nonexistent or obsolete and the teachers were poorly educated and trained. Most important, however, was the inadequacy of teacher preparation which resulted in ineffective teaching. To remedy the situation would seem to call for better teacher preparation, but this would take many years to achieve. Teachers could be recruited for the system. However, several hundred teachers are not likely to be found readily in addition to the cost of transporting and housing so many. Therefore, the suggestion of the National Association of Educational Broadcasters that the extended use of television be employed was the alternative accepted by Lee and Congress.

Basically, the method used was to transmit the primary content of instruction from the United States making use of highly competent teachers whose work then the Samoan teachers would reinforce according to methods set down in a guide. Rote learning methods were abandoned and problem solving and individual study used. A team approach was used in that the competent teachers were used in a maximum of classrooms via television while the classroom teacher sought to give individual attention to the student. The development of the educational system did not depend on the education and training of all the teachers in the system. The educational gap was not closed but "jumped."

The all-pervasive deficiencies of the Samoan schools enabled such a revolutionary technique to be employed readily but in a more sophisticated system, integration of such a system would require it to be modified. Surely, it might be a manner in which our better teachers could be put to more comprehensive use in a system.

As could be expected, the cost of the incorporation of technology in Samoan schools raised operating expenditures. An initial $360 per child and a yearly $380 per child are the costs for incorporation and operation, respectively. However, the cost can only be evaluated in terms of providing similar quality of instruction through different means. If revamping the system were begun with adequate training of teachers, the system would have had to wait fifteen years. This is unthinkable, and surely a false economy. The importation of teachers has already been shown to be economically unfeasible. No other method save the use of technology seems more economical than maintaining the status quo and ignoring the absence of learning. Thus the cost of technology cannot be determined apart from totality of the educational system. Learning and the lack of learning must be put into dollar and cents figures if the real dollar cost of technology is to be determined.

The extra absolute cost of providing technology for the Samoan schools was provided by the federal government which leads to the question of: What do locally supported school systems do to acquire the increased revenues needed to pay for the inclusion of technology? Many are too small in area to have a tax base sufficient to support the extra funds needed. Other districts are already approaching the limit of the capacity of the property tax to absorb the cost of education. Yet, other districts find State laws prohibiting the taxing power of the local government to be exercised in certain areas. Federal funds have been a relief in providing monies for new equipment and experimental programs. State funds have been allocated more to keep local boards of education solvent than to provide for innovation and the purchase of the products of technology.

It would appear that interested citizens should begin to campaign vigorously for more money for better schools. In the poorer states, the Federal government could be exhorted to supply more funds. State governments could guarantee sufficient funds in every school district by redistricting school districts whose tax base is insufficient to support the schools, or allocating monies from the State treasury, or providing new areas in which school revenues could be collected in addition to the property tax. A well-organized citizens committee active on local, state and Federal levels of government could help to bring about the needed improvements in the schools. The question is, how much will it cost? Tantamount to this, however, is how shall the cost be computed?

116

What shall be included in the cost of educating a pupil? If the "cost per unit" method used in industrial cost accounting is applied to education, it would appear that the national average of $607 per pupil per year is fallacious. At present we are taking into account only the cost of *teaching* the pupil. This would be comparable to industry computing the cost of only the "operable unit" and the "development costs" in the "cost per unit" figure. However, there are units produced which are inoperable and their cost must be included in the total "cost per unit." Education's "inoperable units" are those who have been taught but who have not learned. The cost of these "inoperables" is found on the relief rolls, in the juvenile detention homes, and in our prisons. The cost of maintaining these "inoperables" is much higher than their "teaching cost." Relief costs are three times more than education costs; imprisonment is five times more and the detention home four and one-half times more than education costs. If these costs are included in our cost of education it can be seen that in reality we have been spending a great deal more for educating students and really not producing as many students who have learned as we would like to believe. Thus, although the cost of incorporating electronics technology would absolutely increase the "cost per student taught," a saving will be realized in a reduction of the number of "inoperative units" or those students who fail to learn enough to maintain themselves and must be supported with other tax monies.

Rehabilitation costs can be reduced and the saving channeled into education to offset the increased cost of incorporation of electronics technology in education.

Electronics technology in the schools offers quality *and* quantity at the lowest *possible* cost. If education takes an example from industry and begins a program of intensifying capital equipment investments instead of increasing salaries which is the opposite of the present trend in education, the results will be a better "end product" and an overall lower expenditure per student through reduced rehabilitation costs.

The knowledge explosion which has been much mentioned is a critical problem for all educators. "There is so much to be thought upon," as the primitive man said when he first saw London, that we do not wonder that he, or anybody might give up the attempt to under-

117

stand it at all. But regardless of the debates, uncertainties, and a multitude of errors, we must keep on with keeping the store, or give up and head for the back woods. "Curriculum" is many things, but it is finally whatever we make it. By constant thought, patience and some courage, we may change it as indicated positively in the article by Stevens.

THE LABYRINTH: THE EXPLOSION OF KNOWLEDGE
*William Stevens**

The ideal school of tomorrow will be built on educators coming up with ideas that reflect the best of our culture's values. This will take time, patience, understanding, communication and interaction between the educator and society. It is a conference that takes place while we are all galloping on horseback and in the heat of battle, and the conference concerns not only the generals, but all the privates; not only the battle or the war, but the conditions of peace. The great confusion is created by the current pace and proliferation of educational development.

This paper is an attempt to determine what is taking place between the educator and society in the midst of a fantastic amassing of information.

There is an explosion of communicated and acquired knowledge. This fantastic amassing of information is described graphically in the NEA report of the Project for Instruction:

> Never before have the dynamic forces of change spun with such incredible speed. In the nearly 2,000 years since the birth of Christ, there has been first a very slow and then a rapidly accelerating growth in the accumulation of knowledge. If this accumulation is plotted on a time line, beginning with the birth of Christ, it is estimated that the first doubling of knowledge occurred in 1750, the second in 1900, the third in 1950, and the fourth in ten years later, in 1960.[1]

The report goes on to point out that it is impossible for one person to learn summaries of existing knowledge; not only this, but there is

---

* Graduate Student, Wayne State University, College of Education. Author's unpublished monograph, 1967.

[1] *Schools for the Sixties, A Report on the Project on Instruction*, National Education Association (New York: McGraw Hill Book Company, Inc., 1963), p. 50.

the problem of past and present knowledge rapidly becoming obsolete. We are faced with "the negation of previous understandings and the consequent need for correcting misunderstandings."[2] A realization of these facts is one of the prime reasons that curriculum planners are concerned about the task they face, more than ever before.

Attempting to examine a few facets of curriculum planning is like picking up one or two pieces of a jigsaw puzzle and pretending that a few irregularly shaped pieces of pasteboard represent the whole picture of interlocking parts. A description of some of the parts, therefore, does not serve to describe the whole. This is merely to point out that in order to present some of the problems and issues in curriculum reform, one is forced to neglect a vast array of highly-important related issues. It must not be assumed that the writer is unaware of the influence of topics such as social trends and forces, learning processes, teaching techniques; in fact, a great part of the structure of public education in America is ignored because the list of concerns that affect the decision of the curriculum planner would continue *ad infinitum*.

Definitions. A "semantic jungle" is how John Goodlad aptly describes the curriculum in the school.[3] On the one hand agreement could be reached with the writer who states:

> The commonly accepted definition of the curriculum has changed from content of courses for study and lists of subjects to all the experiences which are offered to learners under the auspices of the schools . . . to all the experiences over which the school has control . . . These experiences may occur in school, school busses, cafeterias and corridors . . . If, in line with Gestaltist thinking, the whole child is said to come to school, teachers must have concern for his attitudes and appreciations as well as for his cognate learning.[4]

The foregoing may be acceptable, in part; however, to best serve the interests of this paper, it will be endeavored to stay out of busses and the cafeterias. Although Arno Bellack concurs that "the school responsibility extends beyond teaching the organized fields of learning and inquiry," and that "it must also serve a multitude of ends and

[2] David Riesman, "Abundance for What?", *op. cit.*

[3] John I. Goodlad, *School Curriculum Reform in the United States* (New York: The Fund for the Advancement of Education, March, 1964), p. 53.

[4] Ronald Doll, *Curriculum Improvement: Decision Making and Process* (Boston: Allyn and Bacon, Inc., 1964), p. 15.

needs created by our society and culture," however, "by universal agreement of knowledge as the stock-in trade of the school," for the most part, this paper will deal with the fields of organized knowledge in accord with the idea that "few would deny that the fields of organized inquiry are significant aspects of our culture that the school is uniquely equipped to introduce to students."[5]

Integration of the disciplines. An impassioned spokesman for the integration of the disciplines, Henry Winthrop, says that a "major task which must be faced by professional educators . . . is to reorganize the curriculum so as to reflect the interdisciplinary emphases which are changing the face of the world."[6]

The interdisciplines that Winthrop describes are but a few of many, he reports. There are examples such as cybernetics, comparing the functions and control and communications in computers, or as the construction of models which simulate large social systems and other human affairs; bionics, a special phase of cybernetics concerned with the efforts to use biological systems as models for machines; general systems theory, related to the first two interdisciplinary areas which, it is hoped, will be a bridge for the disciplines and is mathematical in nature; and operations research, which is aimed at identifying problems to promote a quantitative basis for decisions.

Although these interdisciplines function in the realm of higher education, the downward push will doubtless occur in these fields as it has in others. Winthrop would like to see an *Institute of Intellectual Synthesis* formed by scholars to perform the following functions:

1. Tackle the problems missed by specialists, or problems neglected when they cannot be fitted into the Procrustean beds of traditional subject matter.
2. Acquaint curriculum builders with newer disciplines.
3. Develop methodology suitable for newer disciplines.
4. Build bridges between the disciplines.[7]

The scholars chosen to build the bridges between the disciplines

[5] Arno Bellack, "What Knowledge Is of Most Worth?", *The High School Journal*, XVLII, No. 5 (February, 1965), p. 318.

[6] Henry Winthrop, "Contemporary Intellectual Ferment," *The Social Studies*, XLVI, No. 8 (March, 1965), p. 84.

[7] Winthrop, p. 86.

might follow Oxford University's Professor Peterson in searching for relationships. Bellack sums up these approaches as follows:

> In the first, emphases are on the conceptual scheme and methods of inquiry associated with the broad fields of knowledge, the natural sciences, the social sciences, mathematics, and the humanities. In the second, attention is focused on modes of thought—the analytic, the empirical, the aesthetic, and the moral—that transcend the boundaries of mutually reinforcing conceptions of knowledge that serve well as the basis for curriculum planning.[8]

The present. Today the emphasis is back to the disciplines with the objectives being the understanding of the logical order inherent in knowledge itself, on the structure of concepts and principles of inquiry that characterize the various fields of learning. In his study of recent projects, Goodlad makes the distinction between the *old* and *new* approach as follows:

> In the old, topic followed topic; there were few attempts to reveal what lay behind them. The new arrangement still discusses topics, but interspersed among these are reminders, for example, of the importance of careful observation on, or of the relationship between a topic and a concept which this topic is designed to illuminate.[9]

The justification for teaching the fundamental structure of the discipline is that understanding of fundamental ideas is the main road to adequate "transfer of learning," says Bellak, citing Jerome Bruner's phrase. Another reason why this method of learning is being used is that these projects originate in the universities and the scholars who design them happen to be the leaders in the various disciplines, noted Bellack and Goodlad. The latter reason also explains another important trend—the emphasis on science and mathematics. Of course, the advent of the Sputnik age caused many curriculum planners to agree that, "The citizen must have an improved awareness because of the impact of the resulting technological advances on his social environment."[10] However, at present there is a notable imbalance resulting from this attention to science and mathematics as compared with the

[8] Bellack, "Structure of Knowledge and the Curriculum," p. 35.
[9] Goodlad, p. 56.
[10] Goodlad, p. 57.

development in the fields of social sciences, humanities (especially the arts), health and physical education.

Other trends today. The ways in which curriculum planners are presently attempting to cope with providing more knowledge to more people was observed by McAulay. He noted the downward pressure of course content (primers in the kindergarten), a trend toward homogeneous grouping of students, a departmentalization in elementary schools with specialized personnel in certain fields, an increase in more liberal arts education for teachers, and a tendency toward bigness (the consolidation of school districts).[11]

The future. The future will find us utilizing a longer school day and a longer school year, reports Hazel Lamber. Her research predicts that the bachelor's degree will be outmoded as a basic requirement for teaching: six years of college will be more commonly expected for teachers. Further, the use of teaching aids such as television and teaching machines will be more commonplace.[12]

The following excerpts taken from Changing Times *survey the modern curriculum area. The tone is rather optimistic in telling about the enormous numbers of students who are processed through our schools. Nevertheless, the great success is achieved at the expense of, or at least along with, stupendous losses, and no clear solution is offered.*

HIGH SCHOOLS: ARE THEY DOING THEIR JOB?*

In 1900 fewer than 10% of the 6,100,000 American youngsters between 14 and 18 years of age went to high school. High school was an experience for the intellectually elite, and the total enrollment was only some 519,000 boys and girls, practically all of whom took a classical course. Indeed, that was about the only course offered.

The secondary schools of that period were essentially college-pre-

* High Schools: Are They Doing Their Job?", *Changing Times: The Kiplinger Magazine*, X, No. 7 (July, 1956), 25-31. Reprinted by permission.

11 J. D. McAulay, "Elementary Education—Five Straws to the Wind," *Phi Delta Kappan*, Vol. XLI, No. 9 (June, 1960), p. 384.

12 Hazel M. Lambert, "Elementary Education" (Washington, D.C.: The Center for Applied Research in Education, Inc., 1963), p. 98.

paratory schools, and youngsters who didn't care for classical subjects or were not on their way to college had the alternative of going to work.

Today approximately 80% of American youths of high school age are enrolled in junior and senior high school classes. As nearly as anybody can estimate it, the total enrollment is a whopping 7,200,000 pupils, give or take a few hundred thousand. Literally, almost everybody goes to high school now—not just the academically inclined. In the 1800's a free elementary-school education became the birthright of every citizen. The first half of the twentieth century was the period in which a free secondary-school education was added to that prerogative.

A number of economic and social factors have brought this result about. Technological progress in industry and on the farm has all but eliminated the need for child labor. Higher family incomes also have lessened the necessity of children's having to work. Untrained youngsters are, in fact, neither needed nor overly welcome in the labor market. The place for them to be is in school, and laws have been passed to enforce their attendance. In many states today the minimum legal age for leaving school is 16. Several states won't let students quit till they are 18.

All this has posed an enormous problem for educators. Of the vast new hordes of young people descending upon the public high schools, greater and greater majorities come without interest in the traditional classical subjects or the ability to grasp them. They are not planning to go to college. They couldn't care less about Latin or math or science.

What should the schools teach these kids?

Commercial and vocational subjects began to edge into high school curricula about 1910, when it became obvious that many youths who were not going to college could profitably be taught subjects that would help them make a living.

Commercial training for girls was built largely around shorthand, typing and business English. Vocational training for boys was built around the trades and crafts. Sometimes separate high schools were constructed to house classes in these subjects. More often the high schools were expanded into comprehensive schools that offered all types of courses.

But with the onrush of youngsters that began in the jobless 30's these courses were not enough. Not all girls who planned to work after

123

graduation wanted typing and shorthand. Shorthand was beyond the capabilities of some, and others had no real interest in office work. Not all boys wanted to be electricians or machinists. So the variety of business and technical courses was broadened until today every conceivable commercial and vocational subject is taught in some high school somewhere.

Frequently such courses are supplemented by on-the-job training during the students' last two years in high school. For example, boys and girls taking today's course in "distributive education"—school terminology for wholesale or retail selling—will work in local stores part-time during their junior and senior years. A boy learning gas station management will work in a service station under the eyes of both his employer and his high school principal or counselor.

Naturally, such unscholarly goings-on bring gasps from adults who have been accustomed to thinking of high school in terms of the old college-preparatory institutions. But the fact is that these courses usually find their way into the curriculum because the parents and taxpayers of the community want them there. They are valuable to the students who take them, and they have added vastly to the power of the high schools to hold youngsters that are not academic-minded. Even so, far too many children drop out of school as soon as the law permits. Almost half of those who enter high school fail to graduate. . . .

A typical college-preparatory course includes four years of English, a minimum of two years of foreign-language study, two to three years of social studies (including history), two years of mathematics and two years of science. This makes a total of 12 or 13 of the 16 credits usually required for graduation from high school and admission to college. Three or four other credits should be earned in major subjects for which college entrance credit is given. Credits for minor courses are supposed to be extra.

Successful completion of a course like this will land your youngster in any one of 95% of the colleges in the nation—at least as far as academic requirements are concerned. "Successful completion," however, means that your child should be in the top part of his class. An eastern suburban high school has set this standard as a guide for its students who plan to go on to college: 60% A's and B's in the junior and senior years and no mark below a C. . . .

In answer to the argument that it will soon be necessary for students to attend private schools in order to prepare for college, it is noteworthy that public high school students do better than private school pupils in most subjects in College Entrance Board examinations. Here, for example, are comparative mean scores of all public and private secondary-school pupils who took College Board achievement tests in March 1954, the latest period for which complete figures are available. The possible range in these examinations is 200 to 800 points, with 500 regarded as average.

Public high school youngsters outscored their private-school contemporaries in these fields:

	public	*private*
social studies	525	511
German	509	492
Latin	557	530
biology	508	491
chemistry	540	522
physics	549	518
intermediate mathematics	530	495
advanced mathematics	582	575

Only in English composition, French and Spanish did the private-school pupils do better than the public-school youngsters, with comparative scores of 523 to 521, 526 to 506, and 500 to 486 in the respective subjects.

In aptitude tests the public-high kids beat the private-school boys and girls 484 to 482 in the verbal section, 514 to 492 in the mathematical section and 543 to 525 in the examinations having to do with spatial relations. . . .

Thus far we have presented a number of protagonists whose central concern has been with subject matter and academic issues. Gertrude Noar, however, has a somewhat different emphasis. She sees a most vital aspect of education in the building of good self-concepts and human relations.

INFORMATION IS NOT ENOUGH
Gertrude Noar*

There are many people, in and out of schools, who believe that the primary responsibility of the school is to give children information. They view the teachers, especially of secondary schools, as purveyors of information. Many of them think that the solution to interpersonal and intergroup tensions lies in giving people—both young and old— information about race, about religions, about the social class and caste structure of American society, and about distant lands and cultures.

There is no doubt that information about all these things is important. Any school in which pupils fail to get facts, and fail to learn how to get facts, is not as good a school as the American public demands. Nevertheless, current evidence in the field of education points to the fact that information is not enough—*not enough* to create people with generous outgoing personalities able to lead rich and abundant lives; *not enough* to help people develop and utilize to the fullest extent their own and other individuals' potentialities; *not enough* to give people the courage needed to stand up and be counted in the fight against prejudice, discrimination and bigotry; *not enough* to enable adults of this generation to cure the human relations illnesses which beset our times: delinquency, crime and moral breakdown; divorce and the deterioration of family life; mental illness and emotionally caused illnesses; interracial and international strife.

If information is not enough, then what else *is* required in the classrooms of America? What else must the teacher do besides tell? What kinds of learning experiences do children need besides reading, writing, figuring and reciting?

* Gertrude Noar, *Information Is Not Enough: The Implementation of Human Relations Education in the Classroom.* Published by The Anti-Defamation League of B'nai B'rith (New York, 1958), 5, 6. Reprinted by permission.

First, Schools must help the pupil to create a self-concept that permits him to like himself and, therefore, to like others; one that enables him to move positively toward others who, in one way or another, are different from himself.

Second, Pupils can and, indeed, must learn certain human relations skills. These are as essential for effective living as are the fundamental skills of reading, writing and arithmetic.

Third, Education for good human relations requires the inculcation of positive attitudes toward others, toward differences, toward democracy, toward life itself.

Fourth, The schoolteacher has a primary responsibility for providing minority group children with status-building experiences. This kind of education requires resources and materials which are already available.

How does the teacher help to create *an adequate self-concept* in the child, a concept that will enable the child to relate well to others and to do his best? This goal can be achieved by making the child *know* that he is liked, needed, accepted and wanted—no matter whether his skin is light or dark, whether he is fat or thin, whether he goes to church, cathedral or synagogue, whether he lives on the hill or across the tracks, whether his forefathers were born in the British Isles or in Italy....

We explain why curriculum cannot profitably be considered as an isolated subject. Curriculum must be human-centered, because for good or ill, man learns through motivation tied in with the structure of human nature. Only by being thoroughly human in his learning can he at times seem to transcend himself.

CURRICULUM: THE LEARNING OF CULTURAL SETS
*Wilfred R. Smith and August Kerber**

The problem of curriculum can be approached on a number of levels. We can concern ourselves, if we wish, only with the efficiency

* Wilfred R. Smith and August Kerber, "Curriculum: The Learning of Cultural Sets." Unpublished monograph, Wayne State University (Detroit, 1961).

of learning of the students in the courses we have prepared. Supposedly, if they are not interested, or not mastering the content of the courses, the fault lies with the courses themselves. The task for educators would be seen as making the subject matter more intelligible, more stimulating, and of greater impact on the neural structure of students.

A more encompassing level would be concern with the general appropriateness of the content of the courses. In this view the goals of education, the kinds of people in our society, the movement of greater knowledge, and the broad sweep of human affairs would have to be taken into account in constructing the content, or "what" of learning.

A view of still greater inclusiveness for curriculum goals would be what we would call the cultural approach. In this view, curriculum would be considered a part in a dynamic whole, considering the individual, the learning content, and the total society as a dynamic totality, intertangled and only abstractly separable. This view has been presaged by psychological schools of thought and so-called progressive education. The broad emphasis in institutions preparing teachers has been on the "whole child" and "teaching children, not subjects." Dewey had insight on the social nature of learning, but he lacked modern knowledge of the structure and function of the society and the individual.

The concern for curriculum in modern education is very real, and very understandable. It would be disastrous if we decided the issue was of small consequence and could be ignored or evaded. Those who have a rigid curriculum for the perfect society and those who "don't care what you teach, as long as you love children" are to be distrusted. The feeling that all is not well in the state of Delaware is basically a hopeful sign, because from it may come constructive action.

Modern Western education came from the Greeks and, in a truly awesome measure, bears the stamp of the cultural complex they contributed. Learning, in the Greek notion, was the absorption of certain symbols into the tablet of the mind, which was strengthened by the discipline and praxis of this activity. The symbols were carefully selected to have lasting value to the learner. These symbols were good for him and for society. In the Renaissance, learning was extended to other subjects, and to a certain extent to skill and vocational training. Just as the medieval Christians inherited the problem of teaching Christian parables via pagan models, modern education has wrestled with the opposing views in curriculum of the eternal verities and making it pay its way in the market place.

Our knowledge of man today makes us believe that such oppositions are based on ignorance. Each view has some part of truth, or of clear knowledge. Equality, freedom, beauty, goodness, and truth are not meaningless abstractions. They are universal ideals that all men who use symbols, who communicate, and who participate in a common world can understand. Yet each person is unique. He comes from a different culture, and has a different perceptual base with which to learn. He learns the speed of light, the theorems of Euclid, the Gettysburg Address as objective, public facts; but he learns these things if his culture is literate, if he has had enough rice to eat in the morning, and if the teacher has not berated him for having torn trousers.

We have now progressed in social science enough to know that the "how" and the "what" which is learned are inseparable. We therefore state that we need a philosophy of education to make adequate criticism of the content of education, and we need an expansion of and application of the social sciences to get the child to learn. The core learnings, the amount and quality of the general subjects, and the kinds of specialized learnings needed in the modern school we shall not discuss here. This is by no means to indicate a belief of lesser importance in this aspect of learning, that which is traditionally known as curriculum. We would rather state some principles to be realized in the learning process. If these principles are realized, then we shall have a basis for a good curriculum in school and in life.

1. The child should get to know the culture in which he lives. He perceives this culture by means of previous culture sets which he attains in the learning process. He can be blocked in the expansion of his cultural sets, and today very often is, by the cultural set of the school. (A cultural set is the perceptual framework of a child produced by his previous enculturation, the acculturation his present cultural environment has given him, and the present objects of cultural significance which engage his attention.)

2. He should be engaged in a continual process of communication. No

person can resign from the human race, and no child can democratically elect *not* to communicate. This principle bears upon the ideals of equality, freedom, truth, and individualism; it bears also on ultimate purpose. Culture is inculcated, that is, enforced upon him. The only way he can express himself against coercion, fear, crime, and stifling of the self is *through* freedom, truth, and creative intelligence. He must, therefore, communicate. He must learn that the holocaust of war, the fleeting currents of hate, and the dull ear turned to eager entreaty are alike anticommunication and antilife.

3. His most effective learning will be in small groups who accept him. Cooley called primary groups the "nursery of human nature." Infants lacking attention of mothers do not develop even physically, to say nothing of their emotional complexes. Each child has a right to be accepted by others, and he will be accepted by them, because he fulfills needs in them—unless walls are interposed by society. In education, the presence and support of others who recognize him and know him as a self is not merely a help to learning. It is an integral part of it.

4. The learning of content, of a new occupation, of a new cultural context is a social enterprise. The poet addresses someone, as does the statesman, and the scientist isolated for a year in an outpost in a scientific experiment. We are engaged in eternal conversation; that is the quest for knowledge, and the value of the bridges and sealing wax. We do not seek beauty in itself, nor knowledge in itself. We seek knowledge because we are convinced others somewhere, sometime will live better and communicate better because we have learned the particular facts represented in the symbols swimming before our eyes.

Editors' Summary

Democracy, or at least our democracy in the United States, is a battleground for many diverse groups, and these differences of opinion cannot neatly and clearly be settled by our collection of words here. Those who have such neat solutions walk where angels fear to tread. The solutions turn out to be of the nature of descriptions of unicorns, perpetual machines, and schemes on "how to beat the horses."

Ask the average man what he believes. Sound him out on cosmology and politics, and he will usually come up with only the vaguest notions or meaningless platitudes about these topics. Submit a list to him of the subjects being taught in high schools, or better still tell him why and how these subjects are taught, and he can, and often does, give specific, animated reactions. He has many crystallized opinions when shown all the lineaments of the cultural expression of the school. He senses that the school expresses his values, shows his selections and priorities of information, his image of society, and his ideals of human relationships.

Since every man in a democracy sees things differently and has different ideas concerning learning theory, it is small wonder that curriculum is a battlefield. Notice that the battle itself is really an insignificant part of curriculum, but that curriculum is the battle site. The causes lie in the past, the vested interests, the clash of dogmas, and the lack of mutual support of institutions in our whole society.

The problem cannot be solved by statistical norms, appeals by silvery-tongued public relations men, the shibboleths of adjustment or mass media exposure, or appeals of youth, the experts, crackpots, or formulae peddlers. Nor can the battle be escaped. It is the struggle of a society realizing itself, and we are all in it together.

We shall be educating for democracy when we help the immature grow into the skills, the knowledge, and the attitudes needed by free men. We must make education the source of a democracy which stimulates the teachers, the students, and all others in the realization that life is fulfilled and goals achieved at every moment. Ralph Barton Perry has said:

> *To live appropriately in a democratic society requires that one shall prefer this form of association to the company of the servile and obsequious. It is this interplay of freedoms—this living among the free—that creates the zest and exhilaration of democratic social relations.*

RELATED READINGS

Anderson, V. E., and others. "Lay Participation in Curriculum Development," *Educational Leadership*, XV (April, 1957), 398-431.

131

Benjamin, Harold. "Whose Fundamentals?" *Phi Delta Kappan*, XXXIII (1951), 87-89.

Bode, Boyd H. *Progressive Education at the Crossroads*. New York: Newson & Co., 1938.

Bryce, James. *Modern Democracies*. New York: Macmillan, 1921.

Champlin, Nathaniel L. "The Attacks Upon Public Education: Their Significance for Philosophy of Education," *Educational Theory*, VIII (July, 1958), 157-61.

de Tocqueville, Alexis, *Democracy in America*. New York: Vintage, 1954.

Dewey, John. *Experience and Education*. New York: The Macmillan Co., 1939.

Ekirch, Arthur A., Jr. *The American Democratic Tradition: A History*. New York: Macmillan, 1963.

Flesch, Rudolf. *Why Johnny Can't Read*. New York: Harper & Brothers, 1955.

Foley, Louis. "Defenders of Grammatical Heresey," *Phi Delta Kappan*, XXXIV (1952), 101-03.

Justman, Joseph. "Wanted: A Philosophy of American Education," *School and Society*, LXXXIII (May 12, 1956), 159-61.

Kaplan, Louis. "The Attack on Modern Education," *Phi Delta Kappan*, XXXII (1951), 223-26.

Kyte, George C. "A Core Vocabulary in the Language Arts," *Phi Delta Kappan*, XXXIV (1953), 231-34.

McGrath, Earl J. "Language Study and World Affairs," *Phi Delta Kappan*, XXXIV (1953), 144-48.

McNeill, Wm. H. *The Emergence of the West*. Chicago: University of Chicago Press, 1963.

Melby, E. O. "Where and What Are the Educational Wastelands?" *School and Society*, LXXXIII (March 3, 1956), 71-75.

Michael, Donald M. *Cybernation: The Silent Conquest*. Santa Barbara, Calif. Center for the Study of Democratic Institutions, 1962.

Moore, W. "Causal Factors in the Current Attack on Education," *American Association of University Professors Bulletin*, XLI (December, 1955), 621-28.

Piel, Gerard. *Science in the Cause of Man*. New York: Knopf, 1961.

Riesman, David. *Constraint and Variety in American Education*. Lincoln: University of Nebraska Press, 1956.

Sheviakov, George V., and Fritz Redl. *Discipline for Today's Children and Youth*. Washington, D.C.: National Education Association, 1958.

Smith, Mortimer. *Public Schools in Crisis: Some Critical Essays*. Chicago: Henry Regnery Co., 1956.

Smith, T. V., and Edward Lindeman. *The Democratic Way of Life*. New York: Mentor, 1951.

Von Neumann, John. *The Computer and the Brain*. New Haven: Yale University Press, 1963.

Woodring, Paul. *A Fourth of a Nation*. New York: McGraw-Hill Book Co., 1957.

PART III

THE EQUALIZATION OF EDUCATIONAL OPPORTUNITY

Probably the greatest achievement America has shown the world, with the exception of the total idea of the democratic society, is that of the public school system. It is in this institution that society makes good its promise to provide opportunity for all regardless of genetic structure, condition of birth, or "race, creed, color, or previous condition of servitude." While creating further diversities in every moment of the attempt, the least man of the society recognizes the nobility of the effort.

The statement that "all men are created equal" is regarded by all who have thought a little about the nature of democracy as an over-generalization of what the ideal should be, if ideal specific conditions existed. This does not make the statement meaningless or ridiculous. True, universal agreement is never attained on whether specific policies or measures square with the ideal. Yet everyone who believes in democracy quickly identifies and objurgates anything that would militate against this ideal. The reason this is possible is that "equality" is a convenient, shorthand symbol for many values, constantly working and constantly appreciated, in our society. When any of these core values are flouted, a public outcry of hurt arises.

These values are received from many streams of Western culture, and we are beholden to the Greeks, Romans, British, and others for them. But the unique synthesis and the day-to-day working of these values across the land is both our burden and treasure. The values center in the core notion of the supreme worth of man, instanced and implemented in the individual man, but caused by the paradigm of culture. The briefest, clearest way to state the ideal of these values is that each man is human, and the culture is dedicated to bring to each his ultimate of humanness.

To search for and implement formulae of legal, economic, social, spiritual, or even physical equality is to flee at once from the greater good of building the society so that each may become more human, who correlatively may make the society stronger and more securely grounded in the enterprise which succeeded in him. That there is an absolute distinction between men and animals is known, but the ways in which the qualities of humanness may be amplified among men, the course of history shows to be fraught with peril. Each age brings its problems, and each new structure of government or society may bring immoral or amoral men into control. It is always easier to divide poverty equally, or to make all underlings equally subject to coercion, than to build the individual and the society simultaneously.

Our society has made the major commitment of endeavoring to enculturate the individual to his full potential. Why then, do we not forge ahead quickly with this universal mandate? There are several great obstacles. We shall oversimplify them in explaining the difficulties of the search for equality.

1. *Definition.* Most of us would agree that all men are physically, mentally, socially, and idiosyncratically unequal. Yet we equally vote, have equal privileges and immunities, and we most fervently demand our equal rights. There is a world of difference between me and thee on what equality means for the whole range of humanity in our society. Some look for certain absolutes of equality, and others search for formulae to apply to sex, age, grade, and station. Some have no specific idea, but a pious hope.

2. *The means of attainment.* Even if we could all agree that equality in the society should have certain conditions, for example political equality, how shall we go about getting this equality? One vote does not mean equal political power with your neighbor, who may be running a well-oiled political machine. A college B.A. degree cannot be achieved by some, and others wish to exceed it. Even if we

should agree on the narrowest local means of some measure, for instance, health, you may think the program must be headed by an M.D.

3. *The conditions change.* Even if we were to agree on a particular scheme for equalization, the new conditions arising would necessitate new planning among us which would bring disagreement. To take an oversimplified example, suppose that all of us were demanded to carry an equal burden for a day's journey. After elaborate meetings and plans, we might decide to exclude the infants, old, lame, etc., and give all the rest *proportionate* burdens. But in the course of the day, some would hurt themselves, fall into swamps, or meet with unusual difficulties. What should be done? The pressure might be to elect a czar to settle all problems.

We have purposely referred the problem of equalization to the level of equality, to show how enormously complicated the real problem is. It would seem at first blush to be insuperable. But no matter how difficult it is, we must at all costs keep trying. Seeking easy formulae and rationalizations is the start of deterioration, which is cumulative and adds to the new problems.

Our knowledge of man and of our culture has so advanced that we know what our challenges are and what our work must be. We see that each person must be educated—that is encultured—to his full power. Our society has traditional institutions and age-old ways of dealing with individuals which do not square with enlightened, democratic views of equality of opportunity. To have a fair chance, each child should have equal opportunity to gain the rewards of our culture. This immediately makes the problem greater than the one of obtaining strict equality in several departments—but in no whit removes our responsibilities as fellow human beings in making these opportunities more equalitarian.

The moment we step off from our general principle and deal with specific issues, as for instance, the education of the gifted, we run into knotty arguments. It is not a problem of whether to have or not have a program for the gifted, but one of priorities in a situation in which many other worthy claimants put forth their demands. Even if we all agree to give the gifted program a top priority, the controversy is not settled. We argue among ourselves on a thousand and one ways to accomplish the program.

The outlook is one of a long-term, many-faceted struggle. This is not in itself discouraging. What is most important is that we strive to maintain the struggle on the ground of the general ideal of equality, which as we have said really means the elevation of the *humanness* of each man in the society.

We have seen fit to present the issue of equalization of opportunity in three chapters. At first the topics may seem quite disjointed, yet the discriminating reader will soon discern the equalization *leitmotif*. We pose the question: Can the public schools of the United States long exist only partially integrated? The last cannonade of the Civil War has long since died, but many of the mores of the old ante-bellum plantation days remain with us. The latest assault on that system was the toppling of the walls of the 1896 "separate but equal" decision of the U.S. Supreme Court.

A problem that has burgeoned into proportions unforeseen by many, and tied in with racism, desegregation, and the whole press of urbanism—a very general movement in our society—is that of inner city schools. The success or failure of inner city schools is intimately related with democratic opportunity in our society. The traditional theory is that education gives mobility to individuals. The evidence now is that the inner city schools have failed to abate the movement toward the crystallization and demarcation of a large, disfranchised, economically and socially defeated inner city Negro class. This is discussed in the second chapter.

Our third chapter deals with educating the exceptional and the handicapped. Some people, because of accidents unavoidable to them as individuals, are blind or otherwise handicapped. We all agree on helping these unfortunates, but to what extent? A far larger handicapped group are those who came from deficient or destructive social backgrounds. Statistically, large numbers of these culturally different children fail in school. What can we do that will make large numbers succeed? Should we educate for the upper, the middle, the lower groups, or all children? It is a question with much disagreement among us. The Sputnik success in 1957 strengthened the pressure for us to increase our quality of output. An obvious source of immediate higher scholarly attainment is among our academically talented, whoever they are. The pros and cons of the notion of special help for the gifted, or about various programs for the gifted, are presented in this chapter.

VI

The Desegregation Issue

Editors' Comment

The radical Republicans at the close of the Civil War made the ratification of the 13th and 14th amendments by the seceded states a condition of their readmission into the Union. Theoretically, it would seem that these amendments, plus the 15th, gave the Negroes all the fundamental rights of the whites. Such pertinent passages as the following were written with this purpose in mind.

(Article XIII, Section 1) Neither slavery nor involuntary servitude . . . shall exist within the United States. . . . (Article XIV, Section 1) All persons born or naturalized in the United States . . . are citizens of the United States and of the State wherein they reside. No state shall make or enforce any law which shall abridge the privileges or immunities of citizens of the United States; nor shall any State deprive any person of life, liberty, or property without due process of law. . . . (Article XV, Section 1) The right of citizens of the United States to vote shall not be denied or abridged by the United States or by any State on account of race, color, or previous condition of servitude.

But as we know, many discriminations against Negroes exist in our society, including the overt flouting of these amendments; the

137

voting franchise up to now has been extended to only a small percentage of Negroes. Some facets of this discrimination, however, have drawn more attention than others. So much value has been placed on education in our society that it is quite natural that the educational discrimination against Negroes has been a focal point of conflict in the mores of groups of Americans.

The courts, supposedly the weakest of the three branches of the government, have initiated the greatest stroke for desegregation in our modern history. The decision revolving around the famous five cases of May 17, 1954, does not immediately make illegal all similar cases of discrimination. A narrow interpretation would have it that every single case of discrimination would have to be tried in the courts on its own merits. In a way this famous decision has stretched the process of the Supreme Court considerably; universal litigation has been avoided and lower courts have been directed to command school boards to integrate "with all deliberate speed." In effect, the courts are turning themselves into executive bureaus for the interim of the crisis—that period of time in which it looks as though the states may not integrate.

Though we have faith in the power of law to make real changes and know of the great prestige of the Supreme Court, we have grave doubts about the power of the Supreme Court to direct the whole desegregation movement. What is needed is an alignment of the other parts of our government and all the institutions of our society with the decision of the Supreme Court or, put more broadly, the dissolution of all legal and illegal discrimination.

The story of the Negro in America is one of continued crisis and conflict of values of Americans. Other groups, like the Irish and Italians, have been able to assimilate into the mainstream of the culture. Groups classified as Caucasian have also fused into the melting pot with somewhat more difficulty. The Orientals and American Indians have had much greater obstacles. We believe the latter would not have had such difficulties if the racist formula had not been so widely and intensely applied, bringing the other non-whites into the vortex of the racist maelstrom created by Negroes.

From the beginning, the Negroes have posed a basic problem of ethics to Americans. They came as slaves, and though in colonial times concensus on the ideals of democracy had not been clearly written down

138

or stated by the vox populi *as a coherent set of principles, many of those of earnest thought and concern felt that slavery was inimical and insupportable as part of democracy. They knew that the ideal was true without exception, or it was meaningless.*

About 200,000 slaves were imported into the territory of the United States before 1807. They came from many tribes on the West coast of Africa. Typically in the southern plantations, the Negro families and tribal groups were broken up. They were shorn of their culture and given just enough of their masters' culture to function as slaves. Most of them served as field hands. A fraction in time became freedmen, artisans, and house hands before the Emancipation Proclamation.

After the Civil War, the Reconstruction era operated for a short time—probably more effectively than most historians give credit for— to educate and bring economic independence to the former slaves. But by 1870, most of the Old South was instating, or reinstating a system more compatible with their mores.

For this was a human problem, not a problem of cold logic, nor an objective scientific problem appealing to invention or creative design. Logically, the Negroes could have been annihilated, deported to Africa, or relegated clearly to a subcaste. Theoretical tendencies and actual practices moved toward such solutions, but really, the reservoir of culture had too many cross currents. Our society could not conscientiously accept the kind of solution the Nazis had for the Jews prior to World War II, for example. The total result was one in which the Negroes, as a group, have had to accept a smaller, discriminatory share of the rewards in our society. The practices may have varied from community to community and between the South and the North, but the end result was one of discrimination. Using income, education, and voting rights as general areas of comparison, we notice that Negroes have an average family income of sixty percent that of the whites, their education is about three years behind the white average, and they are almost totally excluded from voting in five of the Old South states.

Historically and sociologically, the Negro problem is that of assimilating the four million Negroes emancipated in 1863 into American culture. The Irish, Germans, Italians, Poles, Jews, and others of Southeastern Europe, and even from Asia, have done it. They have been helped by their own groups. This has been done by Irish power and

German power, and power of the other groups, even though their names were not given. They also were helped by the mores of the country to motivate themselves to rise individually. But the sons, grandsons, and great grandsons of the field hands have remained largely unassimilated.

The problem of the assimilation of the field hands has taken a new dress in fastmoving, technologically revolutionary urbanized Twentieth century. Many of the unassimilated Negroes have moved to the inner city. The tempo of the times has masked the problem, but it is basically the same. Because of the pace of movement, it has become more aggravated.

Uneducated, culturally unassimilated Negroes of the inner city are in relatively worse shape than they were a generation or two ago. No longer is there a demand for brawn in the cotton fields, or as unskilled laborers in the labor market. To be competitive today, one must be educated enough to absorb refresher training to make up for obsoleted skills three times in the career of a technician. Most inner city Negroes lack the minimal skill or entry education to run with the pack.

Bringing the problem up to date, becoming aware of its enormity and portent, is the prerequisite to solution. The stopgap programs, the myriad kindly, but unintegrated measures to help the Negro have badly failed.

To apply the words of Lincoln, perhaps in a way he had not intended, we are now engaged in a great contest testing not whether the nation may endure, but whether the principle of liberty and the proposition that all men are created equal may endure. For if we imagine that sonorous affirmations on the statute books, abetted by piddling programs in public schools, increased welfare allotments and a host of noisome poverty programs are adequate to the task of bringing the Negro group into assimilation, we are deluding ourselves. And the consequences of this delusion will become more exacerbated as we move through several more decades of technological revolutions like solving the problem of getting a man to the moon. We need much more simple social equity for the great grandson of Sambo on Colonel Slade's plantation, sitting and listening to a modern teacher in a modern classroom in the inner city.

The sins of the fathers may be visited unto the sons for several generations. As Franklin saw that slavery was an institution which would rise to threaten our existence as a free nation, so now many see the inner city Negro as a juggernaut of destruction proceeding with a kind of superorganic inevitability over the castellated towers that rise for the millenium of the Common Man. We must therefore, not con ourselves with thinking that middle class etiquette, modernized ladling of free soup or verbal affirmations come up to the stature of the problem. We must realistically admit the problem in all of its manifestations and act with courage and resolution to its full measure.

The following is a report about a report. The original report is of 737 pages and relates how the Negro is doing in American schools. The answer—badly. The reasons, and the total picture are somewhat surprising in specific details, but a couple of salient facts stand out: (1) Negroes, as a group, are below whites in achievement all along the line, and, of course, the gap is greatest in public school at the twelfth grade level; and (2) the role of language is crucial in academic achievement. After looking at all the facts, we should be able to implement some desirable changes.

EDUCATION: THE RACIAL GAP
Christopher Jencks

Equality of Educational Opportunity
by James S. Coleman, *et al.*
(Government Printing Office; $4.50)

Equality of Educational Opportunity is not light reading. Prepared as a US Office of Education report to Congress, it is written in the workmanlike prose of an Agriculture Department bulletin on fertilizer. Well over half its 737 pages are filled with tables, charts, and questionnaires, most of which will be virtually incomprehensible to those who are not trained in statistics. Recognizing that neither educators nor laymen would be willing to struggle through such a morass, the Office of Education issued a summary (Government Printing Office, 35 cents), but this is hardly more satisfactory. It omits some of the most interesting findings of the larger Report, and gives no more sense of the social and personal realities which lie behind the statistics.

Despite its defects as literature, the Report is the most important piece of educational research in recent years. To begin with, its scale is unprecedented. The study surveyed more than half a million students and 60,000 teachers in 4,000 schools, at a cost of $1.5 million. The survey was nominally intended to document the extent and effects of racial segregation, North and South, but it actually did far more. It does not, after all, take $1.5 million to show that Americans of different colors usually attend different schools, and that those with darker skins usually have worse facilities, worse teachers, less varied programs and less stimulating classmates. The revolutionary thing about James Coleman's study is that it went beyond this well-known if depressing fact to ask what effect different school characteristics had on what individual students, white and black, actually learned. Shocking as it may seem, this question had never before been examined in a systematic way. There has been a lot of speculation and some small-scale research about the relative influence of genes, family background, personal values, school facilities, school programs, teachers and classmates on individual achievement. But Dr. Coleman and his collaborators are the first sociologists with the interest and the resources to investigate this problem on a national scale. Their findings are as relevant to white middle-class schools in Scarsdale and Peoria as to Negro schools in Harlem or Lowndes.

While the authors themselves make no policy recommendations, their diagnosis of what makes students learn is at odds with almost everything legislators, school board members, and school administrators have believed in recent decades. Not only that, but it is at odds, with what most contemporary curriculum reformers believe. If the Report's analysis is correct, then most of the money now being spent to improve the public schools is going down the drain.

The Report begins by describing some of the differences between schools attended by Negroes and whites. Schools attended by Negroes generally have inferior facilities and programs, but the differences are not very large. Indeed, Negroes are in some respects better off than the average white. In the South, for example, the average Negro attends school in a newer building than the average white, reflecting the fact

142

that most Southern school boards built "modern" facilities for whites before World War II, while they did not build them for Negroes until more recently. In the urban North, on the other hand, Negro school buildings are older than white ones. Nationwide, the average Negro is more likely than the average white to have a library and a full-time librarian. He is slightly more likely than the average white to have new textbooks, slightly more likely to get them free, but less likely to have an adequate supply of them. The typical Negro is in a slightly larger class than the typical white. Overall, however, the striking fact about school facilities for Negroes and whites is how alike they are. The gap between Negro and white schools is significantly less than the gap between rural and urban schools or the gap between Southern and Northern schools.

When one turns from facilities to staff, much the same picture emerges. Teachers of Negroes are on the whole inferior to the teachers of whites, but the differences are generally small and far from uniform. Teachers of Negroes score lower on tests of verbal ability, think worse of the colleges they attended, have lower morale, and are more eager to transfer to another school. (This desire is, however, apparently frustrated. Schools catering mainly to Negroes keep their teachers slightly longer than schools catering mainly to whites.) On the other hand, teachers of Negroes claim more activity in professional organizations, more reading of professional journals, and more time spent preparing for classes than teachers of whites. They are equally likely to have majored in an academic subject as against Education, equally likely to have a graduate degree, equally experienced as teachers, and equally badly paid (though there are significant regional variations in pay, with teachers of Negroes earning more than teachers of whites in some places and less in others).

One reason why Negroes have less sophisticated and verbally adroit teachers is that very few school boards seem to assign teachers on a color-blind basis. In the South, of course, most Negro students still have Negro teachers and vice versa. But even in the urban North, Negro students have about one chance in three of getting a Negro teacher, whereas white students have less than one chance in fifty. As more Negroes enter colleges, earn degrees, and begin looking for middle-class jobs in the North, the number of Northern Negro students with white teachers may actually decline rather than increase. On the average, Negro teachers are drawn from around the middle of the Negro ability distribution, just as white teachers are drawn from the middle ranges of the white ability distribution. This has evidently been true for a long time, and continues to be true among the young men and women now entering the profession. The best Negro college students are not becoming school teachers, any more than the best whites are. Since Negroes as a group have developed their academic and verbal ability less than whites, this pattern of teacher recruiting ensures that the average Negro teacher will remain less competent than his white counterpart for some time.

In addition to facilities, programs, and staffs, the survey collected information on students themselves. Some of the findings are startling, at least to those whose pictures of lower-class attitudes and behavior were formed by college sociology prior to 1960. For a long time students of the urban slum focussed their attention on immigrant sub-cultures, especially sub-cultures rooted in Southern and Eastern Europe. They found a great deal of overt hostility to American schooling, and they saw lower-class students' poor academic performance and high dropout rates as a by-product of this hostility. But times have changed. The USOE survey suggests that while the old stereotype may still apply to lower-class Puerto Rican youngsters, it does not apply to lower-class Negroes.

To begin with, the dropout rate among 16- and 17-year-olds, while higher among Negroes as a group than among whites, is not higher among many particular kinds of Negroes. In the rural South, for example, Negro men are more likely to be in school at 16 and 17 than white ones. Perhaps this reflects the fact that most of these rural Negroes want to move to a city, preferably in the North, and want a diploma to help them find work. The whites, on the other hand, usually plan to stay in the rural South, and do not need a diploma to take over the family farm or store. In the urban South, Negro girls stay in school slightly longer than whites, perhaps because they expect to go on working after marriage and therefore care more about having a diploma. Similarly, in the nation as a whole among families whose head has less than eight years of education and earns less than $3,000, Negro children are more likely than whites to stay in school. Presumably this reflects the fact that the Negro poor are more urbanized than the white poor.

Furthermore, while Negroes as a group are more likely than whites to drop out of school, and are less likely to go to college, they are no less *eager* to stay in school, and they express more *desire* to enter college. Negro students also report more interest in school, more time spent on homework, more books read outside school, and less truancy than whites. These startling results may project wishes rather than reality, or may even be deliberate attempts to con adult interrogators. Nevertheless, it is clear that Negro students are anxious to conform outwardly to their teachers' expectations, even if they don't really do so. The problem, in other words, is not lack of motivation but lack of performance.

Contrary to much recent research and speculation, Negro students showed no less academic self-confidence than the average white, at least in their questionnaire responses. They did not, however, show as much conviction that their personal behavior would affect what happened to them. Negroes were more likely than whites to feel that "people like me don't have a chance to be successful in life," more likely to feel that success depended on luck rather than hard work, more likely to report that "every time I try to get ahead, something or somebody stops me."

What does all this mean? How do these conditions affect what students actually learn? To answer this question students were tested for verbal and non-verbal ability, reading comprehension, mathematical achievement, and general information about the natural sciences, social studies, humanities, and "practical arts." The authors' first conclusion was that despite the rather small external differences between Negro and white schools, Negroes were learning substantially less than whites. About a sixth of the Negro first graders score above the national average on tests of verbal ability. The same is true of Negro high school seniors. The picture is not substantially different when one examines non-verbal ability, reading, mathematics, or general information. Twelve years of schooling, in other words, does nothing to narrow the initial gap between Negroes and whites. In the South, schooling actually seems to widen the gap slightly. (Kenneth Clark's research suggests that the gap also widens in Harlem, but this is evidently not typical for Northern cities.) This same pattern evidently continues in college, though here the Report's sampling was very limited. (In interpreting this finding, the reader should remember that if Negro scores average 75 percent of white ones in fourth grade, the typical Negro will be one grade behind. If Negro scores still average 75 percent of white ones in twelfth grade, the typical Negro will be three grades behind.)

The authors' second conclusion was that of all the tests they administered, the best measure of school effectiveness was the verbal ability test. This test was at one time thought to reveal a pupil's innate biological potential, and is still commonly used to measure IQ. Today it is generally recognized that no paper and pencil test reveals very much about the individual's genetic endowment. But this realization has not reduced the importance of verbal ability. Ours is, after all, a middle-class country, and the primary mission of the schools, accepted by both the middle and lower classes, is to prepare the young for middle-class jobs. Of all the things taught in school, verbal facility is probably the most important in finding such a job and getting promoted. Furthermore, even if one rejects occupational success as a primary goal of education, and insists that the schools exist to develop the intellect, verbal facility remains critical. Verbal ability is vital to almost any sort of intellectual attainment (and is in any case highly correlated with non-verbal ability). Colleges, for example, have found that of all the tests they use to predict college performance, verbal ability is the most reliable—much more so than subject-matter tests.

Verbal fluency is not only the most important skill developed in school, it is also apparently the skill with which schools have the most varied success. This means that scores on verbal ability tests make an excellent index of a school's overall effectiveness, separating good from bad schools more effectively than reading, mathematics or general information scores. This is presumably because most schools, good or bad, teach reading, math, and other subjects in much the same way, with somewhat similar results. They do not usually teach verbal skills directly, and so their influence is more varied.

The authors then set out to isolate the characteristics of both individuals and their schools which influenced verbal scores. This is by no means easy. We know that verbal ability usually develops in small increments over long periods of time. Verbal scores are therefore influenced not just by the school a student is attending when he takes a test, but all the other schools he has ever attended. It is extremely difficult to get accurate retrospective information about these schools. Since the authors could not spend twelve years following various sorts of students through school, observing all the salient features of each institution, they had to assume that a student who was in a particular kind of school at the time of the survey had probably spent most of his academic life in similar schools. While there is a good deal of empirical evidence to support this general assumption, there are plenty of exceptions. Each exception reduces the relationship between a student's current attainment and the characteristics of his current school.

Given their method, it is perhaps not surprising that the authors found a fairly modest relationship between students' test scores and the characteristics of the schools students attended. Family background, for example, seems to exert more independent influence on verbal ability than the schools do. So do individual attitudes, especially the feeling of being able to control one's destiny. Such attitudes may, of course, be somewhat influenced by the characteristics of a school, but the Report does not turn up much interrelationship. Overall, the Report makes a convincing though not definitive case for the view that student achievement depends largely on forces over which today's schools exercise little control. Whether they could exercise more influence if they were organized and run differently remains an open question.

To the extent that schools do influence what a student learns, their facilities and programs are evidently the least important factors in the equation. If the quality of teachers and students is held constant, a luxurious physical plant contributes nothing to the development of verbal skills, and an inadequate plant does nothing to inhibit them. Nor does it matter whether the textbooks are old or new, whether there is a library or a librarian, whether the classes are large or small, or whether the school groups children in separate tracks or not.

Good teachers seem to contribute somewhat more than bad ones to their students' verbal ability, but it is hard to tell how much. Partly this is because able teachers are usually found in the same schools with able students, so that it is hard to separate the influence of teachers from that of classmates. Partly it is because the statistical analysis in the report is poorly explained and seems at times contradictory. *One thing is clear, however, namely that good teachers are much more important to Negroes than to whites:*

However much difference teachers may make, the student culture evidently makes more. *Again, the difference is far greater for Negroes than whites.* Negroes do much better if they have middle-class school-mates, while whites do little worse when they have lower-class ones. Those of our forefathers who pushed for the common primary school, and later for the comprehensive high school, were evidently on the right track. Such a melting pot seems to help the disadvantaged without appreciably hurting the advantaged. (In the light of this finding, it is hard to see why internal segregation, in the form of ability grouping and tracking, should not promote student achievement, but the report found that it did not.)

The finding that able teachers and able classmates matter more for Negroes than for whites raises a basic question. It is hard to believe that this is really a racial difference, and tempting to assume that it is an economic one. Unfortunately, the Report provides no separate tabulations for middle-class Negroes or for lower-class whites, so the question cannot be answered directly. Indirect evidence does, however, suggest that it is the poor in general, rather than Negroes in particular, who respond strongly to good and bad schools. The Report finds, for example, that Negroes respond to good teachers, regardless of race. They do not respond to white teachers per se. Similarly, the Report finds that Negro students do better in predominantly middle-class schools and worse in predominantly lower-class schools, but that racial integration has little or no independent effect. Integrating poor Negroes with poor whites, in other words, probably does no good. Integrating poor Negroes with middle-class Negroes might do as much good as integrating them with middle-class whites, but as a practical matter there aren't enough middle-class Negroes to go round. (One reason for this is that 40 percent of all white-collar Negroes send their children to private schools—an incredible finding which deserves study.) For the foreseeable future class integration will be impossible without racial integration as well.

The best working hypothesis for explaining these findings is probably that virtually all American children, regardless of race, know they will need verbal skills to get ahead, and acquire them if given half a chance. If they come from good homes they pick these skills up from their parents and neighboring children, and even a good school adds relatively little. If they come from poor homes, however, they cannot acquire verbal skills from their parents or on the streets. In that case school, and more especially schoolmates, are crucially important.

Yet before discounting race entirely, we must take account of a finding which the Report notes but does not stress. A Negro child's achievement is very highly correlated with his feeling that he can control his own destiny (but not with his academic self-confidence, perhaps because the questions asked in this survey did not really measure self-doubt and self-hatred very well.) Negroes are somewhat more likely to feel they can control their fate if they attend racially integrated schools. While the *average* Negro test score is about the same in a segregated as in an integrated school (once class differences are taken into account), averages can be misleading. The integrated schools are not in fact the same as the segregated schools: they are either considerably better or considerably worse. The Report did not investigate what made the difference between a good and a bad integrated school. One can, however, guess that the good schools were those in which Negroes felt more or less accepted, and therefore felt that they had a chance of making it in white America. The poor ones, on the other hand, were probably those in which Negroes felt beleaguered and excluded, and were worse off than they would have been in an all-Negro school. *If this hypothesis is correct, a really superior school for Negroes must indeed be racially integrated*, even though the risks of integration are indeed considerable.

Taking the Report as a whole, three tentative conclusions seem warranted:

First, America's present school system is doing nothing to narrow the gap between Negroes and whites. If the gap is narrowing at all (all that is certainly debatable), the credit must go to forces outside the school system.

Second, pouring more money into Negro schools will probably accomplish little or nothing. While the Report does not prove that as yet untried improvements in school facilities and programs (e.g., computers) would have no significant effect on learning, it does provide a good deal of indirect evidence that this kind of innovation has made very little difference in the past.

Third, closing the gap between whites and Negroes would require radical changes in the present system of matching teachers with students, and students with one another. Barring truly open housing, mixing classes as well as races, equality of opportunity would require abandoning the neighborhood school. Not only that, it would require mixing students from the inner city with those from the suburbs, perhaps in educational parks. But neither parents nor educators will believe the Report's finding that white, middle-class children do as well in heavily integrated schools as elsewhere. The necessary changes will therefore be strongly opposed by both suburban and small-town educators, and by white parents. They will only be possible if the federal government ignores those people's protests and intervenes directly in an area traditionally reserved to local government. Such intervention is unlikely. But that is only another way of saying that white America is not ready to do what would have to be done to integrate Negroes into the mainstream of society.

American educators are traditionally concerned about equality of education. Any proposals for a realistic solution to the problem of inequality in education must be sought through a total cultural approach. Family life, the economic patterns, religion, government and mass media are some of the variables besides education relevant to a societal problem of inequality. Educators therefore need to assess the family in many aspects as they design the educational experience. This means the family as an institution of total society, seen in its broadest trends as an interrelating part of society. It also includes the family of the local district, and the families of individuals the teacher is concerned with. The following article assesses the causal interrelationships involved in the family, especially the lower-class Negro of the inner city, vis-a-vis the school.

THE NEGRO URBAN FAMILY AND THE SCHOOL
*Phyllis Freeman**

Early American family life was characterized by its stability. Knowledge was agreed upon by most individuals and passed on from father to son. Families were productive units and roles were well defined. While doubtless a relatively small difference occurred between generations, there was general consistency in what was taught in the home,

* Graduate student, Wayne State University; unpublished monograph, 1968.

school and church. The values of each institution reinforced the others. Divorce was not an acceptable alternative to marriage and the vow "till death do us part" was taken literally. The family usually lived where the parents had grown up. The early pioneers moved West, but with the intention of remaining permanently in one location. Hard work was seen as a mark of good character. Other than local communication was limited to letters, an occasional newspaper, and limited books.

Rapid change or transition are evident in all segments of life today, and the family is no exception. The family has become a unit of consumption rather than of production. Inconsistencies often exist among the values taught by the home, school and church. The nuclear family continues to function as an institution, but has lost many of its previous functions, i.e., recreation, production, and education. Divorce has become a socially acceptable alternative. Families move more frequently than ever before. The United States Census indicates Automation and cybernation are making it impossible for men to work in the same way as in the past, but a substitute value ethic has not emerged. The media of mass communication serves both to make the population more conforming and to bring conflicting ideas to the public.

The change from rural to urban life has affected the total population. Members of various cultural and ethnic groups have been at the bottom of the socio-economic ladder upon their arrival in urban areas. Gradually, they were assimilated into the mainstream of society often losing their cultural identity, but often retaining much. The Italians, the Jews and the Irish each become full-fledged members of the dominant society. This has not been true for the Negro.

E. Franklin Frazier (*The Negro American Family*, University of Chicago Press, 1939) predicted that Negroes "will crowd the slums of Southern cities or make their way to northern cities where their family life will become disrupted and their poverty will force them to depend upon charity." In 1967, we see his prediction a reality. This shift from rural to urban life has taken place in the total population. The Negro occupies the lowest rung on the socio-economic ladder and, kept there by a society which perpetuates this practice, has lost most. Perhaps rather than considering the "pathology of the ghetto" we should consider the "pathology of the society" which continues to produce large numbers who are liabilities both to themselves and society. Some continue to romanticize the poor, like the "noble savage," but in reality poverty does not produce "happy, child-like individuals" but the group in which psychosis is most prevalent, and human despair is part of existence.

The Negro Family published by the United States Labor Department (1966) under the direction of Daniel P. Moynihan suggests that Negro family instability is a basic cause of Negro inequality as reflected by unemployment statistics and census data. Instability of the Negro family is indicated by the high number of female-headed households and high illegitimacy rates. Moynihan's critics tend to argue that the female-headed household, the matriarchial family, is adaptive rather than pathological, and is a result of conditions imposed by the dominent, white culture. William Ryan ("Savage Discovery," *Nation*, November 27, 1965) says "a systematic inequality of access to a variety of services and information" rather than "a careless acceptance of Negroes of promiscuity and illegitimacy" account for the Census Bureau statistics on illegitimacy for white at about 3 per cent and Negroes at about 22 per cent. The problem is not the matriarchial family or illegitimacy, *per se*, but families which are operating on a different family policy than the majority. Children are produced which begin life with the disadvantages of a family pattern fairly unique to the subculture of poverty in addition to the disadvantage of pigmented skin. This is not to suggest that a change in family organization to coincide with the dominant culture will yield equality or that change in family structure is attainable without change in the structure of the total society. The difficulty in attempting to do away with matriarchal family, if one accepts the soundness of the proposal, is that there is no feasible alternative under the existing pattern of high unemployment for Negro males. In addition, the ADCU program makes financial aid dependent on the absence of the male, therefore acting as a stimulus for additional female-headed households. The cycle of unemployment, family disorganization, and poor children continues; working on any one variable will do little to break the cycle. The total conditions which perpetuate a society which disadvantages and demoralizes the Negro must be attacked.

Many solutions have been suggested. The public school has often been seen as an institution relevant to the problem. After all, many have argued, once laws are made to stop discrimination in employment, all the schools need do is prepare Negroes through education. Primarily, this has been attempted through compensatory education, the spending of large amounts of money without any change in the existing institutional or social structure. The U.S. Office of Education report to Congress in 1966 (*Equality of Educational Opportunity*, James S. Coleman, et al.) indicated that positive results are negligible for Negroes in schools which continue to be segregated because of housing patterns regardless of funds allocated. Housing patterns are one more indication of the attitude of the dominant culture toward Negroes.

The relationship between education and employment for Negro males is not as expected. A study in 1960 ("Social Structure and the Negro revolt," James Geschwender, *Social Forces,* 1964) reveals that whites are twice as likely as Negroes to get professional jobs with some college or a college degree. Herman Miller (*Rich Man, Poor Man,* Crowell, 1964) states that a white man with eight years of school can expect to earn more than a Negro college graduate in his lifetime. Paul M. Siegal ("The Cost of Being Negro," *Sociological Inquiry,* Winter 1965) shows the average annual cost of being black if you have four years or more of college is $3800.00. Conditions may be somewhat changed in 1967, but most would accept that the total efforts of the Federal poverty program, compensatory education programs, and legislation have not come close to disproving the international accusation that the United States does not practice the equality of opportunity it idealizes. Furthermore, it is not surprising the Negro boys' and girls' aspirations are lower than whites', or that educators are unable to convince Negro youngsters that equality of opportunity exists if they receive an adequate education.

The educator analyzing the many programs and their ineffectiveness is apt to take the position that it just takes more time, or more money, or more staff . . . but rarely can he see beyond the accepted way of doing things. This is no revelation recognizing the school and its personnel are part of the so-called Establishment, the dominant white culture, which has caused the problem. Therefore, in effect, educators have often reacted to change in order to perpetuate their own institution. Some seem overcome with professional importance, rather than recognizing candidly they are only one spoke in the wheel, and perhaps not the most important.

Educators have often accepted, with little defense to the contrary, that the school system can in some way make the difference to a minority which has been historically disadvantaged. Little bold innovation has taken place within the educational institution. Fads regarding methods change, but a classroom today is much like a classroom of one hundred years ago with the addition of "technological hardware." The lack of success in attempting to destroy inequality must be faced honestly. Blinders to the many variables operating in the culture must be removed. The responsibility for breaking down the cycle of poverty, deprivation, and lack of education must be recognized as a product of the society and not of the school. It is not suggested here that educators revert to the position that their job is instruction, i.e., teaching the basic skills, and the responsibility of the school stops there. Rather, the complexity of the societal problem must be analyzed through interdisciplinary study and cooperation.

The family role in the socialization of youngsters has diminished and the trend seems likely to continue. Assuming this to be true, what social response will educators make? Will they continue to be servants of the public, doing as they are told, and avoid responsibility for necessary social change? Or will they continue to accept more and more responsibility with little or no structural change in the institution? Or instead, will educators make value decisions and cooperate with others on all levels, both politically and professionally, for the development of a sound social program which meets the needs of the society? The future will answer these questions, but there will be no middle ground. Either educators will join with others in promoting realistic integration of social agencies, of which the school is one, or they will continue to have minimal effect in the solution of America's social problems.

The "long hot summer" of 1967 saw an outbreak of "riots" that threw American society into turmoil. These "riots" were outbreaks in the Negro sections of the inner cities of many great American metropolises. One of the worst outbreaks of the kind, and one of the worst in American history, occurred in Detroit on the days of July 23 to July 27, 1967. Property damage up to $500,000,000 was estimated, and a loss of 42 lives occurred.

American society was rocked by this and the other riots. (The term "riot" is sociologically inappropriate because the outbreaks could not have spread by crowd contagion over such a wide area so quickly.) The important question now is, "What are we going to do about it? A survey of news media and of opinions of individuals from many sectors of society tell us, unfortunately, that people are reacting predictably to the problem. That is, their viewpoints are understandable in terms of their previous conditioning and values, and few seem to rise to the level that the problem requires for solution.

Some take a smug attitude of "I told you so," arguing that "inborn" nature of Negroes, or excessive coddling in their environment brought the disorganization. Others believe that it was the fault of Christianity; the schools, the churches, family, economic discrimination or various discriminations were causal. No one, especially the social scientists, and certainly the Negroes themselves (including actionist Black Muslims, etc.) were able to well predict the dimensions and patterns of the disorder.

Predictions, though, are unimportant compared with principles and ideals which are the stuff of social motivation. Something went wrong. The summer riots of 1967 are symptomatic as well as both cause and result of that wrong, and it is the duty of American society to correct that wrong.

Almost all of the reactions to the riots of the inner cities, summer of 1967 have been of little value toward the solution of the problem, because they come from the same value-attitude schemes almost unchanged in which the conflicts arose. Some changes are necessary. As an example of insights which take a broader, more insightful perspective of the problem, is submitted herewith the views of Daniel P. Moynihan.

THE AMERICAN CRISIS:
A LIBERAL LOOKS AT THE ASHES OF DEAD DREAMS AND ISSUES A MANIFESTO FOR SURVIVAL
Daniel P. Moynihan

These failings have been accompanied, moreover, by a formidable capacity for explaining them away.

In the aftermath of Newark one could already detect our self-defense system at work. Newark, we were beginning to say, was after all a backward city, doubtless run by the Mafia. Unemployment was high. The mayor was fighting with the poverty program. The police were brutal and corrupt. Newark, we were almost saying, deserved a riot.

But Detroit . . . what have we to say after Detroit?

Detroit had everything the Great Society could wish for a municipality. A splendid mayor and a fine governor. A high paying and, thanks to the fiscal policies of the national government, a booming industry, civilized by and associated with the hands-down leading liberal trade union of the world.

Moreover, it was a city whose Negro residents had every reason to be proud of the position they held in the economy and government of the area. With two able and promising Negro congressmen, Detroit, at the time the rioting broke out, actually had one-half the Negro membership of the House of Representatives. Relations between the Negro community and City Hall could hardly have been better. Detroit Negroes held powerful positions throughout the city administration, and to cap matters, the city was equipped with the very model of a summer task force, with a solid program and a 24-hour watch to avert violence.

How then could Detroit riot?

The answer lies in the question "Who rioted?" The studies that will be made have not appeared. And yet a partial answer seems warranted.

The rioting was begun, and probably largely continued by, young persons sociologists would describe as an urban lower class. They happen in this case to be Negro and American. Yet, their counterparts are to be found in the slums and in the literature of nations throughout the western world. (Whether they exist in the East is an interesting and unresolved question.) Marx called them "lumpenproletariat," and despaired of getting any help for his revolution from persons whose main impulses seemed to be so destructive, both to themselves and the society around them.

Where did this lower class come from? How did it form?

There does not seem to be any satisfactory answer, save that something like it has always been present in most cities in America, and that there are reasonably good signs by which to detect it.

The basic conditions that would appear necessary for the formation of such a class have clearly existed in our cities for a generation.

First, and uppermost, is unemployment. The Depression has never ended for the slum Negro. In how many ways have American liberals sought to state that fact so that somehow the nation would listen and believe? We have failed, or rather the nation has failed. And yet neither have we—in deference to the callous stupidity of the public on this subject—come forward with programs that would match the dimension of the problem.

To unemployment, add low wages, add miserable housing, add vicious and pervasive forms of racial discrimination, compound it all with an essentially destructive welfare system, and a social scientist would have every ground on which to predict violence in this violent country. Moreover, there were many specific warnings sent our way.

Five are perhaps most prominent:

1. *The increase in welfare dependency.* Beginning in the 1950's the number and proportion of Negro women and children living on welfare began to climb quite sharply, so that today something like six out of every 10 Negro youths reaching 18 have at some time been supported by the Federal Aid to Families of Dependent Children program.

2. *The increase in certain types of crime.* For the crimes of burglary, larceny, and auto theft, the Negro crime rate increased 33 percent between 1960 and 1965. White rates also increased, but not as much and from a very much lower base.

3. *The missing men in the census count.* At least three years ago we began to realize that the number of Negro males enumerated in the 1960 census was far fewer than it should have been. We now know that altogether we missed 10 percent of the Negro population, with a much higher loss rate in young adult males. Something like one male in six had in effect simply dropped out of organized society.

4. *Educational failure.* For five years or more we have known that Negro children were doing very badly even in schools that would have to be described as quite good. For some time we have known that the net results, the failure rate on Selective Service examinations, were near horrendous; until recently, something like 56 percent of Negro youths called up for the draft have been failing the mental test—a sixth grade examination.

5. *The steady deterioration of family structure in low-income Negro neighborhoods.* Probably not more than a third of the children of low-income Negro families now reach 18 having lived all their life with both their parents.

The task is to devise programs that will avoid the weaknesses of the past, that will confront the reality of our social problems, that will insist on the great effort needed to solve them . . . and will avoid letting that effort get lost in the thickets of bureaucracy.

One further point: The more programs, the less impact. The 1966 White House conference "to fulfill these rights" produced a hundred pages of recommendations, which meant that the conference was a failure and a disaster. If it had produced three recommendations, it might have been a success.

I will propose three.

First. The United States Government must become the employer of last resort, so that anyone looking for work and not finding it is automatically given a job. Put to work.

If this is done stupidly it will turn out to be a W.P.A., but with just a little administrative energy such jobs can be distributed throughout the labor market so that in fact they are not visible as such. The worker himself need not know that he is being subsidized. The temptation is to elaborate on such proposals, and that must be resisted. The U.S. Government must see to it that everyone looking for work finds work, and correspondingly that those without work have no excuse for their situation. It is as simple and profoundly important as that.

Second. We have got to get more money directly into the hands of the poor.

The best way to do this, or at least the best known way, is through a family (or children's) allowance. The United States is the only industrial democracy in the world that does not have such a system of automatic payments for families who are raising minor children. A payment of $8 per child under 6 and $12 for those between 6 and 17 would have a significant impact on the income of low-skilled family men, and it would have the further advantage that everyone will get it, not just a special segment artificially defined as below a certain income line, or across a certain racial line.

158

We need programs that stress the unity of the nation and not its divisions. We also need programs that can run automatically without creating yet another monster bureaucracy looking into clothes closets to see if there is a man in the house. The children's allowance would be both those things. It has worked well all over the world, including Canada, and for $9 billion a year, it would be a sound investment in the future as well as the present.

Third. We must rebuild, or at least clear, the burnt-out neighborhoods.

The Federal Government has a dozen ways to do this, and it must. Otherwise the ruins remain a symbol of the injustices that led to them. In Detroit a number of churches are banding together to preserve one of the burnt-out buildings for just that purpose, and well they might be saved; in Watts the ruins are still there, and likely to remain so until a new highway is needed. Accompanying such a clearance and rebuilding program, we simply must enact a form of federal reinsurance of small business in such areas. Otherwise they will become deserts.

The problem, of course, is that it is unlikely we will do any of these things, or any other things.

Never has the national instinct and the national interest appeared more divergent. The mood of the administration in Washington is one of paralysis. There is no political will for the executive branch to move in any direction, and nothing but fear as to what direction Congress will take if it should seize the initiative.

This paralysis derives from several sources.

The first, understandably, is disappointment, and not a little bitterness at what has happened. This is a mood tinged as well with exhaustion. Many men in Washington have been at their desks for eight years. The first few were exhilarating, but of late an entirely understandable exhaustion seems to have set in.

The second source of paralysis is the conviction within the administration that the public mood is one of fierce dislike for Negroes and adamant determination that there be "no reward for rioting."

But the third is the decisive one: There is no money.

The war has used up all the available income, and taken us beyond that to a massive deficit. It was enormous this year; responsible men estimate that it may reach 25 billion next year, an unheard of amount.

159

Washington does not dare spend another nickel and indeed appeared to be in the process of quietly cutting back many domestic programs when the rioting resumed in June.

The result has been a curious process of backward reasoning. First: "We can't do anything." Second: "We don't do anything." Third: "We shouldn't do anything." Everyone must keep a stiff upper lip— "no flinching" as the British used to say when the natives got restless. "Never apologize, never explain." And, above all, not giving ammunition to the Republican enemy by suggesting perhaps there were some deficiencies in our approach to date.

Beyond that, we are to pray and to wait the report of the presidential commission, which will solemnly reassure us that the FBI has found no evidence of Communist conspiracy, and that the problem of rioting lies in despair, and hopelessness in the ghetto.

We might get away with it. Just possibly. Or we might march directly into a political crisis that will spoil the rest of the 20th Century for the American people. Such a disaster would be the election, next year or five years from now, of a determined right-wing President.

The task of American liberals would seem to be clear. We can not do anything without the President, and the President seems determined to do nothing. The administration seems to feel that the Congress is not going to do anything and that therefore it will be useless and worse to ask and be refused. Not only will the obstructionist majority say "no," but from elsewhere there will come a chorus of charges that the war in Vietnam is the reason he will not move. This is true, but also irrelevant. The President dares not and will not scrap the war in order to save the cities. Somehow, he must be enabled to scrap other things, and raise new funds, in order to proceed with both.

The experience of the Vietnam protest will hardly encourage the thought that he responds to pressure, much less to name-calling. (And much less to articles such as this.)

The only serious option open to us would seem to be that of trying to persuade the public at large that we can do something about the causes of Negro violence that will not only help the rioters but everyone.

It is time for this fabulously rich nation to declare a dividend. A family allowance would be a good beginning, guaranteed full employment programs that will work in the slums, and yet assert the unity of the nation. Let us look for them.

The riots in the big cities in the summer of 1967 have underlined a fact that existed, but was little known or heeded. The fact is that another class has arisen in our midst. The obliviousness of scientists, leaders, Negroes, and the general public to this fact is deplorable but understandable. All our groups have their own tribal gods, shibboleths, and vested interests. Few have been able to analyze the situation, and fewer still have proposals for solution pitched to the magnitude of the problem. The world will go on, of course, but the penalty for not understanding and solving the problem in its true meanings as a threat to democracy may be retroaction and the monolithic state dedicated to "law and order." We all have to realize that a new class has risen in our society. The warning is in the wild, anarchic destructiveness of the frustrated lumpenproletariat. *The challenge is to surmount the crisis by bringing equalitarianism to all of our society—equalitarianism in the fully cultural sense. August Kerber here analyzes the implications of this American crisis.*

THE UNHEEDED WARNING
August Kerber

If a mild-mannered, stable citizen in our society, as for instance a Casper Milquetoast bookkeeper, were suddenly to murder his wife with a broadaxe, society would be greatly shocked. People would be shocked because the unpredictable in its most terrible form occurs. All the devices to ward off the evil eye, and the regular customs and safeguards of society, are momentarily set at naught. We become pawns to mere chance, or mischance, in a universe that has no personalistic concern for our safety.

We immediately cast about for explanations. Tumor of the brain? Genetic defects? Passion and intrigue including the boss's wife? Late weaning? It does not matter what assignments of cause are made, as long as they are sufficiently rational to pass muster and bring the world back into a harmonious system. Once an explanation becomes acceptable we can contemplate the harmonious system without fear that the great axis of the cosmos will shake loose.

The recent breakdowns of law and order in the big cities in this summer of 1967 were unpredictable—like a homicide by an apparently non-homicidal individual. And the end result of most of the words,

161

researches, fact-finding sessions of the vulturine investigators, the apologists, claptrap orators and calamity howlers will be just about as useful in our society. Hardly an atom will be displaced in the cosmos by the most massive head counting and multivariate analyses of ecological variables in the Negro ghettos of our inner cities.

A number of great facts and conditions should be noted about these summer 1967 riots. In citing these facts, I will blame social scientists, political leaders, the general public, and the Negroes themselves. My purpose, however, is not to twit the ignorant but to edify all concerned so that we can apply positive and humanitarian principles to the situation.

First I must condemn the general run of social scientists and educators about their overall lack of understanding and concern about the problem area. If we examine the literature we find only vague rumblings about the reservoir of social dynamite that existed. The space and wordage appropriate to the imminent peril in life and social structure was negligible. Any predictions were inaccurate. And now the solutions are only more intense reiterations of previous clichés, programs, and positions. There is a lion in the streets and the social scientists never even predicted mice.

The political leaders are frenetically name-calling and dashing about like cats on hot bricks to escape blame. To avoid ruination, they are trying to use each other as scapegoats while disavowing to high heaven any responsibility or negligence on their own part for the whole tragic mess. The federal government and leaders blame local political leaders and police for incompetency, cowardice, and vilification. Local politicos voice recriminations about lack of federal action in massive emergency. Whites blame Negro political leadership, who return the compliment. Tempers flare, knots bulge in foreheads, fists bang on desks, but little occurs of constructive program or understanding.

A number of fallacies and hardy stereotypes are bandied about by the general public. Let us consider a few:

(a) Riots start because some significant incident which implicates Negro rights occurs—as for instance, a case of police brutality.

(b) A great deal of complicity and conspiracy attended the riots. They were organized in advance.

(c) Negroes spared Negro lives and property.

162

(d) Negro leaders involved have some fairly clear view of aims and ends.

(e) Most Negroes are involved in the riots, at least to the extent of offering no resistance to fellows.

The answers to these statements are now fairly clear.

(a) The "incident" that begins a riot is insignificant and irrelevant as a precipitating cause. Once such a riot starts it feeds on itself.

(b) Evidence shows little of any kind of social organization or planning in the usual sense. All that seems to have happened is that a rather few individuals determined to be very destructive once the riots started.

(c) The overwhelming destruction of life and, to a large extent, of property too, was against Negroes by the destructive Negroes.

(d) The riots had almost no leaders in the sense of a military or conventional social group, though at times they showed effective co-operation. The public pronouncements of Carmichael and the like cannot be used to prove any ideological aims in the course of the riots.

(e) Most of the Negroes were as ignorant and helpless as the whites about what was going on. Many of them did attempt to restore law and order.

The Negroes to whom the whites now look for understanding and articulation of what happened are no more useful now than they were before. The professional groups like NAACP will not change their basic policies (though they may feel more intensively). Preachers and editors will continue their established lines. The bulk of the Negro groups will each pursue its independent way. The feelings of the groups will support and move them when crises occur, but they have no inner knowledge of plots or designs, or what to do specifically in time of crisis.

What has happened is that a new social group, fairly well defined in terms of the criteria of group alignment, has arisen in the inner cities. This group is composed of Negroes, and amounts to a subculture. But the problem in relation to this group is not primarily racist. It is one of class. If it were racist all Negroes would think and act similarly, and complementarily all whites would think and act in ways defined by racist dogma. The Negroes of the inner city think, act, feel, and socially participate in ways that are part of a class-oriented group.

163

The awareness of, implications, and threats of this recently crystallized group were sufficiently plain, but there was no overall objective awareness of its threat to the stable middle-class urban society. The segments of our society which dealt with inner city Negroes had their limited and correct views, but their relations and understandings did not amount to effective means of checking the destructive potential of hate and frustration building up. Society rested in pluralistic ignorance of the total phenomenon.

The figures tell much of the story.

The Negroes as a group have made great strides since the beginning of World War II; relatively, they increased their incomes more than the whites from 1940 to 1950, and from 1959 to 1964. But the inner city Negroes have been getting worse off. And their condition is worse than the figures show, because the dispossessed and uneducated man today is more of a liability than ever before.

Consider some of the facts about inner city Negroes as reported by the Detroit Urban League in a study called "The Detroit Low Income Negro Family."

"Nearly one-third of Detroit area non-whites under 18 live in broken homes." "The non-white illegitimacy ratio rose from 138.0 per 1000 live births in 1950 to . . . 228.4 in 1964." "About 20 per cent of Detroit area non-white females who ever married are divorced or live apart from their husbands." The educational level of these Negroes is well known to be low. About 56 per cent of Negroes called up by the draft fail the educational tests—requiring a sixth-grade level. And the inner-city Negroes are much worse off. Some Negro inner-city elementary schools fail to pass 5 per cent of their group on to college. Unemployment is increasing in the inner city. There are many missing men in the inner city. These dispossessed men consider it an advantage to be unmarked and unknown.

One could go on and on citing facts. Even the supermarkets discriminate against the inner city. The price of staples goes up on days the welfare check comes out. But supermarkets are few, and the many independent stores set high prices to multiply their profits. Crimes of all kinds occur more frequently, and some kinds like burglary much more frequently in ghettos than in white middle-class neighborhoods.

But the most important fact of all is the affective emotional condition of these inner-city people.

These people have no native or indigenous culture. They draw their values, their world view, their images of self and themes of the good, true, and beautiful from the white middle-class society. But they are forced to live among themselves, largely cut off from effective, meaningful, primary group communication with the rest of society. If the division were clear; if super and sub-ordination were part of the mores—then they could adjust. As it is, the psyche of each individual Negro is assaulted thousands of times a day by the misery of recognizing the gap between the real and the yearned for.

Add to this the recent civil-rights activism, the rise of SNCC, CORE, and the Black Muslim movement, and we have within us the condition for conflagration. It is not determined, or fatalistic, but the conditions are explosive. Any small spark may ignite a forest fire. The conditions are not in any existing buildings, ecological structures, or marks on pieces of paper. The conditions are in the feelings of people who meet us daily, and who misunderstand each other mutually. But the Negro of the inner city does not misunderstand or assess wrongly the values of the hypocritical majority, who have worked diligently since this country's birth to find formulae to create the form without the substance of democracy.

The inheritance of this long record of woe and discrimination was not forever to be ignored, nor explained away by bromides, nor palliated by a thousand fragmentary programs (mostly benefiting their directors). The inheritance burgeoned in the long hot summer. There was a warning, but the warning went unheeded.

Editors' Summary

Democracy exists on communication. It is a dialog among men as they press forward in their environment. In America the Negro group of the inner city had lost communication with the great white middle-class urban community—including the majority of Negroes who qualify as internalizing WASP middle class mores. Because the census had counted them, and they paid taxes, attended school, rode public transportation and worked in factories, it was assumed that they were "soul brothers" in the eyes of the U.S. Constitution and democratic ethic.

The truth is that our inner cities have become ghettos to contain a group with whom we cannot and will not communicate. And with a subtle alchemy that blinds the eye of the mind we dispossessed and disenfranchised them in every social way, regardless of law and official policy. Our grants-in-aid, urban renewal, compensatory education programs and euphonious urban associations and leagues have been sops to our consciences in lieu of the genuine communication which is the lifeblood of democracy.

*Economics, the usages of civil rights and voting, the folkways of social participation and sexual mores are important and have effects— but these are secondary to communication which raises, hallows, modifies, or destroys the usages as the body politic decrees. Economics, or the sharing of the rewards of life, is the most important manifestation of the results of communication. But communication comes first. If we freely agree to an inequalitarian allocation of rewards—*and can change the allocation at any time by orderly communication—*then we have democratic communication.*

The "Negro problem" does not arise alone from the Negroes' having less income, education, housing, recreation, social stability or ideational mobility than the whites, although improvements in these areas are in the right direction. However, such improvements are useless and futile as long as we tolerate the gap of communication. As long as the white middle class think they deal "correctly" with Negroes, but do not communicate with them, we will continue to have the great urban Negro crisis.

We have created a great enclave of Negroes in the inner city with whom we do not communicate. Sociologically, communication means the sharing of culture, sharing of the nature of being human as culture defines it; it is not simply the intoning of the Great Verities of Law, Religion, and Americanism. Since the Negroes had no share in the great society, they created their own subculture. And though many of them tried hard to believe the Great Verities, when the riots of Detroit (or Newark, Milwaukee, Podunk) came, they grabbed Molotov cocktails and mail-order guns and expressed their rage and frustration.

What, then, is the answer? We have to build up communication with the Negro inner-city subculture. The end is to destroy that part of Negro urban culture which breeds hate and violence. We do so by giving them jobs, housing, education, health aids, and positive help toward becoming fully functioning citizens. But the means are not the ends or essences of the program. The end is the acceptance of the Negroes as first-class citizens and whole human beings in a democracy.

RELATED READINGS

Ashley, Walter E. *The Society of the Streets.* Ford Foundation (477 Madison Avenue, New York 22, N.Y.) 1962, 49 p.

Bettelheim, Bruno. "Sputnik and Segregation," *Commentary,* 26:332-339, October, 1958.

Butler, Broadus N. "The Negro Self-Image," Publication of a Speech Before the Booker T. Washington Business Association, June 28, 1961 (Detroit: Booker T. Washington Business Association, 1961).

Byerly, Carl L. "Pupils Who Do Not Respond," *Educational Leadership,* A.S.C.D., pp. 309-314, February, 1963.

Clark, Kenneth. *Dark Ghetto,* 1965.

Clift, V. A., Anderson, A. W., and Hullfish, H. G. (eds.). *Negro Education in America.* Sixteenth Yearbook of the John Dewey Society. New York: Harper and Brothers, 1962.

Cohen, Albert. *Delinquent Boys: The Culture of the Gang.* Glencoe: The Free Press, 1955.

Conant, James Bryant. *Slums and Suburbs.* New York: McGraw-Hill Book Company, 1961.

Eddy, Elizabeth M. *Urban Education and the Child of the Slum.* New York: Hunter College, City University of New York, 1965.

Eells, Kenneth, et al. *Intelligence and Cultural Differences.* Chicago: University of Chicago Press, 1951.

Hansberry, Lorraine. *A Raisin In The Sun.* New York: Random House, 1959.

Havighurst, Robert J. *Education in Metropolitan Areas.* Boston: Allyn and Bacon, 1966.

Krugman, Morris. "The Culturally Deprived Child in School," *NEA Journal,* 50: 23-24, April, 1961.

"Negro American." *Daedalus.* Fall and Winter Issue, 1966. American Academy of Arts and Sciences.

Newton, Eunice Shaed. "Verbal Destitution: The Pivotal Barrier to Learning," *Journal of Negro Education,* 29:497-499, Fall, 1960.

Rainwater, Lee. *And the Poor Get Children.* Chicago: Quadrangle Books, Inc., 1961.

Riessman, Frank. *The Culturally Deprived Child; and His Education*. New York: Harper and Brothers, 1962.

Sexton, Patricia Cayo. *Education and Income*. New York: Viking Press, 1961.

Weaver, Robert. *The Negro Ghetto*. New York: Harcourt, Brace and Co., 1948.

Warner, W. L., Robert J. Havighurst, and Martin B. Loeb. *Who Shall Be Educated?* New York: Harper, 1944.

Wright, Richard. *Black Boy*. Ohio: The World Publishing Company, 1945.

VII

The Inner City School

Editors' Comment

W. I. Thomas, famous sociologist of a generation ago, talked of the "strain toward consistency" in culture. Cultures tend to be all of one piece, because they cannot usually synthesize widely different values and ways of life. Sometimes conflict cannot be avoided—as for example the Civil War, fought because the North and South found their views to be irreconcilable.

Our society would be less unsettled if we could maintain subcultures and unique individuals among us, with positive advantage to all. Unfortunately, we cannot have a whole territory taken over by people of a much different culture from the rest of us middle class, educated, urbanized Americans. The pressure to conform, as it is called, is basically a pressure to relate constructively with the total society. A man is not free to choose that he sit by the side of the road today and contemplate mundane mutation. A policeman, a tax collector, various salesmen and do-gooders will approach and bedevil him. He will be forced to go out and earn some money to live.

There is the rub. In a simpler era, he could get by with simple skills and willingness to work. Now he has to relate with dozens of people in a complex and expensive way to get to a job and work at it, with specialized skills. The people who cannot relate in this way become dispossessed of all means of subsistence, and become a charge on society, if they do not obligingly perish. Our culture is breeding a large number of such dispossessed persons.

All persons who are handicapped in some way so that they cannot translate their working energies into a livelihood are part of this group. They are the unemployed, underemployed, unfit, old, and discriminated against, and they are numerous—from a fifth to a third of our society, depending on the measuring stick used.

The most prevalent, and the most embarrassing problem according to our set of values, is the culture of poverty of the inner city. Our urbanization is now well nigh universal. The movement has been an ill-planned or unplanned one which is fast making U.S. one great metroplex. The movement has been marked by one unwholesome trend: as the megalopolis (Jean Gottman calls it) spreads, the ecological change has been largely one affecting the middle class, relatively well-off residents moving to rather exclusive de facto ghettos of suburbia, while lower socio-economic and dispossessed people remain in, or move to, the inner city. This has been seen strikingly in the high concentration of poor Negroes. The problem has been aggravated by the dysfunctional nature of American education in the inner city. Although our American myth is that education should offer opportunity to all for social mobility, a combination of factors interact to set the "culture of poverty" in an insoluble residue. The educators give up trying to educate, and the pupils respond in counterreaction to make bad matters worse.

According to Thomas Linton in an article we are presenting in example, for the lower-class child, "deprived of meaning" or one living in a "disadvantaged urban area" as he describes it, the whole educational system must be a "radically redesigned school program which is specifically structured to work directly with slum-area children." These children, he argues, are treated as individual deviants, and are punished by our middle-class society—through our agents the teachers—by being treated to individualized clinical and therapeutic procedures as if they were individual "bad" middle-class children.

SOCIAL AND CULTURAL FACTORS IN DEVIANT CLASSROOM BEHAVIOR

Thomas E. Linton*

The Problem

This article will discuss the social and cultural factors which produce a mass-based form of deviant classroom behavior. Broad scale social deviancy and failure in the schools to "succeed" is the direct result of social factors which perpetuate these conditions. The deviant classroom behavior, as such, is not deviant, but normal behavior for the area in which it occurs. The behavior is deviant only when one views classroom behavior from an academic and very traditional position. This is the core of the problem. Vast numbers of disadvantaged children are being approached with obsolescent and rigid curriculum standards. The teacher selection and methodology processes are essentially similar for disadvantaged social areas and affluent areas. The common cry of school people is that disadvantaged children are not motivated and not concerned with achieving in the "mainstream" fashion as are the suburban children. But rarely does one see a radical revamping of the traditional school approach to slum children. What one does see is the standard clinical approach to deviant behavior as long emphasized by education, social work, and psychology.

The widespread clinical approach to deviant classroom behavior is seriously in error. The problem, by and large, is not only of pathological behavior on the part of the child. If anything the pathological behavior is more characteristic of the adult authorities. These authority figures such as political leaders, board members, school officials and teachers frequently deny the seriousness of the problems and refuse to openly examine the basis for deviant classroom behavior. This retreat from reality is indicative of a kind of social pathology which characterizes many of the social and civic leaders of our time. More importantly, most of the professionals directly involved with maladjusted and delinquent children refuse to examine the implications of the social psy-

---

* Director, Emotionally Disturbed Children's Program, Department of Exceptional Education, The University of Wisconsin-Milwaukee, Milwaukee, Wisconsin.

chological deficits imprinted on millions of children. School officials, teachers, psychologists, and psychiatrists are fond of detailing a child's deviations from acceptable social and classroom behavior. One has only to attend such conferences as the Orthopsychiatric Association meetings to observe the extreme emphasis given to individual pathology. These meetings commonly deal with maladjustment and social deviancy, but they rarely emphasize the social causes of these conditions.

There is a great involvement with clinical measurement and personality evaluation of deviant children. Many of these children are displaying behavior which is mass based and not unique to the individual examined. By rescuing and salvaging a few children from the mass with therapeutic techniques we are able to enlarge our occupational domain. We are able to have more and more specialists who focus on the clinical domain. We are able to have more and more specialists who focus on the clinical personality needs of the child while we carefully manage to avoid any involvement with the conditions which breed the mass-based social maladjustment.

What are some of the major theoretical formulations which support the idea that deviant classroom behavior is not a clinical entity but a mass based social condition. The central purpose of this article is to examine some of the theoretical factors which condition the child's behavior toward what is called deviant classroom behavior.

Intelligence and Environment

It is common knowledge that the largest group of "educable" children in most urban areas come from what is often termed the inner city. This area is usually the most socially fragmented, the most decayed, and the lowest income part of the city. Many of the residents of these districts are migrants from southern and rural communities. They are usually minority group members who have been prevented from normal participation in the "main stream" of American and Canadian life. They have been utilized as inexpensive labor by concerns not required or able to pay normal wages. They are released from employment first in slack periods and hired last in periods of increased employment. In essence, their abilities have not been fully utilized by the society in several major ways such as education, employment, housing, and social activity.

172

Yet granting these conditions the schools apply standard I.Q. and achievement testing procedures to a population that has difficulty in producing normal range results. The evidence is abundant that intelligence is strongly affected by environmental factors. Not only is intelligence strongly affected by environmental factors, but also motivation, language development, interest pattern, cognitive growth, and perceptual patterning of one's environment.

The relationship between social class and I.Q. has been clearly established in numerous studies. These studies indicate that as social class rises so does I.Q. and school achievement. In a study done by the author on a Canadian population there was a clear and significant relationship between income and occupation on the one hand and school achievement on the other. The research examined 525 boys in the ninth grade who were required at this point in their schooling to take an examination. The results of the exam determined their school placement in subsequent years. The sample was divided into three groups, those who failed the examination, those who received average passing marks, and those obtaining honor marks. With few exceptions, the failing group, some 120 boys, were from lower income working class families. With some exceptions, the honors group were from more affluent, higher status occupation families. There was a direct linear relationship between fathers' occupations and the scores the child obtained on the examination. As the status of the parental occupations rose, so did the boys' performance on the departmental examinations.

These ninth grade examinations perform a selecting out process in terms of who goes on to higher level schooling. It is felt that these exams serve as a fair means of screening students on the basis of intellectual ability and achievement. The study would indicate that the exams serve instead to reinforce pre-existing social prejudices against the lower income groups. They do not sort on the basis of actual intellectual difference, but rather on the basis of social class conditioning.

This study was concerned with why lower class students test at lower levels, not merely with establishing the well known fact that I.Q. varies with the rise in social class. The IPAT test of nonverbal reasoning was utilized as a criterion measure against the standard verbal and quantitative measures used in the examination. While the IPAT results were not significant, there was a marked trend for the IPAT scores to reflect higher capacity than was indicated by the students' examination marks. In several cases the IPAT scores were higher than would be expected by their results on the examination. Personality testing of the students as well as parental interviewing further substantiated the importance of lower social class conditioning as a key determinant in school failure.

Masland, Sarason and Gladwin made an extensive review of the research on the relationship between intelligence and environment. They concluded that the I.Q. scores were not valid measures of intelligence.

> The I.Q. is unstable over time, cannot be reliably measured by any agreed upon single instrument and has strong environmental determinants, and its genetic determinants are sufficiently multi-factorial that they do not lend themselves to existing techniques of genetic research.[1]

[The multi-factored aspect is taken from psychometric studies which have elicited forty factors involving differing intellectual functions.

> The question: 'Is intelligence inherited or is it acquired' makes less sense than it ever did. Such a question must be asked regarding each and every factor.[2]]

The schools operate as though the achievement and intelligence tests are fair measures of academic potential. They do not alter the curriculum, the teaching methods and the counseling approach to benefit a disadvantaged population. The schools act as though only a small number of these intelligence factors are the concern of education.

These factors are the ones utilized frequently by the more successful members of the community. These abilities are deliberately articulated and fostered by the parents of the more successful students. When these students come to school they experience a behavioral expectation pattern which is very similar to the one they have learned at home. Hence, the transition is from acceptable behavior to acceptable behavior. But for the disadvantaged child, the transition is from acceptable be-

[1] Sarason Masland Gladwin, *Mental Subnormality*. New York: Basic Books, 1959, p. 211.
[2] Ibid.

havior to non-acceptable behavior as labeled by school authorities. This, in turn, is then viewed as deviant social adaptation to the school's expectations. What is needed is not classroom management of deviant behavior, but rather a radical changing of the schools approach to the education of culturally and intellectually deprived children.

The schools have tended to associate intelligence and achievement with a very narrow range of human abilities. School teachers and officials are inclined to believe that the higher achievement results found in suburban schools are the product of essentially superior genetic endowment. They may not state this publicly, but they do express this in private conversation. For example, superintendents in suburban areas like to quote statistics from their high schools indicating the low drop-out rate, the high percentage of those graduating, and the large number going on to college. They rarely indicate in these discussions an awareness of the social conditioning factors which produce these figures. They appear to believe that the efforts of their schools are the significant variable in these figures.

What personality features are developed through deprived environmental experiences? Since there has been a good deal of writing on this topic, we will attempt to tie these together into a personality style which is frequently associated with deviant classroom adjustment. The individual operates from a generalized base of hostility and suspicion towards the outside world. His experiences with his parents and other adults have conditioned him to expect manipulation and personal rejection. He feels that violence and its expression are a commonly accepted means of resolving conflict situations. His conscience is undeveloped and his morality is unique to his group. He is more inclined to express his actual feelings when provoked than to manage, control and repress them which is more common for the teacher. His stronger concern for his virility demands early sexual experience, and a more primitive approach to heterosexual involvement. His group does not sanction the equal sharing of family control, nor the complex and academic relationship which characterizes white collar marriages. He views highly verbal males as "chickens," and lacking the "guts" required for action. The world he has experienced approves direct gratification of impulse whenever this is possible. The idea of delay, of planning for advanced goals has no place in the real world he inhabits.

Most of the teacher's activities involve relating symbolic concepts and utilizing abstractions as learning devices. As Bernstein has pointed out, the development of abstract language is a long term cognitive process. It is a matter of early auditory conditioning, of imitation and of learning to value symbolic behavior in an intrinsic self-rewarding manner. This opportunity is not available to the slum child. The language patterns, the values, and the learning process are geared to action rather than conceptualization. The emphasis is on an overly simplified vocabulary and negative feeling is attached to careful verbal articulation. The child's observations are conditioned to concrete items in his perceptual field. His conceptual growth is poorly developed for he has had little experience with abstract ideas.

He was fortunate if he was able to survive his home and his neighborhood without being involved with narcotics, crime, early sexual involvement and adult retributory actions for minor infractions of rules.

In the school process from the beginning he experiences an alien world rarely adjusted to his unique learning problems. Usually the attempt is made to lighten the regular curriculum and teaching methods. Specifically developed curricula and teachers for children of this type are occasionally found, as in the St. Louis program for deprived children. What is needed is teacher training and recruitment programs designed to equip teachers with conceptual and methodological approaches for these children.

The child enters school with difficulty in the motive, creative and cognitive areas. These have been restricted in development, yet he is required to follow a pattern of learning responses created for children with cognitive experiences of a very different sort. He is soon again failing to perform, the teacher lowers his expectations and may assume he is a "slow learner." He feels the rejection; and the school and the teachers reinforce his anxieties about what he perceives accurately as the punitive adult world. His lack of ego strength over the years makes a simple adjustment to a negative classroom situation very difficult.

For many non-slum children, the rigid curricula requirements and dullness of teaching make many classrooms a very boring place to be. But they are able to handle the dullness and drabness of the academic school day. They have been conditioned to passive acceptance of adult punitiveness, and they have internalized the extrinsic reward system utilized by their parents. However, the slum child has not learned this set of responses. He views his failure and boredom in the school as further evidence of his own incapacity. In this sense the school adds a final day-by-day destructive touch to this already alienated personality.

Implications for the Management of Deviant Classroom Behavior

Since the problem is a broad scale one involving a large number of children what implications may be drawn for the classroom management of these children.

1. These children cannot be 'managed' within the traditional curricula structure of the schools. Specifically designed teaching materials and methods are required for this group.

The slum child has a developmental pattern in terms of experiences, which is very different from the non-slum child. If the deprived child gains more success experiences these will be offered by the schools, not by the families, or by the physically depressed surroundings in which they live. Hence it is requisite for the schools to make radical changes in their present ritualistic and unimaginative school programs in disadvantaged urban and rural areas.

The key point is that the changes that are of major importance for lessening deviant classroom behavior are fairly well known and documented over a long term period. The problem is essentially not what innovations are called for, but how does one effect social change in the educational establishment to permit the utilization of this knowledge. The major problems, whether in the field of education, delinquency, social maladjustment, or related community issues is not what is requisite to lessening the problem, but how does one get frightened and insecure adults to cross professional disciplines and honestly confront these major social problems.

2. Teacher Training Programs for the disadvantaged group should be established by Faculties of Education. This training should emphasize the social, physical and psychological background of these children. The selection of teachers from the deprived areas should be based on specific personal and educational qualifications. The present system of placing new teachers in slum areas on a time serving basis should be discontinued. Both the administrative and the teaching group in the poverty areas should be specifically trained and personally interested in this kind of endeavor.

177

It may be commonly observed that many teachers in the slum schools are both hostile and prejudiced toward their assignments and the children they teach. The traditionally employed formula utilized by urban boards of education has been to place new teachers in the less desirable neighborhood schools and to reward the conforming and non-critical teacher by a preferential school placement after several years of indenture in the poverty districts.

It is obvious that this kind of policy does not produce an effective staff for disadvantaged schools. The result is that over the years the inner city poverty belt schools become characterized by a kind of apathy and inertia which is a direct reflection of the school boards in inadequate and punitive personnel policies regarding the staffing of these schools. It is common knowledge among school people that the teachers in the slum schools represent a very different group from those teaching in the more desirable neighborhoods. The teaching group in the urban slum area is made up of (1) young and inexperienced teachers in their first job placement, (2) old timers who have been in the school for years and have no desire for change, (3) committed and concerned teachers who have chosen to work with deprived children, (4) those who find it far easier and less taxing to teach in slum areas because of the lack of parental involvement and the absence of high academic expectations for the students, and (5) those who feel that the opportunity for becoming an administrator is greater in these schools because of the severity of the problems and the lack of identity and concern by the staff for the welfare of the school. This last factor is important because the slum school, unlike the suburban school, does not involve the staff in a meaningful way in the daily life to the school.

This could all be changed by the school board by drastically altering the dreary and unimaginative personnel policies which have long dominated slum schools. Specifically this would involve several operational changes in the management and recruitment policies of these schools. Among these changes would be the following.

1. A realistic understanding of and concern for the specialized problem of education in deprived areas. It is time for the School Boards to admit that slum area schools require specially designed programs, rather than "hand me down" curriculum approaches developed for high achievement school neighborhoods. The new school programs

would be based on a diagnostic and prescriptive approach to the academic and social problems which characterize the deprived student population. The key would not be a "tight-ship" military kind of school operation, but rather a highly flexible and adaptive program and staff who were constantly seeking ideas and effective educational approaches to motivate and interest the students. Small classes of ten and fifteen students, tutorial and remedial work would be required, a heavy emphasis on basic language and reading skills, a program of cultural enrichment through experiences in the community, and a general level of excitement and concern by the entire staff for the important work in which they are engaged.

2. The school board could develop this kind of staff feeling and school support if they deliberately chose to develop the ideas and approaches already being utilized in the Toronto Main Street school. In addition certain realities should be faced by those administering the program. People do not generally seek to work or remain under adverse and hostile conditions unless there are specific and positive reasons for doing so. Our society is one which rewards those who perform a service which is more difficult or less desirable. Teaching and administering a slum school should provide certain conditions which make the position more attractive.

It is indeed very peculiar to expect good results from a staffing policy which forces inexperienced teachers to work under adverse conditions, and without special salary consideration. The results are very obvious and depressing to anyone who listens carefully to the after shop talk of young teachers who are serving their time in the slum schools. They are often full of contempt and hostility for the children they teach, and racially bigotted toward these same minority group children. They moan about the "miserableness" of their students and how they can't wait to get married or to be transferred out to a suburban 'mainstream' school. It is no wonder that the staff as well as the students are alienated toward each other under these war-like conditions.

3. The teaching and administrative staff should be specifically selected and trained for work in slum area schools. This would include far more careful screening of an applicant's interests, values and background for this work, as well as the expressed feeling that the assignment was highly regarded by the school board. This regard would be

visible both in the lessening of teaching load and clerical responsibilities and in the significantly higher level salary attached to all staff positions in these schools. Further, the staff would be evaluated and rewarded or released from this service as their performance indicated, the idea being that this kind of teaching, as was indicated recently by Lyndon B. Johnson in his inauguration of the National Teacher Corps, was only for selected and highly able teachers, rather than for the inexperienced and alienated teachers in the establishment.

4. The school board's operation in the larger cities becomes so involved in its own bureaucratic mechanisms and traditional orthodox procedures that it loses its actual purpose for existence. Its central purpose is not that of bookkeeping, maintaining bus schedules, cafeteria supplies and rigidly enforcing the status quo, but rather that of providing educational leadership and programs where the present school approaches are terribly inappropriate, as in the slum areas of our large cities.

The school boards need to drastically alter their present approaches to the disadvantaged population. They should begin to employ educational designs in slum areas which are specifically and rationally developed for this purpose. They should discard the ritualized formula which places similar curricula and academic expectations on schools with grossly different kinds of student populations.

We include the next article on language improvement in the chapter because it is peculiarly appropriate to the learning problems of inner-city children. The author has had signal success in motivating and successfully teaching such lower-class children. She suggests a captivating series of lesson plans and activities. Basic to the success of the program is getting the children to unlearn one language habit system (lower class dialect) and learning another (standard academic). The main trick is in getting them to identify themselves with, and aspire to, middle-class career levels. The reader will notice that she gets the whole group motivated to learn standard communication practices, and the individuals of the group are both sustained by and aspire to the new transvalued and internalized peer group goals.

WAYS TO IMPROVE ORAL COMMUNICATION
OF CULTURALLY DIFFERENT YOUTH*
Ruth I. Golden

Mark Twain once said in a sarcastic moment, "Nothing so needs reforming as other people's habits." Yet, I believe he would approve of our interest in the problem of how to reform the speech habits of culturally different students, for our purpose is to break down language barriers and to help each individual acquire a language proficiency that will help him to achieve his greatest potential. As Thomas Pollock has said, "Civilization depends upon communication. Language is the basic instrument through which human beings share their thinking. If a youth is to develop as an individual, contribute to society, and participate in its benefits, he must have command of the social processes of language."[1]

The schools and all the institutions in a democratic society exist for the purpose of promoting the growth of the individual. For his growth

---

* From *Improving English Skills of Culturally Different Youth* (Washington, D.C.: United States Government Printing Office, 1964), pp. 100-109. Reprinted by permission of the editor. Ruth I. Golden is with the Detroit Public Schools, Detroit, Michigan.

[1] Thomas Clark Pollock, et al. "The English Language in American Education," A Report of the Modern Language Association Commission on Trends in Education, 1945, *Issues, Problems, and Approaches in the Teaching of English*, George Winchester Stone, Jr., ed. New York: Holt, Rinehart and Winston, Inc., 1961, p. 137.

in oral communication, most public high schools offer elective classes for improving the speech arts. These attract mainly those who already possess some speech proficiency. Most schools also have speech correction classes which are staffed with specialists to take care of those with severe defects. If we define a speech defect as any deviation from normal speech that calls attention to itself or to the speaker in a negative way, the specialists could not possibly accommodate in their speech correction classes all the students who need help.

This problem of reforming, or changing, language habits, then, concerns all English teachers and particularly those in urban centers where we find a great many students of foreign extraction or of various ethnic backgrounds for whom English is either a second language or like one. For the student whose native speech, even though it is American English, contains a great many structural, articulatory, and intonational differences, learning to speak a language that is acceptable on the high school level is surely like learning a second language, which is not an easy task.

Virgil Anderson, who wrote *Improving the Child's Speech*, estimated as far back as 1953 that there were approximately 2,500,000 speech-defective children of school age in the United States—over 40,000 in a city the size of Los Angeles, for example, and around 350 in a small city of 20,000.[2] The number today far exceeds that of 1953 because of continued immigration and migration, along with growth in language awareness. During the past 10 years, Detroit's population alone has increased by more than 200,000 because of the influx of southern and foreign migrants who have brought with them their own speech habits. It is, therefore, increasingly important for the classroom teacher to be cognizant of the individual speech needs of his students and to have some means of coping with them.

I emphasize the speech aspects of language, for the oral symbols are basic and the child's written expression is likely to reflect his speech. Two examples of this from my own class papers are: "All people should be treated like *beans*," spelled b-e-a-n-s (these students seldom use the sound of *ing*) and, "Use the right *can* of language," spelled *c-a-n* (*kind* was pronounced *can* following their usual substitution of

[2] Virgil A. Anderson, *Improving the Child's Speech*. New York: Oxford University Press, 1953, p. 7.

182

the low front vowel *ae* for the dipthong *ai*). If we can improve spoken language, written language should also improve.

In adult life we spend at least 90 percent more of our time expressing ourselves orally than we do in writing; therefore, it is deplorable that so little emphasis is placed on improving oral communication in the English classroom.[3] Of course, the aim is to develop in the learner to the best of his ability the four basic aspects of any communication arts program—listening (or understanding), speaking, reading, and writing. These are interrelated and all have to do with developing language expression. Although for many pupils they can best be taught concurrently in integrated language arts units, for children with special problems special practice drills are needed.

My own teaching experience has been devoted to meeting the needs of large numbers of pupils, particularly migrants or children or grandchildren of migrants who are mainly at a low socioeconomic level. Although the pupils speak American English, they speak and continually hear one distinctive variety of it at home or in the neighborhood, where they may continue to speak it for rapport. However, if they are to become employable or to succeed in business, they must learn to shift into the more dominant patterns of the area in which they may later live and work. For these pupils many of the techniques of second-language learning are applicable.

I cannot recommend too highly the book by Mary Finocchiaro entitled *Teaching English as a Second Language in Elementary and Secondary Schools*.[4] This book is full of practical ideas that would enrich teaching in any situation. For good oral drill games particularly suited for the junior high school level, I might suggest *Good English Through Practice*[5] by Marjorie Barrows.

Before we discuss method, let us review some of the factors we know about this very complex phenomenon called language. Because we express our individual personalities and communicate our wants and de-

[3] Lecture by Preston H. Scott, head of the Speech Department, Wayne State University, Detroit, Michigan, 1940.

[4] Mary Finocchiaro, *Teaching English as a Second Language in Elementary and Secondary Schools*. New York: Harper and Row, 1958.

[5] Marjorie Wescott Barrows, *Good English Through Practice*. New York: Henry Holt and Co., 1956.

sires through language, and because we are judged partly by what we say, language is a very personal possession and we become highly sensitive about it. As English teachers, we must be aware of this sensitivity. It may help if we remember that, when we point one finger at someone else, we are pointing three fingers at ourselves.

We know that language is a living, changing set of symbols and the better we know the code, the more effectively we can communicate in it. Part of our job as English teachers is to preserve the basic code and to maintain respect for it. However, unlike the Morse code, there is no one exact set of symbols. Instead, there are many acceptable variations of what may be considered the standard code, and there are different levels of language which may fit various situations. To be most effective, one must be socially mobile in his use of language so that the listener's attention is on *what* one is saying, not on *how* he is saying it. A visit to the United States Senate convinces us of the many acceptable varieties of American English typical of the particular areas from which the senators come. These variations are mainly in the pronunciation and enunciation of vowels.

To some people of one area, the variations used by those of another area may be very amusing. I'm reminded of the Yiddish dialect stories, the lovable Hyman Kaplan, the minstrel shows that depend on Negro dialect, and the comparisons of the Boston dialect of President Kennedy and Senator Lodge made by Frank B. Gilbreth in his "Dictionary of Bostonese." Whether we have positive or negative reactions to slight variations depends upon the personality of the individual, his educational and cultural level, and his freedom from structural deviations. So long as the speaker is effective in various situations, and so long as there are positive reactions from his listeners, we would not wish to change his language. Should a Bostonian come to live in the Midwest for any length of time, or vice versa, he might adjust his speech unconsciously through imitation, or consciously to avoid being conspicuous. More than anything else, as human beings, we want to be accepted, to be approved, and to be recognized, each as an individual.

That variations will decrease and one common standard American language will, in time, prevail seems likely because of our humorists, our television commentators, and the fact that we are a Nation on the move. In one recent year, approximately one of every five Americans pulled up stakes and changed residence. Three and one-tenth percent of these moved to another state. It is already possible to move from the Pennsylvania-Ohio line all the way across to the Pacific Coast without being aware of dialect differences. This is one of the largest dialect areas, or speech communities, in the world and represents the General American dialect that will probably become more or less standard for the Nation. This is the dialect that is used in teaching English to foreigners here and in teaching abroad through the United States Information Service, which has 389 cultural centers in 80 countries of the world.[6] There is, then, little chance of disagreement on what dialect we should teach.

We know, too, that speech is an overlaid process. Each organ that contributes to the speech mechanism has another primary purpose. Speech is a learned activity; it is not biological or racial. Only about 15 percent of those said to have defective speech have any physical basis for it, and only about 10 percent more have speech defects which could be classed as complicated or involved. In fact, about 75 percent of all speech defects, according to Anderson, are the result of bad habits based on poor listening, carelessness, laziness, indifference, or imitating poor models.[7] Within this 75 percent are most members of the ethnic groups in the process of acculturation. They provide a challenge to the English teacher. Anderson does not include the challenge of grammatical or structural errors with which the English teacher has always been concerned.

Our Nation has progressed to an unequalled extent because of our principle that each individual is entitled to rise to his highest potential. In our public schools we hold that no child shall be handicapped by artificial restraints in his struggle to rise. It, therefore, becomes the task of every teacher to participate in helping each student to equip himself with the language habits used in conducting the affairs of our country and in making himself acceptable socially.

The teacher, however, can only point the way; it is the child who must change. His language is definitely related not only to his success in school, but also to his possibilities for subsequent employment. Much of the urge to change depends upon the child's concept of him-

[6] Lincoln Barnett, "The English Language," *Life*, March 2, 1962, p. 75.
[7] Anderson, op. cit., p. 13.

185

self and of his place in the democratic society. What he does, what he learns or avoids learning is related either to building up or defending his self-concept.

How do we go about setting the climate so that the child will want to make the effort to change? For one thing, we must broaden his self-concept by giving him pride in his own culture and by making him aware of the heroes and leaders of his own ethnic group who have mastered his same problems. An assembly speaker, a book, or a picture on the bulletin board may provide the initial motivation.

We must let him retain pride in the language he already has, even guide him into taking classes in Spanish, German, or whatever foreign language he understands so that he can increase his proficiency in it. In the case of those who have retained through historical, regional, and social class influences a brand of English that contains many unacceptable structural deviations, the learning of a foreign language helps to focus attention on language as a tool and skill and to develop facility in usage. But we should encourage pupils to assume the responsibility of speaking English proficiently. We may say to them, "This brand of English you are using is a language in itself, which may have its uses for you. It is like an old suit of clothes that we don't throw away because we may still want to wear it on some occasions. But we would not think of wearing the old suit for a job interview or a dance, if we have something better to wear. Here in class you can acquire the language used by most Americans in the business world. This language will then be yours to use when you want and need it."

This is the approach I use with my students, many of whom use such structural deviations as "he have," "they is," "he taken," and "that's mines," adding the s sound, but saying, "ten cent," omitting the s. They may substitute f for th as in bofe, i for e as in pinny, the low front vowel ae for ai to confuse rat with right, and use a great many non-standard expressions. We must offer them alternate usages and so strengthen them that the English language of the business world will be for them a second language into which they can move for upward social mobility.

Let us review the speech process in order to arrive at a technique to improve these students' speech. As talking animals, we learn to communicate verbally through various stages of development from crying to babbling to lallation (the first ear-voice reflex), on to the stage of echo-lalia where we echo, or imitate, the sound patterns we hear about us. As Donald Lloyd says, "We learn to speak at our mother's knee and at other low joints."

It is in this latter stage, the echolalic, that the special sound pattern of the child's native language becomes established. As he goes on into articulate utterance, his speech becomes more refined and fixed so that by the time he is about 6 years old, the habits that will form his adult speech pattern are already set. To reeducate and build new habits, we must take him back to the stage of lallation, sharpen his ear-voice reflex, and carry him on through echolalia, giving him good standard forms to imitate. The language laboratories for teaching foreign languages have been successful in our schools because they have been established on this premise. It is time we English teachers had them, or at least time we began to make greater use of their techniques for the teaching of English to these pupils.

A year of independent study as a Ford Fellow led me to this conclusion. Part of the study included a questionnaire given to 11th- and 12th-grade students in six Detroit high schools. The study showed that the selected list of 102 nonstandard usages, which the students were free to check or not to check, were both heard and used at least four times more frequently by students in schools representative of Detroit area patterns. The results of this study were published by Wayne State University Press for the National Council of Teachers of English. The book is entitled *Improving Patterns of Language Usage*.[8] It is divided into three parts: "The Problem," "Possible Ways To Meet It," and "Suggested Remedial Lessons and Exercises."

The time needed to develop and test English lessons on tape geared to meet this problem was provided by the U.S. Office of Education in a 2-year grant. During these 2 years I have been relieved of school duties in order to direct, to test by analysis of covariance, and to evaluate a research project under Title VII of the National Defence Education Act.

The set of 14 taped lessons we developed are of the listening-repeating type, but they incorporate some writing. They serve as a type of

[8] Ruth I. Golden, *Improving Patterns of Language Usage*. Detroit: Wayne State University Press, 1960.

teaching machine to explain the structure of the language as well as to change particular usages by giving the student the opportunity to imitate and to practice using better forms. Skinner's theories are involved in that the tapes give immediate reward and reinforcement. The taped lessons are also built upon linguistic concepts, but retain some traditional terminology. To hold interest, because each tape runs just under 30 minutes, we use a variety of rich voices, both male and female, and a variety of teaching techniques and student activities.

Ideally, the tapes could be used in the foreign language laboratory, but we included them as an English classroom activity in a three-group plan with the groups rotating their activities of speaking, reading, and writing during the 3 middle days of the week, while still carrying on other language arts units.

We find that the tape recorder has so many valuable uses for teaching English that we think there ought to be one in every classroom ready for use at any moment. There is much wasted time if you have to requisition a recorder from an audiovisual room or get one out of a closet and set it up. Bolting the recorder to a table seemed to be our best solution.

We have our basic spelling words recorded on tape. If a teacher expects to give the same spelling lesson more than once, he might as well hold a microphone in front of him the first time he dictates it. Thereafter he is free to take the roll or to do other work as he wanders around the room while the spelling test is on and the students are getting training in listening. If the teacher's voice over the tape sounds natural to the students, they will then believe that their own voices, which sound so unreal over tape at first, really do represent the way they sound to others.

Hearing one's own faulty articulation and structural errors over tape can be one of the greatest motivating forces for pupil self-improvement that I can imagine. After there is pupil awareness and desire to improve, the next logical step is to give pupils good forms to imitate and to give them practice in hearing themselves saying the approved forms.

Along 2 walls in the corner of our classroom are 2 phonojack boards, making 12 earphone stations in all, partitioned with plywood. Under the rotating group plan, one group will be at the corner using earphones for listening and repeating lessons. Another group will be reading, since lack of reading background is at the heart of much of the language problem. The third group will be in individual contact with the teacher in a small circle while working on their writing or speaking difficulties.

For the reading group, we have tried various materials including the *Practical English Magazine*, the *SRA Reading Laboratory*, and a Scholastic Magazines' reading kit which provides a classroom library of two shelves of books on a thematic unit. The unit we chose at Central High School was *Mirrors*, which pointed up our semester's theme of taking a look at ourselves, and particularly a look at our language.[9] One of the two books for common learning, *Best Television Plays*, edited by Gore Vidal,[10] contains a wealth of third-person singular verbs in the stage directions. Our students especially need to strengthen such forms of agreement between the subject and verb as in, "John laughs as he crosses the room and opens the window."

This three-group plan is conducive to creating an atmosphere of trust, cooperation, and a feeling of interest in the individual, which is what these students need so badly. Somehow through the earphones, which the students enjoy using, they also get the feeling that they are being individually instructed, and we have purposely tried to make our tapes seem warm and personal. The small circle contact is invaluable. This work, however, is not for an inexperienced teacher; it takes a calm, well-organized, friendly but firm attitude to manage any three-group activity successfully.

The experiment involved four classes, two control groups and two experimental groups. There were two oral and two written tests and an attitude inventory, all given before and after the special series of lessons. All groups were taught in the same way with the same material, the only difference being that the experimental groups went to the booths to hear the taped lessons while the control groups went to the booths to read the same material from scripts without hearing it. All groups had use of the tape recorder for recording the oral tests and for other speech activities, but we found that the special taped lessons in addition were highly effective in improving speech.

[9] Since the preparation of this paper, other useful educational materials, as well as revisions of the above titles, have become available.

[10] Gore Vidal, *Best Television Plays*. New York: Ballantine Books, 1957.

The teaching ideas I'd like to share in the rest of this paper are partly those used in the experiment, but mainly the result of almost 20 years of teaching in 4 Detroit high schools where there are culturally different students.

Much of the success of an English language laboratory class depends upon the attitudes and the individuals' aims set at the beginning of the semester. In the orientation period, we discuss the purposes and the need for education. We discuss all aspects of language, stressing in realistic terms the need for effective language in all walks of life. To clinch the discussion, students write letters to the teacher in which they introduce themselves and state their aims for the semester. This setting of aims paves the way for breaking into speech drills later whenever the need arises. We plan introductory talks to be taped, and individual or group projects to be presented later to the class.

These projects provide most of the composition work for the semester, although purposeful letter writing is engaged in as frequently as possible. A sheaf of letters, usually written to an individual or to an organization within the school, will actually be mailed so that good writing is made meaningful. Replies to the letters lead to some informal conversations later. The presenting of the booklets or other individual projects gives practice in strengthening needed forms such as, "This picture" not "Dis pitcher" and in stressing agreement as in "This shows" and "It has."

To orient students to the use of the tape recorder for critical listening, we first give names or one-sentence introductions into a traveling mike from a relaxed sitting position. Even in so simple an exercise, we can learn the importance of emphasizing the surname so that it can be repeated in an introduction. Then we may try a sentence or two in "class on parade" order and hear a playback before giving introductory talks about our hobbies and interests.

"Class on parade" is a device I use frequently for many types of brief oral presentations. A whole row of students will rise at one time and take positions at the side of the class. Each student then waits for his turn, makes his brief presentation, moves to the other side of the room, and waits for his group to finish so that all can take their seats as the next group comes up. Barring illness, there are no exceptions. Anyone who is not prepared says so when his turn comes, but the moral support given when several rise at one time and the atmosphere of encouragement and informality seem to eliminate procrastinators.

This procedure works well and saves time during speech activities such as: the Inquiring Reporter, in which one student reporter asks each student two or three questions from a long list which they have all had time to consider; famous sayings, in which as a part of a unit on biography each student presents an adage or quotation and tells in his own words what it means to him;[11] memory work, such as a few lines from "The Gettysburg Address" in a ninth-grade Lincoln unit; or the explanation of a rule of courtesy.

Other classroom speech activities include various extemporaneous talks, introductions, business interviews, and panel discussions. A taped business interview with questions designed purposely to bring out deviations, if used, comprised the second oral test of our experiment. For choral reading, with the ninth grade, I especially like Alfred Noyes' "The Highwayman" because my particular students need practice in improving the *ai* sound through the repetition of *highwayman* and *riding, riding*. The correction of this one sound may be a key to changing the entire speech pattern. As students change this frequently used sound, they are often reminded to change other less desirable usages.

We have made up a little nonsense story about "The Rat Named Kite" which introduces the idea of having the students write what we call "stupid stories" to bring in the repetition of sounds or usages they particularly need to practice. We emphasize final consonants and the past tense signal *ed* by listing substitutions for words like *walked* and *said* and by classifying these words according to whether they have a *d* or a *t* sound at the end.

Besides the taped group lessons for usage drill practice, we frequently spend a few minutes on general oral drill. If someone says, "fave cent," we may take a minute to count in unison from "one cent, two cents," up to "ten cents," stressing the *s* sound. When trouble occurs in agreement of third person singular noun and its matching verb, or if we hear "seen" instead of "saw," we may take time out to drill on the

[11] We have typed a large collection of these sayings on 5- by 8-inch cards, and find them excellent for extemporaneous speech training as well as for uplifting values.

conjugation of the verbs, jazzing up the rhythm to make the activity fun as well as to reinforce it in the memory.

For extracurricular motivation, we participate in speech contests and put on plays and variety shows. In two schools we have organized a speech and personality improvement club called "The Teen Talkers and Tapers." One club sponsored a schoolwide Better Speech Campaign complete with Tag Day, daily homeroom lessons in speech improvement, and colorful hall posters and bulletin boards.

We now have some proof of success, but one never knows how truly successful such speech efforts are because so much of the learning may be a delayed action process. If we hold to high standards, yet make speech activities pleasant and memorable, there will be positive results. We cannot change the student's speech habits for him, but we can help him to become aware of the need for change by becoming a more critical and discerning listener; we can give him good examples to imitate; and we can encourage his efforts at self-improvement.

The beauty and good of education is so dinned into the ears of Americans that almost no one would verbally doubt the value of going on to the high-school diploma, at least. Behaviorally, the story is different. About a third of 18-year-olds are dropouts. Ten percent of these will be chronically jobless. What would happen if these dropouts had been persuaded to stay in school? The article raises some doubts as to whether the lives of the dropouts would have been changed much if they had stayed in school. It also suggests some successful plans.

WHY DROPOUT CAMPAIGNS FAIL*
Bernard Bard

Two years ago the U.S. Office of Education spent a quarter of a million dollars in twenty major cities to identify dropouts, and to persuade them to go back to school. Some 30,411 dropouts were identified, of whom 10,015 agreed to come back. To this date, no one knows how many of those ten thousand stayed until graduation, and how many

* Taken from *Saturday Review*, September 17, 1966, p. 78.

dropped out again. "There has been no follow-up," said Leroy V. Goodman, information director for the Office of Education. "School districts operated on their own."

The information gap about the fate of the ten thousand typifies much that has been said, written, and researched (or not researched) about the multiplicity of anti-dropout drives in progress across the nation. On the whole, there has been no systematic evaluation of their success or failure.

The campaigns come in many packages, from the rehabilitative Dropouts Anonymous to the humanitarian Operation Second Chance to the mundane Stay-in-School. Virtually all suffer from the same basic weaknesses. The school officials who mount these efforts are often more concerned with the image than the reality of their dropout drives. And, in many major cities, while the bus placards warn marginal students not to chuck it all, principals are chucking them out of school by the tens of thousands. Often the school districts are either unable or unwilling to follow up on their own propaganda. The returning dropout may be confronted with red tape, hostility, and constant reminders that he failed once and no one in authority expects much more from him the second time around.

Washington, D.C., persuaded hundreds of dropouts to come back in the fall of 1963, but didn't know what to do with them once they got there. At Spingarn High School, overcrowding was so severe, ninety dropouts were shoe-horned into a room. Some sat on radiators or stood in the rear. Other classrooms were overloaded with fifty and sixty students. At McKinley and Eastern High Schools, the dropouts were assigned to the same schools they had quit, depositing them, in effect, into the same environment of failure. Six out of ten quit again.

A premise of the anti-dropout mechanism is that getting the victim back to school is most of the battle. It is wrong, if nothing significant has changed about school to keep him there. And, as a rule, nothing has been changed. A growing body of expert opinion among youth specialists and sociologists holds that working on the dropout problem via the dropout is rather phony. Such an approach assumes the dropout is at fault, when actually he may have made his own shrewd appraisal of what school and the high-school diploma is worth in terms of his own future. Negroes and Puerto Ricans know that their diploma is often useless on the job market. Statistically, there is practically no difference in the unemployment rates of minority-group youngsters who finish high-school and those who drop out.

Dr. Abraham Tannenbaum, a consultant to New York's Mobilization for Youth and an associate professor at Teachers College, Columbia University, says, "Society is resorting to the Big Lie and using a convenient excuse when it employs the label—'the dropout problem.' We tell youngsters to stay in school so they can earn more money. This is all very well if you're talking about a white kid, but for the Negro it will only make a little bit of difference, not much. By conning the sixteen-year-old to stay in school for another year or two, we know or should know that it's not going to make a great deal of difference in his chances. This is baloney; it's like putting a Band-Aid on cancer."

The scope of the dropout problem dulls the senses. The statistics are already a cliché. Of the 3,800,000 Americans who reach age eighteen every year, at least 1,200,000 will be dropouts. Ten percent will be chronically jobless. A year ago, the number of jobless youths between sixteen and twenty-one stood at 730,000. In five years, if present trends hold up, the figure will more than double.

What schools are doing about it—while often irrelevant—covers a wide range of approaches. Galveston, Texas, organized a Dropouts Anonymous, with groups meeting once a week. When a member shows signs of defeatism, a group leader talks him out of dropping out again. Of those participating, there is an 85 percent holding-power. Denver runs a Metropolitan Youth Education Center, which arranges a flexible work-study program. Potential dropouts can proceed through school without grades, and without time limit. Houston has a Talent Preservation Program; Albuquerque, a Lincoln Project; Memphis a Youth Corps; and Chicago, an EE (Education-Employment) Program. The list goes on and on, but what does it add up to? Frequently, nothing.

At the root of the so-called dropout problem, of course, is this statistical indictment—schools in the big cities spawn far more dropouts than can be salvaged. The nation's five largest cities, New York, Los Angeles, Chicago, Detroit, and Philadelphia, have a combined average dropout rate of 24 per cent. (Philadelphia is the champ, with a whopping 46.6 per cent.) In general, the larger the city, the higher the dropout rate, according to the NEA. Even the job of compiling dependable dropout statistics is made next to impossible by the duplicity of some school districts. The NEA, in its dropout project, found that some school officials only keep dropout records on a nine-month basis. Since about 25 per cent of the dropouts occur over the summer, the nine-month casuality list is artificially depressed.

Some other systems compute the dropout percentage against the "total school population," which means first grade through high school. Since few pupils are precocious enough to call it quits in the third, or fourth, or sixth grade—even if compulsory attendance laws allowed them to—this approach is a statistical lie. To obtain accurate dropout percentages—measured against high-school enrollments—the NEA found it had to throw out figures supplied by many districts and work instead from raw U. S. census data. The same schoolmen who are in part responsible for the dropout tried, in other words, to camouflage the number of victims.

How great is the distance between what school officials say and what they do concerning the dropout? The case of Laura M., from the files of Mobilization for Youth, suggests the disparity. She became pregnant, and dropped out of Washington Irving High School in lower Manhattan. After she had her child, she tried to go back under Operation Return, a city program aimed at the 27,000 city students who quit school each year. At first, she was told by an assistant principal at Irving to try another school. She did. The new school sent for her records, but weeks elapsed before their arrival. Meanwhile, Laura was advised to seek counseling for one of the maze of agencies working on dropouts. She selected MFY, which bombarded Irving with phone calls in an effort to obtain her records. Finally, as a last desperate act, a project director called Board of Education headquarters, and was told: "Laura is not acceptable because of motherhood status." MFY had never heard of such a regulation. A check with the Bureau of Attendance produced the information that it did not exist. "In fact, we encourage them to come back," said a functionary. "No one can take that right away from her."

Laura's rights had been taken from her, of course. Her enthusiasm for school had long vanished, crushed by the "get-lost" attitude at her old school and the inertia of the record-keepers. She abandoned the idea of returning to high school, and became a dropout statistic.

The biggest stumbling block is the school principal. In Harlem, a youth worker reported that "ninety-nine times out of a hundred the principal won't take the kid back." Similar conclusions were reported by the NEA in connection with its Project: School Dropout, despite the assertions of the official propaganda issued by various boards of education. Daniel Schreiber, former director of the project, found the prevailing attitude among principals to be one of hostility and suspicion. "The principals were most afraid the dropout would become a discipline problem," said Schreiber. "Their biggest worry was that the dropout might endanger the education of the others if he came back."

What about the dropout who doesn't drop out a second time? Does his perseverance pay off? Rarely. Pittsburgh recently inaugurated a month-long course for dropouts on how to get and hold a job. Ten Negroes signed up. At the windup, only one found employment. This was true, despite the fact that the course was planned by Pittsburgh businessmen who said they would help place the dropouts. School officials decided it would be cruel and pointless to bring dropouts back for more of the same.

The business community is ambivalent toward the dropout. On the one hand, hundreds of the nation's leading firms are cooperating with work-study programs aimed at luring him back to school while giving him a part-time job. On the other hand, there is substantial resistance on the part of many industrial giants. The rub apparently is that there aren't enough jobs to go around. In a recent nationwide sampling, the Wall Street Journal found a fear on the part of some firms of creating ill-will if dropouts were signed on. "If we let it be known we were hiring dropouts and then have to turn down a youngster who's got a high-school diploma, how do we explain it to him?" asked a personnel officer for a large insurance company. One of the nation's Big Three auto manufacturers (Ford) proposed that each of its 9,000 dealers provide a part-time job for a dropout, provided he returned to school. But dealer reaction was "pretty negative," so the plan was put on the shelf. "I'm frankly disappointed," said a company executive, "it would have helped 9,000 boys get back on the right track."

The anti-dropout effort, no matter how novel the approach or what combination of alphabet-soup the agency is packaged in, invariably comes at least five years too late. The dropout usually becomes visable in the third through the fifth grades. From that point on, he usually keeps stumbling—right out the schoolhouse door. It is quite often the school that has failed as much as the dropout.

"They are bored, tremendously bored," says Aramis Gomez, director of the East Harlem center of Job Orientation in Neighborhood (JOIN) in Manhattan, a $3,000,000 program co-sponsored by the city and the U.S. Labor Department. "They yawn their way through school," says Dr. Tannenbaum of MFY.

Despite New York's many sided approach to the problem, counselors still find in talking to dropouts that principals and teachers are "throwing them out arbitrarily." Many counselors at anti-dropout agencies find fault with the Board of Education on several counts—shoving out dropouts in filing-case batches, offering outmoded courses in obsolete skills at vocational schools, and permitting near-illiterates to get as far as the sophomore and junior years of high school. "We shouldn't be in business," asserted an official of a dropout agency with branches in the five boroughs. "Why should we have to offer courses in remedial reading and arithmetic? This is supposed to be done by the Board of Education—and yet it forms the biggest part of our job. We're taking on what they messed up in the first place."

A high Board of Education official admitted that it was standard practice to promote children who should be left back. She conceded, in fact, that as many as 25 per cent of the "graduates" of junior highs do not graduate at all, but are merely handed certificates of attendance, stating they have been there, and that's about all. "This is a fake," she said.

The pupil who is too old, then, for junior high is passed into senior high school without a diploma, and further shoved along the route to becoming a dropout. It is left for agencies such as JOIN, MFY, and others, to pick up the pieces. MFY, for instance, runs a nonprofit service station and luncheonette to give realistic training to youngsters who need help in finding a job. But it has been found that many flunk the training courses because they can't handle enough arithmetic to add the city sales tax to a customer's bill. Much of the work of anti-dropout agencies boils down to patchwork educational remediation, or random efforts at finding jobs for a handful of trainees whose numbers are dwarfed by new "push-outs" and "squeeze-outs" and other categories of school rejects.

For the agencies, it is an up-mountain fight. New York's Neighborhood Youth Corps, for instance, obtained 4,500 full-time and 900 part-time jobs for dropouts last year—but the city that year produced five times that number of new dropouts. "This program is intended specifically as an aid to the high-school dropouts. Yet it would not affect the total dropout problem if it were magnified five-fold," said Professor Robert A. Dentler of the Center for Urban Education and a faculty member at Teachers College, Columbia University. "It is hard to grasp how it could be magnified at all, or even repeated in a second or third year of operation, since 40 per cent of the jobs being offered are for posts in city departments. There is a fallacy inherent in such programs. They may supply a limited number of jobs for pupils fresh out of pilot programs, but they are very apt to be like the jobs available now for dropouts, scarce in number and good for one filling per generation."

While most dropout campaigns are too little and too late, there are some rays of light in the generally dismal picture. They may be seen usually, in more imaginative school districts that saw past mistakes and completely overhauled programs. Washington, D.C., which muffed its earlier drive, tried again last year and found it was able to hold on to virtually all the returnees. Instead of shipping dropouts back to their old schools, they were installed in special night classes at Spingarn High School. The program is called STAY (School to Aid Youth). Classes run from 3:30 to 10 p.m., some lasting two hours so a student can take more credits in fewer trips to school. Classes are small (under twenty), all homework is done in school in recognition of the fact that many dropouts have no desk at home, and a full range of academic courses is offered. Students may take as many or as few courses as they wish. "There isn't any formula," said STAY director William F. Carpenter. "That's just the point. We find out what the kids need and give it to them. It's simple."

STAY officials made an interesting discovery—one that may have national implications. Students came into the program weeks before transcripts arrived from their former schools. They were asked to write down their own grades, so they could be placed accordingly. Later, when the records arrived, teachers were astonished to find that some of the hardest working students had been rated "absolutely incorrigible" or otherwise hopeless. Knowing that their past records of

198

failure had, in effect, been erased the dropouts gave themselves a clean slate and made good. School officials decided to ignore the old records altogether and to judge each returnee on the basis of current performance.

One of the miracles wrought by Assistant Superintendent Samuel Shepard, Jr., in the 95 per cent Negro Banneker District in St. Louis, has been a reversal of dropout trends among the 15,000 pupils in his twenty-three schools. Shepard reduced the rate from more than a third to less than one in ten by motivating parents as well as pupils. Parents were signed up as homework managers, as aids on field trips, as counselors to run study-ins. "You've heard of sit-ins and teach-ins," said Shepard. "Well, these are the same, except they're for studying." The parents were asked to sign pledges to turn off the radio or television during homework hours. They promised to sign each day's homework, or to check with the school when a child said there was none. Teachers who complained of too-large classes were told the class size would be cut, and it was now up to them to "deliver or get out." Dropouts in Banneker today average well below the St. Louis citywide average of 13 per cent.

B. Frank Brown, principal of the 1,500-student Melbourne High School, Melbourne, Florida, faced a different sort of problem. His school, near the Cape Kennedy space center, accommodates children of mechanics as well as those of propulsion experts with Ph.D.'s. In 1959, he had an 18 per cent dropout rate. Today it is down to 4 per cent. He combatted dropouts through a non-graded high school program in which traditional grade levels are abolished and "phases of learning" are substituted. Students are taught in small and large study groups, and encouraged to progress at their own pace. Time is made available for individual research projects.

The inner-city family is a growing problem, and the short-term prospect is that the slums will continue to get worse. Present-day plans are on the order of urban housing that calls for bulldozing the slums to provide for economical housing. The results have been a worsening of conditions for dispossessed families. Alternative plans that get to the cultural roots of the problem are necessary.

Sociologists are quite convinced that the family of the inner city is the ever-growing and persistent source of difficulty with the students of the inner-city schools. Most people agree that the family is a sacred cow that cannot be assaulted in any way. The following article suggests a modification of the typical family group. The underlying significance is that, if this modification succeeeds, a number of other modifications may be possible.

AN INNER-CITY SOLUTION: THE URBAN KIBBUTZ
*David H. Loebl**

We read each day of American families being broken up by divorces. Newspapers carry articles of children sniffing glue for "kicks." Fathers dodge their responsibility by deserting their families. Even the upper class cannot escape being murdered by their offspring. These and other transgressions represent the failure of the modern-day American family. No longer is it true that only the poor must suffer these afflictions; the rich are victims as well.

Perhaps, though, the most outstanding characteristic of these problem families is that they fail to perform the functions normally associated with family life. Children can hardly be properly indoctrinated with community norms of behavior when the parents have never learned them. By example, if not intent, children learn the advantages of lying, distrustfulness, and general indifference toward others. A number of authorities now claim that the notion of social workers that the natural family is superior to any other social form for child care is incorrect. They believe the most important aspect of rearing children is the socialization of the child, i.e., meeting the psychosocial criteria for the development of a healthy personality. The facts are that the American family tends more and more to fail in meeting these criteria. It is the author's plan to present a more effective solution to family problems than those currently being offered.

The real victims of broken families, conflict families, or problem families are the children. Generally they are removed from the home by the courts and placed in foster homes which are designed to meet

* Graduate student, Wayne State University. Unpublished monograph, 1968.

their need for the security of family life when it is not possible for them to live with their natural parents. Usually the foster parents receive payment for their services, and supervision from the child-placing agency. The foster family assumes responsibility for the physical care and education of the child. It is considered good practice for the foster family to help the child understand the circumstances that made the placement necessary. The agency on the other hand should assist the foster parents to understand that they will not be taking the place of the child's own parents. This is basically the foster home as it should be.

The terms collective, commune, and cooperative are used often interchangeably but separately in this paper. The author's concept of the above-named institutions encompasses two basic forms of child-rearing institutions. The first, often referred to as the pseudo-family type, groups children of various ages into a single, relatively self-contained unit. Usually several such units, each with its own "mother," are grouped together. The children are often involved in the responsibilities of the household and participate in the education program of the entire institution. Heavy emphasis is placed on self government and group control of members' behavior. The second is the kibbutz-style youth program which is similar to the first but utilizes frequent parental contact. This form also encourages its participants to marry and remain with the institution.

The idea of collective living is not novel. It dates back to the biblical period when whole villages found it necessary to consolidate their entire productivity for survival. But it has not been until the last century that group living has been seriously considered as a way of life, except possibly among primitive families. Previously individuals turned toward communal living as an economic resource. Today, societal experts are scrutinizing the collective as a positive substitute for the modern-day family.

The local regulations governing living conditions in the kibbutz are issued by a general assembly elected for a limited period of time by all members over the age of eighteen. The assembly elects committees to function on such matters as labor, housing, education, culture, work assignment, and management. The general assembly passes final judgment on the admission of new members and makes final decisions on the expulsion of undesirables.

Public opinion is used to force members to live up to the code of the kibbutz. Members who fail to produce for the good of all are ostracized socially. Work is allocated from the central committee, which bases its judgment on the proved ability of the individual. For example, a woman who shows an aptitude for cooking will study nutrition.

A central kitchen in each kibbutz and a central dining hall provide for all adults who participate in serving the food on a rotation basis. Adults are able to participate in group activities, in drama, and dances, and they also travel to see films, plays or sporting events. Full medical, dental, and hospital care is provided for members at no expense to them.

The child is dependent on the community rather than the family. Motherhood no longer entails the abandonment of a vocation, because the commune takes over all responsibilities for the children from the moment of birth, even to their feeding. Children are taught from the cradle onward to live with and love their intimate age group, regarding individualism as anti-social.

There are no rigid timetables in education. Subjects are taken up spontaneously and treated intensively and from many points of view. Lessons start with visual presentations and proceed as projects. Children work in the kibbutz for two hours a day at age ten. By age fourteen they are employed in kibbutz activity for four hours a day.

Stress is placed on wide humanistic knowledge and scientific education. Teachers are encouraged to use the project method of teaching, making it possible to introduce geography, history, agriculture, biology, chemistry, physics, mathematics, and economics, thus creating opportunities for individual effort and collective work.

There are no examinations, no marks, and no punishment. Children advance with their peers. The children themselves demand discipline and responsible behavior from the members through a junior counterpart of the general assembly. There is a relationship between the teacher and the pupil based on mutual trust and respect for the personality of the child. The teacher tries to win over the child by explanation and persuasion. The kibbutz educator bears full responsibility for the child's development, not just during school hours. Attention is paid to every child who discusses his problems with the teacher, whose function is to help the child overcome clashes between the individual and society.

Teachers must participate in kibbutz living and receive special training in the aims of the organization before undertaking their positions. In time, kibbutz children now receiving their basic education will be able to return as full-fledged teachers to continue the work of educating the children.

A form of communal living, then, is offered as a method of solving the human problems of those persons who live in abject poverty in the central core of urban areas. We cannot afford to sit back complacently while a huge portion of our urban population does not have the opportunity to gain self-respect, or acquire decent housing, an adequate education, or the opportunity for economic advancement. The losses to our society are too great.

What I propose is a series of agricultural collectives to house the children normally placed in foster homes. In brief, each section of a collective would have a "mother" for each fifteen children. Placement would be permanent until adulthood except in unusual cases. Financing of the project would be a minor problem if some of the 30 billion dollars a year we spend on Vietnam could be diverted after the war's completion. It would be expected that the project could eventually operate at a profit.

The proposed land is desert or wasteland owned by the federal government; thus securing the property rights would not be a problem. Israel utilized water conduits and canals for its irrigation needs. Depending on finances, the same could be done in this plan. If far less expensive means are necessary the camp members could do much of the irrigation planning themselves. The area is drained by the Gila, Salt, and Colorado River systems as indicated in the accompanying map. Pipelines from fresh-water areas and salt-water conversion plants could be utilized in the future if the camps prove successful. Once irrigated, the area should prove quite productive, as it is not lacking in mineral content.

It would be expected that much of the knowledge gained from the Israel Kibbutzim could be passed along to the administrators of the project. Schools, medical needs, and recreational activities would be offered the children and personnel of the establishment. Upon reaching adulthood, participants could leave or remain with the program. It is even hoped that marriages would take place and families reared within the confines of the institution. Granted many unforeseen problems would appear, but they could be solved just as problems were solved by the Israelis. We know it took stages, retreats and painful struggles to overcome the dilemma of the Kibbutz.

In conclusion, the author believes that the collective form of child-rearing is vastly superior to the foster-family program as it now stands. Children reared outside the family structure appear to grow to healthy maturity and to fit into their societies as responsible, constructive adults. There are flaws and problems in all types of child-care settings, yet the collective appears to be the most promising solution to these problems. It merits at least a future experiment.

Editors' Summary

What to do? It becomes apparent that unifactorial or piecemeal approaches will not greatly help. It also becomes apparent that the approach which makes sense at the level of such a problem is a cultural one: the outworn mode of treating "the unfortunate" as single objects of charity is inhumane and futile. What we need is an education that enters into the ether of the culture of poverty, and culturally changes the individuals thereof in a way that is conscionable to our best ideals and values, and scientifically effective in doing so.

VIII

Educating the Exceptional and Disadvantaged

Editors' Comment

    Every society transmits its culture through the current crop of babies. Every culture has a greater or lesser success in the transmission, depending on the physical bodies, the mode of transmission, and the content of transmission. The existence of idiots, criminals, unhappy, mis-utilized or underutilized individuals is a problem for any society. Our society magnifies the problem and makes many failures highly visible, because we must place people in specialized jobs, which usually require a long apprenticeship. Our handicapped, institutionalized people, welfare recipients, unemployed, socially disorganized and people in obviously poor mental health show (and cause) our obvious failures. Another failure, more insidious but perhaps more significant for productivity, is the underutilization of human beings. Most of us are never really tested by our work, or have a chance to show the stuff we are made of.

    Concern for the academically gifted has risen greatly in the last few years, and the air is rife with proposals for educating these gifted, talented, or exceptional children as they are variously called. In advocating programs for the gifted, a body of rather vague misgivings about democracy had to be referred to. Are the gifted any better that they should be given preferential treatment? Might we not suborn a new elite of I.Q. snobbism, with concurrent inferiority complexes among the excluded masses? Might not democracy call for everyone getting equal expenditure of educational energy, even if they could not absorb it equally? Once you set up inequality as an ideal, even in the name of democracy, there is no clear prediction as to where it could end.

Arguments to soothe, evade, or explain away all these misgivings were found. Empirically, inequality is the law of life. Gifted children give back to the community greater service and value for the dollar spent on them than do the less-talented children. And the cultural ethos is more sympathetic to the loss of stars, geniuses, and champions than to their plebeian brothers who earn a four-line obit.

But perhaps the real reasons for the pressure to educate the academically talented are more tacit than admitted. We live in times of dreadful stress and urgency. In such times, the genius, the man of unparalleled wisdom, the inventor and leader are most highly prized. They can save us; they can solve our problems. Any kind of financial outlay that will uncover for us such leadership is well spent.

Some ill-founded presumptions about the nature of society and man catalyze such dreams of cultural salvation through the anointed few. Our understanding of culture, though not as extreme as Leslie White who says that culture is everything and the individual nothing, greatly emphasizes the importance of the total culture in any progress of men. No man or group of men is brilliant, charming, or ingenious enough to make many fundamental changes in the culture.

The important questions to ask, therefore, relate to what this or that measure can do for the quality of our culture. If we as a group decide that we shall have queen bees who reign and are recognized as superior, we shall have them. If we want a generation of sensation-seeking lowbrows, we shall have them. All depends on the nature and interpretation of the goals we set for ourselves. We can so magnify the importance of the gifted that we may minify more fundamental goals of the good life for the common man, and thus kill the goose that laid the golden eggs. We could have a new elite of stars fawned on by their grateful, low I.Q. compeers, or we could have higher standards for all and a thoroughgoing challenge of purpose for everyone including the more capable. It is this difference of emphasis which is all important.

A tremendous loss of our intellectual resources is a matter of fact. For example, only a third of the high school graduates enter college; of the two thirds who do not, many are more qualified than those who enter, on the basis of I.Q. A drop-out of high ability continues from grade school through the Ph.D. graduates. "Only a fiftieth of the young men and women with AGCT scores over 123 will earn Ph.D's." Dael Wolfle has the figures:

INTELLECTUAL RESOURCES
Dael Wolfle*

The scientific and intellectual advances of a nation are generated by a comparatively small number of people. These few—the inventors, scientists, thinkers and scholars—who have given us the Declaration of Independence and atomic energy, railroads and radar, antibiotics and masterpieces of music and literature—have contributed to civilization out of all proportion to their numbers. In the U.S. we think immediately of such giants as Thomas Jefferson, Benjamin Franklin, Josiah Willard Gibbs, Thomas Hunt Morgan, Alexander Graham Bell, John Dewey, Mark Twain and Walt Whitman. But the geniuses represent only a part of a nation's intellectual resources; for every genius there are hundreds of less eminent but highly competent men and women who also contribute significantly to the nation's intellectual progress.

The first step in appraising the intellectual resources of the U.S. therefore, is to try to define just what group we are talking about. We cannot define it simply in terms of education, for our intellectual manpower certainly does not include all of the six million college graduates in the U.S. Some of them have retired from work; some are in non-intellectual occupations; some, though they have obtained degrees, can hardly be classed as capable of high-level mental work. Conversely, there are many people making important intellectual contributions who never went to college.

As a rough definition of our intellectual manpower let us say that it comprises all those who work primarily with their brains. We do

* Dael Wolfle, "Intellectual Resources," *Scientific American*, CLXXV, No. 3 (September, 1951), 42-46. Reprinted by permission.

not know how large this number is, because no exact census of them has ever been taken. Efforts are now being made to do so: the Federal government, professional societies and other agencies have been compiling rosters of specialists in the sciences, humanities and various professions, and the 1950 Census made a number of new tabulations of scientific specialties.

It is estimated that we have about 400,000 engineers, 209,000 doctors, 200,000 college teachers and 175,000 scientists. If we add the architects, editors, lawyers, social scientists and persons in other high-level fields, the total number of brainworkers is perhaps a million and a half. Even if the actual number is twice that, we are still considering only two percent of the total population and five percent of the nation's labor force.

Individually the members of this group vary greatly in their intellectual contributions to society. But in general these are the people who have ideas, develop new inventions, processes and products, manage the nation's social, intellectual and administrative machinery, run its industry and commerce and train others for these complex tasks. They are a growing resource. Through their work they have greatly increased the demand for people like themselves. Their scientific discoveries, inventions and social improvements have created new demands for engineers, scientists, social scientists, historians, scholars and other men of ability and training who can manage our ever-more-complex society.

Our problem is: Where are we to find the resources to meet these additional demands? How many people have we who are capable of making creative contributions? How effectively are we discovering and utilizing our intellectual potential? Can we increase our intellectual manpower?

To answer these questions we must have some reliable measure of intellectual ability. No one will pretend that this can be determined by a simple formula. Intelligence alone is not enough for effective intellectual work: to make creative contributions in a scientific or scholarly field one must also be endowed with interest in it, industry, persistence, strength of character, confidence and some spark of originality.

. . . .

If intelligence is not a sufficient condition for creative intellectual work, at least it is a necessary one. Some minimum level of intelligence is necessary to master the basic concepts, problems and techniques of a specialized field. The minimum level varies, of course, with the difficulty of the field. It turns out, for example, that people who go into work in the pure sciences score higher in intelligence tests, on the average, than those in applied fields; within the field of the basic sciences the physical scientists average a little higher than the biologists. Remember, however, that we are speaking only of averages; there are very high I.Q.'s in all fields.

. . . .

The story is even less favorable [about the number of talented who get educated] when we examine what proportion of able people obtain the Ph.D. degree—today a requirement for many of our top-level intellectual occupations. During the 10 years from 1941 through 1950 U.S. universities conferred an average of about 3,300 Ph. D.'s a year. According to the best available information, the median score of Ph.D.'s on the AGCT is probably in the neighborhood of 134, and the score exceeded by 75 per cent is approximately 123. About 12.5 percent of the total population scores above 123. Of this group, who possess the intelligence to earn a Ph.D., only 1.5 percent actually do so. The proportion will probably increase during the next 10 years; perhaps the figure will be 2 percent instead of 1.5 percent. But even so only a fiftieth of the young men and women with AGCT scores over 123 will earn Ph.D.'s.

This is not to imply that everyone with an AGCT score above 109 should graduate from college or that everyone with a score above 123 should get a Ph. D. Bright people are needed in some fields, e.g., in business and the highly skilled crafts, where college training is not necessarily the most effective preparation, and the Ph.D. is not generally needed in such high-level fields as medicine, law, engineering, schoolteaching, business administration or social work. Nonetheless, we have serious shortages of people in many specialties that do require college or Ph.D. training. Consequently we need to give serious attention to the large potential of intellectual resources that we fail to use to full capacity because of lack of the necessary education.

Clearly the raw material is available for training more engineers, more scientists, more people in other important fields. Just how many more we might realistically expect is hard to estimate. It is easy to see, however, how the numbers could be increased substantially; we need only look at the reasons why so many bright youngsters fail to go to college.

We could not add greatly to the number of potential intellectual workers by attempting to keep in school those who drop out before finishing high school; the great majority of these drop-outs are only of average or less than average ability. It is at the point of high-school graduation that the biggest single loss of bright students occurs. Only a third of the high school graduates enter college, and of the two thirds who do not, a large proportion are above average in ability. The attrition among bright students continues in college, for half of the people who enter fail to graduate. Most of the drop-outs, to be sure, are in the lower-ability brackets, but many are brilliant; even among that rare company who score about 150 on the AGCT more than 20 percent leave college before graduating.

There are two main reasons why bright students fail to go to college or quit before graduation if they do go: lack of interest and lack of money. Of these, lack of interest is the more common one. A great many able students forego college because their parents do not expect them to go, because they decide early on a vocation that does not require college, because they prefer to marry or because their friends are not planning to go to college.

If the country wants to use the abilities of its ablest youngsters at the highest possible level, it must somehow encourage more of them to go on with their education. The first step, of course, is to identify these best brains. Fortunately this is not too difficult. The people who possess the talent for academic work and scholarship of a high order can be picked out at a fairly early age. Dr. Cox pointed out that the eminent people she studied gave evidence of their unusually high I.Q.'s in early childhood. Voltaire wrote verses "from his cradle." Coleridge could read a chapter from the Bible at the age of 3. Mozart composed a minuet at 5. Goethe produced grown-up literary work at 8. Nowadays intelligence-test scores and school achievement records make possible reliable early selection of the able children. Indeed, whether a youngster will be successful in college can be predicted about as well by tests given at the ninth-grade level as at the time of college admission.

210

The next step is to give active encouragement to those who show the greatest promise. In some cases it is necessary to offer financial help. At the highest levels of training considerable help is becoming available. The Federal government, concerned about shortages of scientists and engineers, has started several new scholarship programs. The Atomic Energy Commission grants fellowships to graduate students in the sciences related to atomic developments. The Veterans Administration gives subsidies to college graduates interested in careers in clinical psychology. The new National Science Foundation plans to make a scholarship and fellowship program one of its chief activities. But I suspect that graduate fellowship programs will be less effective in increasing our intellectual manpower than their supporters hope. To qualify for a fellowship one must first finish college. If the goal is to enlarge the total pool of highly trained talents, money offered as scholarships to help bright youngsters start to college would probably be more effective than fellowships awarded to graduate students. There is no doubt that we need a great many more scholarships at the undergraduate level.

We have an even greater need, however, to improve our efforts to interest the brightest youngsters in pursuing an advanced education. In this task our schools frequently fall down. Despite the widespread school use of intelligence tests, too frequently the results are not used as a basis for encouraging the most promising. More school systems should follow the example of that in the State of Iowa. Each Iowa child is given the Iowa Test of Educational Development at several points during his school career. The most promising are actively encouraged by their teachers to continue their education, and their parents are notified of their promise. The Iowa psychologist Leo Phearman found that 92 percent of the Iowa high school seniors who scored in the top 2 percent of these tests, and 75 percent of those in the top 10 percent, continued their educational careers into college.

. . . .

No one knows how much is lost to science and creative scholarship by holding brilliant youngsters back to the pedestrian pace of the typical school and college. They can develop faster. As S. L. Pressey has effectively demonstrated at Ohio State University, they can do so without damage to health, without appreciable loss of opportunity to participate in extracurricular activities, without loss in quality of work and with the very positive benefit that a larger percentage of these accelerated students graduate from college than is true of equally bright but nonaccelerated students. They can start graduate work earlier and can begin contributing sooner to society and to their chosen field of work. . . .

In a Dionysian culture such as ours, the tendency is to reward strength, merit, and talent far beyond what these attributes would receive in an Apollonian culture. (These terms, from Nietzsche, mean respectively an egoistic and competitive culture, and one which is altruistic and co-operative.) This means that those who are not handsome, capable, and mentally and physically sound will suffer disproportionate handicaps in reaching their goals. What rationale can we have in educating the handicapped? We advance some arguments on this question.

THE SOCIALIZATION OF THE MENTALLY RETARDED
August Kerber and Wilfred R. Smith*

The underlying philosophy for educating the handicapped is the belief that in a democracy, all children are entitled to education according to the limit of their capacities. The understanding is that all are equal before the law and have equal rights to an education even though they do not have equal abilities to learn. The mentally-retarded child has an equal right to receive to the full potential of his unequal ability to learn. This statement of individual rights is well accepted now, and is paralleled by a social principle of equal importance. Only through the attainment of the highest dignity and worth of the individual can society reach its full stature. What society does to the individual, it does to itself. By condemning the lowest and meanest among us, the whole society falls from its state of grace.

* August Kerber and Wilfred R. Smith, "The Socialization of the Mentally Retarded." Unpublished monograph, mimeographed, Wayne State University (Detroit, 1960).

The slow learner, as a human being with but one life to live, is entitled to and must have as many experiences educationally as his ability will allow. An actual experience in living that is related to his immediate interests and environment will provide for him a richer and more vital life. Beginning with the birth of the individual, society reacts to him as an individual until his death.

Whether it be in the family or in society, attitudes toward the individual develop. The fact that learning plays such an important part in attitude formation has long been recognized. The problem of the social adjustment of the mentally retarded is not solely one of their making. Social behavior is interactive. The education of the mentally handicapped differs from the education of the average child in its lack of emphasis placed upon academic achievement in contrast to the emphasis placed upon the development of personality and adequacy in the occupational and social areas.

Education is a public function and has been since the days when parents paid for the education of their children under the old "rate bill." Since that time public responsibility for furnishing educational opportunities has been rapidly extended. In the same way that public education is responsible for the education of normal children, it is responsible for the education of handicapped children. Unfortunately many of our cities and localities are not now able to finance an adequate program for the education of their handicapped children. The educating of these children has thus been recognized and established as a function and responsibility of our individual states, and now more than twenty of our states are aiding in the support of special classes and schools for handicapped children.

The economically-minded person might be concerned with what these people actually are able to contribute to society when many of them may never become self-supporting. Had we taken this attitude from the time of Aristotle until the present day we would never have made progress in the area of health or in the fight against disease. Fortunately this has not been true, and we have made significant gains. It is well to note that many marvelous contributions have been made by the afflicted and the handicapped throughout the ages. Demosthenes, whose fame as an orator in ancient Greece has lasted through two thousand years, had defective speech. Beethoven, who composed some of our greatest music, did much of this when he was completely deaf. Milton, who wrote *Paradise Lost*, was blind. Steinmetz was a hunchback. The achievements and fame of Helen Keller and Franklin Delano Roosevelt are nationally known. It is not difficult to see that the afflicted and the handicapped have and continue to make their contributions too. Therefore, treatment, rehabilitation, and education for them are not, as many people might believe, charity. Our obligation is to make education available for all and to utilize to the utmost the potentialities of each individual.

The reason we know that the mentally retarded *must* be educated is from our knowledge that culture is only advanced by participants. If we have people segregated, isolated, or otherwise identified as incapable of cultural participation, we withhold this cultural participation from them. No man is good enough to rule another, nor one people to rule another. Each human being must be free to communicate with his fellow human beings with all his capacity, and with all the creativity he can muster. There is an unseen calculus which acts with iron determination against all those who arrogate to themselves the right to make the terms for others under which they shall be members of society.

Recidivist is the term applied to the prison inmate who returns to jail again after serving a sentence. Most criminals become recidivists. Evidently something goes wrong with our system of handling criminals. The modern theory is that criminals should be rehabilitated in the penitentiary. They should have "seen the light" after being duly punished, and they should have gone on as good citizens after seeing the error of their ways.

The trouble is that most criminals belong to a criminal culture, and the ways of this culture in molding behavior may be as effective as the major culture. Any effective rehabilitation must therefore succeed in changing the cultural patterns, i.e., the usages and beliefs of the individuals who uphold the criminal culture. These individuals must be "resocialized"—develop images of themselves as good citizens and proceed to behave as such. The following article suggests some ways in which this might be done.

RESHAPING CONVICT BEHAVIOR
Burton H. Wolfe*

While prisons should rehabilitate, they often don't: up to two thirds of those in state prisons have been convicted before. Now, experimental techniques being tried in federal and state prisons indicate that rehabilitation is not hopeless. Here is an inside look at one promising experiment in Alabama.

By mingling with the inmates of Draper, Watkins ascertained that there was a "convict culture" at work, that it was in direct conflict with the culture of the free man's world, and that it prevented any meaningful interaction between prisoner and prison keeper. As a result, the efforts at rehabilitation, including psychotherapy sessions, were often going to waste.

The concept was not a new one to sociologists and did not originate with Watkins. As early as 1940, criminologist Donald Clemmer described a "living community" within the prison walls that he termed a "prisonization culture." Clemmer's thesis was in turn based on sociologist Robert Merton's concept of "anomie," a social situation which

---

* Reprinted by permission from *Think*, October, 1967.

contains no norms and is in conflict with the norms of the governing body. Other sociologists gradually came into agreement with the Clemmer-Merton viewpoint, but made few attempts to put it to practical use in prison work.

Watkins believed the concept, with modifications, could be used as the basis for a rehabilitation program. He saw the convict community as a culture that *does* contain norms and is not sheer anarchy. In fact, this convict culture, Watkins maintained, appeared to be conservative, with an elaborate set of rules for conduct, rules in direct opposition to its governing body, the prison authority. In many prisons these rules govern the kinds of associations the convicts can form, the proper subject matter for conversation, the parts of the prison on or off limits to different individuals, the prevention of race-mixing, the proper time to fight, the food to be eaten, and the extent of cooperation with the authorities.

"This force," Watkins explains, "is so powerful that it transcends all efforts at treatment (I prefer that word to punishment or correction) or even a prisoner's relationship with his family and loved ones on the outside. For example, a prisoner has a 'brother,' a fellow prisoner in the convict culture, who is about to escape. Even though the prisoner is convinced that his brother will be killed if he goes through with the attempt, he cannot bring himself to tell the custodial people. He will not inform either to save his brother or speed up his own release. He would consider it immoral.

"This is the way the laws within the convict culture function to protect the system. It is very immoral to inform or in any way betray the culture to the administration. But sodomy or robbery may be proper conduct if the group approves, and sometimes a beating or even murder can become the *right* thing to do. In one institution the 'law' provides that when a 'rat' (or stool pigeon) is wounded in the yard, he cannot be assisted by another prisoner even though the man may die as a result. In another prison culture, the convicts provide a watchman who keeps a constant surveillance of the office of the captain of the guard, and reports back to the system the names of any prisoners who visit this office."

In the convict culture within the prison, therefore, the inmates learn that behavior approved by their fellow inmates is rewarded with

their esteem and good will, while disapproved behavior is punished—
by isolation, beatings, or even knifings and murders.

"Now," Watson says, "pit that against what you see happening in
the average prison, which is run like an army. You have discipline and
punishment, and all that does by itself is make the criminal rebel
against authority. It hardens him, makes him more bitter toward you
and the whole free world, and convinces him that you just don't understand and his only friends are the other prisoners. No interaction or
interanalyzing between him and the prison authority can take place.
Instead, the convict culture takes over.

"Then you have psychologists and social workers running around
the prison, and they may get the inmate to learn a few facts and say
he has a better understanding of himself now, and 'you're helping me,
and I'm getting better,' and all that. This is what they call 'putting
the hat on the man' (prison argot for convincing psychiatrists, social
workers or prison officials that they are on the mend). Anything to get
paroled. But the inmate isn't changing because you haven't done anything about the culture to which he owes his first loyalty and from
which he gets his only true rewards. So, the whole prison experience
is only training him to become a better convict."

The Watkins Approach

Watkins' approach to a successful rehabilitation program is, therefore, based on the need to break up the convict culture that prevents a
change in the prisoner's behavior, establish a different kind of culture,
and win inmate cooperation that stems from a real desire to change
and not just to get out.

For three years, 1958-61, he experimented with individual prisoners. Then he called in a psychologist, Dr. John McKee, former Director
of Mental Hygiene in Alabama, to help set up a formal two-part rehabilitation program: (1) reconditioning (or "reconstructing" as Watkins puts it) of a prisoner's personality by reshaping both his own
values and attitudes, and the convict society to which he belongs: (2)
education, primarily by programmed instruction, to provide new goals
and prepare the prisoner for a non-criminal life in the outside world.

The program is placed within the context of the prison as a "treatment community" and an "educational community" in lieu of an insti-

tution of punishment with its unbreakable convict culture really running the show and even, in effect, controlling the behavior of the prison authorities. In this treatment community, everyone from prisoner to warden is supposed to participate in a cooperative effort toward better lives for the inmates. Watkins has in mind "group dynamics such as those of Alcoholics Anonymous and Synanon, in which alcoholics and drug addicts help to reconstruct each other's behavior."

This is the program being developed by Watkins and McKee at Draper, the education part of it under annual grants totaling nearly half a million dollars from the National Institute of Mental Health and the Manpower Development and Training Act.

Paradoxically, it is Warden Watkins, basically a sociologist, who handles the conditioning therapy part of the program at Draper, while Dr. McKee, a clinical psychologist, administers the educational phase. Both believe the warden of a prison is in a better position to handle the conditioning, if he can learn the techniques, than a social worker, psychologist or psychiatrist.

To begin the conditioning, Watkins singles out the toughest prisoners, the so-called "solid convicts." They are usually products of low-income neighborhoods, broken homes, little education, and a life of crime that began with the boy gang. (To Watkins, there is "no dysfunction of the psyche" in the vast majority of criminals, but only an "arrested development that made them internalize a rebellion." In his theory the popular psychological and sociological views of the convict as a psychopathic or sociopathic personality, as "asocial" or "dissocial" individuals, are played down.) The solid convicts hate all authority, and they are respected by the other convicts as men to be trusted in efforts to subvert the prison staff. These "incorrigibles" almost automatically assume the role of leader among various inmate cliques that carry on illegal, anti-prison administration activities within the culture: gambling, peddling dope, smuggling in liquor.

"Before you can do anything to change the culture," Watkins says, "you have to get to the solids and convert them to your side."

For this task he mixes some psychology with his conditioning techniques. He gets to the prisoner when he is under particular stress; for example, he first breaks through to some of them when they are in solitary confinement. They may say, "Warden, you got to get me out of here," and he'll say, "All right, but you've got to change."

218

In continuing talks with the solids, he explains their own behavior to them, that they started "running with the gang," as they put it, in order to escape a female-dominated home. All the time they were looking for a father figure, but could not find one at home because the man of the house was himself a criminal, had fled or died, or he was too weak—drunk, uneducated, unskilled, incompetent in one way or another to raise a family. As long as the solid convict keeps trying to seek his maleness in the boy gang, Watkins tells him, he will remain in trouble and keep winding up in prison.

Once Watkins gets the prisoner to understand this, he gradually induces the solid to transfer his identity from the gang to himself, the warden, as the father figure. (Some of the prisoners call him "Pop.")

There is, of course, some backsliding: The transfer does not happen overnight, but takes weeks or months, depending on the individual prisoner. As the process continues, the prisoner begins to pick up words like "development," "improvement," begins to build a new vocabulary—an important step as he learns to verbalize his feelings and attitudes. Meanwhile, Watkins reinforces the switchover with appropriate rewards: special privileges, trips outside the prison, a great deal of freedom and trust. Without this reinforcement of proper behavior, Watkins believes, the Freudian transference of identity would be meaningless.

Learning Without Teachers

Most prisons base their educational programs on standard classroom or on-the-job instruction. There are a teacher who teaches, standard textbooks that supplement the teaching, and students who take notes and eventually display learning or non-learning on a test. At Draper the situation is different. There are no teachers because convicts have been conditioned to detest them as the result of boyhood school experiences. (As McKee points out, "teacher" is one word they try to eliminate from the Draper vocabulary.) There is no instruction at the same pace for an entire class, because convicts are conditioned to hate the competition for grades and teacher approval involved in the traditional schoolroom situation—that, in fact, is why many of them became dropouts. Instead, there is individually paced self-instruction.

The "textbook"—really a learning book—in a programmed course consists of "frames," that is, a series of related studies followed by questions and answers. This enables the student to proceed at his own rate of comprehension. Each course is programmed so that if the student gets wrong answers, he must correct himself before proceeding to the next frame. The programs are designed to enable the student to give the right answers most of the time, and this gives him a feeling of success.

"Ordinary school programs," Dr. McKee explains, "require of a student perseverance that can be sustained only by the expectation of success. The Draper inmate brings with him a conviction that he can only be a failure. Programmed instruction is able to overcome this defeatest attitude and maintain the trainee's active involvement in a learning situation. For a man who hates teachers, who has failed every major project he ever undertook in his life—even crime, or why else would he be in prison?—success can be a sweet and exhilarating experience."

For his subject matter, the convict may choose from 350 programmed courses that cover a broad spectrum—for example, word analysis, Russian, computer mathematics, atomic physics, basic electronics, growing spiritually, psychiatry, social studies, fingering movements on the trumpet. Some of Draper's courses have been programmed by student prisoners in the experimental school's technical writing class. A second-degree murderer, studying to become a professional technical writer, took a six-month course in welding so that he could then program a self-instructional method that is now in use at Draper. (McKee expects this man to be paroled within a year, to complete college, and to become a valuable asset to society.)

Throughout his schooling, the convict student is offered rewards for improving his rate of learning: free time, personal chats with his favorites on the education staff, and so forth. "He is then motivated to keep on improving to gain these free-time rewards," McKee explains, "and we keep trying to reinforce him with better ones."

There is, for example, the attempt to improve learning by use of stimulus, response and reinforcement. The prisoner negotiates a contract, that is, he sets down on paper the projects he intends to accomplish—read a book, for example—and signs it with the education staff member. If he finishes the project, fulfills his contract, he is allowed to take part in activities he has listed on a separate sheet of paper, called a reinforcement technique menu. These activities are chosen by the prisoner, though the time allowed them is determined by the counselor. A prisoner might be allowed 10 minutes to sit and simply gaze out the window, if this is what he has specified. Draper is setting up a reinforcing event room where the prisoner can indulge in desired activities —read magazines, play a pinball machine—*if* he fulfills his part of the contract. Watkins and McKee believe that such techniques have made the difference between a large percentage of failure in other prison educational programs and a high percentage of success in Draper's.

Since Draper's school is designed specifically for convicts, the students also undergo self-instruction in etiquette, personal grooming, posture, social attitudes, management of a family budget, and job interview techniques—all extremely important to an individual who has been part of a convict culture with norms opposed to those of conventional society, and who now has the task of entering that society to earn a living after he "graduates." Draper inmates may also attend an experimental seminar in spoken English, where they all correct each other, and then learn to correct themselves. They are trained in grammar, pronunciation, widening vocabulary, and in sensitivity—learning to listen for mistakes.

After the Draper experimental school completed its fifth year, McKee was able to report the following results: Students who have taken and retaken a standard measure of education level, the California Achievement Test, have registered an average gain of three grades after only six months in the program. High school diplomas have been obtained by 75 inmates while still in prison. Thirteen paroled inmates have entered colleges in various parts of the country on scholarships for ex-prisoners, and one of them is eligible for Phi Beta Kappa. Around 65 percent of the students have been granted early parole dates, while another 25 percent have voluntarily postponed their parole to finish their training program. Only 7 percent of the prison school enrollment have become "dropouts," and some of these men reentered the course of study.

. . . .

221

What happens to the boys who dropped out of school in high school and before? In most cases, it is a sad relation of frustration and defeat. In various ways they make kinds of adjustment, in themselves and situationally, but in the large they represent red marks in the ledger of our society. The Job Corps was set up with an aim of doing something for these boys. The fact that in the following example the educational program succeeds in advancing their education at the rate of one school year per month in Job Corps is heartening for us in relation to this program; at the same time it makes us wonder about the overall effectiveness of public education.

THE JOB*
Charles S. Carleton

Some 3,000 youths are enrolled in the Gary Job Corps training Center at San Marcos, Texas. Three thousand dropouts, many of them unacceptable for the Armed Forces because of poor education. Most of them—because of their lack of skills—unemployable except in the most menial jobs. Three thousand young men unable to compete. Three thousand vocational and academic pariahs.

The job of educating these young men, of providing them with the bare bones of knowledge needed to find employment and keep it, is formidable. It is a job that has been left undone by elementary and secondary schools across America—a job akin to staging Pygmalion with a cast of thousands all in the role of Eliza.

"Let's face it," says Al Calkin, chairman of the Gary math department, "you walk on base and see these guys with long hair and shirts unbuttoned and huge tattoos and you say to yourself, 'In a few days *that's* going to be in my class.' "

Calkin and Ben Ledbetter, Gary's instructor of personal finance, and Ray Schulze, director of the remedial math lab—all in their late twenties or early thirties—were talking about teaching at Gary as they had lunch one day last April. They had driven from the camp to a cafe on the outskirts of nearby San Marcos and were downing enchiladas, chicken fried steak, guacamole salad, and iced tea as they talked.

* From *American Education*, "The Job," V. 2, No. 10. Health, Education and Welfare Office of Education, Washington, 1966.

The previous June (1965) when he arrived at the camp, Calkin recalled, "there were three math teachers and no program and we were just scratching around. We did things by trial and error and some of the things we tried just flat haven't worked. But the main thing is we were trying to do something that had never been done before."

What has evolved through trial and error and continues to evolve at Camp Gary is a completely pragmatic approach to education. The function of the Job Corps is to make competent, employable citizens out of incompetent, unemployable kids. Academic instruction operates within that framework, with no flourishes. As one Gary administrator puts it: "This is education from the ground up, and it's education designed specifically to prepare them to get decent jobs. Shakespeare, Chaucer, they don't have any meaning here."

Gary's academic courses (math, science, communication skills, and citizenship) are presented without tests and without grades and are geared to the 39 shop courses offered at the camp—in effect creating 39 subtly different academic programs. Thus, reading material for a class of meat cutting students differs from reading material for would-be photographers, even though both classes might be at the same reading level.

So, stated very simply, the academic side of instruction at Gary is a means to an end: get a job. You can't train a boy to be a good transmission and differential man if he can't read a parts manual or can't compute gear ratios. So you teach him to read and to work with figures. If, in the course of class work, a fire is kindled that makes a corpsman want to pursue education farther (and it has happened), so much the better. But that's gravy.

"I'll be honest," said Schulze, "after my first week here, I would have swapped my way out with no holds barred. I was discouraged most when I sat in on classes and wondered if I could do this kind of teaching. At first it was, hell, confusing, but now I wouldn't think of doing anything else."

Calkin took up the conversation. "After a while we found out what worked and what didn't. At first we tried standing up at a blackboard and lecturing, but when you have one kid over here that can't do fractions and one over here that can't multiply, you can't lecture. It

223

has to be individualized. And you have to be patient. One of the big problems is getting rid of their apprehensions. It's the same in class and out. We had one boy who would take three or four cartons of milk and loaves of bread with him every time he left the chow hall. He was afraid it wouldn't be there the next time he came by."

Ledbetter chimed in. "Most of these kids have never had anyone listen to them, it's always been, 'shut up.' The teacher, whoever he is, is the Enemy, but by being relaxed with them, and patient, we can overcome that. When you get one like that in class the main thing is selling the old boy—letting him know that you're not going to push anything on him."

This day in April, just after lunch, a tractor was towing a mowing rig near the military-style entrance to Camp Gary and the smell of the cut grass was intense and sweet, but almost acrid. Bluebonnets, the state flower, blanketed acres of land beneath the warm sun. It was a bad day to have to be inside one of the barrack administration buildings at Gary, but it was there that June Davis, in charge of Gary's citizenship courses, joined the conversation, comparing Gary with the public schools of the country.

"You know," he said, "we have all the same problems here as in the public schools but the schools can at least group the students by grades."

We can't gear them into 12 different groups," said Gil Herrera, Gary's coordinator for education and training. "We have to innovate constantly, and we have to fit the program to the men."

"The men," said Davis. "When they come in here, some have a suitcase, some a sack, a lot of them have nothing. Some of them have little cards from their mother with their names and home addresses. Here's the United States leading the nations of the free world and we have men 20 years old who can't write their own names. Well, when they get here it doesn't matter how little they know," and he echoed what Calkin had said earlier and what others were to say later: "Some of these fellows have done more in six months here than they did in five years of public school."

"You just don't know how bad it is," said Herrera. "Written English is a foreign language to these boys. We had one fellow from

Maine who was paying his friends 10 cents to read his letters to him, and 25 cents to write letters for him."

Instruction in reading and writing, so obviously basic to a corpsman's success after graduation, yet just as obviously neglected before his arrival, are the responsibility of the Communication Skills program.

During their second day at Gary, corpsmen are given a standardized reading survey to determine their grade-equivalency level. Those who read below the fifth grade level are referred to the Reading and Communication Skills Center, presided over by Don Gore, featuring a reading lab run by Lem Railsback.

The Gary philosophy, the approach to academic instruction, permeates the reading lab. Said Gore, "We reinforce here what they have in classes in the morning. By concentrating on high-level, interesting material, we obtain a school year's progress per month for them. This is a new approach and we're the only ones that have it. We coordinate hearing, speaking, writing, and seeing on an individual basis."

In the 36-station lab, for instance, students at different grade-equivalency levels, taking different shop courses, sit side by side working with the tape decks before them. One may be listening to an essay on the automobile power train, following the spoken word by reading a simple text on the subject. Another may be listening to a tape prepared by Railsback (the Center has put out nearly 200 hours of tape so far), at the behest of June Davis, on Texas liquor and driving laws.

"At first," said Gore, "we had to use outside materials—textbooks and so forth—for our format. But now, everything originates from here." "Here," is the Gary recording studio—a large closet in the depths of a quonset hut. "We write our own scripts, too. But we haven't changed the psychology of reading instruction, we've just acclerated it. These are adults we're working with and even the slow ones can learn faster than a child. They already have a speaking vocabulary."

Back in the administration barracks Davis, Herrera, and Counselor Joe Leonard tried to explain what makes Gary tick.

"As I see it," said Davis, "it's the change of emphasis that makes it work. We stress the learning, not the diploma. We make a big fuss about a specific skill and what goes with it. As far as techniques go, these kids are action oriented and so we have to gear our classes to doing. In our citizenship classes, for instance, when we cover the court system, a lot of these guys have been in court, so we work out skits with them. It's action, and they learn.

"Now in your regular schools, outside, failure was built in for these kids. Even though they never had any plans for going on to college, the courses, the attitudes, everything they were exposed to, was geared to college."

Joe Leonard broke in. "In high school it's always the honor student who gets the praise. Or the football hero. Well these guys were certainly not honor students and most of them were so alienated by the system they didn't even go out for football. All they had on their backs was middle-class social pressure. Here, we praise them for every little thing they do right. It makes a difference."

"We've failed in some places," said Herrera. "Getting them to adjust is a long hard process and motivation is still the secret whether it's here or in the public schools. Some of them we're never going to motivate. That's one reason why the counselors are so important. Although, actually, everyone out here has to be a counselor."

Leonard, the counselor, explained how the counseling system evolved at Gary. "At first, the counselors were based just in dormitory areas. We didn't know what to do at first, we were spread too thin and our contact with the boys was almost non-existent during the day. Now we're attached to the vocational areas, too. We work on a consulting basis. We don't have to be sent for: we're there.

"But about this motivation. That's not the only reason guys don't make it out here. You talk with them and you realize that for some of them the group living is just too much, or they've come in to San Marcos from Harlem and the cultural shock is too much or, very simply, they're 16-year-old boys who have a bad case of homesickness."

Said Davis: "Last week I took several teachers along with me and visited the separation center and we talked with some of the boys that had separated voluntarily, and only one out of twenty said he quit because it was too much like school. I think that's a good sign."

One of the major techniques of the Gary approach seems to be to instill pride in the corpsman: a pride in self and a pride in what he's doing. In fact, one of the most impressive aspects of Gary is the "academic" enthusiasm and the interest that the students have in their classes. It is doubly impressive when you realize that most of the corpsmen comprise the dregs of America's classrooms: dropouts, push-outs, slow learners, what have you—these are the students who sat in the back of their classrooms and were passed over by America's middle-class oriented education.

"It's amazing," Calkin said, "they don't wait for the class to start. If the instructor is late, the majority of them will start without him. Sometimes we have to chase them out of class at the end of the period. And then they say something like, 'Well, can I take my book back to the dorm?' We know we're not succeeding with all the boys. But we are succeeding with an awful lot of boys that the public schools had a crack at for eight or nine years—and didn't make it."

Said Don Gore: "The thing is, for the first time we have the money and the chance to do what people have been talking about for years."

Editors' Summary

In previous ages and in more undeveloped societies the salvation of man was largely sought in the supernatural. Hard conditions of life decimated the crops, carried off friends and neighbors with disease, and made every voyage a wager with fate, with the percentage favoring the house. They tried to make the wheat grow with all the practical means they knew, but generally placed final reliance on their religions.

The secularization of the age has made man believe that both the newly opened areas of life and their means of assurance lie with natural means, pursued within the scientific, this-world framework. Therefore we believe that where we fail the cause is in deficient knowledge and application.

So it is with our great secular enterprise of education, that universal means to providing every man-jack with know-how in hewing wood and drawing water. We have to believe therefore that our solutions to the problems of the existence of a vast breed of poor, handicapped, and underutilized must lie in our secular hands.

The reason that the Eskimos do not produce Einsteins, and the

227

Arunta of Northern Australia, Beethoven, is that the individuals of these societies have not been stimulated by a culture in which they can learn the complicated endeavors associated with such activities, and have not communicated with people who could inspire, criticize, and support the aims and goals that Einstein and Beethoven represent. This observation is quite apparent when applied to primitive cultures, but only recently have we turned the lesson inward upon ourselves. We now know that the environment of the child, which among human beings means significantly the cultural environment, is most influential in his success in that culture. Statistically speaking, there is no question about this.

To believe that we must therefore equalize the cultural opportunities is something that most democratic people would agree with in principle. But many think that this would be too radical, completely unworkable, or only of limited effect if applied to the hilt. These are all good arguments, but we cannot let the matter rest there. To maintain our culture and values, we must grow and reapply the values in new ways consistent with the light of the times. The society, through its more complicated features and monstrous developments has unequalized opportunities of the individual, and now is a better time than any other to do something about it. This is a great secular thrust that we must believe can be done in basically the same way that we make electric current and measure stars.

As matters now stand, we are aware of the tremendous waste of talent in this country. We are all in favor of salvaging the geniuses who might otherwise be doomed to the assembly line, cotton picking, or thirty-year corporalship. However, we have to take the most practical stand possible which is still capable of producing results framed in idealism. This was Franklin D. Roosevelt's axiom—to make the best of the objective situation of human beings and use this situation to further goals. In other words, our minds must be in the clouds, but our feet on the ground.

We are not yet sure who the talented are. We are still learning to test I.Q. and interpret the results with more care. We find that at times talent is poorly correlated with I.Q., and if our culture changed greatly, a considerably different group would be considered bright and talented. This remark has more than academic implications if we apply it to our whole culture, rather than merely the school. If our culture changes, our standards and criteria of giftedness will change correspondingly because of the broader base of assumptions determining the nature of talent. A different culture would put a premium on many different talents than those we now reward. If we had a different type of education, we would have a different group of talented children. What we are suggesting is that the higher priority should be given the problem of establishing educational goals and means for our society. We must first set up the goals for our whole society insofar as education has a voice in determining those goals. We believe education is the institution which is pre-eminently fitted by logic and essence to determine the goals for society. Only then can we meaningfully determine the various parts and structure within education. The problem of the gifted, although important, is a subsidiary issue; and, as such, cannot be solved as an isolated issue.

Our programs of cultural help have been piecemeal and directed without clear rationale to the obviously misfit, down-and-out, and defective. We have allotted certain works and institutions to palliate the most painful detriments to worthwhile lives. We "dig down" when the hat is passed for the blind beggar and the widow whose house has burned. When we are convinced that a new home for epileptics, or apprenticeship program for orphans is deserving, we approve certain sacrifices for these projects. Such shortsighted programs lack an over-all rationale and are basically demanding for ourselves and the recipients. Nor is the pure economic argument sufficient, proving that scholarships, homes, counseling, family advisory service, clinics, apprenticeships, and "social work" programs (still stigmatic in connotation) pay for themselves. We do not need the old concept of charity in the modern, democratic world. What we do, we do with enlightened selfishness because we make ourselves better. As Carver observed, to hold the slave down in the mire, the master must get down with him. To help the mentally retarded, we do not have to think like imbeciles. We do not need to raise anybody by lowering ourselves. We do not need to share our possessions with the slum children to prove our belief in equality. What we do need is to open some doors, some golden doors to the excluded and uninvited so the self-enslaving slaves may drop their shackles and glory in the dream-enfranchised destinies.

RELATED READINGS

Association for Childhood Education. *All Children Have Gifts.* Washington, D.C.: The Association for Childhood Education, 1958.

Bereday, George Z. F. "Intellect and Inequality in American Education," *Educational Record*, XXXIX (July, 1958), 202-12.

———. "Selective Education versus Education for All," *Teachers College Record*, LVIII (January, 1957), 198-206.

Brandwein, Paul. *The Gifted Student as Future Scientist.* New York: Harcourt, Brace & Co., 1955.

Brown, B. Frank. *The Non-Graded High School.* Englewood Cliffs, N.J.: Prentice-Hall, 1963.

Counts, George. *Dare the School Build a New Social Order?* New York: The John Day Co., 1932.

Frampton, Merle E., and Elena D. Gall (eds.). *Special Education for the Exceptional*, 3 vols. Boston: Porter Sargent Publisher, 1956.

French, Joseph L. (ed.). *Educating the Gifted: A Book of Readings.* New York: Henry Holt & Co., Inc., 1959.

Gardner, John W. *Excellence: Can We Be Equal and Excellent Too?* (CN/3) New York: Harper Colophon Books.

Ginzberg, Eli, John L. Herma, et al. *Talent and Performance.* New York: Columbia University Press, 1964.

Glicksberg, C. J. "The Lost Generation of College Youth," *Journal of Higher Education*, XXVIII (May, 1957), 257-64.

Grace, H. A., and N. L. Booth. "Is the Gifted Child a Social Isolate?", *Peabody Journal of Education*, XXXV (January, 1958), 195-96.

Hill, Arthur S. *The Forward Look—The Severely Retarded Child Goes to School.* Washington: Department of Health, Education, and Welfare, 1953.

Hollingshead, August B. *Elmtown's Youth.* New York: John Wiley and Sons, Inc., 1949.

Hoyt, Kenneth B. "Guidance and School Dropouts," *Education*, Vol. 85, No. 4, December, 1964.

Lee, Dorothy. "Equality of Opportunity as a Cultural Value," *Merrill-Palmer Quarterly*, II (Summer, 1956), 146-58.

Linton, Ralph. *The Cultural Background to Personality.* New York: Appleton-Century-Crofts, Inc., 1945.

Schlesinger, Arthur. *The American as Reformer.* Cambridge: Harvard University Press, 1951.

Schmuck, R. "Sociometric Status and Utilization of Academic Abilities," *Merrill-Palmer Quarterly of Behavior and Development*, Vol. VIII, No. 3, 1962.

Sprinthall, Norman. "A Comparison of Values Among Teachers, Academic Underachievers, and Achievers," *The Journal of Experimental Education*, Vol. 33, No. 2, Winter 1964.

Taba, Hilda. *School Culture*. Washington: American Council on Education, 1955.

Wallin, J. E. Wallace. *Education of the Mentally Handicapped Child*. New York: Harper & Brothers, 1955.

PART IV

FREEDOM AND CONTROL
IN EDUCATION

Most people, authorities and the "intelligent layman" alike, are not quite aware of the dimensions and nuances of the role of the teacher as an inculcator of children's values. They might be surprised to find the full sweep of the problems facing the teacher in guiding the child. For though ideally the teacher is attached to the precept to teach freedom, the teaching constantly runs afoul of nice considerations of judgment in actual situations. Shall the child be taught that we are not all free in this democracy; that his parents have wrong ideas about sanitation, disease, and nutrition; that he was not spontaneously generated; and Abraham Lincoln was not more nor less than a man? If he is free, why does he have to go to school, why don't his parents have a million dollars, and why does the school have to be named after that old skinflint, Tucker?

The answers to most of these questions are obvious to a practiced teacher, or they can be side-stepped and evaded a dozen times a day. Other answers are more difficult, and public hearings are sometimes required to "settle" the issue. Some feel so strongly that the methods of educating their children are wrong that they take them out of public schools, placing their offspring in parochial or private schools. Even then, the state constrains the parents to meet certain requirements. Many parents simply refute "false ideas" and enjoin their

233

children to be on the alert against instructors who endeavor to capture their minds. For the truth is, the teacher has a license to range the cosmos for material, and the parent has no rigid guarantee what his child will be taught. Most particularly, the parent cannot secure immunity for some of his biases, prejudices, and demonstrably false theories, or even tenets of the most sincere orthodoxy.

When the parent sends his child to church, or to an agency, association, or club of some sort, he is fairly familiar with the kinds of experiences, the kinds of doctrines and beliefs the child will encounter. The public schoolteacher may talk of anything from wigglers to angels, or that Grandpa Silas was not much of a hero in charging up San Juan Hill.

The idea of democracy is founded on rights and privileges as an inextricable correlative of freedom. Parents then claim the rights of their beliefs to be given full respect and immunity. They look upon the school as a possible threat to their rights as parents. To many of them, the public school seems a "hotbed of modernity" which industriously undermines some of their most precious parental beliefs.

Historically a number of principles and formulas have been applied to make the parents and the community feel an assurance about the role of the school. Religion is not officially taught. Courses are known and publicly selected by the school board and the administrators. The parent can complain about specific instances of malpractice of the teacher. Nevertheless, the teacher still has the child in a uniquely vulnerable position, and apparently even a math teacher can indoctrinate Communism unbeknownst to all his charges.

The answer, many think, is to have more rigid controls over the teacher. It is not enough that he did not assault tradition in the past, and has a moral character "pure as the driven snow," but he must put up guarantees that he will behave in the future. Only in this way can the values of the community, product of a long tradition freely and reverently held, be kept intact. For if Sir Schoolmaster seems to subscribe to the modern error that the world is fair game for his little bad-boy pranks of destruction, there is no bottom or anchor in the universe. If, however, all our preceptors are properly registered, stamped, and labeled as approved purveyors of "sound doctrine," then we can know which way the world wags, at least for the time being.

The age-old fear of thought and freedom as the acids dissolving the pillars of tradition is well taken. Change is irreversible, and thought is impartial about the men and interests who get the nod. God has not seen fit to load the dice in favor of the man who has everything now, nor does he uphold the well-established belief that does not want to change.

Parents are responsible for their children, but they do not have the right to put shackles on their minds or on anyone's including the teacher's. The feeling they have for their children can be well expressed by giving them the best the culture offers. In the case of education, some of the values at least are delegated to the schoolteachers to inculcate. To preserve freedom, to achieve the cornucopia of ever-rising values, the precious springs of that freedom must be unroiled and undisturbed.

This does not mean unlimited license of the teacher to teach anything, the minister to sermonize in any way, or the publisher to print everything. A piece printed solely to blueprint a crime or incite a socially destructive act can be seen as such probably more quickly and more surely by those who are most attached to freedom, because the mind works better under its aegis.

It does mean that the precious elixir of freedom cannot flow when the pipes are frozen and all the channels predetermined. The quality of good teaching is least served, and in the long run there is most destruction, when the pedagogues have to register at the police bureau to guarantee pristine purity (and inanity) backwards and forwards in time. An ultimate before the final toppling of democracy is the schoolmaster putting himself in pawn so that he may not offend the tender minds of schoolgirls.

It has appeared to us that freedom and control of education and in education can be covered under the following related topics:

1. *Academic Freedom and Democracy.* In this chapter we present opinions and practical ideas about the freedom of the teacher to teach.

2. *Censorship and Loyalty Oaths in a Free Society.* The centuries-old problem of who, what, how, and when to censor is made pertinent to modern education, and some representative stands are given. The purposes and implications of loyalty oaths are illuminated in argument.

3. *The Separation of Church and State.* The meaning and application of the American formula of separation of church and state is debated in the modern context, now that the whole area of human knowledge and interdependence, and the troubled mood of the times requires that the formula be carefully reappraised.

4. *Community Interest Groups and Power Affecting Educational Policy.* The pragmatic concept of freedom requires a delineation of the whole network of power whereby human behavior is effected and affected. The kinds of influences affecting education, and their helpful and damaging effects, are discussed in this chapter.

IX

Academic Freedom and Democracy

If all mankind minus one were of one opinion, and only one person were of the contrary opinion, mankind would be no more justified in silencing that one person, than he, if he had the power, would be justified in silencing mankind. Were an opinion a personal possession of no value except to the owner, if to be obstructed in the enjoyment of it were simply a private matter, it would make some difference whether the injury was inflicted only on a few persons or on many. But the peculiar evil of silencing the expression of an opinion is that it is robbing the human race; posterity as well as the existing generation; those who dissent from the opinion still more than those who hold it. If the opinion is right, they are deprived of the opportunity of exchanging error for truth; if wrong, they lose what is almost as great a benefit, the clearer perception and livelier impression of truth, produced by its collision with error.

—JOHN STUART MILL

Editors' Comment

In all the articles and selections in this chapter, the writers are agreed on the vital need for academic freedom. On the everyday, empirical level they may disagree. There is a human tendency to suppress the views opposing your own, not of course intending to curtail the freedom of other men nor deny a hearing to differing ideas, but because we believe our freedom requires that others be muzzled. We constantly battle to shackle each other in the name of freedom, that greatest good. But when there is so much difference of opinion about the nature of freedom, can freedom be said to exist in any sense?

The freedom of everyone to be able to speak his mind is not in itself a guarantee of achievement of the highest ideals of democracy. The theory that we individually think our best thoughts about beauty, goodness, and truth because we are free, and that we then submit these thoughts to the crucible of the process of consensus may be merely a shifting of authority from the gods to the market place. Forty million Frenchmen can be wrong, and the idea that the majority is always right, because majority rule is a democratic principle, is absurd. There is danger of tyranny, loss of social sensitivity, and genocide in a democracy, too. A feeling of determinism akin to magic can accompany democratic patriotism. In fine, democracy does not in itself guarantee the noblest human lives, nor shift our responsibility for all our acts of volition, from the smallest specific individual one, to the collective drives of the nation.

The idea that dialectic (the argument from several minds) discovers truth is an old one. It entails a presumption that until recently, with pragmatic philosophy and a broader knowledge of science, has never been seriously questioned. Is there the truth, the method, the body of principles which is hiding, awaiting discovery? We doubt that there is any one truth or one way to that truth, including the democratic way. It is for this reason that we can agree that one man may be right, and the rest of mankind wrong. Or we can agree that all men can be right though viciously opposing each other.

This would seem to some democrats and all authoritarians to be an inconsistent and indefensible anarchy of ideas, and a prescription for chaos in the body politic. With this we disagree because it seems to us that we can offer more order, stability, and meaning in a community of free inquiry which adheres to attestable standards than do either authoritarianism or laissez faire democracy. Authority has to be rejected at the outset because it has its own warrants for truth and cannot therefore be self-correcting. Laissez faire *democracy gives up hard thinking and testing and substitutes the "will of the majority" —which may be merely a pooling of ignorance.*

The search for knowledge and a better life is not easy. No majority vote, no popularity contest of confidence nor appeal to the supernatural will guarantee it. The real meaning of democracy we would say rests on an article of faith. It trusts that when a large number of sincere and educated men, using rigorously tested devices of gaining knowledge, attack the arch of reality they will be able to piece together the summative knowledge that reality is an arch. It happens that nobody really knows that nature is harmonious and will yield up its secrets to the proper methodology. On the other hand, this is far from giving the franchise to uncorrected independencies of intellect to describe reality in any way.

What we are saying is essentially Dewey's idea that there are no absolutes. We will not say absolutely that the electro-chemical epoch will not end, that the United States is better than Russia, Christianity better than Zoroastrianism, or local controls better than centralization. To inherit values and a vast heap of claptrap and old wives tales is easy. To see these only as a source of possibilities for a better world requires earnest and unrelenting, even dangerous effort.

The longing for the security of absolutes is psychologically based. Sometime in the past we pushed off from the womb-like security of authority and supernaturalism and entered the era of the scientific method. In this new world we did not destroy anything in the sense the traditionalists understand. We created a new world, a world of infinite portent and possibility. We have learned that the absolutes (where we will conveniently if not logically include freedom, democracy, beauty, goodness and truth, etc.) are included in a relativism. This is a greater understanding than that of provincialism, supernaturalism, or any kind of "ism" because we can place the limited insights of all "isms" into some kind of setting according to their truth values. We do have an ultimate in a sense: All is relative; there are absolutely no absolutes which are not included in the relative!

Freedom has no meaning out of a social context. The freedom of the teacher is a part of a general principle which we hold is good for a democracy. General human freedom and the freedom of the teacher have two aspects, each of which is vitally necessary to be fulfilled if freedom is to exist. The first aspect is the freedom to search for knowledge. This implies open avenues, co-operation, and absence of taboos. The second aspect is the freedom to communicate the knowledge to society. These two aspects are tied together, and are inseparable even in abstraction. The important condition to notice is that the freedom takes place in society, so that everybody, every moment, is experiencing the successes and failures of freedom in all the ventures of man. Freedom is everyone's business, and the freedom of the teacher is a part of you like the air you breathe.

The freedom of the teacher, says philosopher Boyd H. Bode, consists in inculcating democracy in his students. This may seem like a delusion to authoritarians, who understand democracy as opposed to their methods, and suppose that beliefs are not inculcated in a democratic society. Bode sees democracy as the main teaching of the schools; the whole movement of civilization is in part that of democracy. Civilization also contains a movement toward authoritarianism, and these two ways of life have an essential ambivalence. It is most important that the teacher understand the nature of democracy, which has its means and methods and is very far removed from the "anything goes" theme that dictatorships use in arguing against democracy. Bode argues that it is democratic to be authoritarian about democracy. To successfully accomplish this seeming paradox, he says, we need a group of teachers so attached to the "absolute" of democracy that they will successfully inculcate these values in their students. When the teaching of democracy goes on in the schools, this is really what we mean by "freedom of the teacher."

WHAT IS THE MEANING OF FREEDOM IN EDUCATION?
*Boyd H. Bode**

. . . Underlying the whole question of freedom in the schools is a basic issue which requires careful attention. The issue is whether or not the schools should be expected to protect certain beliefs at all costs. It is scarcely an exaggeration to say that the obligation of the schools to furnish such protection has ordinarily been taken for granted. The beliefs in question may be theological or political or social in character, but in any case they are commonly regarded as being entitled to preferred status, and so it becomes the business of the schools to see that they retain their privileged character. These beliefs are "absolutes" and can claim immunity from destructive

* Boyd H. Bode, "What Is the Meaning of Freedom in Education?," in Harold B. Alberty and Boyd H. Bode (eds.), *Educational Freedom and Democracy: Second Yearbook of the John Dewey Society* (New York, 1938), 8-17. Reprinted by permission of Appleton-Century-Crofts, Inc. Copyright, 1938, by D. Appleton-Century Co., Inc.

criticism. In other words, it is the business of the schools to get these beliefs accepted. Within limits these beliefs may, indeed, require re-interpretation as time goes on, yet this does not alter the fact that the chief concern of the schools is with inculcation, with the fixing of certain prescribed beliefs. Perhaps the reaction against such intellectual and spiritual tyranny is the chief reason for the view that the right and the duty to set the pattern belong, not to an outside authority, but to the teacher.

It does not follow, of course, that either view is correct. To prescribe what people are to believe, is in essence, the principle of dictatorship. In a dictatorship the schools have furnished to them a sketch or blueprint of what is officially regarded as an ideal social order. This social order may have as its purpose the elimination of the profit motive, or the glory of empire, or the glory of race, or what not, but, in any case, it sets a pattern for belief and conduct, and conformity to the pattern is rigidly enforced. In other words, education becomes a means for developing the younger generation according to a predetermined model. . . .

There is a third alternative. As was said previously, human nature is not fixed. It is developed by means of social relationships, through which the individual acquires language and the capacity for conceptual thinking, and through which he achieves moral, social, religious, and other predispositions and insights. Accordingly, it is plausible to suppose that the purpose of education is to bring him into conformity with certain selected patterns and that these patterns have a certain absolute authority and sanctity. From a democratic point of view, however, they were evolved from certain give-and-take relationships. The whole idea of the "social" implies mutual recognition of interests, with corresponding obligations. In this mutual recognition each individual finds an avenue for the development of his capacities. The patterns which happen to be evolved in any given society derive their justification from the fact that they serve as instrumentalities for maintaining and promoting reciprocal relations, or common interests among men. Democracy thus opens up a new road to the question of social organization and to the question of freedom in the schools. With respect to social organization, it holds that all existing forms of organization should be held subject to modification whenever such modifications will further the continuous extension of common interests and purposes. . . . It emphasizes the need of examining our cultural heritage for two reasons: first, such examination leads to a clearer recognition of the nature and range of the interests that are involved in the confusion of patterns; and, secondly, it affords an opportunity to show that for democracy there is a higher obligation than the protection of any specific patterns for belief and conduct. Freedom in a democratic school system, then, means the right to carry through a program of this kind.

From this point of view it is not difficult to see why democracy places so much emphasis on the method of discussion, conference, and agreement. If the procedure is genuinely democratic, the participants achieve a wider view of the subject in hand; the quest for an acceptable solution becomes an attempt to harmonize, as far as possible, all the divergent interests; and the final outcome is a heightened sense that the mutual recognition of interests and the adjustment of conflicting values are of major importance. If these results are achieved, errors in decisions become less serious because a disposition has been cultivated which makes it possible to correct these errors. The method is all important because it has an educational quality, which is to say that democracy is primarily concerned with the development of the individual that results from the democratic procedure.

. . . .

To promote an understanding, then, of what is meant by *democracy* becomes the major responsibility of the schools. In terms of our previous discussion, this understanding requires emancipation from the bondage of traditional beliefs and modes of thinking, in so far as these rest on a basis of authority. . . . The whole movement of modern civilization, including the development of the natural sciences, the social sciences, political and industrial relations, art and literature, has embedded in it the ubiquitous issue of authoritarianism *versus* democracy. A school program designed to bring this issue out into the open is a necessity to a nation that is concerned to preserve and clarify its tradition of democracy.

Freedom in the schools then, means the right of the school to do its appropriate work. . . .

. . . Since the transmission of racial and national heritage inevitably calls for interpretation, it seems reasonably obvious that there are and can be no neutrals in education. Perhaps the most unedifying spectacle in present-day education is the persistent and fatuous attempt to avoid the whole issue by a specious claim of neutrality. . . .

To remain on the fence comes to mean that we are indifferent to moral and spiritual values. A teacher who believes in democracy does not pretend to be detached and indifferent. If he is honest and discerning, he will recognize his personal bias and undertake to assume responsibility for it.

This leads into another question. If there are no neutrals in education, is the difference between the two kinds of teachers [democratic and authoritarian] as great as has been made to appear? Every teacher has his own pet beliefs which he seeks to promote. Why not be candid, then, and admit that all education is indoctrination?

For present purposes it is unnecessary to go into an extended argument as to what constitutes indoctrination. It is sufficient to recognize that there are certain similarities in all teaching and also certain important differences. Every teacher with real convictions is in a certain sense an advocate of those convictions, no matter how painstakingly he may try to be fair and impartial. His method of conducting classes and organizing his work is inescapably affected by these convictions. So far there is similarity. The differences emerge when we consider the values which the teacher is concerned to protect and promote. Authoritarianism places these values in the acceptance of certain habits for the guidance of belief and conduct. Democracy stresses the importance of keeping intelligence free for the continuous remaking of beliefs. The justification for this emphasis is the conviction that intelligence should function as a means of the "abundant life" and not as a means to the discovery of eternal and immutable truth. The underlying philosophies are far apart. One seeks deliberately to keep intelligence in leading strings; the other seeks to set it free. . . .

In stirring and beautiful prose, Henry Steele Commager reminds us of the historical contributions of the school to the greatness of America. First, it provided the necessary level of education to make democracy work. Second, it united the country, providing a sense of "we-ness" "stretching from every battlefield and every patriot grave to every living heart and hearthstone." Third, much of the acculturation of tens of millions of immigrants after 1840 was done by the schools. Fourth, the schools have helped inculcate those common values and standards through which "this most heterogeneous of modern societies" has been able to maintain the characteristics of e pluribus unum—from the many, one.

Unfortunately the whole article is not reproduced here. The reader would be edified by reading it in its entirety.

OUR SCHOOLS HAVE KEPT US FREE
Henry Steele Commager*

No other people ever demanded so much of education as have the Americans. None other was ever served so well by its schools and educators.

From the beginning education has had very special, and very heavy, tasks to perform. Democracy could not work without an enlightened electorate. The various states and regions could not achieve unity without a sentiment of nationalism. The nation could not absorb tens of millions of immigrants from all parts of the globe without rapid and effective Americanization. Economic and social distinctions and privileges, severe enough to corrode democracy itself, had to be fought. To our schools went the momentous responsibility of inspiring a people to pledge and hold allegiance to these historic principles of democracy, nationalism, Americanism, and egalitarianism.

Because we are a "new" nation we sometimes forget how very old are some of our institutions and practices. The U.S.—today the oldest democracy in the world and the oldest republic—also has the oldest public school system in the world. The famous Old Deluder Satan law of 1647 which set up a system of community-supported schools in Massachusetts Bay Colony was, in its day, something new under the sun. "As a fact," wrote Horace Mann, himself one of its later products, "it had no precedent in world history, and as a theory it

* Henry Steele Commager, "Our Schools Have Kept Us Free," *Life*, XXIX, No. 16 (October 16, 1950), 46-47. Reprinted by permission.

could have been refuted and silenced by a . . . formidable array of argument and experience. . . ."

What compels our interest, however, is not only the daring of that law but the accuracy with which it reflected our national character and foreshadowed our history.

How did it happen that this little frontier colony of some 15,000 or 20,000 souls, clinging precariously to the wilderness shelf, should within a few years have established a Latin School, Harvard College and a system of public education? Why this instant and persistent concern for education—so great that education became the American religion? For it is in education that we have put our faith; it is our schools and colleges that are peculiar objects of public largess and private benefaction. Even in architecture we have proclaimed our devotion, building schools like cathedrals.

None of this reflects any peculiar respect for learning or for scholarship. There has never been much of that, and there is probably less of it today than at any previous time in our history. Only in the U.S. could the term "brain trust" be one of opprobrium; only here is the college professor a stereotype of absent-mindedness and general woolliness.

Yet the paradox in all this is more apparent than real. It is not because education advances scholarship that it has been so prized in America—but rather because it promised to bring to real life the American dream of the good society. So declared the great Northwest Ordinance of 1787: "Religion, morality, and knowledge, being necessary to good government and the happiness of mankind, schools and the means of education shall forever be encouraged." And the generation that fought the Revolution had energy enough left to create a dozen new colleges, establish state universities and provide for common schools by munificent land grants. Even the Encyclopaedia Britannica could observe sourly of this generation that "notwithstanding their addition to those occupations of which lucre is the sole object, Americans were duly attentive to cultivate the field of learning, and they have ever since their first foundation been particularly careful to provide for the education of the rising progeny." And, in our generation today, when the critical pedant of the Old World disparages American academic traditions, we are prone—and with

246

much reason—to answer tartly: it has never been the American who succumbed to the evil and meretricious appeals of Fascism, Nazism or Communism.

Let us look at the specific tasks which our triumphant faith in education imposed on our schools. The first and greatest task was to provide an enlightened citizenry in order that self-government might work. Though the earliest settlers in New England used the word democracy only as a rebuke, they had in fact embarked upon an experiment in democracy. With independence the problem of self-government became urgent. It is important to remember that self-government had not been tried before on such a scale. The founding fathers confidently believed they had found the key. "To be long-lived," as Benjamin Rush observed, "republics must invest in education."

Has our investment succeeded? None can doubt that it has. Americans have, in short, made democracy work. They established a nation, held it together, and expanded the original 13 to 48 states—while steadily pursuing the grand objectives of the framers of the Constitution: their "more perfect union" *did* establish justice and domestic tranquility, and secure the blessings of liberty. Through all their history they elected some mediocre presidents but never a wicked or a dangerous one; they never yielded to a military dictator; they avoided revolutions; they settled all problems by a compromise except the greatest one, slavery, and perhaps that could not be settled by compromise; they revealed in every crisis an ability to select able leaders. Only a people taught self-government could record these achievements.

The second great task imposed upon education and on the schools —the creation of national unity—was equally difficult. In 1789 no one took for granted the blessing of the "more perfect union"—for what, after all, was the basis for an American nation? Its geographical basis was so large as to defeat itself, for how hold together an area of continental dimensions thinly inhabited by some four million people? The historical basis was almost nonexistent: differences that separated South Carolinians from Connecticut Yankees seemed to be greater than the bonds that united them.

Yet we created unity out of diversity, nationalism out of particularism. Powerful material forces—the westward movement, canals and railroads, a liberal land policy—sped this achievement. But just

247

as important were intellectual and emotional factors—what Lincoln called those "mystic chords of memory, stretching from every battlefield and patriot grave to every living heart and hearthstone." These were the contributions of poets and novelists, editors and naturalists, historians and jurists, orators and painters—and the medium through which they worked was the school. Through the whole 19th Century, novelists like Cooper and Sims and Hawthorne, poets like Bryant and Longfellow and Whittier, painters like Trumbull and Stuart and Peale, historians like Jared Sparks and George Bancroft, schoolmen like Noah Webster with his Spellers and the McGuffeys with their Readers—all these and scores of others created and popularized that common group of heroes and villains, that common store of poems and stories, of images and values of which national spirit is born. These men gave to Americans, old and new alike, a people's common language with which to voice a people's common heritage:

> God sifted a whole nation that he might send choice grain over into this wilderness; As for me, give me liberty or give me death; If they mean to have a war, let it begin here; One if by land, and two if by sea; These are the times that try men's souls; I only regret that I have but one life to lose for my country; I have just begun to fight; Millions for defense, but not one cent for tribute; Don't give up the ship; We have met the enemy and they are ours; Liberty and union, now and forever, one and inseparable; I propose to fight it out on this line if it takes all summer; Damn the torpedoes; Government of the people, by the people, for the people; With malice toward none, with charity for all. . . .

"The barber shaves every man in the village who does not shave himself: Then who shaves the barber?", is an old paradox. Allowing academic freedom to the Communists has a paradoxical nature for most of us. Harold Stoke argues that the Communists must be suppressed because they do not believe in academic freedom. We would agree with Stoke on the general principle that any dogma which is inimical to freedom in general, and academic freedom in particular, should not be allowed in the market place of ideas. To disbar any member of a group categorically from the freedom to state his case, is, we think, an unwarranted extension of the principle of expediency because

of a supposed crisis, overriding the Anglo-Saxon juridical principle that a man is innocent until proven guilty. We believe every man should be tried individually on the merits of his case. He must individually state that he is against the principle of academic freedom before he is denied freedom of exercise thereof. He should not be allowed to pull us toward his level by making us judge him on the basis of his group membership.

In an article, which we are sorry to present only in parts, Arthur Kornhauser deals with such issues as service versus pure research, utilitarianism versus scholarliness, specialization versus liberal education, busy work versus professional standards, hypocrisy versus guts, and the general image of the university in the modern community. In all this, academic freedom is an extremely relevant question. Particularly significant, we think, is Kornhauser's stress on the university as a community of scholars who have an obligation to communicate and check each other so that the highest standards of the critical search for knowledge may be maintained. A powerful insight of Kornhauser's is that the really meaningful studies and idealistic movements of the universities can be bought off by an inbuilt "carrot" of promotion, privilege, etc., that diverts "questionable thinking" into "good, safe research" by liberal grants and added encomiums. Bribes still the voice of social protest.

The picture of the university here presented is one of intellectual compulsion and moral majesty.

THE UNIVERSITY AND THE COMMUNITY IN OUR TIMES
*Arthur Kornhauser**

. . . If we are going to face up to the challenging questions which I think exist, there is no escape, first of all, from taking a position as to what the university essentially is—and should be. The university must understand and clearly define its role in order to have a rational basis for determining and assessing its relationships to the community.

* Arthur Kornhauser, "The University and the Community in Our Times," *Graduate Comment* (Wayne State University), II, No. 5 (July, 1959), 2, 3, 4, 5. Reprinted by permission.

Lacking such a guiding conception, the university is reduced to a policy of opportunism and expediency in response to whatever community pressures play upon it.

My own answer . . . is that the university does have distinctive, unique functions which should define its activities and relationships and which should determine what it is expected to do and not expected to do in the community. The university, as I see it, is a center of intellectual activity; its business is scholarship; it is devoted to the independent search for truth and the communication of truth. All its activities, including its community relations, should be conducted as fully as is socially possible on the level of research and in the spirit of independent scholarly thought. . . .

My basic premise is that the advancement of knowledge, the persistent devoted search for truth, the creative and critical examination of old beliefs and new ideas—that these things are good for the whole society. . . .

The question of concern is how community influences interfere with the university's performance of its role as a true university. Of the numerous points at which differences occur between the university's requirements and the pressures of the community, I have singled out four of the most important. They are as follows:

1. Freedom of inquiry and learning versus limitation upon, and infringements of, this freedom.
2. Devotion to the intellectual pursuit of truth, the basic quest for knowledge versus insistence on practical, utilitarian values.
3. Thorough, liberalizing general education of future leaders, citizens, and scholars versus either specialized vocational and professional training or shallow college programs for great numbers of students.
4. Primary effort concentrated on scholarly work, basic and applied, versus popular demands for direct service to various community groups. . . .

First of all, does our society accept and believe in academic freedom? The most striking evidence on this is fresh in our memories if we let ourselves recall the recent history of legislative investigations, governmental security checks, loyalty oaths, and indiscriminate charges of Communism, atheism, radicalism, socialism, New Dealism in the colleges—often lumping these all together as one and the same. The point of particular relevance for present purposes is the small amount of popular opposition to these encroachments, the fairly widespread endorsement they received. They were "good politics. . . ."

But the point under discussion reaches far beyond the present state of public opinion. A different, more adequate, phrasing of our question would ask: How much freedom of thought and inquiry *can* our society, or indeed any society, grant, and in regard to which of all the things it holds dear? Freedom of inquiry and teaching *are* dangerous. Society must constantly weigh the disadvantages against the gains, and in some crude manner it does so. This very process by which the community makes and remakes its collective decision as to the limits on intellectual freedom is bound to involve "agonizing reappraisals" and accommodations of discordant views. I see no good alternative to this unending debate as a way of arriving at a workable condition of academic freedom at any given time and place. The issue is never settled. . . .

Regarding the first [point on academic freedom], the point I would stress is that groups rarely attack academic freedom as a whole; they specialize, each focusing its objections against alleged transgressions on a particular front. Business groups concentrate on anything that might undermine faith in private capitalism; patriotic societies are against everything remotely critical of the American way of life and America's place in the world, as they define these; the churches attack godless teaching; and similarly for all the other groups, each according to its lights.

I am not suggesting that this is bad. On the contrary, it would be very good if. . . . The big "if" arises because of inequalities of power and differential access to channels of influence open to persons holding diverse views. What is bad, as I see it, is that there is no sufficient airing of answers to the attacks, no adequate countervailing influences to assure a fair hearing on the issues. Even groups which favor certain unpopular thoughts today are likely tomorrow to oppose the expression of other unpopular views which run counter to their own cherished myths. The usual argument that our pluralistic society provides protection is only partially convincing in matters of this kind. The weakness of the protection lies to some extent in the inequality of group power already referred to but is also due to the fact that frequently the expression of unpopular views attracts *no* substantial organized support; *no* offsetting group feels its own interests are involved. The economist or law professor who comes under attack for his position on some labor-management issue is pretty sure to receive approval and backing from one side or the other; but what of the hapless academician whose analyses lead him to conclusions sharply critical of organized religion or private capitalism?

My remaining point concerning academic freedom seems to me most important. It can be stated in the form of a suspicion that perhaps the direct attacks on freedom in the colleges are really secondary, a diversional battle occurring while the main ranks of the erstwhile defenders of freedom are being quietly and unsuspectingly enveloped, scattered, and disarmed by other forces. Let us begin by making a distinction between the academic rights involved and the exercise of those rights. Our concern about the individual's freedom to step out of line becomes an empty shell if no one desires to step out of line. In that event, the most exacting drill sergeant imposes no restraint upon freedom. The disturbing doubt sometimes forces itself upon me that more and more academicians in the present period experience no interference with their intellectual freedom because they think no thoughts that are out of line. They are so thoroughly assimilated into the community, so conforming, so innocent of ideas which anyone could object to, that there is no longer any problem of freedom for them.

Perhaps this represents a conservative society's most effective method for handling "dangerous" thinking or any form of heretical inquiry and teaching. If one were a sophisticated power holder opposed to too much free thinking in the universities he could follow either of two courses of action. One would be to use his influence to punish or threaten professors, administrators, and institutions which stepped out of line; for example, he might stop donations, encourage legislative investigations, insist on having the radicals fired, whip up public opinion against the university. But this means a fight. An alternative course might be to use the carrot instead of the stick. Why not make "good, safe research" and "sound teaching" so rewarding—through promotions, consulting jobs, research grants—that almost any fool (even college professors and administrators) would be enticed? To the degree that the professors can

252

be kept occupied on valuable, interesting, exciting, and at the same time "respectable" projects, they will have neither time nor inclination to go off on tangents in silly pursuit of answers to such fundamental questions as how our industrial society is doing and how industry can best be run in the public interest (including its direct effects on working people): whether there are better uses for our minds than watching television; why there is so little genuine debate about the life-and-death issues of our times; or what has happened to the social idealism and militant liberalism and reform movements of earlier decades. I am sure that there has been no deliberate plot of the kind I suggest. But, however unplanned, the developments of our generation may be taking a course which ominously leads to the same end results.

The important question is whether university faculties, for whatever reasons, are being seduced away from their function of radical criticism and bold exploration of crucial issues which, being crucial, are also controversial and "dangerous." Academic freedom is a mere fetish unless it means not simply freedom to stay in line but freedom to be heretical, to penetrate into and speak out on vital issues which the community prefers to keep buried. Imperative as are the formal, legal defenses of teachers' liberties against external pressures and constraints, this is but half of the battle. The greater threat may be the spread of *internalized* deterrents and alternative attractions which keep the professors safe in a painless manner, without any need for imposition of crude controls or visible pressures by government or community. Perhaps the influences which foster this internal acquiescence are the forces most to be feared, the really effective interferences preventing the actual exercise of academic freedom. . . .

Editors' Summary

All of the selections in this chapter show the most earnest concern for academic freedom. Indeed, democracy and freedom are universally loved; democracy is the officially-declared form of government of the Soviet Union. Since there is such general agreement in principle, it might seem strange that such an area of contention arises on these matters.

The difficulty is that we do not live in a vacuum, but in some kind of relationship with each other. These relations have been growing more complex and numerous, and we are increasingly interdependent for our welfare. We are intrinsically bound together, and we must work out our fate in common. Everything I do affects you in some way. If we were all omniscient, had absolute egos, and were not harmed or retarded by each other's wrongful decisions, we would all declare for absolute freedom.

My freedom to be an actor depends on an audience; to get a million dollars from coal mining requires that others be willing to dig for me; to rear my children as anarchists has a necessary condition that society be willing to allow me to inculcate this particular ideology in my children. Many of the freedoms which have been prized traditionally even in our democracy entail some kind of restrictions of the freedoms of others—in time, space, behavior, or ideational mobility. That others are not aware of this curtailment does not alter the fact. The growing awareness of these relationships is creating many problems in maintaining the corresponding freedom.

The greatest freedom is that of thinking. Again, this cannot be done in a vacuum. We can tell a room full of students to "think!" and all we will get are a random sample of ideas that have no focus, and, if not communicated, are lost. The thinking takes place in an environment, and produces reactions, if only in communication in a "bull session." For man, the most meaningful environment is his net of social relations; this environment has an objective reality, and in times of slow change almost determines the lines of thought.

In times of rapid change, reflective thinking and creative thinking become heightened in significance; it makes the difference between an organism that merely responds unreflectively and mechanically, and one interacting meaningfully with that environment.

To achieve this creativity of thought, the human being must have the necessary conditions. A poorly socialized, handicapped, ignorant child cannot become a thinking adult in the modern world. Of course, many educated and socially powerful adults are muffled and oppressed and do not have freedom of thought, but this is another, more manageable level of the problem.

The essential ground of human thought is education. Education is a social activity, and requires a lifetime in its fullest meaning. Freedom of

254

the press, speech, religion, and assembly are vital safeguards, and must be written in the law of the land; but they are empty phrases without the people equipped to use them. The appreciation and implementation of freedom is of slow, sometimes painful, growth, and, we agree with Bode, inculcated to a degree. It is not merely absorbed because it is pleasant, but requires an enforcement of tough standards. You have to inculcate the notions of walking straight, speaking the truth, having a sense of pride, and feeling a sentimental attachment to democracy.

Because ours is a dynamic, complicated world, the critical freedom is found in the school. Other freedoms are sustained, explained, and strengthened by the freedom to think. As we take years to become educated, able to react in a responsible, creative way, so we take years to learn how to think. And as our families, neighbors, church brethren, employers, and other groups know us and respond to us in patterned ways, we cannot depend on them to teach us to think.

But the schoolteacher has the moral obligation to teach us to use knowledge rationally. Our greatest meaning of self, our highest and greatest experiences as sentient beings depend on this; and so does society as it is related with each of us. So we owe it to the teacher as a moral obligation to promote the conditions which will enable him to fulfill his task.

Any restraint or impediment tending against freedom to teach is immoral, and any measure promoting this freedom is progressive if we want further light and reason. Freedom of the teacher, therefore, is not only a necessary moral principle, but an ineluctable means of making a better life for all of us.

RELATED READINGS

Ahrens, Maurice. "Freedom to Learn: Censorship and Learning Materials," *Social Education*, XVII (April, 1953), 165-70.

American Association of Universities. "The Rights and Responsibilities of Universities and Their Faculties," *Atlantic Monthly*, CXCI (June, 1953), 44-46.

Can America Lose Her Free Public Schools? Virgil M. Rogers. (Orig.) Syracuse University Press, University Station, Syracuse, N.Y.

Commager, H. S. (ed.). *Living Ideas in America*. New York: Harper & Brothers, 1951.

Dahl, Robert A. *Preface to Democratic Theory*. Chicago: University of Chicago Press, 1956.

Ebenstein, William. *Today's Isms*. Englewood Cliffs, N.J., Prentice-Hall, Inc., 1958.

Education and Democratic Ideals. Gordon C. Lee. (Orig.) Harcourt, Brace and World, 757 Third Ave., New York.

Education and Freedom. Hyman G. Rickover. (D47) Dutton Paperbacks, E. P. Dutton and Co., 201 Park Ave. South, New York.

Education and Liberty. James Bryant Conant. Random House, 457 Madison Ave., New York.

Education as Power. Theodore Brameld. Holt, Rinehart and Winston, 383 Madison Ave., New York.

Greenberg, L. "A Critique of Classic Methods of Identifying Gifted Children," *School Review*, LXIII (January, 1955), 25-30.

"Hell Breaks Loose in Paradise," *Life*, Vol. 54, No. 17, April 26, 1963.

Hook, Sidney. *Heresy, Yes!—Conspiracy, No.!* New York: The John Day Co., 1953.

Kennan, Richard B. "Freedom of Thought in American Life," *Social Education*, XVIII (April, 1954), 149-54.

Kirk, Russell. *Academic Freedom: An Essay in Definition*. Chicago: Henry Regnery Co., 1955.

Laski, Harold J. *Liberty in the Modern State*. Revised Edition. New York: The Viking Press, Inc., 1949.

Locke, John. *On Civil Government: Two Treatises*. New York: E. P. Dutton & Co., Inc., 1924.

Lynes, Russell. "The Importance to Our Society of High Level Talent," *Education Digest*, XXIII (January, 1958), 19-13.

MacIver, Robert. *Academic Freedom in Our Time*. New York: Columbia University Press, 1956.

McCord, William. *The Springtime of Freedom—the Evolution of Developing Societies*. New York: Oxford University Press, Inc., 1965.

Newman, E. S. *The Freedom Reader*. Revised Edition. New York: Ocean Publications, 1958.

Smith, T. V., and E. C. Lindeman. *The Democratic Way of Life*. Revised Edition. New York: New American Library of World Literature, Inc., 1951.

Westby-Gibson, Dorothy. *Social Perspectives on Education*. New York: John Wiley and Sons, 1965.

Woody, Thomas. "Affirmation versus Negation in American Education," *School and Society*, LXXIX (February 6, 1954), 33-39.

256

X

Censorship and Loyalty Oaths in a Free Society

Editors' Comment

The problem of censorship is an old and vexing one and by the nature of things will never be finally settled. In a restricted sense, censorship refers to legal control over printed material, but the ends and effects of censorship are tied up with systems of control, and particularly with coercive prohibition by others.

Some kind of restriction of our expressive behavior is intrinsic in our physical constitution, the limitations of our psyche, the physical conditions of the environment, and the folkways and mores of culture. Culture, in fact, is one grand inhibition. But it is more than that, and therein lies the problem which led us to state that censorship, as one of the kinds of cultural repression, will always be with us.

Culture is an invitation, a challenge to the individual as well as a situation of negative control. Culture offers the individual opportunity to play the game, and without rules and regulations the game would not be enjoyable. Culture does more: it gives the individual an opportunity to create new games. In these opportunities for expression lie freedom. Notice that without culture, without the games to play, the individual would have no freedom. He would not be able to understand the concept.

257

Some kinds of prohibitive controls are necessary in all cultures: murder, incest, and robbery are well-nigh universal taboos. Almost all societies protect the weak, infirm, and immature against exploitation. All cultures must restrict and coerce individuals to some degree to achieve the ends of maintenance, security, education, and social control. The amount and severity of these controls varies from culture to culture. In some, called Apollonian, the social controls are so internalized by the individuals that the degree of deviance from the dictates of the tribal gods is small. In others, called Dionysian, because of the value placed on individual expression, the individual is often at odds with society. But even in our society, the expression takes place within culture.

Our American democratic ethic is basically Dionysian. We believe that culture exists for the aggrandizement of the individual. The culture does not feel; the individual does. This is our rationale for making culture subserve the individual. Therefore, any kinds of unnecessary restrictions on the individual, even if imposed in the name of culture, religion, the national honor, or good taste, are suspect as detractive of the highest good of individual expression. Even when the restrictions are visited on the body politic for more immediately pragmatic reasons, such as the protection of reputations, the overcoming of flagitious and licentious behavior, the stemming of drivel and sensation, we have to scrutinize all these strictures very carefully.

For in the end, we always find that it is individual men who have decided that other individual men are to be cozened, lectured, and herded from one culturally sanitized area to another, in the name of all that is great and holy. And the ones who are fed the predigested pap and fitted with blinders are rightly drawn to inquire: Since our culture is one of equal men in an unknown world which we exploit from equally valid viewpoints, what gives you the gift of the gods to order my comings in and goings out? The great weight of evidence shows that when individuals are given to prohibit the expressive behavior of their fellows, they are seldom able to curb their own unrestricted drives. Then we behold the spectacle of a population bound and gagged, though the censors will tell you with dirgeful solemnity that these measures were necessary to keep the mob from rushing over cliffs like ravening, senseless beasts, held back only by the cool, high minds of the favored few, who are fitted to know what is best for the others.

258

It is this admittedly difficult wavering line of creative control versus destructive control that society must watch and establish with consummate care. In the case of censorship and loyalty oaths, our sympathies are with the view of educating the individual to the degree that he is able to make an intelligent determination of the kinds of control necessary for himself and society.

In 1644 John Milton summed up his thoughts on the licensing of printing to the British Parliament in a speech entitled "Areopagitica." With slight changes of wording his arguments would be timely and the best available today. This illustrates the universality and timelessness of Milton's basic principles. It also reminds us of the persistence of the threats to our liberty. The essence of his argument is that reason and liberty go together, and one cannot exist without the other.

MILTON'S PROSE WORKS
Areopagitica

I deny not, but that it is of greatest concernment in the Church and Commonwealth, to have a vigilant eye how books demean themselves as well as men; and thereafter to confine, imprison, and do sharpest justice on them as malefactors. For books are not absolutely dead things, but do contain a potency of life in them to be as active as that soul was whose progeny they are; nay, they do preserve as in a vial the purest efficacy and extraction of that living intellect that bred them. I know they are as lively, and as vigorously productive, as those fabulous dragon's teeth; and being sown up and down, may chance to spring up armed men. And yet, on the other hand, unless wariness be used, as good almost kill a man as kill a good book. Who kills a man kills a reasonable creature, God's image; but he who destroys a good book, kills reason itself, kills the image of God, as it were, in the eye. Many a man lives a burden to the spirit, embalmed and treasured up on purpose to a life beyond life. 'Tis true, no age can restore a life, whereof perhaps there is no great loss; and revolutions of ages do not oft recover the less of a rejected truth, for the want of which whole nations fare the worse.

We should be wary therefore what persecution we raise against the living labours of public men, how we spill that seasoned life of man, preserved and stored up in books; since we see a kind of homicide may be thus committed, sometimes a martyrdom, and if it extend to the whole impression, a kind of massacre, whereof the execution ends not in the slaying of an elemental life, but strikes at that ethereal and fifth essence, the breath of reason itself, slays an immortality rather than a life. But lest I should be condemned of introducing license, while I oppose licensing, I refuse not the pains to be so much historical, as will serve to show what hath been done by ancient and famous commonwealths against this disorder, till the very time that this project of licensing crept out of the inquisition, was catched up by our prelates, and hath caught some of our presbyters.

In Athens, where books and wits were ever busier than in any other part of Greece, I find but only two sorts of writings which the magistrate cared to take notice of; those either blasphemous and atheistical, or libellous. Thus the books of Protagoras were by the judges of Areopagus commanded to be burnt, and himself banished from the territory for a discourse begun with his confessing not to know "whether there were gods, or whether not." And against defaming, it was agreed that none should be traduced by name, as was the manner of Vetus Comoedia, whereby we may guess how they censured libelling. And this course was quick enough, as Cicero writes, to quell both the desperate wits of other atheists, and the open way of defaming, as the event showed. Of other sects and opinions, though tending to voluptuousness, and the denying of Divine Providence, they took no heed.

And thus ye have the inventors and the original of book-licensing ripped up and drawn as lineally as any pedigree. We have it not, that can be heard of, from any ancient state, or polity or church; nor by an statute left us by our ancestors elder or later; nor from the modern custom of any reformed city or church abroad; but from the most antichristian council and the most tyrannous inquisition that ever inquired. Till then books were ever as freely admitted into the world as any other birth; the issue of the brain was no more stifled than the issue of the womb: no envious Juno sat cross-legged over the nativity of any man's intellectual offspring; but if it proved a monster, who denies, but that it was justly burnt, or sunk into the sea? But that a book, in worse condition than a peccant soul, should be to stand before a jury ere it be born to the world, and undergo yet in darkness the judgment of Rhadamanth and his colleagues ere it can pass the ferry backward into light, was never heard before, till that mysterious iniquity, provoked and troubled at the first entrance of Reformation, sought out new limbos and new hells wherein they might include our books also within the number of their damned. And this was the rare morsel so officiously snatched up, and so ill-favouredly imitated by our inquisiturient bishops, and the attendant minorities their chaplains. That ye like not now these most certain authors of this licensing order, and that all sinister intention was far distant from your thoughts, when ye were importuned the passing it all men who know the integrity of your actions, and how honour Truth, will clear ye readily.

But some will say, What though the inventors were bad, the thing for all that may be good? It may be so; yet if that thing be no such deep invention, but obvious, and easy for any man to light on, and yet best and wisest commonwealths through all ages and occasions have forborne to use it, and false seducers and oppressors of men were the first who took it up and to no other purpose but to obstruct and hinder the first approach of Reformation; I am of those who believe it will be a harder alchymy than Lullius ever knew, to sublimate any good use out of such an invention. Yet this only is what I request to gain from this reason, that it may be held a dangerous and suspicious fruit, as certainly it deserves, for the tree that bore it until I can dissect one by one the properties it has. But I have first to finish, as was propounded, what is to be thought in general of reading books, whatever sort they be, and whether be more benefit or the harm that thence proceeds? . . .

[In a vision, God said to churchman Alexandrinus in 240 A.D.] Read any books whatever come to thy hands, for thou art sufficient both to judge aright, and to examine each matter. To this revelation he assented the sooner, as he confesses, because it was answerable to that of the Apostle to the Thessalonians. Prove all things, hold fast that which is good. And he might have added another remarkable saying of the same author: To the pure, all things are pure; not only meats and drinks, but all kind of knowledge whether of good or evil; the knowledge cannot defile, nor consequently the books, if the will and conscience be not defiled.

For books are as meats and viands are; some of good, some of evil substance; and yet God, in that unapocryphal vision, said without exception, Rise, Peter, kill and eat, leaving the choice to each man's discretion. Wholesome meats to a vitiated stomach differ little or nothing from unwholesome; and best books to a naughty mind are not unappliable to occasions of evil. Bad meats will scarce breed good nourishment in the healthiest concoction; but herein the difference is of bad books that they to a discreet and judicious reader serve in many respects to discover, to confute, to forewarn, and to illustrate. Whereof what better witness can ye expect I should produce than one of your own now sitting in Parliament, the chief of learned men reputed in this land, Mr. Selden; whose volume of natural and national laws proves, not only by great authorities brought together, but by exquisite reasons and theorems almost mathematically demonstrative, that all opinions, yea errors known, read, and collated, are of main service and assistance toward the speedy attainment of what is truest. I conceive therefore, that when God did enlarge the universal diet of man's body, saving ever the rules of temperance, He then also, as before, left arbitrary the dieting and repasting of our minds; as wherein every mature man might have to exercise his own leading capacity.

How great a virtue is temperance, how much of moment through the whole life of man! Yet God commits the managing so great a trust, without particular law or prescription, wholly to the demeanour of every grown man. And therefore when He Himself tabled the Jews from heaven, that omer, which was every man's daily portion of manna, is computed to have been more than might have well sufficed the heartiest feeder thrice as many meals. For those actions which enter into a man, rather than issue out of him, and therefore defile not, God uses not to captivate under a perpetual childhood of prescription, but trusts him with the gift of reason to be his own chooser; there were but little work left for preaching, if law and compulsion should grow so fast upon those things which heretofore were governed only by exhortation. Solomon informs us, that much reading is a weariness to the flesh; but neither he nor other inspired author tells us that such or such reading is unlawful: yet certainly had God thought good to limit us herein, it had been much more expedient to have told us what was unlawful than what was wearisome. As for the burning of those Ephesian books by St. Paul's converts; 'tis replied the books were magic, the Syriac so

262

renders them. It was a private act, a voluntary act, and leaves us to a voluntary imitation: the men in remorse burnt those books which were their own; the magistrate by this example is not appointed; these men practised the books, another might perhaps have read them in some sort usefully.

Good and evil we know in the field of this world grow up together almost inseparably; and the knowledge of good is so involved and interwoven with the knowledge of evil, and in so many cunning resemblances hardly to be discerned, that those confused seeds which were imposed upon Psyche as an incessant labour to cull out, and sort asunder, were not more intermixed. It was from out the rind of one apple tasted, that the knowledge of good and evil, as two twins cleaving together, leaped forth into the world. And perhaps this is that doom which Adam fell into of knowing good and evil, that is to say of knowing good by evil. As therefore the state of man now is; what wisdom can there be to choose, what continence to forbear without the knowledge of evil? He that can apprehend and consider vice with all her baits and seeming pleasures, and yet abstain, and yet distinguish, and yet prefer that which is truly better, he is the true wayfaring Christian.

I cannot praise a fugitive and cloistered virtue, unexercised and unbreathed, that never sallies out and sees her adversary, and but slinks out of the race, where that immortal garland is to be run for, not without dust and heat. Assuredly we bring not innocence into the world, we bring impurity much rather; that which purifies us is trial, and trial is by what is contrary. That virtue therefore which is but a youngling in the contemplation of evil, and knows not the utmost that vice promises to her followers, and rejects it, is but a blank virtue, not a pure; her whiteness is but an excremental whiteness. Which was the reason why our sage and serious poet Spenser, whom I dare be known to think a better teacher than Scotus or Aquinas, describing true temperance under the person of Guion, brings him in with his palmer through the cave of Mamon, and the bower of earthly bliss, that he might see and know, and yet abstain. Since therefore the knowledge and survey of vice is in this world so necessary to the constituting of human virtue, and the scanning of error to the confirmation of truth, how can we more safely, and with less danger, scout into the regions of sin and falsity than by reading all manner of tractates and hearing all manner of reason? And this is the benefit which may be had of books promiscuously read.

But of the harm that may result hence three kinds are usually reckoned. First, is feared the infection that may spread; then all human learning and controversy in religious points must remove out of the world, yea the Bible itself; for that ofttimes relates blasphemy not nicely, it describes the carnal sense of wicked men not unelegantly, it brings in holiest men passionately murmuring against Providence through all the arguments of Epicurus: in other great disputes it answers dubiously and darkly to the common reader. And ask a Talmudist what ails the modesty of his marginal Keri, that Moses and all the prophets cannot persuade him to pronounce the textual Chetiv. For these causes we all know the Bible itself put by the Papist into the first rank of prohibited books. The ancientest fathers must be next removed, as Clement of Alexandria, and that Eusebian book of Evangelic preparation, transmitting our ears through a hoard of heathenish obscenities to receive the Gospel. Who finds not that Irenaeus, Epiphanius, Jerome, and others discover more heresies than they well confute, and that oft for heresy which is the truer opinion?

Seeing therefore, that those books, and those in great abundance, which are likeliest to taint both life and doctrine, cannot be suppressed without the fall of learning and of all ability in disputation, and that these books of either sort are most and soonest catching to the learned, from whom to the common people whatever is heretical or dissolute may quickly be conveyed, and that evil manners are as perfectly learnt without books a thousand other ways which cannot be stopped, and evil doctrine not with books can propagate, except a teacher guide, which he might also do without writing, and so beyond prohibiting, I am not able to unfold, how this cautelous enterprise of licensing can be exempted from the number of vain and impossible attempts. And he who were pleasantly disposed could not well avoid to liken it to the exploit of that gallant man who thought to pound up the crows by shutting his park gate.

Besides another inconvenience, if learned men be the first receivers out of books and dispreaders both of vice and error, how shall the licensers themselves be confided in, unless we can confer upon them, or they assume to themselves above all others in the land, the grace of infallibility and uncorruptedness? And again, if it be true that a wise man, like a good refiner, can gather gold out of the drossiest volume, and that a fool will be a fool with the best book, yea or without book; there is no reason that we should deprive a wise man of any advantage to his wisdom, while we seek to restrain from a fool, that which being restrained will be no hindrance to this folly. For if there should be so much exactness always used to keep that from him which is unfit for his reading, we should in the judgment of Aristotle not only, but of Solomon and of our Saviour, not vouchsafe him good precepts, and by consequence not willingly admit him to good books; as being certain that a wise man will make better use of an idle pamphlet, than a fool will do of sacred Scripture.

'Tis next alleged we must not expose ourselves to temptations without necessity, and next to that, not employ our time in vain things. To both these objections one answer will serve, out of the grounds already laid, that to all men such books are not temptations, nor vanities, but useful drugs and materials wherewith to temper and compose effective and strong medicines which man's life cannot want. The rest, as children and childish men, who have not the art to qualify and prepare these working minerals, well may be exhorted to forbear, but hindered forcibly they cannot be by all the licensing that Sainted Inquisition could ever yet contrive. Which is what I promised to deliver next, that this order of licensing conduces nothing to the end for which it was framed; and hath almost prevented me by being clear already while thus much hath been explaining. See the ingenuity of Truth, who, when she gets a free and willing hand opens herself faster than the pace of method and discourse can overtake her.

It was the task which I began with, to show that no nation or well-instituted state, if they valued books at all, did ever use this way of licensing; and it might be answered, that this is a piece of prudence lately discovered. To which I return, that as it was a thing slight and obvious to think on, so if it had been difficult to find out, there wanted not among them long since who suggested such a course; which they not following, leave us a pattern of their judgment that it was not the not knowing, but the not approving, which was the cause of their not using it.

If we think to regulate printing, thereby to rectify manners, we must regulate all recreations and pastimes, all that is delightful to man. No music must be heard, no song be set or sung, but what is grave and Doric. There must be licensing dancers, that no gesture, motion, or deportment be taught our youth but what by their allowance shall be thought honest; for such Plato was provided of; it will ask more than the work of twenty licensers to examine all the lutes, the violins, and the guitars in every house; they must not be suffered to prattle as they do, but must be licensed what they may say. And who shall silence all the airs and madrigals that whisper softness in chambers? The windows also, and the balconies must be thought on; there are shrewd books, with dangerous frontispieces, set to sale; who shall prohibit them, shall twenty licensers? The villages also must have their visitors to inquire what lectures the bagpipe and the rebeck reads, even to the ballatry and the gamut of every municipal fiddler, for these are the countryman's Arcadias, and his Monte Mayors.

Next, what more national corruption, for which England hears ill abroad, than household gluttony: who shall be the rectors of our daily rioting? And what shall be done to inhibit the multitudes that frequent those houses where drunkenness is sold and harboured? Our garments also should be referred to the licensing of some more sober workmasters to see them cut into a less wanton garb. Who shall regulate all the mixed conversation of our youth, male and female together, as is the fashion of this country? Who shall still appoint what shall be discoursed, what presumed, and no further? Lastly, who shall forbid and separate all idle resort, all evil company? These things will be, and must be; but how they shall be least hurtful, how least enticing, herein consists the grave and governing wisdom of a state.

To sequester out of the world into Atlantic and Utopian polities which never can be drawn into use, will not mend our condition; but to ordain wisely as in this world of evil, in the midst whereof God hath placed us unavoidably. Nor is it Plato's licensing of books will do this, which necessarily pulls along with it so many other kinds of licensing, as will make all both ridiculous and weary, and yet frustrate; but those unwritten, or at least unconstraining, laws of virtuous education, religious and civil nurture, which Plato there mentions as the bonds and ligaments of the commonwealth, the pillars and the sustainers of every written statute; these they be which will bear chief sway in such matters as these, when all licensing will be easily eluded. Impunity and remissness, for certain are the bane of a commonwealth; but here the great art lies to discern in what the law is to bid restraint and punishment and in what things persuasion only is to work.

If every action, which is good or evil in man at ripe years were to be under pittance and prescription and compulsion what were virtue but a name, what praise could be then due to well-doing, what gramercy to be sober, just, or continent? Many there be that complain of Divine Providence for suffering Adam to transgress; foolish tongues! When God gave him reason, He gave him freedom to choose, for reason is but choosing; he had been else a mere artificial Adam, such an Adam as he is in the motions. We ourselves esteem not of that obedience, or love, or gift, which is of force: God therefore left him free, set before him a provoking object, ever almost in his eyes; herein consisted his merit, herein the right of his reward, the praise of his abstinence. Wherefore did He create passions within us, pleasures round about us, but that these rightly tempered are the very ingredients of virtue?

What advantage is it to be a man, over it to be a boy at school, if we have only escaped the ferula to come under the fescue of an Imprimator, if serious and elaborate writings, as if they were no more than the theme of a grammarlad under his pedagogue, must not be uttered without the cursory eyes of a temporising and extemporising licensor? He who is not trusted with his own actions, his drift not being known to be evil, and standing to the hazard of law and penalty, has no great argument to think himself reputed in the Commonwealth, wherein he was born, for other than a fool or a foreigner. When a man writes to the world, he summons up all his reason and deliberation to assist him; he searches, meditates, is industrious, and likely consults and confers with his judicious friends; after all which done he takes himself to be informed in what he writes as well as any that writ before him. If, in this the most consummate act of his fidelity and ripeness, no years, no industry, no former proof of his abilities can bring him to that state of maturity, as not to be still mistrusted and suspected (unless he carry all his considerate diligence, all his midnight watchings and expense of Palladian oil, to the hasty view of an unleisured licenser, perhaps much his younger, perhaps far his inferior in judgment, perhaps one who never knew the labour of book writing), and if he be not repulsed or slighted, must appear in print like a puny with his guardian, and his censor's hand on the back of his title to be his bail and surety that he is no idiot or seducer, it cannot be but a dishonour and derogation to the author, to the book, to the privilege and dignity of Learning.

And what if the author shall be one so copious of fancy, as to have many things well worth the adding come into his mind after licensing, while the book is yet under the press, which not seldom happens to the best and diligentest writers; and that perhaps a dozen times in one book? The printer dares not go beyond his licensed copy; so often then must the author trudge to his leave-giver, that those his new insertions may be viewed; and many a jaunt will be made, ere that licenser, for it must be the same man, can either be found, or found at leisure; meanwhile either the press must stand still, which is no small damage or the author lose his accuratest thoughts, and send the back forth worse than he had made it, which to a diligent writer is the greatest melancholy and vexation that can befall.

And how can a man teach with authority, which is the life of teaching, how can he be a doctor in his book as he ought to be, or else had better be silent, whenas all he teaches, all he delivers, is but under the tuition, under the correction of his patriarchal licenser to blot or alter what precisely accords not with the hidebound humour which he calls his judgment? When every acute reader, upon the first sight of a pedantic license will be ready with these like words to ding the book a quoits distance from him: I hate a pupil teacher, I endorse not an instructor that comes to me under the wardship of an overseeing fist. I know nothing of the licenser, but that I have his own hand here for his arrogance; who shall warrant me his judgment? The State, sir, replies the stationer, but has a quick return: The State shall be my governors, but not my critics; they may be mistaken in the choice of a licenser, as easily as this licenser may be mistaken in an author; this is some common stuff; and he might add from Sir Francis Bacon, That such authorised books are but the language of the times. For though a licenser should happen to be judicious more than ordinary, which will be a great jeopardy of the next succession, yet his very office and his commission enjoins him to let pass nothing but what is vulgarly received already.

Nay, which is more lamentable, if the work of any deceased author, though never so famous in his lifetime and even to this day, come to their hands for license to be printed, or reprinted, if there be found in his book one sentence of a venturous edge, offered in the height of zeal and who knows whether it might not be the dictate of a divine spirit, yet not suiting with every low decrepit humour of their own, though it were Knox himself, the Reformer of a Kingdom, that spake it, they will not pardon him their dash: the sense of that great man shall to all posterity be lost, for the fearfulness or the presumptuous rashness of a perfunctory licenser. And to what an author this violence hath been lately done, and in what book of greatest consequence to be faithfully published, I could now instance, but shall forbear till a more convenient season.

Yet if these things be not resented seriously and timely by them who have the remedy in their power, but that such ironmoulds as these shall have authority to gnaw out the choicest periods of exquisitest books, and to commit such a treacherous fraud against the orphan remainders of worthiest men after death, the more sorrow will belong to that hapless race of men, whose misfortune it is to have understanding. Henceforth let no man care to learn, or care to be more than worldly-wise; for certainly in higher matters to be ignorant and slothful, to be a common steadfast dunce, will be the only pleasant life, and only in request.

And as it is a particular disesteem of every knowing person alive, and most injurious to the written labours and monuments of the dead, so to me it seems an undervaluing and vilifying of the whole Nation. I cannot set so light by all the invention, the art, the wit, the grave and solid judgment which is in England, as that it can be comprehended in any twenty capacities how good soever, much less that it should not pass except their superintendence be over it, except it be sifted and strained with their strainers, that it should be uncurrent without their manual stamp. Truth and understanding are not such wares as to be monopolised and traded in by tickets and statutes and standards. We must not think to make a staple commodity of all the knowledge in the land, to mark and license it like our broadcloth and our woolpacks.

What is it but a servitude like that imposed by the Philistines, not to be allowed the sharpening of our own axes and coulters, but we must repair from all quarters to twenty licensing forges? Had anyone written and divulged erroneous things and scandalous to honest life, misusing and forfeiting the esteem had of his reason among men; if after conviction this only censure were adjudged him that he should never henceforth write but what were first examined by an appointed officer, whose hand should be annexed to pass his credit for him that now he might be safely read; it could not be apprehended less than a disgraceful punishment. Whence to include the whole Nation, and those that never yet thus offended, under such a diffident and suspectful prohibition, may plainly be understood what a disparagement it is. So much the more, whenas debtors and delinquents may walk abroad without a keeper, but unoffensive books must not stir forth without a visible jailer in their title.

Nor is it to the common people less than a reproach; for if we be so jealous over them, as that we dare not trust them with an English pamphlet, what do we but censure them for a giddy vicious, and ungrounded people; in such a sick and weak state of faith and discretion, as to be able to take nothing down but through the pipe of a licenser? That this is care or love of them, we cannot pretend, whenas, in those popish places where the laity are most hated and despised, the same strictness is used over them. Wisdom we cannot call it, because it stops but one breach of license, nor that neither: whenas those corruptions, which it seeks to prevent, break in faster at other doors which cannot be shut.

And in conclusion it reflects to the disrepute of our Ministers also, of whose labours we should hope better, and of the proficiency which their flock reaps by them, than that after all this light of the Gospel which is, and is to be, and all this continual preaching, they should still be frequented with such an unprincipled, unedified and laic rabble, as that the whiff of every new pamphlet should stagger them out of their catechism and Christian walking.

This I know, that errors in a good government and in a bad are equally almost incident, for what magistrate may not be misinformed, and much the saner, if liberty of printing be produced into the power of a few?

Censorship can take many forms, as the commentary below on Act 888 of Alabama shows. Through the satiric tone, one detects the question: Once some tyranny and injustice is allowed, where can we logically stop?

ALABAMA BOOK-TOASTERS
Renwick C. Kennedy*

In 1953 . . . the Alabama house of representatives secured the passage of Act 888, now more notoriously known as the "poison label bill." The preface to the law states that its purpose is to "prohibit the use of certain textbooks and writings in public schools, institutions of higher learning and trade schools" in the state of Alabama. A more fantastic scheme for regulating the instruction of youth has probably never occurred to the mind of man than is contained in this ineffable law. . . .

This act means that every book used in the colleges, the public schools and the trade schools of the state must be labeled. The label must indicate that the author is or is not an advocate of communism or socialism, is or is not a member of a Communist party, is or is not a member of any communist-front organization. It also must give the same information about the author of any writing cited in the book. The bill also provides that any citizen may take court action to prohibit the use of any book he thinks violates its provisions. . . .

The law applies to all textbooks used in classes from the first grade to the graduate division of state schools. It applies to all library books that may be assigned for reading or reference. It applies to books owned by teachers and pupils if such books are used in the schools. It even applies to publications of the state department of education and the departments of government that may be used in any way in the public schools. It applies to all books in print and to those out of print.

Presumably Shakespeare's plays will have to be labeled. Was John Milton tainted with communism? Who knows? Who shall say? A strict interpretation of the law would almost certainly eliminate the Bible as a socialist document. Many people already so regard it. Who

* Renwick C. Kennedy, "Alabama Book-Toasters," *The Christian Century*, LXXI, No. 4 (April 7, 1954), 428-429. Copyright, 1954, *Christian Century Foundation*. Reprinted by permission.

wrote the Mother Goose rhymes? How safe are they? There are scholars who do not regard them as simple rhymes but as veiled social and political lampoons. Who shall certify them as sound?

The University of Alabama has about a half million books in its library. Other colleges in the state have thousands of books, and there are other thousands in the public schools. Each must be labeled with a safety brand lest youth may be contaminated. . . .

Some aspects of this insane law are amusing. Not only must the author of the book be cleared of leftish taint, but *the author of every citation in the book* must also be cleared! The writer talked with a history professor who stated that the American history tome he uses as a textbook in his college classes has more than 1,000 references to other books and authors in the text, the footnotes and the bibliography. The author of each of these citations must be certified as pure before the book can be safely and legally used.

One might expect propaganda, perhaps, in a social science book. But an algebra textbook or a treatise on atomic physics must also be cleared or it is unsafe to use. Probably no college physics department could remain open, for some scholars who have done important work in physics live behind the iron curtain.

No provision is made in the law for books whose authors are dead or whose publishing firms have gone out of business. The law requires that the firm or the author supply the statement that the book is pure. Books whose publisher and author are no longer extant will perhaps be burned. Books like the Bible and Shakespeare can presumably be cleared, since present day publishers have an interest in their continued circulation.

The law makes it possible for any crackpot, screwball or sorehead to challenge any book he dislikes. By so doing he could attack a teacher, principal or superintendent he happened to dislike by challenging a book used in his school. He need not even be able to read. . . .

An editorial writer on the *Montgomery Advertiser* coined a neat term. He said of a supporter of the law that he "seems but one degree removed from a book-burner—which, we suppose, is a book-toaster."

Many times in the past, works of genius and talent, and even of whole cultures, have been obliterated in the name of various righteous principles. The Germans killed millions of Jews to prevent contamination of their race. Over the years mountains of books have been burned to insulate minds from the vicious thoughts they contain. Conquering peoples have torn down all the structures that might be harmful in the cause of holding people in subjection. Fear and ignorance have been the springs of all measures that aim at annihilation and obliteration of man or the works of man. A good mind in a healthy body is the strongest proof against tyranny, debauchery, crime, and prurience. The end of achieving that mind and body should be our dedication. To destroy a heathen temple so that our dogmatism remains more secure is the most sacrilegious of acts. And if your mind is pornographic, you will find pornography wherever you go—your id will see to that. The following article by editor Wilfred Smith spells out the general argument against book-burning.

THE BANNING OF BOOKS
Wilfred R. Smith*

Ever since the invention of writing, man has been concerned with the effects of written symbols on the mind of fellow man. One who is engaged in an act of depravity will be quickly corrected or punished. The man need not be killed or held in jail. The cause of his depravity should be determined and he should be given therapy. A book has an eternal life. As long as one copy remains, it may be endlessly reproduced, to affect the minds of people new to the written word, and generations yet unborn.

Books, like all the artifacts and "mentifacts" of man may be bad or good, colorful or sterile, noble or debased. The same basic question of values faces us in relation to books, therefore, as in the problem of "the good" in nuclear fission, the telephone, folk epigraphy in lavatories, and the various ideologies in the world. It is quite true that man may destroy himself by the atomic bomb. Many people misuse the telephone, for idle gossip or the planning of crimes. Artistic expression may reach down into "the blue" as well as up to the gates of paradise. Whole systems of thought of man may be evil. To sum it all up, there is evil in the world.

* Wilfred R. Smith, "The Banning of Books." Unpublished monograph, Wayne State University (Detroit, 1961).

273

One ancient method, born of a primordial striving for survival, is simple attack and annihilation. In some cases this may be a necessary emergency measure. A much better principle is to make good use of nuclear power, writing, and the media of mass communication. We destroy evil by building the good. The existence of evil is a fact of life, and the greatest evil is to become immolated by contemplation of it.

The banning of books, under whatever proclaimed purpose, is caught in a gross error. A crime is not purged by another crime. Men fear their habitual thinking; their way of life may not have in it the strength of survival, of greater development. Their hostilities are their frustrated loves. Their fear of obscurity is awareness of needs established by their lack of wholesomeness. Their hatred of political opinions expressed by others measures the insecurities of their beliefs in their own ideology. It is much easier to condemn, burn at the stake, and put under the ban of the dictator or the League of the Lily Whites, than it is to drive the enemy from the field in open debate.

All the bannings of books from the time of the invention of writing till today have been founded on weakness and ignorance. What men wished to preserve by their ban of the Tyndale Bible, the *Decameron*, Robin Hood, *Das Kapital*, and the *Adventures of Huckleberry Finn* was not worth saving. Rather, that which brought about the ban should have been destroyed, not the books. "Death is so final" has often been said. The loss of ideas of a book, however wicked the intent of the man who wrote the book, is a loss of our general treasure. We can make good use of ideas and artifacts some time and some place, but only if they exist.

In the words of George Moore, "If all the books objected to by censors as sexually stimulating were swept from the face of the earth, the spring breeze would remain to awaken desires in man and woman." And the evil in books, or anywhere is not destroyed by fire but by good books, dear thoughts, and a great society secure in its freedom.

Robert Hutchins makes a plea for freedom of the teacher on the basis that such freedom is necessary for competence. We simply cannot teach competently, which in his terms means to teach students to think, without the freedom to inquire and explore issues. Whenever others

*outside of the teaching profession dictate areas of inquiry and proscribe
others, or arrogate to themselves the hiring and firing of teachers on
their surmise of the teacher's "right thinking" or "wrong thinking,"
then no academic freedom exists. The ones who suffer most of all are
the rising generation.*

ACADEMIC FREEDOM
Robert M. Hutchins*

. . . Man is a learning animal. The state is an association the primary aim of which is the virtue and intelligence of the people. Men
learn by discussion, through the clash of opinion. The best and most
progressive society is that in which expression is freest. Mill said,
"There ought to exist the fullest liberty of professing and discussing,
as a matter of ethical conviction, any doctrine, however immoral it
may be considered."

. . . In such a society the intelligent man and the good citizen are
identical. The educational system does not aim at indoctrination in
accepted values, but at the improvement of society through the production of the intelligent man and the good citizen. Education necessarily
involves the critical examination of conflicting points of view; it cannot
flourish in the absence of free inquiry and discussion. . . .

We have been stifling education in this country because we have
been asking the wrong questions. To ask the right questions, one asks
whether or not a subject is important. Students should not be forbidden
to discuss a subject, like the entry of Red China into the United Nations, on the ground that it is too important. The right question about
a subject of research and the methods of investigation is whether competent scholars believe that the subject should be investigated and that
this is the way to investigate it. . . .

The right question about a textbook is whether competent people
think it can make a contribution to education. One does not ask

* Robert M. Hutchins, *Freedom, Education, and the Fund: Essays and Addresses,
1946-1950* (New York, 1956), 36-45. Copyright © 1956 by Robert M. Hutchins.
Reprinted by permission of the author and Meridian Books, Inc.

whether incompetent people are going to be offended by passages taken
out of context.

. . . .

Academic freedom comes and goes because of some conviction
about the purpose of education on the part of those who make the
decision in society. The Kaiser gave professors freedom of research
because he believed that this was one way to make Germany strong
and prosperous. This freedom did not extend to professors who wanted
to engage actively in politics on the wrong side, the side of the Social
Democratic Party. The Kaiser did not set a high value on independent
criticism. . . .

If the people believe that independent thought and criticism are
essential to the progress of society, if they think that universities are
centers of such criticism and that the rest of the educational system is
intended primarily to prepare the citizen to think for himself, then
academic freedom will not be a problem, it will be a fact. Under these
circumstances teachers would not be second-class citizens subject to
limitations of expression and behavior that show the public thinks the
teacher of today is the nursemaid of yesterday. A teacher would be
appointed because he was capable of independent thought and criticism
and because he could help the rising generation learn to think for
itself. He would be removed only if those who appointed him proved
to be mistaken in these matters. The proof of their error would have to
be made to persons who could understand the issue—an out-of-hand
administrative removal approved by a board of laymen without participation by academic experts is a denial of academic freedom.

*Much fuzzy thinking is apparent about the democratic ideology.
It is also apparent that many people think that democracy has no
ideology. Even those who can formulate ideas about the mechanics of
government and the doctrines of rights as guaranteed in the Constitution often feel "Democracy's system is that it has no system," or that
"It is a means of exploring alternatives."*

*In a time of crisis and disorganization, people are out to stop the
conflicts, breakdowns, and obvious signs of ruin that they see around*

276

them. The minds and hearts of men are difficult to see, but the acts of loyalty or disloyalty can be described so that they are obvious to all. Thus if you wear a leak in your hat and march with the king, you are loyal. All those who do not become suspect, and in times of extreme stress can be cut down.

The expediency of head counts and tribal rites undoubtedly has tactical value at times, but the view that they can be extended as the means of preserving the society, especially in some of its more creative aspects, soon leads to stultification. Worse, the bully boys who like jackboots, torchlight parades, and midnight executions soon rise to the top.

Henry Steele Commager says that loyalty first becomes identified with conformity. It is deceptively easy. You are not required to do much —just conform.

WHO IS LOYAL TO AMERICA?
Henry Steele Commager*

. . . What is the new loyalty? It is, above all, conformity. It is the uncritical and unquestioning acceptance of America as it is—the political institutions, the social relationships, the economic practices. It rejects inquiry into the race question or socialized medicine, or public housing, or into the wisdom or validity of our foreign policy. It regards as particularly heinous any challenge to what is called "the system of private enterprise," identifying that system with Americanism. It abandons evolution, repudiates the once popular concept of progress, and regards America as a finished product, perfect and complete.

It is, it must be added, easily satisfied. For it wants not intellectual conviction nor spiritual conquest, but mere outward conformity. In matters of loyalty it takes the word for the deed, the gesture for the principle. It is content with the flag salute, and does not pause to consider the warning of our Supreme Court that "a person gets from a symbol the meaning he puts into it, and what is one man's comfort and inspiration is another's jest and scorn." It is satisfied with membership in respectable organizations and, as it assumes that every member of a liberal organization is a Communist, concludes that every

* Henry Steele Commager, "Who Is Loyal to America?," *Harper's Magazine*, CXCV (September, 1947), 193-199. Reprinted by permission.

member of a conservative one is a true American. It has not yet learned that not everyone who saith Lord, Lord, shall enter into the kingdom of Heaven. It is designed neither to discover real disloyalty nor to foster true loyalty. . . .

The concept of loyalty as conformity is a false one. It is narrow and restrictive, denies freedom of thought and of conscience, and is irremediably stained by private and selfish considerations. "Enlightened loyalty," wrote Josiah Royce, who made loyalty the core of his philosophy, "means harm to no man's loyalty. It is at war only with disloyalty, and its warfare, unless necessity constrains, is only a spiritual warfare. It does not foster class hatreds; it knows of nothing reasonable about race prejudices; and it regards all races of men as one in their need of loyalty. It ignores mutual misunderstandings. It loves its own wherever upon earth its own, namely loyalty itself, is to be found."

Justice, charity, wisdom, spirituality, he added, were all definable in terms of loyalty, and we may properly ask which of these qualities our contemporary champions of loyalty display. . . .

The effort to equate loyalty with conformity is misguided because it assumes that there is a fixed content to loyalty and that this can be determined and defined. But loyalty is a principle, and eludes definition except in its own terms. It is devotion to the best interests of the commonwealth, and may require hostility to the particular policies which the government pursues, the particular practices which the economy undertakes, the particular institutions which society maintains. "If there is any fixed star in our Constitutional constellation," said the Supreme Court in the Barnette case, "it is that no official, high or petty, can prescribe what shall be orthodox in politics, nationalism, religion, or other matters of opinion, or force citizens to confess by word or act their faith therein. If there are any circumstances which permit an exception they do not now occur to us.". . .

There are further and more practical objections against the imposition of fixed concepts of loyalty or tests of disloyalty. The effort is itself a confession of fear, a declaration of insolvency. Those who are sure of themselves do not need reassurance, and those who have confidence in the strength and the virtue of America do not need to fear either criticism or competition. The effort is bound to miscarry. It will not apprehend those who are really disloyal, it will not even frighten them; it will affect only those who can be labeled "radical." It is sobering to recall that though the Japanese relocation program, carried through at such incalculable cost in misery and tragedy, was justified to us on the ground that the Japanese were potentially disloyal, the record does not disclose a single case of Japanese disloyalty or sabotage during the whole war. The warning sounded by the Supreme Court in the Barnette flag-salute case is a timely one:

> Ultimate futility of such attempts to compel obedience is the lesson of every such effort from the Roman drive to stamp out Christianity as a disturber of pagan unity, the Inquisition as a means to religious and dynastic unity, the Siberian exiles as a means to Russian unity, down to the fast-failing efforts of our present totalitarian enemies. Those who begin coercive elimination of dissent soon find themselves exterminating dissenters. Compulsory unification of opinion achieves only the unanimity of the graveyard.

Who are those who are really disloyal? Those who inflame racial hatreds, who sow religious and class dissensions. Those who subvert the Constitution by violating the freedom of the ballot box. Those who make a mockery of majority rule by the use of the filibuster. Those who impair democracy by denying equal educational facilities. Those who frustrate justice by lynch law or by making a farce of jury trials. Those who deny freedom of speech and of the press and of assembly. Those who press for special favors against the interest of the commonwealth. Those who regard public office as a source of private gain. Those who would exalt the military over the civil. Those who for selfish and private purpose stir up national antagonisms and expose the world to the ruin of war.

Editors' Summary

A military axiom is that to attack is the best defense. To remain in the citadel fending off attacks is the way to final defeat. The best security we can achieve comes from building our strength and moving forward at all times. To seek absolute security is to ask for the grave.

Inevitably we have to deal with crime, sickness, unhappiness, and suffering in society, as an invariable concomitant of life. We do this

279

with whatever efficiency we can muster, and expend our major energy in growing, maintaining and creating. At time of extraordinary emergency and crisis, we take unusual measures for survival. We go to war and annihilate the enemy, and declare martial law in unsettled areas. These emergency situations are regarded as temporary, and we strive to get back to our normal footing as soon as possible. We do not like having curfews, seizures without warrant, and summary arrest.

We live in an age of permanent crisis. A free-floating neurosis pervades the society. Conformity, rededication, return to tradition and a greater reliance on coercion are symptoms of a fear, an anxiety about the many threats we face.

The positive reaction of making the society stronger intrinsically, of bureaucracy identifying all the problems and dealing with them courageously is the crusade we need. We need confidence in ourselves and an understanding of the workings of our society to do this. Failing this, a common tendency is to suspect everybody, doubt our own conviction, and punish those who would make us fear more by castigating our negative reaction.

Censorship and loyalty oaths belong to the measure of fear and reaction. Lacking confidence that people can read what they want, say what they believe, teach to raise doubts, and live as individuals in a "right little tight little world," the armament of society is brought out to make people conform. The conformity is demanded to the image of the true and good society.

The disillusioning reality is that this paranoid heaven is a façade housing the very Black Death from which the oath prescribers attempt to flee. To insure freedom, all are counted and required to sing songs of freedom. The penalty of refusal is hinted at by the rattle of chains in the abattoirs of the police state. To insure loyalty, all are made to repeat vows that turn to unvoiced imprecations.

The way to morality, and taste in reading, writing, speaking, thinking, and teaching, comes from the free exercise of expression in a socially responsive setting. Murder, illness, lust, and treason come from unwholesome oppression of the individual. The answer to the problem is not more censorship, book-burnings, and public recantations, but the resolute strengthening of a whole society. Where good books, a happy

280

home, intellectual power, and confidence in the way of life exist, the problems of repression will tend to be eliminated.

RELATED READINGS

Association of the Bar of the City of New York. *The Federal Loyalty-Security Program.* New York: Dodd, Mead & Co., 1956.

Blanshard, Paul. *The Right to Read.* Boston: Beacon Hill Press, 1955.

Braden, Tom. "I Was the Target of a Hate Campaign," *Look,* Vol. 27, No. 21, October 22, 1963, pp. 54-60.

Cloward, Richard A., and Lloyd E. Ohlin. *Delinquency and Opportunity: A Theory of Delinquent Groups.* New York: The Free Press of Glencoe, 1963.

Commager, Henry S. *Freedom, Loyalty, Dissent.* New York: Oxford University Press, Inc., 1954.

Crucial Issues in Education. Ehlers and Lee. (3rd Ed.) Holt, Rinehart and Winston, 383 Madison Ave., New York.

Fisher, John. "The Harm Good People Do." *Harper's Magazine,* CCXIII (October, 1956), 14-20.

Gardiner, Harold C. *Catholic Viewpoint on Censorship.* New York: Random House, 1958.

Gellhorn, Walter. *Security, Loyalty, and Science.* Ithaca, N.Y.: Cornell University Press, 1948.

Grodzins, Morton. *The Loyal and the Disloyal.* Chicago: University of Chicago Press, 1956.

Hook, Sidney. *Common Sense and the Fifth Amendment.* New York: Criterion Books, Inc., 1957.

Howe, Irving, and Lewis Case. *The American Communist Party: A Critical History.* Boston: Beacon Hill Press, 1958.

Konvitz, Milton R. *Fundamental Liberties of a Free People.* Ithaca, N.Y.: Cornell University Press, 1957.

Lasswell, Harold D. "Censorship." Article in *Encyclopedia of the Social Sciences.* Vol. III, pp. 290-94. New York: The Macmillan Co., 1930.

McKeon, Richard P., R. K. Merton, and W. Gelhorn. *The Freedom to Read.* Published for the National Book Committee. New York: R. R. Bowker Co., 1957.

Myers, Gustavus E. *History of Bigotry in the United States.* New York: Random House, 1943.

Shimm, Melvin G. (ed.). "Obscenity and the Arts," *Law and Contemporary Problems,* XX (Autumn, 1955), 521-674.

Taylor, Telford. *Grand Inquest: The Story of Congressional Investigations.* New York: Simon and Schuster, Inc., 1955.

XI

The Separation of Church and State

Of all the differences between the Old World and the New this is perhaps the most salient: Half the wars of Europe, half the internal troubles that have vexed European States, from the Monophysite controversies in the Roman Empire of the 5th Century down to *Kulturkampf* in the German Empire of the 19th, have arisen from theological differences or from the rival claims of church and state. This whole vast chapter of debate and strife has remained virtually unopened in the United States.

—JAMES BRYCE, 1893

Editors' Comment

Man is unique among the animals in his ability to create new needs. The slaves who spent their days fanning their masters luxuriating in canopied palanquins, the serfs, prisoners, and exploited minorities may not have felt any urge to rebel against their lot. Yet Buddha, the young prince of a potent empire, supreme ruler of a storied kingdom of castles, servants, soldiers, and concubines gave all of it up for a life of contemplation of the higher good.

This restless search for higher purposes and greater values to which to dedicate lives has been the life's blood of progress as well as the juggernaut of destruction. Opposing societies may battle each other to near annihilation or a new faith may take over several cultures without a struggle. The long history of wars, oppressions, enslavement, and constantly expanding areas of conflict has caused many with the teleological view of history to believe that man can never really live at peace or without violent conflict.

This view is of some significance in that men are today willing to fight and die for ways of life that were unknown a century ago. Men have been able, nevertheless, to subject many of their conflicts to orderly processes of settlement. They have learned that their problems can be settled by peaceful means, which are the essence of government as expressed in the "compact" of the eighteenth century rational-idealists. We would believe that a publicly understandable and demonstrable ethic requires that the processes of government be democratic to hold for the best hope of individual growth and social solidarity in the most liberal sense. In all things that pertain to man's relations with man, including his use of the resources of nature, we believe it is possible to obviate conflict and channel discontent into an orderly social process of expression.

Religion poses a problem. True, men are religious, and the church is an institution having tangible things and empirically knowable experiences. The religious experience is not of the kind, however, that may be submitted to a human process of testing, debate, or adjudication. The United States was a product of European civilization, profiting from its cultural heritage but also inheriting its problems. Europe had its annihilating religious wars, its pogroms, massacres of the Huguenots, and the fires of the faith. Many sincere men were sure that, suffering death or not, their respective faiths must be promulgated. They recognized that a weak and banal spirit of compromise would work in religion as in any other area, but they felt that not only would they be weak and cowardly to agree to this, but they would put their eternal souls in torment.

One cannot help but admire the sincerity and courage of martyrs. We cannot deprecate their willingness to die for principle. A life uselessly lived or, worse yet, lived to destroy those things in which one really believes, has no moral claim to existence. As Patrick Henry said, "Is

283

life so dear, and peace so sweet that it must be purchased at the price of chains and slavery? . . . Give me liberty, or give me death!" If then, we serve a great good by dying for a principle, what can we say about the "two and seventy jarring sects" who are willing to defend their ideas to the death against each other?

We can say that these men may be brave, but they need not die for their beliefs. This is a lesson of history, and shows the development of clearer concepts about the nature of religious beliefs. We can be heroic, and religious, and human in every conceivable way, and still grant to each other freedom of religion. This is a higher morality; instead of tyranny over others, we grant each other freedom to communicate and the privilege of making up our own minds. We have learned to avoid one particular kind of tyranny in the United States. An important part of the American formula of tolerance, which we have been in effect iterating, is that we do not use the power of the state to inculcate religion.

The belief developed in the United States was that the religious feeling could be expended at full pitch, but need not contravene or overcome the rational processes of thought or the means of regulating society. It could be exercised in the fallible human way with a full panoply of "pealing anthem and fretted vault," declaring, as the anthropologist Malinowski observed, "the triumphant testimony of man's weakness." The American formula decided that religion was not to have the decisive or pre-eminent sway in the orderly maintenance and productivity of values that constitute society. Terms such as "tolerance," "freedom of conscience," and "the separation of church and state" have been used to express the American formula.

In times of stress, crime, or disorganization, whenever people are ill at ease or need assurance, it is natural that they seek solace and meaning outside of the forms of orderly civil government afforded to them. This is no danger and even has great pragmatic value. When the people begin to distrust the secular social processes of government in themselves, however, then that way of life which has been a living tissue of transmission for thousands of years is in peril. For when we go outside of worldly wisdom and philosophy to find the answers, the records show that the way becomes open to those who claim ultimate solutions, and these people generally hold their fellows in low regard. They are apt to see them as fallible and accursed if they do not agree, and give them to the thumbscrew and the rack for the glory of the Lord. These measures can be effective. We must lament that dogma and tyranny have often driven out freedom and persuasion. In our society, the movement may come with a cult of conformity.

Leonard Gordon takes a brief look at the recent trend toward shared time in the public schools and notes the arguments pro and con as to the probable effects on all education, public and parochial. The problem at issue is not the right of parents to send children to other than public school, but the right of parents to get governmental support when sending their children to private or sectarian schools. The crucial question is whether public education, dedicated to preserving freedom against sectarianism, majority rule, and other influences, including government, can maintain freedom when the purse strings are opened to other kinds of education.

SHARED TIME—ANALYSIS AND EVALUATION
Leonard Gordon

In his senate address of May 20, 1963, on the religious controversy in education, Senator Abraham Ribicoff referred to the concept of "shared time." He suggested that the shared-time plan could be one of the techniques to break the deadlock between public- and parochial-school supporters over federal aid to education. Senator Ribicoff's presentation is symptomatic of a major discussion of what public aid, if any, should be given to religious educational institutions.

Shared time is the term for an arrangement whereby parochial-school students attend public schools for some of their schooling, the subjects usually being those with the fewest theological implications; for example, math, physical sciences, shop, home economics, gymnasium, and vocational courses.

The most extensive program began in the fall of 1963 in the Cherry Hill School District near Detroit. This particular plan and others have caused widespread comment.

Shared time is part of the constellation of church-state concerns as to the proper relationship between religion, education, and government. Examples of other issues are the use of tax funds for parochial-school construction and salaries for parochial-school teachers.

Only shared time involves no direct aid to religious educational institutions. It has attracted much attention and aroused conflicting ideas involving the following three considerations:

I. *Would a Shared-Time Plan Abrogate the Traditional Principle of Church-State Separation?* Protection of the principle of church-state separation is generally argued on constitutional grounds. Although there has been no court test of a shared-time plan, it appears to be constitutional on the basis of the *McCollum* and *Zorach* "released time" decisions, as parochial schools would receive no public funds. Yet, the Constitution can be changed by amendment; therefore it is necessary to consider the importance of church-state separation and whether or not the shared-time concept affects it.

The separation principle is designed to protect the religious conscience of each citizen and is vital for minorities. It contains the essence of Jeffersonian democratic theory, i.e. the right of anyone to hold views contrary to prevailing custom and thought. It is unlikely that any shared-time proposal would be accepted if it clearly breached the principle of church-state separation. It is argued that with certain qualifications the shared-time concept can meet this test. While the First Amendment guarantees the "free exercise of religion" it also prevents the government from aiding or hindering any "establishment of religion." The free-exercise clause would not be touched so long as there were no religious observances in public schools.

From the "establishment" clause arises a conflict between church-state separation and the substitution of parochial education for public-school education. This, supporters say, need not be altered. Children would depend on privately supported parochial establishments for religious instruction. They contend that, by allowing school children to substitute parochial education for public education, we have sanctioned indirect government support of an establishment of religion.

There is a contrary view. Public-school officials are responsible to all the people. Public schools deal with individuals, not ethnic or religious groups. It appears inherent in shared time that public-school officials would be working with parochial-school officials who are responsible to a particular group, not the entire public.

II. *Would the Aid Afforded Parochial-School Systems Strengthen Them to the Detriment of Public-School Education?* The public-school systems have proved valuable as an educational and social meeting ground for the various elements in our pluralistic society. One argument is that allowing parochial-school students to attend public schools would add such intolerable expense to the public-school system that it would result in impossible administrative complications. Supporters say that this argument is nullified by our commitment to the principle that the public-school system is open to all regardless of expense. Supporters go on to say that shared time would work to the advantage of both parochial-school and public-school students. In such classes as physics and home economics, parochial-school students would have the benefit of better facilities and staff. At the same time, public schools would probably enjoy more enthusiastic tax support from parochial-school parents.

Opponents think that shared-time programs would injure the public schools. They say that shared time, by relieving church schools of the financial burden of the subjects cited above would enable them to create more parochial schools. The effect could be such a proliferation of parochial schools that administrative costs would mount to the point where it would have a deleterious effect on all education, public or parochial. Also, the public schools might become merely vocational centers. Shared time could lead to joint operation of the public-school system, which would be fatal to its integrity.

Another point concerns interracial tensions. It is argued that shared time would cause many white people to take their children out of desegregated public schools for part of the day, making shared time a stepping stone to abandonment of the public schools.

III. *Can a Shared-Time Proposal Help Break Deadlocks over Needed Additional Taxes?* As property-tax rates reach saturation levels, it becomes more obvious that additional federal and state aid to education is needed. Attempts to provide this generally have been blocked by controversies over school desegregation and aid to parochial schools. Shared time, for the above-stated reasons, could be one of the techniques for resolving the second controversy. If this occurred, perhaps support would be forthcoming to pass appropriate school-aid bills; furthermore local millage and bond issues might stand a better chance of passage.

Opponents argue that parochial schools give little indication that demands for aid would cease if shared time were provided.

The constitutional principle of separation of church and state seems simple and clear, and one might think that the application of this principle in particular cases should be obvious. However, the particular instance is never obvious as a logical subdivision of the main idea. Men differ in their opinions and biases relating the main idea to the particular instance. The democratic process is our only solution to this logical problem. The following is a recounting of the recent decisions involving the separation-of-church-and-state principle.

THE SUPREME COURT DEFINITION*

Four decisions—in 1947, 1948, 1952 and 1962—provide the juridical groundwork for assessing current trends in church-state relations as applied to public education.

Everson v. *Board of Education:* In February 1947, the Court in a 5-4 decision, held that the state could provide free bus transportation to children attending private—including church-related—schools. While granting the legality of free bus rides to parochial schools, under the specific conditions of the New Jersey act, the Court enunciated a far-reaching interpretation of the separation principle:

Neither a state nor the Federal Government can set up a church. Neither can pass laws which aid one religion, aid all religions, or prefer one religion over another. Neither can force nor influence a person to go to or to remain away from church against his will or force him to profess a belief or disbelief in any religion. No person can be punished for entertaining or professing religious beliefs or disbeliefs, for church attendance or non-attendance. No tax in any amount, large or small, can be levied to support any religious activities or institutions whatever they may be called, or whatever form they may adopt to teach or practice religion. Neither a state nor the

* Philip Jacobson. *Religion in Public Education—A Guide for Discussion*, pp. 9-10. Reprinted by permission of American Jewish Committee, Institute of Human Relations.

Federal Government can, openly or secretly, participate in the affairs of any religious organizations or groups and vice versa. In the words of Jefferson, the clause was intended to erect "a wall of separation between church and state."

This sweeping definition provoked immediate and prolonged attack, especially from many churchmen, both Protestant and Catholic.

McCollum v. *Board of Education:* In March 1948, the Court reaffirmed its position, and declared the released-time program of Champaign, Illinois, unconstitutional. The response again was very sharp. The July 1948 statement of the 27 Protestant leaders, stimulated by this decision, condemned the "misleading metaphor" of a wall of separation. In November, a statement by the Catholic Bishops of the U.S. labeled the language of the Court a "shibboleth of doctrinaire secularism."

Zorach v. *Clauson:* In April 1952, in a 6-3 decision, the Court upheld the validity of the New York released-time program. This caused some confusion. Even though the Court did say, "We follow the McCollum case," which had struck down a released-time program in Champaign, it also stated, "We are a religious people whose institutions presuppose a Supreme Being." The New York program was distinguished from the Champaign practice in that classes were not held on school premises; nor, it was said, was there pressure on children to participate.

While the Court said there can be no doubt "that the first amendment reflects the philosophy that church and state should be separated," the decision added that it does not follow that "in all and every respect there shall be a separation of church and state." As a caution, the majority opinion also stressed that public authorities may not "undertake religious instruction nor blend secular and sectarian instruction."

The dissenting judges expressed fear that this decision removed the state from a position of complete neutrality in the religious sphere. One of the minority opinions concluded that "state help to religion injects political and party prejudices into a holy field"; and that "Government should not be allowed, under cover of the soft euphemism of "cooperation," to steal into the sacred area of religious choice."

Engel v. *Vitale* (see also, School Prayers, p. 27). In June 1962, in a 6-1 decision, the Court declared unconstitutional the recitation in the public schools of a prayer composed by the New York Board of Regents. This decision marked the Court's fourth reiteration of its interpretation of the establishment clause, first enunciated Everson. The other three cases were McCollum (discussed above); Torcaso (ruled out requiring a public official to swear a belief in God); and McGowan (upheld Sunday closing laws).

Moreover, Mr. Justice Douglas, on two separate occasions (McGowan and Engel), took pains to explain what he had meant by: "We are a religious people whose institutions presuppose a Supreme Being." He said in McGowan:

> The Puritan influence helped shape our constitutional law. . . . For these reasons we stated in Zorach v. Clauson . . . "We are a religious people whose institutions presuppose a Supreme Being." But those who fashioned the Constitution decided that if and when God is to be served, His service will not be motivated by coercive measures of government. . . . This means, as I understand it, that if a religious leaven is to be worked into the affairs of our people, it is to be done by individuals and groups, not by the government. . . .

The Engel decision provoked sharp public expressions of dissatisfaction. Forty-nine proposed constitutional amendments were introduced in House and Senate, most being designed to overturn the decision by specifically permitting Bible reading and nondenominational prayer in the public schools. Others would permit Congress and the states to assist religious groups, provided aid were extended without discrimination.

In light of the Court's repeated interpretation of the religion clause and its holdings in the several cases here mentioned, it would appear that the separation principle applies to the public schools as follows:

—Mere avoidance of preferential treatment of one religion over another is insufficient; strict neutrality is required of government.

—It matters not whether a religious activity is nondenominational or nonsectarian. Religious activity of whatever nature, such as a school-sponsored prayer, is unconstitutional.

—That a child is afforded the privilege of withdrawing from a religious exercise is also immaterial.

—There is ground for court intervention even if the religious intrusion is small, as in the case of a denominationally neutral prayer.

In sum, the Court's several holdings seem to affirm that public schools must be conducted as a secular institution.

In an attempt to be all things to all people in a democracy, we may be losing some of the best values of our tradition. In the drive to "be well-liked," we allow the school to be used in all kinds of interfaith and intercultural programs. If we do not know what we are about, we will be doing damage both to the most dogmatic and the most liberal of our society, says Don Hager.

INTERCULTURAL EDUCATION AND THE SEPARATION OF CHURCH AND STATE
*Don J. Hager**

Both intercultural education and the field of intergroup relations generally proceed on the assumption that religious controversy and conflict is similar, in substance and form, to racial and cultural conflict. It is also assumed, therefore, that conventional intergroup theory and practice are equally applicable to the study and reduction of interreligious tensions. Characteristically, there is the tendency to lump racial, creedal, ethnic, national, religious, and even class differences together. This process is followed by the assumption that the same psychological and social dynamics that prompt one form of conflict operates in all contexts. We note, for example, that "interfaithism, i.e., understanding, is best taught through firsthand contacts with members of different religious groups," has considerable acceptance in intercultural circles. In dealing with religious differences there is the familiar assumption that "understanding will remove religious tensions, that religious differences and interreligious conflict share the same character, content and consequences as racial and ethnic differences.

More importantly, too few schools and educators have given serious consideration (in their overzealous attempts to "prove" that their schools are not "godless") to the extent to which, if at all, the public

* Don J. Hager, "New Problems in Intercultural Education," *Journal of Educational Sociology*, XXX, No. 4 (December, 1956), 166-67. Reprinted by permission.

schools bear a responsibility for religious education and practices. Most of the educational effort appears to be devoted to a premature concern with how religion is to be managed in the public schools— a concern that will not be satisfactorily nor intelligently fulfilled until the question of responsibility is resolved. It is also important to note that many educators and teachers are unaware that certain proposed devices and techniques designed to contribute to "interfaith understanding" seriously threaten the spirit if not the doctrine of the constitutional separation of church and state. In the interest of "religious harmony," intercultural education often becomes enmeshed in programs aimed at "teaching about religion," the establishment of "common core" teachings, and the promulgation of programs in "moral and spiritual values." The involvement of intercultural education in such programs endangers its more legitimate aims, and particularly if these programs promote the use of religious sanctions for moral behavior. It becomes necessary, therefore, to consider the practical consequences as well as the constitutionality of the following classroom practices intended to foster "interfaith harmony and understanding:"

—religious and joint holiday celebrations
—reading or recitation of prayers
—reading of the Bible
—the distribution of religious literature
—classroom visits to churches and synagogues
—visits of clergymen to classrooms
—singing sectarian or religious hymns
—use of books, cartoons, and film strips describing the beliefs and practices of the various faiths
—interfaith or sectarian meetings on school premises
—display and explanation of religious symbols

When considering the use of intercultural education to promote "better interfaith relations" in the public schools, it is also necessary to point out that such programs frequently rest upon and perpetuate the enormous assumption that contemporary religious conflict and controversy had its roots in "religious prejudice and bigotry." This is a point of view that had long been abandoned by serious students of interreligious conflict. The nature of religion and religious conflict has undergone striking change in the last quarter-century. Contemporary religious conflict flows from dispute over church-state relations (religion in the public schools), issues in religious liberty (Sabbath laws), and from the competing demands of the religious and secular worlds. It has long been observed that these forms of conflict persist in the absence of prejudicial attitudes. It is misleading to suggest, for example, that the dispute surrounding the question of Federal aid to parochial schools is attributable to a resurgence of religious prejudice. It is true, of course, that conflict can aggravate and perhaps stimulate prejudicial behavior; but we should not mistake effect for cause.

If we are to assume that one of the central tasks of the public schools is to create respect for the democratic tradition, a tradition that cuts across racial, ethnic and religious membership, we may be inclined to question the advisability of educational programs that lay stress, however well-intentioned, on the racial, religious and ethnic backgrounds of students. For the most part, these characteristics are a function of status and birth; they are not in themselves a measure of individual merit or worth. The objectives of intercultural education might, therefore, be more realistically directed toward examining and exploiting the pragmatic consequences, expectations, and requirements of life in a constitutional democracy.

Editors' Summary

The importance of the controversy over the separation of church and state principle lies in its test of the cultural heritage of America. The period after World War II has been a time of social stress and disorganization. As an answer to this disorganization, people have been seeking guarantees and sure-fire systems that were not always attainable. The widespread turn to religion as an answer has put pressures on the schools to teach religion, teach about religion, or allow released time and other such devices. Many of these proposals were clearly contrary to the 1st amendment.

The strength of a democracy lies in its ability to hold enduring principle through time, regardless of the transitory character of the immediate society. At times of crisis, many people acting on the pas-

sion of the moment can commit acts contrary to the great values of our society. The institutions of society, the family, church, courts, schools, and others can show their value by righting wrongs, easing tensions, and bringing the power of great symbols to bear on the wills and attitudes of the common citizen.

Clearly the schools have a mandate to tell the public not to throw away any of their most precious heritages, even in the name of the Holy of Holies. On the other hand, some of the questions regarding religion for or against certain programs on the premise that one has the final answers is perhaps as damaging as serving as a doormat to the general community, regardless of inner convictions. For example, the school must not let the community dictate that religious instruction is to be imposed, nor should the schools necessarily oppose lectures about religion or health programs for private schools, without investigation. Those measures which lead to better education and better children should be encouraged.

In the end, the principles we most prize are not to be maintained by rules and laws, but by a common endeavor to improve the quality of our lives. This cannot be articulated in pros and cons, but if the endeavor is envisioned all arguments are seen with a new clarity showing their parts in a greater whole. John Dewey puts it well:

> *The things in civilization we most prize are not of ourselves. They exist by grace of the doings and sufferings of the continuous human community in which we are a link. Ours is the responsibility of conserving, transmitting, rectifying and expanding the heritage of values we have received that those who come after us may receive it more generously shared than we have received it. Here are all the elements of a religious faith that shall not be confined to sect, class, or race. Such a faith has always been implicitly the common faith of mankind. It remains to make it explicit and militant.**

RELATED READINGS

Barker, Sir Ernest. *Church, State, and Education.* (10), Ann Arbor: Ann Arbor Paperbacks, University of Michigan Press.

Blanshard, Paul. *American Freedom and Catholic Power.* Boston: Beacon Hill Press, 1958.

* John Dewey, *A Common Faith* (New Haven, 1934), 87.

Butts, R. Freeman. *The American Tradition in Religion and Education*. Boston: Beacon Hill Press, 1950.

Commager, Henry Steele (ed.). *Living Ideas in America*. New York: Harper & Brothers, 1951.

Conant, James B. *Education and Liberty*. Cambridge: Harvard University Press, 1953.

Educational Policies Commission. *Moral and Spiritual Values in the Public Schools*. Washington, D.C.: National Education Association, 1951.

Haan, Aubrey. *Education for the Open Society*. Boston: Allyn and Bacon, 1962.

Hartford, Ellie Ford. *Moral Values in Public Education*. New York: Harper & Brothers, 1958.

Hay, Clyde Lemond. *The Blind Spot in American Public Education*. New York: The Macmillan Co., 1950.

Howe, Mark DeWolfe. *Cases on Church and State in the United States*. Cambridge: Harvard University Press, 1952.

Keller, James. *All God's Children*. New York: Hanover House, 1953.

Kilpatrick, W. H., and others. "Religion and Education: A Symposium," *Progressive Education*, XXXIII (September, 1956), 129-55.

Maritain, Jacques. *Man and the State*. Chicago: University of Chicago Press, 1951.

Melby, Ernest O., and Puner, Morton. *Freedom and Public Education*. New York: Frederick A. Praeger, Inc., 1953.

Nichols, J. H. *History of Christianity, 1650-1950*. New York: The Ronald Press Co., 1956.

Nixon, Charles R. "Freedom vs. Unity: A Problem in the Theory of Civil Liberties," *Political Science Quarterly*, LXVIII (March, 1953), 70-88.

Pfeffer, Leo. *Church, State and Freedom*. Boston: Beacon Hill Press, 1953.

Stokes, Anson Phelps. *Church and State in the United States*. 3 vols. New York: Harper & Brothers, 1950.

XII

Emerging Power Structures
and the Future of Public Education

Editors' Comment

An oversimplified view of how our democracy works is to conceive of all voters as independent individuals considering the candidates and issues and voting accordingly. A somewhat more sophisticated view is the picture of political parties in contention, with each person accepting a package of candidates and policies. The reality is much more complicated, with a vast number of organized groups exerting many kinds of pressure. The official political process is only partly and often superficially a manifestation of the power press of our society. The wills of individuals and groups determine our fate in levels that often transcend, circumvent, or carry unwittingly along the formal decisions.

The reality we have to deal with in understanding the development of public education is not, therefore, the public and the school, but a great number of groups who want a great many things from something that is itself extremely complicated. The real state of affairs of public education is a tangled web of contending forces. Only from a limited point of view and in a restricted sense can the schoolroom be considered in isolation from the rest of society. The learning

296

that goes on, and the microsocial situation of the classroom can only be understood in the context of the total society. Actually, like the magnetic lines of force that surround the earth, invisible but potently there, a setting of forces of social power pervade and surround the classroom, the teacher, and the groupings to which these all belong.

Education is thoroughly a social process. The success of teaching $2 + 2 = 4$ depends on the social conditions being adequate to sustain this particular teaching-learning process. The teacher must understand the social relations which actually operate in making the students, administrators, fellow teachers, parents, and the general public what they are.

An important phase of the teacher's knowledge has to do with community relations, although as the reader knows the term "community" has become blurred in the "acids of modernity," the many new ways and ideas directing modern life. The teacher needs to know what forces operate for and against the school in order to be an intelligent part of the total process. The teacher is not simply a vessel containing knowledge which is turned on and off like a faucet in the schoolroom, but is himself fundamentally a process, as are the students and the community in terms of John Dewey. These processes become more clarified, complex, and powerful by intelligent social interaction. The teacher then, integrally and intrinsically, is a part of a great social process from which he cannot extricate himself any more than he can resign from the human race.

"Understanding" is not enough for the teacher. In the pragmatic sense knowledge unapplied somehow, somewhere, does not exist. The teacher needs to relate to the forces actually operating upon himself, his students, and on the quality of interrelationships between himself and the students. He must teach the students to look upon themselves as responsible units in a total process. He must be able to actively combat the threats, and promulgate the constructive forces of the whole social process in which the classroom and community are parts.

A most important concept for the teacher to grasp is that of power. Power, briefly, is the ability to control human behavior. All power groups have ends which can be described in terms of control of hu-

man behavior. What Mills[1] calls the "power elite" and Hunter[2] calls the four community groups (business, government, civic associations, and social associations) are groups which have certain ends of social control. Since education is directed to the making of the new generation, the school is a focal point of contention, a most desirable prize.

There is no completely anti-education group, but there are groups whose influence is adverse to good education. Vested interests who "have theirs" are not going to be enthusiastic about any change that might affect them adversely. Religious, political, and social extremists who want to use the schools as instruments for implementing their philosophies are also enemies.

The educational institution has been what sociologists would call a reflective or adaptive institution. Big business and big government are pivotal or formative institutions. Though they may work behind the scenes, and do not send official delegates to the board of education meetings to pound on the tables, it is their decisions and wishes which are most influential in all that is vital in the directions of society. In a sense, the debates in education, the consensus of meetings, and the whole warp and woof of school-community relations have a spurious quality. The school does not really create the values nor control human behavior in the most crucial aspects of society.

Professional educators must realize the limitations under which they presently work. Fully realizing their difficulties and limitations in attaining power in the community is a prerequisite to success in amelioration.

One of the favorite themes of the people who sigh for the "good old days" is the idea of settling things "man to man." The feeling is that an over-all loss occurs in the quality of living with the rise of organized groups and the submergence of each person to a number or a faceless entity in an impersonal mass. Also the feeling occurs, particularly among teachers, that the whole business of social organization for effectuation of power goals is somehow reprehensible, or at least not relevant for them. William Stanley argues that 1) power groups are here to stay, that 2) each man realizes himself today most

[1] C. Wright Mills, *The Power Elite* (New York, 1956).
[2] Floyd Hunter, *Community Power Srtucture* (Chapel Hill, N.C., 1953).

*effectively in groups, and 3) no other means exist for settling differ-
ences among men, and the group process of determining solutions can
be, and generally is, of a high level of morality.*

ORGANIZED INTERESTS AND SOCIAL POWER
*William O. Stanley**

. . . But in the great society created by science and technology the
individual citizen, as Professor Harold Laski has remarked, secures
effective power only as a member of an organized group. Individuals,
to be sure, are still heard but, except for a few outstanding and unique
personalities, they are heard for the most part not as individuals but
as the leaders and spokesmen of powerful interests. Hence, men have
either withdrawn from the arena of public affairs or they have turned
to group action and to group expression of opinion. Consequently, organized associations representing specialized and particular interests
in society are in large measure the media through which individuals
participate in public affairs. The organized interest group, therefore,
has replaced the local community as the effective agency of public
opinion and politics just as special interests and occupation have replaced the neighborhood as the major force in the shaping of the
conduct and beliefs of persons. . . .

. . . The members of pressure groups are also members of society; as such they, no more than other men, can free themselves in
their own minds from the common obligation to respect the public
weal. Moreover, in order to advance the interests which they represent, pressure groups must frequently secure the cooperation of other
groups. Hence, they are compelled both by moral principles of their
members and the practical necessities of the situation to relate their
particular interest to the general welfare. The tendency of men, where
vital interests are at stake, to erect their particular into a universal may
be readily admitted. But that is a principle which is limited to no
single group, and it is pertinent to ask where, in a modern industrial
society, the impartial public is to be located. The fact is that the ex-

* William O. Stanley, *Education and Social Integration*. Teachers College Bureau
of Publications (Columbia University, N.Y., 1953), 7-9. Reprinted by permission.

istence of powerful organized interests in American society is the reflection of the division of that society into significant functional groups, as the existence of group perspectives and points of view is a reflection of the absence, in part at least, of universally accepted standards of public welfare. In the last analysis, the conflict of social philosophies and programs represented by the welter of contending interest groups is a competition of contrasting theories of the public good, undoubtedly conditioned by the particular interests cherished by each of these groups, but not, in any sense, simply a cynical and selfish dogfight conceived solely in terms of purely private advantage. The public interest, in the modern world, is an achievement rather than an original datum; acceptable standards of public welfare must include in some measure, as they must also transcend, the particular interests of the functional groups necessarily involved in the social structure. It may also be added that it is probable that where such standards are achieved, the competing conceptions of public welfare cherished by these organized groups inevitably furnish an important element of the material out of which they are fashioned. While these groups, therefore, are pressure groups, that label does not fully define their meanings; indeed, their primary significance cannot be comprehended at all in such terms. Rather, they must be understood as representatives of important group interests in American society, and as the bearers of pregnant propositions concerning the meaning of the public welfare and the definition of the ends of public policy.

In the last few years the power struggle in the United States has become much more complex and dynamic. The relatively simple models of white collar and blue collar workers of middle class businessmen on the school board directing the lower middle class teachers by few and simple commands have passed away. Now we have many power foci, and the directions they take are not easily understood and predicted. A mixture of unionism, professionalism, and the pressures of rising living costs have created a new militancy among teachers.

The author of the next article gives the "definition of the situation" that teacher militancy has brought out. He sees that teachers will gain power, while principals, and more strikingly, superintendents, are shorn of power. The long-term trend forecast is equality of educational opportunity, and a professionalization of teachers.

CHANGING BALANCE OF POWER IN EDUCATION: TEACHER MILITANCY*
David Strom

Growing teacher militancy is creating great changes in the structure of American education. The small school district locally controlled and financed is now "gasping for breadth." The militancy of teacher unions and associations has demonstrated, anew, the deepening financial crisis of the cities and the decline in educational services within the urban setting.

Teacher organizational demand for a greater voice in determining teacher salaries has shown that local control of the economic purse strings is impossible. The declining ability of property taxes to support good progressive educational districts has helped destroy localism in education. Boards of education while wishing to make policies for the school districts are hampered by their need for money which only the national government and state governments can give. Dependence on monies from sources outside the school district has taken some autonomy away from school boards. To receive they must give. What they give is decision-making power.

Historically, the board of education's role has been that of power maker. When local taxes could and did support quality education the board had no need to act as a pressure group, but today while property taxes are an archaic way of supporting education, boards have been forced to become aware of the legislation in Washington, D.C., and in their respective state capitals. Slowly, as they realized the facts of educational costs, they consolidated into larger and larger school districts, and formed state and national organizations to lobby for better educational legislation and more financial aid.

The small school board has disappeared and what is within the very near future are county-wide school boards. These boards will

* Unpublished monograph, Wayne State University, 1967.

oversee all educational policies within the county and will bargain with a county-wide teacher organization in the areas of salaries, hours, and working conditions.

Teacher militancy is multi-causal. A great deal of progress has been made in the area of civil liberties and civil rights within the past decade through the use of picketing, marches, sit-ins, and other types of demonstrations. Teachers participate, as individuals, in these demonstrations and recognize the value in displaying problems openly and with force before the community. They realize poor communication exists between boards and teachers; they see small pay envelopes every other week; they live and work in districts where school tax laws are archaic and cannot support education of sufficient quality; they recognize entry and exit in the profession is "out of their hands"; they have little voice in how and what shall be taught, therefore, they take their problems into the streets. Thus, long teacher meetings, pamphleteering, professional days, sick days, board packing, sanctions, and strikes are seen as possible methods to their goal of teaching as a profession.

What do teachers mean when they say "teaching is a profession?" They assent:

1. A professional salary of $8,000-$15,000 a year for teachers with a baccalaureate, and one to seven years experience;
2. Control of entry and dismissal or disciplining within the profession;
3. Determination of curriculum, class size, length of school year, length of school day, and textbook selection and the like;
4. Preeminent control over working conditions in general.

The achievement of recognition in being heard and listened to has changed the school power structure. The teachers' voice through the negotiated contract has been broadened, and if teachers have their way will be broadened still further. The power that the teachers have gotten has come mainly from the changing relationship between superintendents and school boards. Teachers are beginning to feel that, as professionals, they ought to have control over their work-a-day world. Who can know more about teaching methods, class size, curriculum and teaching day than they, the professionals, who have to be the educational leaders within the classroom?

What is at stake in the changing relationship within the public

302

educational system? The future vitality of public education! When teachers have a say in curriculum they will bring about needed changes within the school program. As an example, teachers are usually given a city-wide curriculum which has had the "expert" approval, but when it gets down to the classroom "it just won't work." Class size has been talked about, written about, but now the teacher in the classroom is starting to say what the size of the class should be. Many examples of democratization of public education are taking place with the rise in militancy of teacher organizations. This democratization of public education will buttress the sagging prestige of American education. With the breath of freedom in the schools and in its operation the tide and growth of private and parochial schools will be stemmed. Teacher militancy for control of the educational process will save public education.

Clearly, teacher militancy will help in equalizing the educational opportunity of the poorer school districts. Militancy will help in demonstrating the inadequate nature of the property tax for support of education. The poorer district will not be able to compete in good school programs, hiring competent personnel, having adequate physical facilities and the like. They will be forced to consolidate into larger and larger districts. With this will come new methods of support for education. The school monies will be disbursed on a county- and then a state-wide basis, with a proportionate principle insuring that the schools in need of the most funds receive them. Being born and attending school in a poor district will be less and less a handicap.

The traditional role of the superintendent as an educational statesman and leader, the impartial fact-finder and liaison officer to the local board of education, the spokesman of the professional staff, and the public's image of what is the best in public education is at an end. Teacher sanctions and strikes, teacher militancy and the "bigness" of education today has buried that role. The superintendent's role is diminishing because of these factors:

1. Federal government legislation that gives money to the local school district, but restricts the usage of the money to specific programs.
2. Teachers, as professionals, in organized associations and unions, have a bigger say in making educational policies.

3. Principals and other administrators are organizing and determining to bargain as a unit with school boards.
4. The emerging role of the superintendent is that of mediator-compromiser rather than as educational leader and statesman.

Because the superintendent is hired by the board to run the school district, he often is requested to negotiate on the board's team. Oftentimes, he is the main spokesman for the board's bargaining team, and at the opposite end of the table is the teaching staff's negotiating team. He thus, clearly, has broken the "mythical ideal" of his being in either the board's camp or teachers' camp, but is now the teachers' "enemy." The teachers view their former father image as their adversary, someone to be wary of, and someone to take power from. They are effectively doing this.

The new role of the superintendent is that of business manager of the school district and the firm's public-relations man to the community and professional staff.

Growing professionalism of the teaching staff makes it difficult for the principal to assume his former role of educational leader within the building. Decision-making of the principal is severely limited by the negotiated contract. Most of the time a principal is not involved in negotiations and is by-passed when the important decisions are made. He lives and works with a contract agreed upon by his superiors and the teaching staff. His main course of action comes in interpreting the contract. If his interpretation is not in line with teacher organizational thinking, a grievance can and will be filed against him, and then the decision-making matter is taken out of his hands to a higher authority to settle. His decision-making role is so limited in broad educational areas by the contract that only in small unimportant areas of school management can he make his insignificant decisions. This relegates him to taking care of such matters as office management, building maintenance, and school routines. Some teachers feel that with the rise in rank and status of teachers the principals' professional role is diminishing and the locus of decision-making is to rest with the professional staff.

Since about 1960 various teacher organizations have made concerted drives to gain for public-school teachers the right to collective action in negotiating with school boards. Teacher organizations bargain effectively in areas of salary, hours of employment, and other working conditions. Teachers feel that everything involving the educational process is bargainable. With the shift to collective negotiations changes in the decision-making power between boards of education, school superintendents, and teacher organizations are taking place. This changing power relationship has implications for public education in these ways:

1. Consolidation into larger school districts. First, on a county-wide basis and then on a state-wide basis.
2. Economic equalization within the county-wide school system will upgrade education in poor areas.
3. Democratization within the school district will strengthen public education and slow the growth of private and parochial schools.
4. Greater changes in the school curricula will take place with the growing teacher control within their world of work.
5. Local support of education is totally inadequate, and thus more support will come from state legislatures and federal government.
6. School superintendents are mediators of school district conflicts.
7. Principals' main role is that of office management, building maintenance, and school routines.

One of the promising developments of the time is the development of a "hierarchy of professions" concept for teaching. It is born of a stringent need, but the basic principle is one that may prove a cutting-edge pilot project which foreshadows the future.

SUB-PROFESSIONALISM: ITS ROLE IN EDUCATION
*Antone C. Colovas**

Two of the most persistently pressing problems in the American educational community today concern (1) the need to provide classroom teachers with assistance in the discharge of various non-teaching duties, and (2) the need to provide students with more individual attention and aid.

* Teacher, Jr. High School, Dearborn Public Schools—unpublished monograph.

The legitimacy and urgency of these problems are readily apparent. Why is it that teachers must consistently be burdened with responsibilities of a custodial or clerical nature? Why must they be required to supervise recess and lunch-time activities? Why should they serve as hall monitors or operate audiovisual equipment? Tasks of this nature seriously divert the teacher's efforts away from his primary responsibility of teaching and as a consequence deprive students of the benefits of having a full-time instructor.

Concurrently, and even more importantly, why must a student have to compete with thirty or so other youths for assistance from his teacher? Why should a youngster who is capable of doing advanced work be penalized because no one is available to give him direction? Why must a student who is suffering scholastic problems have to fall further behind in his studies because he is unable to obtain extra help? Conditions such as these must certainly be eliminated if the educational responsibilities of the nation are to be met.

One of the most promising solutions to these problems seems to lie in the extensive use of so-called sub-professional workers as aides to the classroom teacher. Experimental projects are providing increasing evidence that such workers, if properly utilized, can help effect dramatic changes in the traditionally conservative instructional process.

The concept of the teacher aide is certainly not a new one. Numerous school districts throughout the country have at times employed such workers and have found them useful in performing a variety of tasks. In most instances, however, this past use of sub-professionals has been a rather limited, relatively unstructured operation and has not been an integral part of the total educational program. In addition, the position of the teacher aide has been somewhat of a terminal one and has offered little opportunity for advancement.

Today, these earlier, somewhat rudderless views of the sub-professional worker are being replaced by carefully organized programs aimed at making the teacher aide a vital part of the classroom structure. The basic notion behind these new programs is that sub-professionals should no longer be lumped into one catch-all category such as teacher aids or teacher assistants. Instead, they should be stratified into a number of separate categories, each having certain functions allocated to it, its own specific prerequisites for entry, and its own pay scale. Furthermore,

306

these categories should not be terminal ones. They should offer opportunities to move from a lower level to a higher one, and should, in fact, afford the worker a chance to move completely out of the realm of the sub-professional and into the position of a full-fledged, certified teacher.

A look at a sample program of this nature illustrates how this revised concept of the sub-professional employee might be implemented. Such a program would divide the different members of the instructional staff according to the following scheme:

1. General aide
2. Instructional assistant
3. Associate teacher
4. Teacher
5. Staff coordinator

The first three categories in this arrangement would comprise sub-professionals while the remaining two levels would be staffed with professional workers. Each position, as indicated earlier, would have its own specific characteristics.

The initial category of general aide would serve as a point of entry into the program and would be open to virtually anyone regardless of educational attainment. The primary prerequisite for this position would be the successful completion of a short four-to-six-week preparatory program that would train the individual for the kinds of tasks he would face as an aide. These might include such duties as operating audiovisual equipment, dictating spelling words or objective tests, reading orally to students, performing clerical work for the teacher, sponsoring certain school functions, assuming responsibility for the maintenance of equipment and supplies, and supervising recess and lunch-time activities. Especially capable aides might even assist individual students with homework problems.

The aide would, it is hoped, strive to continue his own education. Eventually, if he were able to attain two years of college or its equivalent, he would become eligible for the position of instructional assistant. In obtaining the added education needed for this new role, the aide would not necessarily have to earn all his credits through college attendance. A system could be devised that would give him a certain amount of college credit for his on-the-job activities. This credit, combined with the satisfactory completion of a specified number of college courses, would permit him to meet the additional educational requirements for the post of instructional assistant.

As an instructional assistant the sub-professional would have more important responsibilities and duties than he had had as an aide. These might include such things as processing and preparing materials to be used by the classroom teacher, showing and commenting on film strips and movies, tutoring individual students, marking and criticizing student papers, giving demonstrations to the class, working with small groups on individual projects, and assisting the teacher in determination of report card marks. In addition, to the extent of his educational background, he might even help in the actual teaching of specific subjects.

From the level of instructional assistant, the sub-professional could advance to the position of associate teacher. This would require two years of experience as an instructional assistant combined with the equivalent of one year of additional academic training at the senior-college level. The tasks of the associate would be similar in most respects to those of a certified classroom teacher. However, the associate would remain under the direction and supervision of a staff coordinator and would not have the classroom autonomy that is usually extended to a fully qualified person.

Once having become an associate, the sub-professional could then progress to the level of certified teacher by obtaining his college degree.

Thus, through a program of this nature, an individual could create an entirely new career for himself and in a relatively few years could move from the category of the sub-professional to that of the full-fledged teacher. Moreover, during the entire period of his apprenticeship he would be gainfully employed and would be serving in a socially useful capacity.

The implications of a sub-professional career program such as the foregoing are very great. First of all, of course, the classroom teacher would be relieved of many burdensome, non-teaching tasks and would thereby be freed to do more actual teaching. Secondly, an entirely new set of career opportunities would be opened for sub-professional personnel. Of even more crucial importance, however, would be the benefits which could accrue to the child in school. Through the extensive utilization of sub-professional workers, the ratio of students to instructional staff could be greatly reduced and more individualized attention could be focused on youngsters. This could be expected to improve education in our schools.

More specifically, large-scale usage of sub-professionals could play a vital role in the development of intensive education projects for impoverished youths. For example, efforts could be made to hire sub-professional workers who were native to the disadvantaged area they would be serving. These workers, through knowledge of their district's particular subculture, would be in a position to make valuable contributions leading to a better understanding and fuller appreciation of the needs of local disadvantaged students. In addition, through the presence of such local employees, the school could take on a new, more personal meaning for the poor. It would no longer be strictly a middle-class oriented institution but would contain people who understood and were sympathetic to the problems of the disadvantaged.

In ways such as these the sub-professional person can unquestionably play an important role in our nation's future educational efforts. Through proper utilization of his talents new dimensions can certainly be added to the instructional process; youngsters, especially disadvantaged ones, can be given increased attention and new hope for the future; our schools can assume a more dynamic posture and can finally begin reaching all our youths rather than just the more fortunate ones.

The following statement of position is a model of a basic speech made by teacher leaders in meetings organizing teachers to take action in politics. The author says he has made this basic speech in many teacher meetings.

A TEACHER TALKS
William E. McDonald*

A classroom teacher in our public schools is a private in a vast army, an army that wins no battles and follows none of the traditional military procedures.

* Teacher, West Junior High School, Taylor, Michigan.

The school board functions as the general staff. Made up of people with no knowledge of their job it doesn't make any combat plans. The commanding general, the superintendent of the district, spends most of his time pleasing the general staff and the public. The commissioned officers, the school administrators, direct most of their efforts toward protecting their jobs and salary, pleasing their commanding general and hampering the efforts of the lowest-ranking member of this fighting complex—the classroom teacher.

The situation would be livable if the instructor had the private's anonymity and responsibility as well as his pay. There is much to be said for the yardbird's position in our fighting forces.

The enemy is numerous and complex. They attack from all directions. Occasionally they are led by the army's commissioned officers, the administrators, who also sit on the sidelines and applaud the carnage.

Why then do teachers strike? It works! In New York City they have turned a hodge-podge of broken buildings, mobs of illiterate students and harassed, frightened, underpaid babysitters into a system where education is beginning to move.

This educational revolution must be more complete than accepting more salary, a few more sheets of paper and a return to the twiddle-dee-dee–twiddle-dee-dum frustration of our present education fiasco. We must accept our responsibility to society, to educating that society.

Our concern must be with the numerous and faceless mass of society that the teacher deals with every day. Too long we have aped and developed our educational goals to please the small segment of the middle and upper classes.

To educate and lead, we must become part of this large group, know it, organize it and develop leaders for it and be concerned with its economic, political and social development. Next, we must control education, all facets of it; those who engage in the process and the financing. If we believe in the importance of our jobs, we must make sure that only highly qualified people become teachers and that they are well paid. No teacher has taken an oath of poverty, obedience and chastity. To do this we must make sure a proper share of the national income is allotted to education.

This will require teachers to become leaders in our society, leading it toward goals that we develop instead of following or attempting to follow false goals that others set up. We will have to become political creatures using teacher power, not abusing it, but not being frightened or ashamed of it.

In addition to political leadership, the instructor must lead in the reorganization of the school structure. No educator can be an administrator or guardian of the wax, seller of pictures and the cleaning, inspector of rest rooms, and inspector of paper towels and remain concerned with the prime function of the school, education of students. We must separate administration of school buildings and teaching. No educator will be an administrator.

To the upgrading of the teaching profession, the reorganization of the school structure, we must add educational research. We as teachers must stop being the experimental animals of the educational professors. Most research is sold to our school power elite with the promise that it will enable a teacher to handle more students. Team teaching and educational television are examples of this philosophy. Research is needed—much of it—but it must be developed in our public schools, proven in them and used there. Today there are no failures in educational research. It just doesn't work in the public schools. Research developed by public-school teachers in public schools and tested in the fire of the classroom under everyday conditions and in all types of schools will have failures; but there will be successes too. Teachers must clearly bring to the public the purpose of schools, to educate, not to keep a segment of the lower-class population off the street until they can safely be dumped upon society.

Mass public education is one of the greatest earth-shaking ideas ever conceived. Let's make it work. Irritate! Agitate! Educate!

The purpose of citizen participation should be made functional to serving the professionalization of teachers, according to Myron Lieberman. When laymen engage in affairs of the school, the effect is usually one of giving the laymen power in school matters which are against the highest school interests. In the following selection, Lieberman lays down thirteen rules for layman participation. The reader will notice that in Lieberman's recommendations the layman would serve the school, and not vice versa.

EDUCATIONAL CONTROLS AND CITIZEN PARTICIPATION
*Myron Lieberman**

1. Local control of education by laymen should be limited to peripheral and ceremonial functions of education. However, the rights of individual parents and students to make certain basic choices (for example, whether the student takes a college preparatory or a vocational program) must be carefully protected.

2. Laymen can ordinarily make their most valuable contribution to public education in their noneducational organizations. As members of organized groups, laymen can help to protect the integrity of the school program by opposing efforts to use the schools through special holidays, contests, activities, or subjects to advance organizational interests which are not necessary for the educational welfare of students.

3. In view of the fact that the people most active in educational affairs are usually from the upper classes and tend to favor policies which are unfair to less privileged groups, citizens should support school budgets which make all subjects and activities freely available to all students who have the capacity to profit from them. School-wide activities which are theoretically open to all students but which are usually not attended by poorer children, such as junior proms requiring formal dress, should be eliminated unless economic and social class factors in participation can be removed.

* Myron Lieberman, *The Future of Public Education* (Chicago, 1960), 281-83. Reprinted by permission of The University of Chicago Press. Copyright, 1960.

4. Laymen should support proposals to give teachers more authority over students and over parental behavior relating to school problems. A request from school authorities for a parent to discuss a school problem relating to his children should not be something the parent is free to ignore, as is almost everywhere the case at the present time.

5. Citizens should support school boards which are willing to negotiate conditions of employment with representatives of the majority organizations of teachers, provided such organizations have adequate safeguards against administrator domination.

6. School boards should provide contracts of perhaps five years' duration for superintendents. Superintendents hired for shorter periods are too busy building their political fences (to insure reappointment) to provide effective educational leadership; they frequently pass every controversy on to the public, regardless of the professional nature of the issues involved.

7. Citizen participation, like the work of the teachers, needs to be evaluated periodically and critically. It might be salutary for superintendents to reveal the record of citizen participation in their community for each past year. A great deal of this participation consists of pressure to fire an athletic coach after an unsuccessful season, protesting because one's child is not in an accelerated group, criticizing the school cafeteria for not providing home cooking, attempting to get the school bus to make a more convenient stop, and sundry other matters of this nature. Citizens tend to underestimate how ineffective the schools are; at the same time, their own participation and influence upon the school program is often the cause rather than the result of this ineffectiveness.

8. Citizens' committees on public education, PTA's, school boards, and other individuals and groups interested in improving public education should work with teachers through the systematic evaluation of student achievement, diagnosis of what must be done to improve performance, and support for the measures needed for improvement.

9. Respect for teachers should be reflected in support for adequate conditions of educational employment, rather than in annual "Teacher Recognition Days" (which often embarrass the teachers and certainly do not help them materially).

10. Citizens should make an inventory of what parents are doing to help or hinder the educational progress of their children. This inventory should be conducted with due regard for the economic status and living conditions of the families involved. School boards, perhaps in conjunction with PTA's and citizens' committees, should conduct this inventory. The sorts of questions to be answered include the following: (a) Are pupils sent to school with an adequate breakfast? (b) Are pupils accorded a time and a place to do homework at home? (c) How many children work after school and on weekends? At whose insistence do they work, how many hours do they put in, and how is school performance affected by this employment? (d) How many pupils have an automobile or the free use of an automobile? (e) How late do pupils stay up the night before a school day? (f) Are students readily provided with funds for school supplies and equipment? (g) How many pupils are absent on school days before and after holidays? (h) How often are children absent or tardy for trivial reasons with parental knowledge? (i) Do parents have a reasonably adequate understanding of their children's academic aptitude and progress in school? (j) Are the educational policies of citizens' groups formulated with due regard for the less powerful and less articulate groups in the community?

11. Citizens should recognize that the concept of "participation" is one of the vaguest of the many vague terms that make communication difficult in education. Laymen "participate" in helping to solve the medical problems of their children, but the nature and limits of this participation are well understood. Everyone has a stake in a clear-cut delineation of parental, public, and professional authority in public education. It is probably more important that the delineation be clear to everyone than that it be a perfect division of labor between professionals and nonprofessionals.

12. Insofar as elective officials are concerned, the rule is clear: for short-run, relatively minor, but more immediate improvements, concentrate upon local school board elections; for long-range major improvements, concentrate upon the state and national election of education-minded legislators and executives who have the power to shape the context and limits of local action.

13. Laymen who become active in the field of public education

314

should bear in mind the fact that the worst evils of public education are more often due to teacher acquiescence in public opinion than teacher resistance to it.

With a sting of sarcasm and a deceptive flippancy, Max Rafferty takes apart the enemies of education. His categories are not interest groups or sociological types, but stereotypes or caricatures of the enemies of education. As such, we must say in defense of the selection that although Rafferty swings a broad brush rather indiscriminately, he spatters many people, as anyone who has been in public education a season or two should know.

CHILDREN OF URANUS
*Max Rafferty**

Have you taken time out recently to contemplate the enemies of Education? I don't mean to duck; all of us do that often enough, and almost automatically. I mean to analyze the Opposition.

They're quite a crew. Like the legendary Titans, they take many shapes and speak with changing voices, but they were all our children, once. In their day, they swung like amiable gibbons from our jungle-gyms, raced through dusty halls in glad defiance of the rules, and shuffled their feet in immemorial fashion beneath our classroom desks.

What they learned, they learned from us. The specious arguments they raise in the committee rooms of Congress ring with our accent. Their glib pronouncements in the popular periodicals are peppered with our punctuation, garnished with our grammar, and salted with the style we taught them not so long ago. We look on them now with a sort of numb dismay, recognizing in their distorted faces and crooked gestures a macabre mixture of our features and those of the children who once they were, even as reflections in funhouse mirrors give back lethal caricatures of the observer, plus a sinister something more.

* Max Rafferty, "Children of Uranus," *Phi Delta Kappa*, XLII (October, 1960), 20-23. Reprinted by permission.

Examine with me, if you will, these children of ours, grown now to man's estate, and sharpening their sickles.

THE HYPOCRITES

These are the most charming of the Enemy. They wear Brooks Brothers suits. They patronize the best barbers. They are hired expensively and owned completely by the several manufacturers' associations and national chambers of commerce. They are dedicated to the proposition that nothing is too good for Education, except money.

The Hypocrites learned much from us. They turn out slick booklets tastefully designed to show the ardent support of their companies for the schools. They are experts at constructing tables and charts illustrating in living color how (a) Education is good for Business, (b) Business is good to Education, and (c) therefore everything is going to be just dandy.

The smiles become a little strained, and the back-slapping falls off sharply when a move is made to channel a little more of the national income into the schools, however. Need you guess whom we see then before the Congressional committees, damning with faint praise and stifling with sneers of slow disparagement? Their techniques are impeccable, and damnably effective—the two-martini luncheon, the reminiscences about the good old days before life became complex and schools expensive, the raised-eyebrow deprecation of federal controls.

And then there are the slogans. Like Jimmy Durante, they've got a million of "em."

"Support local schools with local taxes."

"Keep the educationists out of education."

"Kids don't need to go to school in palaces."

It works. These gray-flanneled Ivy League types with their Madison Avenue methods have helped keep the United States the only major country in the world which fobs off its educational responsibility on local agencies. They can sell anything but the truth. This is unsalable, because it happens to be that more money spent on education might possibly keep their well-heeled employers from buying that new yacht or taking that annual trip to the Riviera.

Let us leave our false friends, who come before the nation bearing flattering brochures in one hand and the old stiletto in the other.

Dante placed the hypocrites in Gulf Six, Circle Eight of his Inferno. There they were burdened with intolerable weights. I suppose that we may as well derive what comfort we can from the thought that in some future Hell of their own making these smooth, soft-tongued, slippery saboteurs are going to be really loaded.

THE INGRATES

Not too many years ago, a doctoral study was made in Los Angeles which examined the educational pattern of voting precincts. Special attention was given to the way the voters in these districts reacted to school finance measures. Each precinct was identified in accordance with its educational level. If most of its voters were college graduates, it was a "high" precinct. Those made up largely of people with high school backgrounds were labeled "middle," and those benighted areas whose inhabitants had just made it through grade school were, naturally enough, "low."

The results were fascinating.

The "high" precincts turned out *en masse* on election day and used their college-trained minds to vote solidly against school bonds and tax increases in any form, for any reason.

The "middle" voters divided half and half on issues involving more money for the schools. It would be consoling, but probably misleading, to attribute this division to the "suspension of judgment" recommended by certain of the great philosophers.

So it was left to the electors of the "low" precincts to swing the balance for the kids, and they did exactly that. The ignorant, the quasi-illiterate, the cultural Philistine—these least-educated of Americans supported their schools most faithfully.

Here is irony worthy of Dean Swift. Those who had profited most from Education's table, who of all men had most reason to respect and uphold and cherish Education, were the first to welsh out on their bene-factor when the time came to stand up and be counted. Those who had learned the least and benefited the least from Education rallied to its side and upheld a cause otherwise lost indeed.

Extrapolation is perilous here. It leads to the inevitable conclusion that the more people we educate, the less support we can expect to have. The better we teach, the more the schools will be allowed to deteriorate.

The higher the educational level we are able to bring about, the lower will be the national opinion of public instruction. This way madness lies. We had better give up, and quote Mark Twain:

"Feed a starving dog a bone, and he will not bite you hereafter. This is the principal difference between a dog and a man."

It's either grin or succumb to tears of self-pity while ingratitude, more strong than traitors' arms, quite vanquishes us.

THE QUITTERS

When part of any army lights out for the rear in the midst of a battle, it is a tired truism that a greater burden is thrown on the remaining troops. The load is doubly onerous when the deserters have been highly trained specialists.

It distresses me to have you take some of America's churches as an example. For some time now they have been bawling for school money, whining for released time, and pouting because Bible commentaries are not being read daily to school children. This somewhat infantile display of temper has served to conceal but not efface the fact that many of our reverend colleagues have fallen down on the job. A generation or two ago they had no need to clamor for such artificial respiration. They were doing a job, and their churches were full. Today, they seek a captive congregation, and a privileged place at the public trough. They will have abdicated their position in the front rank for a cushy spot in the rear echelon.

There are all kinds of people who want to stop working and let the schools take over for them. Public safety bureaucrats in fifty states don't want to teach their citizens to navigate their highways successfully, so they arrange for the school people to include driver training in an already bogged-down curriculum. Podunk wants organized recreation, but doesn't want the headaches of handling it, so Education wryly welcomes another free-loader. Uncle Sam hesitates to ask too much directly of our Spartan youth, so we get Cadet Corps and R.O.T.C. in our high schools.

All this wouldn't be so bad if we got any thanks for it. But you know what we get.

"Too many frills. Too much money spent on nonessentials. Not enough time spent on fundamentals. The school has its nose in everything."

Of course there is a solution. Let the Quitters take back their babies and nurse them.

You say this will never happen? Oh, well. I didn't say it was a practical solution.

THE PINHEADS

Sooner or later, every school man runs up against the fiery-eyed, gibberish-muttering, rattlesnake-handling brothers and sisters of the Lunatic Fringe. These zealous zanies are visited upon the profession for its sin, as boils were bestowed upon Job.

The Pinheads have a devastating approach. They appeal not to your intellect but to your conscience. This at once places someone like me at a considerable disadvantage, because I have never been entirely certain that I possessed this delicate commodity. And they follow through relentlessly.

Are you building a new gym? You will be buttonholed by a committee of lank-haired elders. They will want a separate, enclosed, coffin-like shower-and-dressing room for each girl, despite the architectural and financial enormity of the mere idea. If you resist the demand, then you are a son of Belial, lustfully relishing the unspeakable thoughts engendered in the minds of fifteen-year-old girls at the sight of each other's naked bodies.

Is your girls' physical education instructor teaching her students the Virginia Reel? She'd better not be, if you have any Pinheads in town. Everyone knows that dancing is a device of Satan. To hear the Pinheads talk, the damned souls in Hell must spend every nonfrying moment tangoing or turkey-trotting. When you stop to think about it, this conjures up a delightfully bizarre picture of the Nether Regions which almost reconciles me to the probability of someday visiting them.

Are you saluting the flag, singing Christmas carols, or studying evolution? Some nut will probably blow the whistle on you.

Did you ever pause to wonder what all these cockeyed crusaders have against the schools? The answer is simple. They hate us and fear us, because Education will eventually destroy them and the creepy causes they stand for. Science and logic and knowledge are anathema to the Pinhead, and for obvious reasons. He stands for bigotry and superstition. We block his path to the minds and hearts of the children.

He hates the schools the way a fly hates the swatter.

There are other enemies of Education, of course. These are the Axe-Grinders and the Profiteers and the Mossbacks. Their eyes bulge out at us from the funhouse mirrors. The congested veins cord like Medusa's snakes from the foreheads livid in the wavy glass. We turn away and go out into the cool of the evening, appalled at the contortions of the masked reflections.

"How," we ask ourselves pathetically, "has a profession which tries only to do good and tell the truth accumulated such enemies?"

Well now, let's not get sickening about it. A lot of this is our own fault. We have striven too long and too hard to be all things to all people. We have been guilty, too, of the sin of Pride. We have been willing to see Education gorged with all sorts of extraneous projects and problems until it swelled like a force-fed goose. Conversely, we have been unwilling or unable to state our case to American people strikingly enough to silence our foes.

But our greatest mistake has been the image of Education which we have presented to the nation. It has been for a generation and more an essentially feminine image—gentle, noncombative, benevolent, maternal, a little fussy.

With all due respect to the thousands of devoted and dedicated women who labor so diligently in our countless classrooms, Education is not feminine. It never has been until just the other day. Since the days of Socrates and Plato, and before, it has been masculine in its outlook and appeal. It seeks to change concepts, to conquer ignorance, to fight evil. It brings not peace, but a sword. In its final, triumphant form, it will sweep the planet like some mighty besom, smashing aside dykes and levees like matchwood, and fulfilling its ancient role as the guardian and mentor of the human race.

In the race to siphon funds out of the public watering trough, of course the weaker fail to get a fair share. The following article tells of the plight of schools and students from the poor districts.

THE RICH GET RICHER AND THE POOR GET POORER . . . SCHOOLS*

"The present allocation of fiscal resources works against education in the central cities. The lesser resources applied to education in the cities apparently hold down educational performance, particularly in the low income neighborhoods. Additional resources, if massive enough, would probably improve educational achievement. The political possibility of finding such resources for central city education is, at the best, uncertain."

In those dispassionate sentences, Alan K. Campbell, professor of political science and director of the metropolitan studies program at Syracuse University, sums up some of the early findings of a series of Carnegie-supported studies of large city school systems. Economists and political scientists are looking at the policies which emerge from school politics and at the ways in which the decisions which produce these policies are made—by whom, how, why, and in what environments.

Professor Campbell gave some of the findings in a paper delivered last summer at Stanford University's Cubberley Conference (copies are *not* available, so please do not request them; however, a list of books and journal articles which are forthcoming from the study will be found at the close of this article). He presented an array of facts, figures, and analyses which add up to a totally disheartening picture of the present efforts and future prospects for financing education in American cities. It is not merely that those that need it most—the city schools —are getting least. That was already known, though how badly their situation has deteriorated just recently relative to the suburbs was not known. It is the portents for the future that are alarming. For if the interested groups in the cities, including the boards of education, perform in the future as they have up to now, it appears unlikely that there will be effective voices demanding the educational resources the cities

---

* "The Rich Get Richer & the Poor Get Poorer . . . Schools," *Carnegie Quarterly*, XIV, No. 4 (Fall, 1966), 1-3. Reprinted by permission.

so desperately require. One may ask: *"Who speaks for the city schools?"*

As recently as 1957, annual educational expenditures per pupil in 35 of the largest metropolitan areas were roughly equal in the cities and their suburbs. By 1962, the suburbs were spending, on the average, $145 more per pupil than the central cities. This differential is primarily a reflection of the fact that during those years the disparity in wealth between cities and suburbs was growing.

The shocker, however, is that state aid to the schools, which one might think would be designed to redress this imbalance somewhat, discriminates *against* the cities. On the average, the suburbs receive $40 more in state aid per pupil than the cities.

Some of the federal aid to education (which came too late to be included in the 1962 statistics) is, of course, aimed directly at disadvantaged areas. But while the federal programs are always referred to as "massive," and while one and a quarter billion dollars per year are a lot of dollars, when they are spread over fifty states, for rural as well as city areas, the impact on any one city—or any one school—is not massive at all.

Whatever the sources of the money, local, state, or federal, the point is that the nation is devoting many more resources to educating suburban children than city children. Or to put it another way, it is spending much more money to educate the children of the well-off than the children of the poor. And every shred of available evidence points to the conclusion that the educational needs of poor children are far greater than those of affluent children. By any measure one wants to use—pupil performance on tests, dropout rate, proportion of students going on to higher education—the output of the schools in the depressed areas of the cities is very much poorer than that of the suburbs. There is little reason to believe that even to equalize treatment would begin to close the gap. To achieve the substance rather than merely the theoretical form of equal educational opportunity requires the application of unequal resources: more rather than less to the students from poor homes.

That knowledge is, of course, what underlies the idea of compensatory education being pushed by the federal government and to a much lesser extent by a very few of the states. The trouble thus far with compensatory education, however, is not the idea but the few funds allocated to it. They are spread so far and so thin that only barely perceptible improvements, by and large, can be made. And barely perceptible improvements have barely perceptible effects on pupil performance.

It does little good to reduce class size from, say, .6 to 30.8 (like the average American family, the average American classroom seems always to contain a number of whole children plus a fraction of a child), or to raise expenditures for pupil supplies from $7.25 to $8.50, or to add one social worker to the staff of a slum high school. The evidence already in on compensatory education tends to prove this.

There is scattered evidence, however, from the few places where it has been tried, that dramatic efforts—placing enormous concentration on the teaching of reading, for example, in very small classes—have dramatic effects. Though this evidence is not conclusive because there is not enough of it, it does suggest that some of the seemingly intractable educational problems of the cities' schools would yield before the infusion of massive resources.

The question is where to find them or, more accurately, how to get them for the city schools. For the money is not hidden, after all. A great deal of it is spent in this country every day, for education and for housing, freeways, war, national parks, liquor, cosmetics, advertising, and a lot of other things. It is a question of the allocation of money, which means the establishing of priorities. That is primarily a political process, and it is heavily influenced by the clarity, vigor, and power with which spokesmen for various interests press their claims.

In education, the decision-making unit at the local level, and the principal spokesman for the schools, is the board of education. Various members of the Syracuse group are making case studies of the role of the school boards in several cities, with particular emphasis on Atlanta, Boston, Chicago, New York, and San Francisco. In the cities studied—and though there may be some striking exceptions, the rule appears to hold for most cities—the boards of education have proved to be more tax-conscious than expenditure-conscious. They have tended to tailor demands to what they calculated the tax traffic would bear rather than to hammer home the needs of the schools and the expenditure levels that would be necessary to meet them.

Since taxpayers' groups have many spokesmen and school children,

323

especially poor ones, have few, one might have expected the boards of education to have attempted more in the way of cajoling, pleading, and demanding. This line of reasoning, however, ignores the composition of most school boards. At any rate, though boards of education might have accomplished much more if they had tried harder in the days when the cities were affluent, the question is now almost academic. Most of the big cities are strapped financially, and although some could raise more locally if they would, it is clear that the kind of money that is needed simply cannot be raised by the cities from local sources alone. Much of it will have to come from increased state and federal aid.

Here the passive role of the school boards is much less easy to understand. If they despair of the possibility of getting adequate tax money at home, it is hard to fathom why they have not been leading the fight for external aid, but they have not. So far, the Campbell group concludes, the boards of education have played a relatively minor role, and "there is no evidence in the studies we have undertaken to indicate that this role is going to undergo any drastic change."

Even if it did, it is obvious that strong and active school boards alone could not bring sufficient pressure to bear on behalf of increased aid to the cities. But a coalition of school board members plus local business leaders, various civic groups, school administrators, and teachers' organizations might be able to.

"No such coalition now exists," Campbell says, though there are signs in some cities that business leaders are becoming increasingly concerned about the quality of education. As their concern grows, perhaps they will serve as rallying points for strong coalitions to speak for the cities' schools.

In the last few years, teachers have become much more militant, and at the present time it seems they are guided much more by what they are against *than what they are* for. *What they are* for *is most often expressed in terms of hours, working conditions, teacher-pupil ratio, and salary. In the following excerpt, the authors make the plea that teachers take advantage of their present victories to advance the general cause of education, and thereby, society.*

THE ROLE OF THE TEACHER IN COMMUNITY POWER
August Kerber and Wilfred Smith

The roles of education and the teacher in this modern welter of power amorality is clear. The great beast of power must be harnessed and brought to the plow. We must avoid the concept that "politics is dirty business." We must not merely adapt to the state; rather, we must shape it. This does not mean that we should all become governors. We must educate our fellows that government requires intelligent followers.

Our educational institution should primarily generate and mediate our values. The individuals who express themselves in the educational institutions must become more free. The institutions which now dominate must become cooperative, meaning that decisions of power must be made with mutual planning and agreement. We need free schools, churches, and political parties. But free and cooperating institutions are not enough. A synthesizing principle, a method of resolving the great issues by preeminent and inclusive power, is needed. This power is necessarily sourced in and legitimized by the state. The morality of power wielding in the state is constantly a question. In the democratic society, we are dedicated to the principle that the source is with greatest morality placed in the whole people, and the acts of expression by specialized government agencies must be constantly overseen and subject to revision.

In this process, education is the handmaiden of the state. Education serves in a mediate but all-important capacity, for it furnishes the ideational content whereby the many problems of the state may be solved.

We should set out to acquire power and use it for the purpose of strengthening the state and the institution of education. We need first the recognition of reality: *Power yields only to power*. We cannot fight if we do not exist. So we must seize the opportunity to fight now with what we have. We must fight to acquire more power to integrate amoral institutions of our time into a moral realm under the state. As men learn to practice power in moral ways, education must continue to teach them to desire efficient social mechanisms which will permit the resolution of issues without resorting to conflict and the abuse of power.

The teacher in the classroom, momentarily insulated in a world of his own, can choose to believe that he is absolutely free under the conditions given him to implant knowledge in the minds of his charges. Or he can be cognizant of his position in a realistic way as one of a certain place in the community, which is subject to identifiable manipulations of power.

Community groups seek to influence schools in a variety of ways. They may be concerned with curriculum in terms of the content, or in goals that are being taught. The curriculum of a given school is always under some kind of revision, since it is determined in content and approach by the community and influenced by many organized groups within the society. Many of these groups become quite articulate with respect to educational policy.

Pressures are exerted by formal organizations during the public hearings of the board of education, where the table pounders who desire to block educational expenditures appear as regularly as the grass each spring. The clearest observation of the toll of education in America comes with viewing it negatively—in seeing what the educators will not do in change and leadership, and what they will do in acquiescence to the forces of the community. Often these community forces are embarrassingly small in number, and of hopeless reactionary stamp. Public hearings of the school, therefore, can hardly be expected to be demonstrative of leadership.

The school, then, is subject to the forces which emerge out of organized groups, many of whom represent business and corporations of the communities spurred to action in the interest of lowered costs. Also there are other groups concerned with curriculum, structural practices, etc. The advent of the Soviet space hardware has emphasized the need for scientific and technical training. Rocketry has caused the

American public to exert pressures on the school to increase its program in the field of science education. The school is therefore amenable to having its policies shaped by the community, not by professional educators.

Primarily sectarian or narrow in nature, other groups, while under the guise of school improvement, are actually interested in modifying and changing school procedures and practices in accordance with their rather narrow, provincial interests. Occasionally, these groups do tend to improve the educational system. Here the task of the teaching profession becomes one of differentiating between the motivations of group action. This calls for a rather continuous appraisal and critical analysis on the part of the teachers and administrators and also for a rather skillful kind of public-relations program maintaining the integrity of the educational program on the one hand, and acknowledgment of positive and constructive community criticism on the other.

Power must be subjected to the searching light of professional analysis. Once we are cognizant of the nature of power, and that this power yields only to power, the dream of the future can be actualized. Whether the teaching profession likes it or not, we must strengthen the relationship between the schools and the community. However, teachers generally owe a loyalty to a broader community than the local community and, therefore, act as interpreters of the larger culture to the more provincial demands of the immediate community.

Leadership Role of the Teacher in the Community

Teachers must have a concept of these matters so that they will know where to yield and where to stand with respect to certain suggestions made by community groups. The procedures and techniques utilized by teachers and administrators will obviously vary from community to community, but there is no substitute for a fundamental understanding of the problems and of community power structure if they are to operate intelligently in this field of forces.

Since the tradition is well settled that local control is exercised by boards of education, the school administrator, who is appointed by the board, recognizes that if he is to achieve a successful record and maintain a satisfactory school program, he must have wide areas of agreement with its members. The lot of the administrator, caught in the middle between the professional community on the one hand and lay community on the other, may be one of reconciling interests and differences. Many administrators, however, desiring to effectuate changes in the school curriculum, believe that an educational campaign aimed at the local board member is, perhaps, the major item of importance in getting any such movement off the ground.

The emergence of more militant professional organizations has brought significant changes in the power relationship between teachers and school boards. The death knell has sounded the passing of an era in which the teacher abstained from political activity and was destined to be a passive factor in the political-social life in the community. Today, teachers have secured significant modifications in school program, financial support, and educational objectives through effective group action in such a manner as to change or transform the American community-school relationships. The leadership of the teacher in the community has become a definite factor in school policy.

In the immediate future, the problem of the teachers is to make professionalism constructive for education. The great gains teachers have made in becoming recognized as legitimate partners in the power decisions relating to education can be continued toward greater growth, or on the other hand may be stultified or reversed. The great, recognized need for education can enable educators to take over the obvious leadership for which they only are fitted, or they can kill the goose that lays the golden eggs by short-sighted selfish demands. Demands related only to salaries and conditions in the framework of educational practice and organization 50 years behind time will only serve to hasten the loss of the war after winning the battle. What is needed is creative leadership from within the group, based on sound modern principles and experimentalism, so that growth accelerates growth in ways that all can understand and profit by.

The long-term goal of education relates to values, with the pragmatic or actual effects of those values in society. Education is that part of human activity which synthesizes our efforts with clear purposes. That purpose, our most enlightened philosophy tells us, is to follow the democratic ethic with intelligence guided by proven method. At the present time, we are prey to antidemocratic forces abroad and at home. The establishment—the power wielders of our society—will of course

328

resist dissolution, as their vested interests uphold institutionalized ways to maintain themselves. Narrow, bigoted, sectarian, and racist biases will maintain themselves as they have always done. The question of meting out rewards and rebuffs will always have fuzzy answers. But if our society is to progress along lines of the ideology of democracy, our best hope of continued progress will be in continuing to make education and life grow together, from age to age more gloriously.

This means that education in the future must increase in quantity and quality. It must be an inextricable part of life from womb-to-tomb. It must be the steersman, on this bank and shoal of time, through troubled waters, with the courage to risk all on the worth of principles, with hope of gain of new life in which those principles are clearer, stronger, and imbued with the quality of experience that makes life meaningful.

Editors' Summary

Cities change gradually and are very seldom radically remade, although many should be. No technological obstacles stand in the way of rebuilding a city from the ground up, but there always remains the difficulty of getting people to agree to such a program. Most often the changes come piecemeal, with better homes, stores, roads, parks, and utilities, and more carefully, esthetically planned communities in the suburbs. In this type of change "we stand on the rubbish heap of our ancestors," and it is a moot question if perhaps a few "clean" atomic bombs might not accelerate progress. The educational system of today is a reservoir of ancient ills combined with modern innovations, and the basic problem is whether to change this system bit by bit or by a concerted and complete rebuilding.

The modern situation of school and society, and of the school's relations with society is confused and ambivalent. One thing is certain—change has occurred. If the school attempts to "adjust" to these changes by "relating with the community" in the sense of giving the local taxing unit what they want, the school has lost the opportunity for leadership by default. It will be operating on the basis of making do by improvisation—like using haywire on a machine that is outmoded. If the school *will help the general society to better assess itself, giving it greater unity and feeling of purpose, the school will be doing both itself and society a service. The more this leadership is asserted, the greater would strength accrue to the educational institution.*

The old community, the old spirit of communalism is gone. Instead of the town hall of yesterday, we now have megalopolises that stretch from Boston to Washington, D.C., and an urbanized state of mind that reaches everywhere. We may beat the drums and engage in fanfare, but we cannot bring back the corpse of the old community. What then? We need to give our students an orientation to living in one world in which all mankind shares a common fate. The school must be integrated and organized on state, national, and world lines, and in step with the tempo, structure, and actualities of the modern scene.

The modern reality is of swift-moving, highly specialized groups that have complicated, specialized dealings with each other and with individuals, but at the same time must address themselves to universals which modern communications and ideologies have formed.

All this means to the teacher that he is now living in a time when groups, blocs, pressures, propaganda, and methods of organizing are part of the essence. To say that he is not interested merely means that he is ignorant and willing to be used as a foil by those who are aware of the realities. One can no more escape the group process than the air we breathe. The intelligent thing, therefore, is to accept the reality fully. Teachers should become a bloc and work with other blocs in making the more complicated democracy we live in, work.

The enemies of education are riding high, wide, and handsome now. The teachers, despite some organization, are a mass, an aggregation of ineffective individuals who are without weapons or experience in attack. If teachers were more aggressive as a group they would be more effective in making the educational institution truly a source of leadership in the modern democracy.

RELATED READINGS

Agger, Robert. "Community Power Structures and Partisanship," *ASR*, August, 1958.

Blau, Peter M. *Exchange and Power in Social Life.* New York: John Wiley and Sons, 1964.

Boulding, K. *The Organizational Revolution*. New York: Harper & Brothers, 1953.

Cahill, Robert S. *The Politics of Education in the Local Community*. Danville, Ill.: The Interstate Printers and Publishers, 1963.

Campbell, Allen K., *Sociology, Politics, and Education Policy: Essays about Decision-Making in Public Education*.

Campbell, Ronald F., Lavern L. Cunningham, and Roderick F. McPhee. *The Organization and Control of American Schools*. Columbus, Ohio: Charles E. Merrill Books, 1963.

Clark, Burton R. *Educating the Expert Society*. San Francisco: Chandler Publishing Co., 1962.

Counts, George S. *Education and American Civilization*. New York: Bureau of Publications; Teachers College, Columbia University, 1952.

Dahl, Robert. "A Critique of the Ruling Elite Model," *Political Science Review*, June, 1958.

Dean, Howard. "The Political Setting of American Education," *The Social Sciences View School Administration* by Donald E. Tape, *et al.* Englewood Cliffs, N.J.: Prentice-Hall, 1965.

Goldrich, Daniel. "Community Power Structures and Partisanship," *ASR*, August, 1958.

Goldstein, Marshall N. "Absentee Ownership and Monolithic Power Structures: Two Questions for Community Studies," *Current Trends in Comparative Community Studies*, ed., B. Swanson. Kansas City, Mo.: Community Studies, Inc., 1962.

Graham, George. *Morals in American Politics*. New York: Random House, 1952.

Hechinger, Fred M. "Who Runs Our Big City Schools," *The Saturday Review*, XLVIII, No. 16, April 17, 1965.

Hunter, Floyd. *Community Power Structure*. Chapel Hill: University of North Carolina Press, 1953.

Jennings, M. Kent. *Community Influentials: The Elites of Atlanta*. Glencoe: The Free Press, 1964.

Kimnbrough, Ralph B. *Political Power and Educational Decision Making*. Chicago: Rand McNally, 1964.

Klapp, Orrin. "Power Structure and Decision-Making in a Mexican Border City," *AJS*, January, 1960.

Kornhauser, A. "Power Relationships and the Role of the Social Scientist," in A. Kornhauser, ed., *Problems of Power in American Democracy*. Detroit: Wayne State University Press.

Lutz, Frank W. "Power Structure Theory and the School Board Decision-Making Process," *Educational Theory*, XV, No. 1, January, 1965.

Lynd, Robert S., and Helen M. *Middletown*. New York: Harcourt, Brace & Co., 1929.
———. *Middletown in Transition*. New York: Harcourt, Brace & Co., 1937.

MacIver, R. M. *Power Transformed: The Age-Slow Deliverance of the Folk and Now the Potential Deliverance of the Nations from the Rule of Force*. New York: Macmillan Co., 1964.

Mercer, Elaine E. *The American Community*. New York: Random House, 1956.

Mills, C. Wright. *The Power Elite*. New York: Oxford University Press, Inc., 1956.

————. *White Collar*. New York: Oxford University Press, Inc., 1951.

Moeller, Gerald H. "Bureaucracy and Teachers' Sense of Power," *Administrator's Notebook*, XI, No. 3, November, 1962.

Monsen, Joseph R., Jr., and Mark W. Cannon. *The Makers of Public Policy: American Power Groups and Their Ideologies*. New York: McGraw-Hill Book Co., 1965.

Mosca, Gaetano. The Ruling Class. New York: McGraw-Hill Book Co., 1939.

Munger, Frank. *The Education of Minorities: Race, Religion and the Large City School.*

Polsby, Nelson W. "The Sociology of Community Power: A Reassessment," *Social Forces*, March, 1959.

Roettinger, Ruth L. *The Supreme Court and State Police Power: A Study in Federalism*. Washington, D.C.: Public Affairs Press, 1957.

Rosenthal, Alan, *Pedagogues and Power: Teacher Organization in Five Large Cities*, Syracuse University Press, 1967.

Rosenthal, Alan, "The Strength of Teacher Organizations: Factors Influencing Membership in Two Large Cities" (*Sociology of Education*).

Rossi, Peter. "Community Decision-Making," in R. Yong, ed., *Approaches to the Study of Politics*. N.W. University Press, 1958.

Thometz, Carol Estes. *The Decision-Makers: The Power Structure of Dallas*. Dallas: Southern Methodist University Press, 1963.

West, James. *Plainville, USA*. New York: Columbia University Press, 1950.

Wirth, Louis. *Ideas and Ideals as Sources of Power in the Modern World*. New York: Harper & Brothers, 1947.

PART V

FINANCING PUBLIC
EDUCATION

"Consequences are pitiless," wrote George Eliot. When we apply this to the deeds of men—not their words—we have the measure of their values. Men have a way of reacting to the façade of words that society puts up around them. Indeed, most people consider this façade the most important part of the environment. In the main, they are right about this, but it is in this mistaking of the shadow for the substance that brings us our most monstrous errors and human tragedies.

Consider the two statements: "He lived in poverty, but had a good soul, and has gone to his just reward," and "He was a wealthy man, born with a silver spoon in his mouth, and I don't believe he ever appreciated it." These statements summarized for most people a multitude of facts and have a ring of finality about them. The flight of the owl of Minerva is made, and there is no point in retracting the passage. Strictly speaking, however, thought begins with the examination of some of the particulars, and moves outward, carefully examining all the evidence.

When somebody says, "There is a tendency for the lower classes not to receive the same quality of education as the upper classes," the mind is left a little unsettled because the statement contains an inference that it would be better for the lower classes to have equitable education. To overcome the dissatisfaction created by these words, two main al-

333

ternatives can be used: 1) Effect some action which will change the situation to which the words refer, or 2) Make up some other words which will relieve the malaise created by the original statement.

Finance, the monetary expenditure of people, is of the same nature as deeds. Many words may be used in getting a person to bet on a certain horse, but once he puts his dollar down, the act becomes history. If a number of petitioners come for money, we can give each one of them a story of sympathy which would make the angels weep, but once we give them their pittance—or nothing—the act remains like the granitic furrows of the great stone face.

In this pitiless irrevocability of the movement of gold counters, we can judge the hearts and minds of men. Each man spends according to his scale of values, and this is reflected in the spending of the general public. The priority rating of values as applied to public education is therefore best described by the expenditures people make. The amount allotted to elementary, secondary, and higher education, and the subsequent breakdown of that allotment into parts is the crystallized reflection of the values of the people.

We seem to speak of an apparent inevitability of the financial picture. We speak as if the currents and forces were predetermined, and the public unaffected. The true situation is far more complex. A dollar spent is history, yes, but the effect of that history on man is future history, and this future, we think, is always open to intelligent choices. This leaves the future amenable to our learning, to results based upon our better nature.

We have thus explained why the financing of public schools is a problem of our society. If what we do in money matters is an inevitable result of our values, and school budget information is merely a recitation of success and failure, we would have a very feeble excuse in considering finance an issue. Nor is the amount of heat of debate on the subject prima facie evidence of the significance of the subject. We could argue that the ends and goals underlying the budgets are most important and that finance is an issue in itself.

It is through the discussion of finance that we are able to see each other's values most clearly, calibrate these values, and set up lists of priorities. We learn what our own values are. We find that as we try to clarify and make our values consistent, we are not dealing with fixed variables but a situation of dynamic disequilibrium in which new features enter as we try to set up the problem. We may often be convinced of needs we did not know existed, and we may often convince others of these needs by a careful study of the costs.

Another reason for the study of finance is that money is the mediator of power. Our society is shaped by the use of power. If our end is to have a school system which meets the challenges of the times, we have to have one which is larger, stronger, and furnishes leadership. This will cost money. The British Parliament, controlling the expenditures of the king since the Puritan Revolution, knows the principle that money is the source of power. Money will not by itself make our educational system great, but money is an indispensable necessity to achieving greatness. Therefore, every responsible citizen should understand the financing of schools. Briefly put, the program of finance is an end in itself. If it were merely a means, it would not be an issue. The modern citizen knows that our greatest capital is our youth, and every dollar we spend on them is immediately repaid severalfold, with the premiums continuing into the future.

Why, then, is there so much opposition to financing of schools, and what improved programs are offered? These are the subjects of this section. In the first chapter, we survey federal aid and examine some of the significant and controversial facets of school finance.

XIII

How We Pay for Our Schools

Editors' Comment

"Perfectly good, perfectly true, and perfectly useless," muttered a professor as he cast another paper onto the pile of corrected sophomore essays. The student must obviously pass; he had put together a potpourri of cheery platitudes with which one could not disagree. He was for God, home, mother, Americanism, and being good.

School finance is usually discussed wtih a cataract of platitudes. Those in the public eye feel they are on the safe side by reminding their audience that everything costs money. This supposedly excuses these advice-givers from having ideas about priorities, values, or responsibilities. They feel that they can hide behind the cliché curtain with impunity.

Not so. We can parry and riposte in general terms without getting down to cases, but when we have to raise taxes and allocate funds, our values and priorities come out as clearly as our "inwards" on the X-ray screen. At this level of salaries and costs we have to show what we believe, in one of the most sincere ways we can in our civilization—by how much we are willing to pay for what we want.

The following series of articles is generally kind toward education. Various proposals and suggestions are made about the expenditure of

336

public monies, and with most of the ideas we can agree. However, at the level where we prepare checks and make contracts, we are perforce committed to a narrower view. We have to take the educational plant as given and try to make the best of it. We talk about the cheapness, in the long run, of ceramic tile in the lavatories. We advocate higher teachers' salaries, better buildings, and scholarships. These are valuable aims but do not come to grips with the basic problems of education.

It will be noticed that most educators in talking about finance deal very specifically with current costs and expenditures. This of course is "practical," and we all are concerned about the housekeeping job. When they talk of bigger proposals, of expansion of schools, curricula, government financing, they take a tone of muscle-bound, benign flaccidity, designed to please all, offend none, and leave everyone unsure about what is to be done, or whether one's particular pocket nerve is to be hit.

We are inclined to think that the level of discourse directed to financing of schools is not that of resolution. To resolve financial issues, we must have bold and clear statements of the ends implicated in education. After reading many articles on finance of education, we are inclined to think that most financiers do not take a very comprehensive or foresighted view about education. They mingle aims popularly agreed upon with pet schemes for improvement. Although they offend no one, neither will they unloose many purse strings.

The mechanism and current status of state-local school finance are explained in the following article. Clayton Hutchins explains that finance is the result of popular will expressed through the pattern of the local board of education. Although the article is titled "Preferred Sources," Hutchins does not make judgments on the advisability of more or less federal, state, or local taxes, or say whether property taxes are better than other sources of revenue. No statement is made concerning the autonomy of boards on finances or the necessity of democratic approval for financial decisions.

SCHOOL REVENUE: PREFERRED SOURCES
Clayton D. Hutchins*

School support patterns in the United States are determined by the people as they choose among the various taxes commonly used for financing the schools and as they decide on the proportions to be supplied by local and State taxation. Citizens express their preferences directly through voting in local elections and through decisions of their elected representatives serving on boards of education and in the State legislatures.

Through these support patterns, about $12 billion, or approximately 3 percent, of all personal income, was made available for public education during the 1957-58 school year. Estimates indicate that local sources provided 55 percent of the total revenues; State sources, 41 percent; and the Federal Government, 4 percent.

The accompanying [table] reports the proportions of non-Federal school revenues derived from property taxes and from other sources and the proportions derived from local and State sources for each State. States are arranged according to the proportion of school funds derived from property taxes.

States listed first in the [table] rely chiefly on local property taxes, while those listed later rely chiefly on State sources for their school revenues. State funds come chiefly from the State sales and income taxes and from the State licensing functions as authorized by State legislatures.

Local Revenue

School revenues represented by the percentages . . . to the left side of the [table] may be regarded as compromises within the approximately 48,000 local school administrative units of the Nation. For each unit, the local board of education approves a school budget. Many participating in this approval want improved educational services and higher budget allowances. Some resist immediate improvements, think-

* Clayton D. Hutchins, "School Revenue: Preferred Sources," *School Life*, XLII, No. 3 (November, 1959), 17-19. Reprinted by permission of the Department of Health, Education, and Welfare, Office of Education.

Non-Federal school revenue from property taxes and other sources, derived from local and State levels, 1957-58

	Percent from property taxes			Percent from other sources		
	Total	*Local*	*State*	*Total*	*Local*	*State*
48 States & D.C.	54.6	53.8	.8	45.4	3.9	41.5
Nebraska	91.3	89.3	2.0	8.7	3.6	5.1
Iowa	85.5	85.5	0	14.5	.9	13.6
New Hampshire	84.6	84.0	.6	15.4	6.1	9.3
South Dakota	81.4	81.4	0	18.6	6.8	11.8
Wisconsin	78.2	78.2	0	21.8	0	21.8
Kansas	77.7	77.7	0	22.3	1.2	21.1
Colorado	74.5	74.5	0	25.5	1.6	23.9
Montana	72.9	72.9	0	27.1	2.3	24.8
Massachusetts	72.4	72.4	0	27.6	0	27.6
Connecticut	72.2	72.2	0	27.8	0	27.8
New Jersey	72.0	72.0	0	28.0	1.4	26.6
Rhode Island	71.3	71.3	0	28.7	2.1	26.6
Indiana	70.1	67.1	3.0	29.9	.6	29.3
Illinois	70.0	70.0	0	30.0	0	30.0
Arizona	70.0	64.5	5.5	30.0	1.8	28.2
Oregon	69.7	69.7	0	30.3	0	30.3
Idaho	68.0	68.0	0	32.0	1.9	30.1
Ohio	67.8	67.8	0	32.2	.9	31.3
Maine	67.3	66.9	.4	32.7	1.2	31.5
North Dakota	67.2	66.7	.5	32.8	0	32.8
Wyoming	66.9	46.2	20.7	33.1	6.7	26.4
Vermont	66.0	66.0	0	34.0	0	34.0
Virginia	59.8	59.8	0	40.2	0	40.2
New York	58.7	58.7	0	41.3	1.1	40.2
California	58.6	58.6	0	41.4	1.0	40.4
Missouri	55.4	55.0	.4	44.6	10.8	33.8
Minnesota	55.2	53.1	2.1	44.8	3.1	41.7
Utah	54.4	50.4	4.0	45.6	4.4	41.2
Nevada	51.9	46.9	5.0	48.1	1.8	46.3
Oklahoma	51.2	51.2	0	48.8	20.2	28.6
Texas	51.0	42.9	8.1	49.0	1.9	47.1
Michigan	50.7	50.7	0	49.3	0	49.3
Maryland	48.3	48.3	0	51.7	15.8	35.9

ing of other urgent public services and the taxes required to finance them. In each community, the school budget adopted represents the will of the majority under the circumstances—higher than some would support and lower than others believe advisable—and local taxes are then levied on the assessed value of all taxable property to supply public funds for the budget.

Non-Federal school revenue from property taxes and other sources, derived from local and State levels, 1957-58 (Cont.)

	Percent from property taxes			Percent from other sources		
	Total	Local	State	Total	Local	State
Arkansas	44.8	44.8	0	55.2	0	55.2
D.C.	40.8	40.8	0	59.2	59.2	0
Pennsylvania	37.9	37.9	0	62.1	12.7	49.4
West Virginia	37.3	37.3	0	62.7	1.3	61.4
Kentucky	36.3	36.3	0	63.7	12.9	50.8
Florida	35.2	35.2	0	64.8	2.0	62.8
Mississippi	34.1	34.1	0	65.9	6.9	59.0
Tennessee	28.4	28.4	0	71.6	5.5	66.1
South Carolina	27.7	27.7	0	72.3	.5	71.8
Louisiana	25.0	21.7	3.3	75.0	6.0	69.0
Georgia	24.0	24.0	0	76.0	0	76.0
Alabama	22.0	17.6	4.4	78.0	4.9	73.1
Washington	20.0	19.9	.1	80.0	28.1	51.9
North Carolina	18.2	18.2	0	81.8	9.5	72.3
New Mexico	14.9	14.0	.9	85.1	.1	85.0
Delaware	5.2	5.2	0	94.8	0	94.8
Outlying Parts of the U.S.	10.9	10.9	0	89.1	3.5	85.6
Hawaii	10.0	10.0	0	90.0	9.6	80.4
Alaska	8.1	8.1	0	91.9	3.9	88.0
American Samoa	1.0	1.0	0	99.0	99.0	0
Guam	0	0	0	100.0	100.0	0
Puerto Rico	0	0	0	100.0	0	100.0
Virgin Islands	0	0	0	100.0	100.0	0

In levying taxes for schools, boards of education operate within certain legal authorizations and limitations. These boards usually have the authority to levy up to a stated limit without electoral approval. If the recommended budget requires additional revenues, the proposal to levy additional taxes beyond the rate limitations may be submitted to the voters. If the proposal is disapproved, the school budget must be reconsidered and a reduced budget proposing the expenditure of no more than the total revenues that apparently will be available is then accepted. If the extra levy is approved at the election, each taxpayer will be required to contribute a larger amount to support the recommended budget.

No estimates are available on the amount of local taxes for schools which are levied by the board "within" its taxing limitations or authorizations and those which are authorized by vote of the people "outside" such restrictions. However, it is presumed that a substantial proportion, a third, for example, of these funds becomes available through frequent references to the ballot and that the voted revenues supplement in a substantial measure the amounts obtained by board action alone, within existing taxation limitations. Practices throughout the United States vary widely on questions of board and voter approval. In some States no proposals to approve school fund levies are submitted to vote, and, in other States, all levies for school revenue are approved by vote of the people.

State Revenue

Similarly, funds represented by the percentages to the right side of the [table] represent the majority opinion of the taxpayers of the State. State funds are appropriated by the State legislatures for distribution to the local school administrative units. Here, also, the amount allotted may be regarded as the result of many compromises. The State legislature considers amounts to be appropriated, noting opinions and reasons advanced by those wanting improvements in the program of the public schools and also by those resisting larger State appropriations for schools.

Final decisions of the legislatures to provide funds for the 1957-58 school year are represented by the State percentages in the chart. States listed early in the chart make relatively small appropriations for schools and depend on local boards of education to levy local taxes for school support, while States listed later provide larger proportions of the school funds from State sources and thereby relieve the local school administrative units of supplying the major proportion of the school support funds.

Freedom of choice on these public questions accounts for the variation in prevailing practices. Requests for funds to finance the school programs are not made to an outside gratuitous entity. Instead, the people in the school districts, the boards of education, and the State legislatures consider the financial requirements of the program they desire and decide on the extent that they will provide their own funds for their public services. This kind of financing has developed the public school systems of the United States, and these school systems have served the communities, the States, and the Nation through the further development of human resources.

State funds for 1957-58 were allotted to the schools through the operation of 411 separate distributions, representing an average of more than 8 school funds to a State. Some of the funds are for the general program of education and may be expended according to the judgment of the local school officials, while other funds are for special purposes and must be expended for the educational purposes specifically designated by the State legislators.

Balanced Support

A partnership relationship between local school administrative units and the States for the support of public schools is apparent in the [table]. Varying practices, exhibited by the [table], in methods of financing the schools are to be expected. Degrees of local and State concern for financing education and interests in financing other public services have important influences. Furthermore, the kind and vigor of the economy affect decisions on the extent to which State funds should finance education and the extent to which it is appropriate to rely on local tax sources.

An economist rather than an educator has penetrated most deeply into the implications of financing public education. He points out that the market is the mechanism which allocates the investment in material capital to the various claimants, but that the formation of skilled workers is in the public domain. Though engineers and scientists may yield a higher return in productivity than the material outlay, a cultural lag has upheld the notion of education as a consumer investment.

Though stated in the depersonalized terms of capital and poverty per se, John Galbraith upholds one of our major themes—that education should be a formative institution. In his terms, he says that education can serve as the means by which capital, land, and labor become more productive and continue to increase in productivity.

EDUCATION IS CAPITAL
John Kenneth Galbraith*

We now come to the nub of the problem. Investment in material capital is distributed to the various claimant industries by the market. If earnings are high (at the margin) in the oil industry and low in the textile business, it is to the oil industry that capital will flow. This allocation by the market works, it would appear, with tolerable efficiency. Among the recognized crimes of economics, any interference with the "free flow" of capital has a very high standing.

But while this flow operates as between different material claimants on investment funds, it operates only with manifest uncertainty and inefficiency as between material and personal capital. Nearly all of the investment in individuals is in the public domain. And virtually all of it is outside the market system. It is the state which, through primary and secondary schools, and through the colleges and universities, makes the largest investment in individuals. And where, as in the case of private colleges and universities, the state is not directly involved, the amount of the investment is not directly related to the eventual pay-out in production. Investment in refineries being higher than in textile

* John Kenneth Galbraith, *The Affluent Society* (Boston, 1958), 177-78, 330-32. Reprinted by permission of Houghton Mifflin Company, Boston 7, Massachusetts.

mills, the refineries will draw investment funds. But engineers to design the refineries may be even more important—in effect yield a higher return. And the highest return of all may come from the scientist who makes a marked improvement in the refining process. These are not imaginative possibilities but common probabilities. Yet the high return to scientific and technical training does not cause the funds to move from material capital to such investment. There is no likely flow from the building of the refineries to the education of the scientists. Here, at the most critical point in the vaunted process of investment resource allocation, is an impediment of towering importance. Characteristically, however, it has received little comment. It is not, like the tariff or monopoly, one of the classic barriers to capital movement. Hence it did not get a foothold in economics in the last century and, accordingly, under the intellectual grandfather clause which has such sway in the science it has no real standing now.

There can be no question of the importance of the impediment. Investment in individuals is in the public domain; this investment has become increasingly essential with the advance of science and technology; and there is no machinery for automatically allocating resources as between material and human investment. But this is not all. As we have seen in earlier chapters, there is active discrimination against the investment in the public domain and hence in any part of it. The investment in the refinery is an unmitigated good. It adds to our stock of wealth. It is categorical achievement. But the training of the scientists and engineers who will run the refinery, improve its economic efficiency, and possibly in the end replace it with something better is not a categorical good. The money so invested is not regarded with approval. On the contrary, it is widely regarded as a burden. Many will judge the magnitude of the achievement in this area by the smallness of the investment. Others will hold this investment in abeyance while arguing the ancient issue of equality. So incredible is the provision for such investment that a considerable part will have to be begged. Even the prestige of the word investment itself is not regularly accorded to these outlays. A century ago, when educational outlays were not intimately related to production, men sensibly confined the word investment to the increases in capital which brought a later increase in product. Education was a consumer outlay. The popular usage has never been revised.[1]

Could it be legally arranged that youngsters were sorted out at an early age, possibly by their test score in mathematics, and the promising then be indentured for life to a particular corporation, the flow of investment into human development might soon be placed on a rough parity with that into material capital. Firms would perceive the need for investing in their scientific and engineering stock much as major league baseball clubs have learned the wisdom of investing in their farm teams. Under ideal arrangements any surplus talent could be marketed. The cost of unsuccessfully trying to educate the inevitable errors of selection would either be written off or partially retrieved by using the individuals as salesmen. Under such a system, which as noted would unfortunately involve the elimination of the liberty of the individuals in question, it is fairly certain that investment in human beings would rise and at a rapid rate.

But so long as free choice remains, such investment must remain largely a public function. The individual, since he is only at the beginning of earning power, cannot himself make any appreciable part of the investment. Whether his parents can and will be willing to do so is a highly accidental matter. His future employer can hardly be expected to invest in an asset that may materialize in the plant of a competitor or another industry. At most he will, as now, distribute scholarships and fellowships in the hope of ultimately influencing the choice of those in whom the investment is nearly complete. This has no appreciable effect on the total of the investment in people. It is a scalping operation. It does, however, suggest the store which is set by the resulting assets.

.   .   .   .

The first and strategic step in an attack on poverty is to see that it is no longer self-perpetuating. This means insuring that the investment in children from families presently afflicted be as little below

[1] Since this was written and under the impact of Soviet scientific achievements there has been considerable discussion of our lag in *investment* in scientific education. However, this is being treated as a kind of aberration, and not as a fundamental flaw in our machinery of resource allocation.

normal as possible. If the children of poor families have first-rate schools and school attendance is properly enforced; if the children, though badly fed at home, are well nourished at school; if the community has sound health services, and the physical well-being of the children is vigilantly watched; if there is opportunity for advanced education for those who qualify regardless of means; and if, especially in the case of urban communities, law and order are well enforced and recreation is adequate—then there is a very good chance that the children of the very poor will come to maturity without grave disadvantage. In the case of insular poverty this remedy requires that the services of the community be assisted from outside. Poverty is self-perpetuating because the poorest communities are poorest in the services which would eliminate it. To eliminate poverty efficiently we should invest more than proportionately in the children of the poor community. It is there that high-quality schools, strong health services, special provision for nutrition and recreation are most needed to compensate for the very low investment which families are able to make in their own offspring.

The effect of education and related investment in individuals is to enable them either to contend more effectively with their environment, or to escape it and take up life elsewhere on more or less equal terms with others. The role of education as an antidote to the homing instinct which crowds people into the area of inadequate opportunity and frustration is also clear. However, in the strategy of the attack on insular poverty a place remains for an attack on the frustration of the environment itself. This is particularly clear in the case of the slum. Slum clearance and expansion of low and middle income housing removes a comprehensive set of frustrations and greatly widens opportunity. There is a roughly parallel opportunity in the rural slum. By identifying a land use which is consistent with a satisfactory standard of living, and by assisting with the necessary reorganization of land and capital, public authority can help individuals to surmount frustrations to which they are now subject. The process promises to be expensive and also time-consuming. But the question is less one of feasibility than of will.

Nor is case poverty in the contemporary generation wholly intransigent. Much can be done to treat those characteristics which cause people to reject or be rejected by the modern industrial society. Educational deficiencies can be overcome. Mental deficiencies can be treated.

Physical handicaps can be remedied. The limiting factor is not knowledge of what can be done. Overwhelmingly it is our failure to invest in people.

In schools, as in shoes, underwear, ships, and sealing wax, you get what you pay for. Probably the most expensive school to run, year after year, would be a tent; a well-designed school of granite would be about the cheapest. In the next selection, Martin Gross tells why, with many illustrations.

BARGAIN-BASEMENT EDUCATION IS NO BARGAIN
Martin Gross*

Parents in the expanding suburbs of Colorado Springs, Colorado, went to the polls early this year and rejected a proposed new junior high school, amid heated charges that it was an "elaborate memorial" that was "too expensive to build."

"The truth," says a local physician who resigned from the school board over the controversy, "is that it was a modern building with labs and a gym—yet it would only cost $13 a square foot, which is average for our area. But opponents distorted the facts so much that we could never catch up with the real truth."

In prosperous, suburban Mount Vernon, New York, a proposal to replace two nearly half-century-old high schools was voted down amid charges that plans called for "plush Cadillac jobs."

In Phoenix, Arizona, a group of citizens defeated a school bond issue by charging that the proposed new $2,500,000 school for 2,000 students—a relatively inexpensive building that utilized the outdoors for an auditorium—was "too fancy." The defeat meant that students in two high schools will have to attend school on the stagger system from 7:30 A.M. until 5:00 P.M.

The startling fact that emerges from these instances is that while the American public has been fighting an eloquent verbal battle for better education in the post-Sputnik era, there has been a tremendous trend

---

* Martin Gross, "Bargain-Basement Education Is No Bargain," *Coronet*, XLIV, No. 6 (October, 1958), 83-89. Copyright by Esquire, Inc. Reprinted by permission.

toward cut-rate education that is endangering the quality of our public school programs.

Throughout the nation, parents have been duped by a strong anti-tax, anti-public-education group who have deceptively, but effectively, been attacking badly needed new schools and modern educational facilities—from auditoriums to audio-visual aids—as "frills" that are "squandering" the taxpayer's money on "elaborate educational castles."

In fact, school communities have defeated more bonds for new schools this year than ever before in recent history. In school elections last May, parents rejected 33 percent of new school proposals—twice as many as in 1957. In the first five months of this year, $173,000,000 for needed schools was defeated at the polls.

"There have been charges of extravagance, but actually economy in school building is unmatched," says C. C. Trillingham of Los Angeles, president of the American Association of School Administrators. "While general construction costs have increased 275 percent during the past 20 years, school buildings have gone up only 150 percent.

"Expensive decorations have been replaced by modern buildings and functional materials. Classroom ceilings have been lowered and corridor space reduced. If there were 'frills,' they were in older buildings with their towers, gables, and parapets."

The new "economy" drive has hit hardest in areas where new schools are needed most. In Mechanicville, an upstate New York industrial town, sorely needed schools were blocked recently by a spacious "economy" argument circulated in a last-minute anonymous letter.

Two of Mechanicville's elementary schools are antiquated Victorian buildings dating back to the 1890s. They are fire hazards, whose roofs often leak. Squinting children study by dull, dim lighting—less than one third normal. There are no auditoriums, books are stacked in the hallway as a makeshift "library." Children must walk down to the basement to reach student toilets. The "gyms" are a converted classroom in one school and a make-do cellar space in another.

"We can't have a proper program in these buildings," says School Superintendent Michael T. Griffin. "We proposed a new 21-room school with average facilities including a library and a combined cafeteria-auditorium. It wasn't a fancy building but some critics called it a 'palace.' One man even said: 'Why do they need a kitchen? When I went to school there, we carried our lunches in paper bags.' "

. . . Can dollars-and-cents economies be made, then, that will *not* jeopardize a school? Definitely, yes.

One of the most important is the consolidation of school districts to eliminate overhead waste and uneconomical small schools. In 1953, there were 77,000 school districts, which have been consolidated to 50,000. However, 25,000 would be even more economical.

Borrowing schoolhouse construction money at good rates can save more than cut-back in facilities. In 1957, the average school-bond interest rate was 4 percent, double that of 1950. In many cases this increased building costs by 30 percent.

A possible solution is State Bonding Authorities such as one proposed by New York. However, one administrator, Howard McEachen of Merriam, Kansas, took matters into his own hands recently. He traveled to Wall Street and successfully convinced financiers that his district's financial record had earned it a lower interest rate. "He saved the taxpayers more money with that one trip than I have in years," says the district's architect.

The economy of entirely prefabricated schools is debated, but experts agree on the value of "modular" or stock parts. In Liberty, Texas, architect Bill Caudill designed a ten-room elementary school with beams of two sizes instead of the usual dozens, and one stock column instead of a half dozen. The school's steel costs were almost 40 percent less, and the school won nationwide recognition, architecturally and educationally.

The intelligent *early* purchase of land for schools is a vital economy. Two towns, one that planned and one that waited, had exactly opposite experiences. Charlotte, North Carolina, started buying land before World War II and recently sold a parcel they could not use at a 300 percent profit. Woodbridge, New Jersey, a rapidly expanding suburb, sold town-owned land to developers ten years ago and is now buying it back for school sites at ten times the price. "And we're taking what's left over," says a disgruntled citizen.

Intelligent economies will undoubtedly help pay our education bill. Meanwhile, it is vital to understand the difference between a supposed

349

"plush palace" and an efficient, attractive school properly equipped to teach our children. It may help defeat the dangerous fallacy of bargain-basement education—as it did in Schenectady, New York. . . . [In Schenectady, the author goes on to say, public opposition to a "dream" high school of $5,500,000 was overcome by a citizens' committee who made a spirited campaign to win a voting proposal on the school by a 684 margin in a city of 100,000.]

* * *

American Education (1966-1967)

About 60 million Americans are in the nation's educational enterprise as students, teachers, or administrators. Important figures are given here:

The Institutions

Elementary	93,000
Secondary	31,000
Universities, Colleges, and Junior Colleges	2,168
Total	126,168

The Learners

Pupils in Elementary Schools
(Kindergarten through grade 8)

Public Schools	31,200,000
Non-Public (Private and Parochial)	5,400,000
Total Elementary	36,600,000

Secondary School Students

Public High Schools	12,000,000
Non-Public	1,300,000
Total Secondary	13,300,000

College and University full- and part-time students
enrolled for credit toward degrees

Public Institutions	4,000,000
Private	2,000,000
Total Higher	6,000,000
Grand Total Students Enrolled	55,900,000

The Teachers

Public School Teachers

Elementary	1,026,000
High School	783,000

Non-Public School Teachers

Elementary	159,000
High School	77,000

College and University Teachers
Public Institutions 257,000
Non-Public Institutions 209,000
   Total Teachers 2,511,000

Administrators and Supervisors
Superintendents of Schools 13,784
Principals and Supervisors 98,616
College and University Presidents 2,168
Other College Administrative and Library Staff 51,700
   Total 166,268

Board Members
Local School Board Members 129,000
State Board Members 492,000
College and University Board Members 35,000
   Total 656,000

The Cost (in billions)
Current Expenditures and Interest
  Elementary and Secondary Schools
    Public $24.4
    Non-Public 3.2
  Higher
    Public 7.6
    Non-Public 5.6
Capital Outlay
  Elementary and Secondary Schools
    Public 3.9
    Non-Public 0.5
  Higher
    Public 2.4
    Non-Public 1.2
    Total $48.8

Figures are based on latest available estimates from the U.S. Office of Education and the National Education Association.

Editors' Summary

The pattern of American education has been one of decentralization in which local school boards carry out the popular will by delegated authority. This system has proven satisfactory in the past because up until quite recently we were largely a nation of farmers. The three R's,

351

the liberal arts, and professional higher education were functional to a high degree in this situation, because the demands of the culture could be satisfied by "on the job experience" after the person had completed his formal schooling.

It was quite possible for a few delegated citizens to build a school, hire teachers, and educate the girls and boys to take their adult stations in life. The pattern was expected to continue in the next generation.

Now the population has increased rapidly; technological developments have altered the conditions of life, and communities, as such, have radically changed or disappeared. The patterns of the horse and buggy era are no longer functional in a modern age. Society's challenge is to revamp education for the purpose of bringing to the citizens an understanding and control of the processes of change.

The financing of public education continues at the local level, since the cultural lag of localism remains. This makes the controversy over finance a misleading one. The public can be whipped into a froth over financial problems because, as is well known in our society, the expenditure of money is agonizing and controversial. The excitement is taken as an indication that "real" problems are being settled. But we think that the real problems are deeper and are not solved by the acceptance of the school budget.

The heat over local educational finance is unfortunate in that people have a mistaken belief that they are making paramount decisions for education. Really, the decisions for education are those which design to make education functional in the modern society. The people are playing with mud pies while the mountains are shifting on their bases. The controversy over finance, on the local level, is so time consuming, so entertaining, that our creative energies are drawn off.

It would be, in our opinion, a waste of time to dedicate ourselves to teaching public-spirited people how to put over bigger millage campaigns in local communities. Making people aware that education must consolidate, modernize, and have adequate and stable funds for its support is of more value.

This idealism, we admit, may not be "practical," although we believe idealism is eminently practical. We admit that tactics for a long time to come must deal with expediency. In this regard, we would say that an enlightened approach for teachers and communities would be:

1) to work for funds from extra-local sources; 2) to enlarge educational systems to make them more efficient; 3) to seek more variety and experimentalism in all phases of education—building, administration, teaching, curriculum, and new departures (for instance exchange students, tours, etc.); 4) to build a stronger teaching profession.

Finally, we must state in all fairness that despite great shortcomings, education in general and teachers in particular have done a monumental service—better in many cases than their corresponding voting units deserve or their critics would admit.

RELATED READINGS

American Council on Education. *Expanding Opportunities.*

Ayars, Albert L. *Administering the People's Schools.* New York: McGraw-Hill Book Co., Inc., 1957.

Beezer, Robert H., and Howard F. Hjelm. "Factors Related to College Attendance." HEW Dept. Of. of Ed., Washington, D.C., 1961.

Burke, Arvid J. *Financing Public Schools in the United States.* Revised Edition. New York: Harper & Brothers, 1957.

Clark, Joseph F. "School Business Is Municipal Business," *Phi Delta Kappa,* XXXII (November, 1950), 102-06.

Cubberley, Ellwood P. *Public Education in the United States.* Revised Edition. Boston: Houghton Mifflin Co., 1934.

Dane, Genevieve O. "Grant Programs for Fiscal 1966," *American Education,* I (July-August, 1965), pp. 5-9.

Frederick, W. L. "State and Federal Financing of Higher Education," *American Association of University Women Journal,* L (May, 1957), 203-06.

Harris, Seymour E. "Financing the Schools," *Education Digest,* XXII (May, 1957), 5-8.

Harris, Seymour E. and Alan Levensohn, eds. *Education and Public Policy.* Berkeley, California: McCutchan Publishing Corporation, 1965. LB 2325 H283.

Hobby, Oveta Culp. "Schools Remain a Local Responsibility," *Phi Delta Kappan,* XXXV (February, 1954), 204-06, 210.

Hutchins, C. D. "Recent Trends in School Revenues," *American School Board Journal,* CXXXVI (January, 1958), 30-32.

Kursh, Harry. *The United States Office of Education.* Philadelphia: Chilton Books, 1965. LB 2807 K96.

Labovitz, I. M. *Aid for Federally Affected Public Schools.* Syracuse, N.Y.: Syracuse University Press, 1963. LB 2825 L14.

National Citizens Commission for the Public Schools. *Financing Public Education in the Years Ahead.* New York: The Commission, 1954.

National School Boards Association, Inc. *Seven Studies.* Chicago: The Association, 1958.

Pierce, Truman Mitchell. *Federal, State, and Local Government in Education.* Washington: Center for Applied Research in Education, 1964. LC 89 P62.

Ruml, Beardsley. "Long-term Problems of Public School Finance." In *American Association of School Administrators Official Report: 1955.* Washington, D.C.: The Association, 1955.

Stevenson, Adlai E. "America's Number One Must," *Vital Speeches,* XXI (August 1, 1955), 1401-04.

Straight, Michael W. "Schools—U.S. Emergency," *New Republic,* CXXXIII (December 12, 1955), 6-13.

Sufrin, Sidney Charles. *Administering the National Defense Education Act.* Syracuse, N.Y.: Syracuse University Press, 1963. LB 2825 S95.

Tax Institute. *Financing Education in the Public Schools: A Symposium.* Princeton, N.J.: Tax Institute, 1956.

U.S. Department of H.E.W. "Higher Education Act of 1965—Section by Section Analysis." Office of Education, Washington D.C., 1965.

U.S. Office of Education. *Cooperative Research Projects; A Seven-Year Summary: July 1, 1956-June 30, 1963.* Washington: U.S. Government Printing Office, 1964. L 111 A 41 no. 736.

———. *Education '65. A Report to the Profession.* Washington: Government Printing Office, 1966. REF 2825 A2775 1966.

XIV

Federal Aid and Public Education

ON HIS OWN TWO FEET

A young man lived with his parents in a low-cost public-housing development in Hamilton County. He attended public school, rode the free school bus, enjoyed the free-lunch program. Following graduation from high school, he entered the army and upon discharge he kept his National Service Life Insurance.

He then enrolled in an Ohio university, receiving regularly his GI check. Upon graduation, he married a public health nurse, bought a farm in southern Ohio with an FHA loan.

Later, going into the feed and hardware business in addition to farming, he secured help from the Small Business Administration when his business faltered. His first baby was born in the county hospital. This was built in part with Hill-Burton funds.

Then, he bought considerable additional acreage adjoining his farm, and obtained emergency feed from the government. He then put part of his land under the Eisenhower Soil Bank Program and used the payments for not growing crops to help pay his debts.

His parents, elderly by now, were living comfortably in the smaller of his two farm homes, using their Social Security and Old Age Assistance checks.

For electricity the Rural Electrification Administration supplied the lines, and a loan from the Farmers Home Administration helped clear the land and secure the best from it. That agent suggested building a pond, and the government stocked it with fish. The government guaranteed him a sale for his farm products.

The county public library delivered books to his farm door. He, of course, banked his money in an institution which a government agency had insured up to $10,000 for every depositor.

As the community grew, he signed a petition seeking federal assistance in developing an industrial project to help the economy of his area.

About that time he purchased business and real estate at the county seat aided by an FHA loan.

He was elected to the office in the local chamber of commerce. It was rumored he joined a cell of the John Birch Society in the county seat.

He wrote his senators and congressman protesting excessive government spending and high taxes, and enclosed John Birch pamphlets, some containing outlandishly false statements.

He wrote, "I believe in rugged individualism. People should stand on their own two feet, not expect government aid. I stand on my own two feet. I oppose all those socialistic trends you have been voting for and demand return to the free enterprise system of our forefathers. I and my neighbors intend to vote against you next year."

—U.S. SENATOR STEPHEN M. YOUNG
Democrat, Ohio

Editors' Comment

Our society has been changing very rapidly in the last few years so that old landmarks, old thoughts, and old institutions have been swallowed up and lost. Still, many common denominators remain and many of the old problems stay with us, aggravated by the rising flood of innovations. The education of the new generation remains a problem, but many of the means and conditions of this education have been radically altered.

Our population has risen by nearly 30 million in the decade between 1950 and 1960. Between 1946 and 1958 the public school population increased nearly 50 percent. The increases of high school and college enrollments are even more spectacular. In 1900, only 11 percent of the 14-to-17-year-olds were in high school. In 1958, 83 percent of this same group were attending. The gross national product has quadrupled in the last quarter of a century. We have seen a depression and the rise of nuclear physics and power devices, thinking machines, Mach 3 airplanes, transistors, automation, TV and vastly increased mass media, two shooting wars, and a cold war of variable temperature. The world has become small, and the problems have become great.

Though much is swept away, more remains. The problem of our society is to take what remains and make it stronger. Education is the touchstone of this movement to a better future.

Most people seem to recognize the importance of education, but when they talk about the means of implementing education, they disagree. We agree about the major goals of our society, but disagree on the means of attaining those goals. We agree on the democratic ethic, but quarrel about what equalitarianism is and how to achieve it.

The federal aid versus local control argument boils down to that of the relative validity and efficiency of local politics versus federal bureaucracy in maintaining and controlling education. We would agree that ultimately the expenditure of money will necessitate some kinds of safeguards and control in education, if federal aid increases appreciably. The arguments of federal aid and local control both urge that the image of democracy is best attained by their respective means offered.

Those who believe in localism hold that: 1) The practice of tradition has sent down roots that have value in perpetuating the present democratic system. 2) Pluralism requires that many subcultures living in one main culture be maintained by the decentralized system of localism for further growth. 3) Localism is more elastic than the great gelid monolith of centralization would be in experimentation, change, and responsiveness to existing demands. 4) The "we-group" feeling of staff and community make them happier and abler in solving all problems. 5) The taxation of the community motivates the people more than any other factor in developing good education.

The arguments of federal aid opposing these points are: 1) A

357

traditional form or institution does not perpetuate democracy, but an ideal which is implemented properly does. Therefore, the structure of education must be made adequate to implement the ideal, and federal aid is the only adequate means available to attain this end. 2) Variety and specialization are always to be maintained and are the inevitable concomitants of progress. More important are the universals and standards which are achieved by wholes of greater inclusiveness. Federally maintained schools would have the kinds of differences and the kinds of similarities which are important. 3) Local politics and communities are hidebound and conservative. The really significant changes and experiments today almost always require a minimal capital, organization, or personnel simply unattainable by local means. Many programs of educational advancement could be done only on a national level. 4) "We-group" feeling is a matter of group dynamics in which localism is a minor factor and becoming less so. Generally speaking, quality, training, conditions of work, and aspirations of the group of educators determine their group morale. 5) The motivation of parents concerning education comes from their understanding of the issues and goals involved and their satisfaction or dissatisfaction with the education their children are getting. Taxation per se is always a negative factor.

The favorite argument used by those against federal aid to education, an argument constantly reiterated and used after learning that facts or figures give scant support to their case, is the danger of federal control. It might *happen, they maintain, and this possibility of the future is held to be sufficient argument no matter how badly off the schools are under local financing. A typical stand is the following sonorous statement lauding the present localism and rendering federal aid anathema, by Nicholas Murray Butler:*

"There is not enough money in the United States, even if every dollar of it were expended on education, to produce through federal authority, or through what is naïvely called cooperation between the Federal Government and the several states, educational results that would be at all comparable with those that have been already reached under the free and natural system that has grown among us.

"Unless the school is both the work and pride of the community it serves it is nothing. A school system that grows naturally in re-

sponse to the needs and ambitions of a hundred thousand different communities will be a better school system than any which can be imposed upon these localities by the aid of grants of public money from the Federal Treasury, accompanied by federal regulations, federal inspections, federal uniformities."

The intent of Title I and Title II is clearly to improve the educational opportunities of poor children. The poor are defined in terms of family income. Since the aim is to help children, not schools public or private, the act says repeatedly in different ways that the money should not go for such things as subsidizing sectarian worship. This statement in language is reassuring, perhaps, to those who desire to maintain the wall of separation between church and state. Nevertheless, it is inevitable that when fairly large sums of money become available for school X, whatever the statement of the giver, it will be impossible to separate the specific effects and uses of the funds into the spoken aims of Title I and Title II and those functions or structures not so regarded. For example, does the child know when he is reading Robin Hood, whether or not this is a Title II book? The result of subsidizing children cannot be separated from the organization for education in which context he receives aid. There will be hassles about this now and in the future.

Another point at issue is the power of the federal agency doing the granting. Although "guidelines" are printed, the giving or withholding of funds rests with the federal people. We can see how this power can be constructively used, and the economic weapon could be turned upon many of the discriminatory sectors of our society. On the other hand, there is no blinking the fact that those sitting there controlling the purse strings have enormous power in controlling how we dance. This is the biggest problem that the public and the educators have to address. It is worth the while of all readers to peruse the following Educational Act of 1965.

ANALYSES OF THE ELEMENTARY AND SECONDARY EDUCATIONAL ACT OF 1965*

The guiding reason for the enactment of both the Elementary and Secondary Education Act and the Economic Opportunity Act has been

* Pamphlet of American Jewish Committee, Institute of Human Relations, 1965.

concern with the underprivileged and educationally deprived youth of our nation. Recognizing that the existence of such youth is at one and the same time a national disgrace and a waste of potentially trained manpower, we have made it a national policy to provide financial assistance to local educational agencies for the education of children of low-income families. In addition, we have taken some initial steps through the operation of the Economic Opportunity Act to give our young people the opportunity to work, have education and training, and live in decency and dignity.

Undoubtedly, these are commendable programs worthy in their broad outlines of our support and assistance. However, there is implicit in their operation a problem of long-standing concern to the American Jewish Committee: the separation of church and state.

Despite the clearly stated intention of Congress in the Elementary and Secondary Education Act to make certain that "Nothing contained in this Act shall be construed to authorize the making of any payment . . . for religious worship or instruction," (Sec. 605) and its similar intention in the operation of the Economic Opportunity Act, problems will inevitably arise.

These Guidelines and Accompanying Analyses are intended to capsulize the content and objectives of these Acts. It is our hope that they will serve as an easy reference for you in ascertaining the amount of adherence there is, in practice, to the above-stated Congressional intention—and a national policy regarding the separation of church and state which has existed since the founding of our nation.

Title 1—*Financial Assistance to Local Educational Agencies for the Education of Children of Low-Income Families*

As is clearly stated in the "Declaration of Policy," the purpose of the act is to provide financial assistance in the form of grants to local educational agencies "serving areas with concentrations of children from low-income families to expand and improve their educational programs by various means . . . which contribute particularly to meeting the special educational needs of educationally deprived children" (Sec. 201).

In determining the amount of aid to these agencies, it has been established in Sec. 203(a), that the child to whom these benefits should flow should come from a family with an annual income of less than $2,000 in recognition of a basic hard core of poverty. Further, it has been recognized that the high incidence of poverty-stricken families in a particular area has an "impact . . . on the ability of local educational agencies to support adequate educational programs . . ." and that to get out of the vicious circle of poverty breeding poverty through lack of educational opportunity, these areas, in particular, must receive federal assistance. To meet this problem, the Act is designed to help *all* children —not merely public-school enrollees.

In its application, Title I provides in Sec. 205(a) that a local educational agency may receive grants upon determination by a state agency that, among other things:

> Payments will be used for programs and projects (including the acquisition of equipment and where necessary the construction of school facilities) "which are designed to meet the special educational needs of educationally deprived children" and (B) "which are of sufficient size, scope, and equality to give reasonable promise of substantial progress toward meeting those needs. . . ."

This falls clearly within the statement of purpose heretofore discussed. It is intended to give encouragement to local school districts to employ imaginative thinking and new approaches to meet the educational needs of poor children.

What is of particular relevance to this memorandum, however, is the following section, wherein it is provided that "to the extent consistent with the number of educationally deprived children in the school district . . . who are enrolled in private elementary and secondary schools, such agency has made provision for including special educational services and arrangements (such as dual enrollment, educational radio and television, and mobile educational services and equipment) in which such children can participate" (Sec. 205(a)2).

As was stated in the Legislative History, the bill contemplates "some broadening of public educational programs and services." However, "no provision authorizes any grant to a private institution" (U.S. Code, Congressional and Administrative News, p. 444). Read together with Sec. 205(a)(3) in which control of funds, title to property, administration of both, reside with the public agency, and Sec. 205(a)(4) in which any construction of facilities must be consistent with overall

State plans, it is clear that the private institution is not to receive funds *per se* under Sec. 205. What is more, under Sec. 206(a)(1), payments under this title are to be used "only for programs and projects which have been approved by the State educational agency . . . and which meet the requirements" of Sec. 205(a). Clearly, therefore, responsibility for the programming of such dual enrollment offerings as are given remains with the public authority. Further, the decision to undertake such programs is discretionary with the public authority.

In the case of dual enrollment plans and special services, both constitutional mandate and national policy forbid segregation of children within the public school on the bases of either race or religion, *Brown* v. *Board of Education* 347 U.S. 483. It is both well-known and well-documented that such emphasis of religious difference as may occur within the public school setting acts as a divisive element within the schoolroom. Therefore, when there should occur joint gatherings of private- and public-school children within the public school under any plan of dual enrollment, "it is to be expected that arrangements will be administered in such a way as to prevent separation by religious affiliation." (U.S. Code, Legislative History, p. 444).

It is particularly in the area of what might be termed these "special educational services" that there needs to be most concern and vigilance in making certain that the First Amendment is not violated. In this regard it is vital to make certain that wherever possible public or non-religiously affiliated premises are utilized for joint programs. Where this is impossible, the tightest safeguards commensurate with the smooth operation of the program should insure that sectarian or religious influence is at an absolute minimum in the materials, the teaching, the grouping, or the premises themselves. And as has been emphasized, in all cases every effort should be made to insure that these services are carried on at non-religious premises. Only in this way would there be assurance that the intention of this act and the Constitution were being fulfilled.

In this regard, it should be again emphasized that dual enrollment programs are not mandatory, but merely are one of "several opportunities . . . afforded local public educational agencies to meet the special . . . needs of . . . school pupils." (Ibid, p. 445).

When teachers or special-service personnel are made available to other than public-school facilities, these must be for the stated purposes of the act, and the presence of such personnel on these premises must be to contribute particularly to meeting the special educational needs of educationally deprived children. This shall take place only where these services are not normally provided by the non-public school.

As in the case of the mobile facilities, provision of these special services are not designed to supplant regular expenditures by the non-public institution. On the contrary, the purpose of the act is to "expand and improve" their programs (Sec. 201), and in no instance shall these services be provided in such a way as to release funds regularly expended by the institution for other purposes. This, of course, would be violative of the intent of the act.

In communities in which there is a community-action program approved pursuant to the Economic Opportunity Act of 1964, programs and projects should be developed in cooperation with the agency responsible for the community-action program to avoid overlap or duplication (Sec. 205(a)7). However, responsibility for carrying out the programs is lodged with local boards of education (U.S. Code Legislative History p. 446).

Title II—School Library Resources, Textbooks and Other Instructional Materials

It has been found that good library resources, textbooks and other printed instructive materials are vital to a sound education. These are often lacking in economically depressed areas, and it is the intention of Title II to remedy this defect as it applies to all school children.

To gain grants for this purpose, the state agency must submit a state plan to the Commissioner of Education to be administered by it or through arrangements with other state or local public agencies. There must be assurance provided that these materials "will be provided on an equitable basis for the use of children and teachers in private . . . schools" (Sec. 203(a)(3)B), and criteria set up regarding the selection and use of such materials by all children in the area. Where there is an approved state plan and there exists no state agency authorized by law to provide printed materials, the Commissioner of Education shall provide for an equitable distribution (Sec. 204(b)). According to the Senate Report, this is in order to insure that there will be made available to children in all states the benefits of this title in instances in which state constitutions or interpretations of church-state separation makes state distribution impossible.

There are safeguards that these materials shall not fall into the ownership of private institutions, for in the words of the Senate hearing, (U.S. Code, Legislative History, p. 458), Title II is "designed *to benefit children and not schools* . . ." (Emphasis is original.)

To use the limitations formulated in Senate Report No. 146, care has been taken to assure that funds provided under the title will not inure to the enrichment or benefit of any private institution by providing that:

"1. Library resources, textbooks, and other instructional materials are to be made available to children and teachers and not to institutions;

"2. Such materials are made available on a loan basis only;

"3. Public authority must retain title and administrative control over such materials;

"4. Such material must be that approved for use by public school authority in the state; and

"5. Books and material must not supplant those being provided children but must supplement library resources, textbooks, and other instructional materials to assure that the legislation will furnish increased opportunities for learning. The state should also assure that the federal funds made available under this title will not be used to supplant or duplicate, inappropriately, functions of the public library system of the State."

Title III—Supplemental Educational Centers and Services

The purpose of this title is to provide these centers and services "to stimulate and assist in the provision of vitally needed educational services not available in sufficient quantity or quality . . ." (Sec. 301a). As the title implies, it is not intended to provide a regular curriculum; rather, its thrust is to benefit "persons broadly representative of the cultural and educational resources of the area to be served" (Sec. 304a), and should benefit not only regular school children, but "persons of varying talents and needs . . ." (Sec. 303b). However, these programs will remain the responsibility of the local educational agency, as is the initiative for their instruction (Sec. 304(A)3).

As in the case of Title I, in the case of the construction of facilities, title to them remains in a state or local educational agency. Further, funds made available are to be used to supplement and, "to the extent practical," increase the level of funds that would have been made available (Sec. 304(A)3). They are "in no case" to "supplant such funds." Again, the material benefit of these programs is not to inure to an institution—such as a private school.

The resources to be utilized would include institutions such as museums, libraries, educational radio and television, universities, private schools, and other cultural and educational resources and are to reflect within the broad composition of the community and its resources.

Our society has changed rapidly, and generally society has accepted the changes. The old community of about 500 people, with a central, tree-shaded square, is no more. Physicians talk with physicians, not the man next door, and the nation is on wheels. The school as a hub of the community, a cohesive, concentrating force, is no more. In fact, schools have changed—probably not enough—to meet the times. However, the neighborhood school is cherished as a democratic goal. Why is it cherished? The following article suggests it furnishes a bastion to carry on the fight for ethnic similarity, with the right of inclusion and exclusion, i.e., discrimination. The real casualty, we would suggest, is the quality of education.

THE NEIGHBORHOOD SCHOOL AND
DEFACTO SEGREGATION
August Kerber and Phyllis Freeman

The U.S. Supreme Court in 1954 stated that "separate but equal" education was not equal. In 1967, thirteen years later, approximately three percent of the students in the South attend desegregated schools. The issue of *de facto* segregation in the North remains controversial and unsettled among both educators and laymen. Data, if gathered, would probably indicate the growing *de facto* segregation in the North far outweighs the small gains in the South—and the trend appears to be growing.

One of the questions being considered by integrationists, segregationists, educators, politicians, and parents is the importance or necessity of keeping the neighborhood school intact. Defense of the neighborhood school may be based on a genuine belief that a school close to home is best, but it often appears to be a smoke screen covering the real issue of *de facto* segregation. Therefore, the outcome of the debate regarding neighborhood schools has great significance in the choice of programs the government will follow in promoting equal educational opportunity. Living patterns throughout America tend to be segregated and are becoming more so. With the few exceptions of "model integrated communities" neighborhood schools will not be integrated.

Similarities exist between the past struggle against consolidation in rural areas and the struggle to maintain the neighborhood school today. The small one-room schoolhouse is no longer a reality in most areas, but at one time it also was defended as educationally sound under the auspices of local autonomy.

The United States Office of Education report to Congress (*Equality of Educational Opportunity* 1966), also known as the Coleman Report, contradicts what most educators and politicians believe and practice about providing equal educational opportunity. The report accepted the hypothesis that a really superior school for Negroes must be integrated, and supports this position with volumes of statistics gathered from half a million students and 60,000 teachers in 4,000 schools. Evidence also indicated that pouring money into Negro schools makes little difference, and that the American school system is doing little or nothing to integrate Negroes into the mainstream of society.

In light of the above, the separatist educational position, i.e., "people should associate with their own kind" or "children can be educated best in their own (segregated) neighborhoods," will continue to perpetuate a segregated, racist society which is far from the ideal of equality of opportunity for all people. This inequality of opportunity will lead to additional social problems and violence, further widening the social and economic gaps in society. The international implications for the future could be devastating, recognizing the statistics on the privileged and underprivileged, white and non-white, peoples of the world.

And so the debate between the proponents of quality education and integrated education rings loud. The question is are they in opposition or are they interdependent? The United States government and other agencies, through funded programs (Head Start, Upward Bound Program, Higher Horizons, Great Cities Project, etc.) continue to spend millions of dollars each year for compensatory-type education programs for the "culturally deprived," who for the most part are also Negro. Compensatory education provides additional services and opportunities for children in ghetto schools without removing them from the ghetto or changing the composition of the school population. This, it is hoped, will compensate for the disadvantages imposed by poverty and discrimination.

Paradoxically, many of those who publically support integration also fight for the neighborhood school idea in its many forms. The two are not compatible in our present housing patterns. But the argument continues among many who indicate they believe in total equality for all. Therefore, it is necessary to examine the neighborhood school concept and evaluate its contribution to a truly integrated society which lives according to the ideals of its constitution.

Throughout the country the reason most heard in defense of the neighborhood school is that it is the most educationally sound. Any drastic change in attendance patterns, which would break down the self-perpetuating segregated characteristic of the country, is seen as an infringement on individual freedom and rights or, equally sacred, local autonomy and control of education.

Numerous proposals and plans have been created to bring about a more equally balanced racial composition in the schools. One plan includes the bussing of children from all Negro schools to all white schools and vice-versa. An open-school policy in which a child may transfer to any school in the city where enrollment figures allow has also been attempted. Large educational parks, which would cut across both racial and class lines and offer the best educational opportunity to all, have been suggested.

These practices and suggestions have been attacked through reference to the importance and fundamental merits of the neighborhood school. Critics have decried the impersonality of the large educational complex while proclaiming the high value of neighborhood peer relationships, local autonomy, and low cost of the neighborhood school. Seldom publically expressed is the belief that segregation should continue. An analysis of the criteria used to attack proposals for breaking down *de facto* segregation shows a selectivity of application.

Parents claim that the large educational complex is impersonal, but research tends to indicate that the size of the educational plant is not significant in determining the quality of the student-teacher relationship. Parents stress the importance of peer relationships, while realistically it is rare that a neighborhood age-mate will be in the same classroom. Rather neighborhood play groups tend to cut across age limits and also include the children who attend schools out of the neighborhood. As students reach adolescence their choice patterns of friends more and more resemble their parents', who drive across town to visit friends with mutual interests, join clubs out of the neighborhood—and may not even know, let alone socialize, with other families in the neighborhood.

The ever-increasing geographic mobility of the American population is one of its most striking characteristics. Whereas at one time it was common for a child to live in one neighborhood throughout his school years, nowadays this pattern is becoming the exception. The rapid growth of private schools in the United States also indicates that the neighborhood school is not unanimously regarded as the most educationally sound. Few have argued that the handicapped should attend their neighborhood school rather than a school which can provide specialized instruction. Special talent schools, such as the High School of Science in the Bronx, New York, have encountered little opposition because they violated the community-school concept. Rather, parents have readily sent their children to a school in which they realized that quality, often integrated education, was being provided. The elite of our population have continued to send their children to private schools out of the neighborhood to receive what they believe to be the best educational preparation. It would be interesting to count the number of parents who argue the importance of the neighborhood school and at the same time would welcome the opportunity to send their children to an "elite" private school out of the neighborhood.

The trend of metropolitan regions and centralized metropolitan government will be accompanied by the break-up of innumerable small school districts surrounding our major cities. This trend makes the struggle for the maintenance of the small, local, autonomous school district unrealistic. The cost of operating integrated schools is high because of the existence of segregated housing patterns, involving additional cost in construction of educational parks or in transporting students. A value decision must be made. Are we to offer equal educational opportunity at additional cost? Or are we to continue to provide segregated and therefore unequal education to much of the population rather than spend to bring about racial balance? (White children are also victims of segregated housing and may reach adulthood with attitudes and experiences not equipping them to live in a world where they are a minority.) Regarding cost, it is interesting to observe that the cost of compensatory education seemingly is mentioned unfavorably less often than the expense of integrating the schools.

The selection of criteria in criticizing programs which would threaten the neighborhood schools strongly suggests that the controversy involves compensatory and integrated education rather than neighborhood schools.

The United States Civil Rights Commission asked Congress in February 1964 to eliminate "racial isolation of children" in Negro schools (*Racial Isolation in Public Schools,* 1967). Like the Coleman Report a few months earlier, they concluded that compensatory education seems to have little positive effect. Urban-suburban cooperation in exchange of students is suggested as one method of overcoming the obstacle of Negro concentration in the cities and white concentration in the suburbs. Even these drastic steps, the Commission states, may not repair the harm done through racial isolation and discrimination.

Whether the government—federal, state, or local—will take heed of the findings and recommendations of the reports of the United States Office of Education or the Civil Rights Commission will depend greatly on the electorate. Although government may act in a leadership role, the tendency is to respond to public sentiment. Any drastic change in attendance patterns seems unlikely while many individuals continue to argue the educational soundness of the neighborhood school, but whatever the decisions regarding integrated educational opportunity, upon these decisions rests the future of all Americans.

The specter of federal control of education has been of concern to those who perceive government as a threat to free public education. Warren Gauerke frames an interesting response to this whole question of federal participation and makes a strong case against localism and for partial centralization in American education.

IS CENTRALIZATION OF SCHOOL SUPPORT AND CONTROL A THREAT TO DEMOCRACY?
Warren E. Gauerke*

. . . There can be no serious advancement of the notion that there be no federal control over education where federal tax dollars are involved. But that noxious control over instruction must be coupled with federal operation is a prime example of *non sequitur* reasoning.

It is foolish to assert that control is inherently bad without reference to what is being controlled or the particular circumstances under which control is exercised. The specter of federal domination over instruction is imagined rather than real. There is no shred of evidence that federal direction of education would result in less local and state school interest, or that education would be swallowed up by a greedy bureaucracy.

There is little, if any, movement toward extension of federal control. To receive federal funds, minimum standards must be met. However, there is simply no evidence of the danger of political propaganda being fed unsuspecting children within the framework of federal control of the public schools.

The belief that the people who would staff federal education offices would be of one school of philosophy is a mistaken one. As in all groups, they would differ widely in their personal values about education. Actually people who work in the field of education for any length of time learn that more than one philosophy can be used effectively in any school situation.

Increasingly, American schools need better leadership than comes from local politicians. Today the national community is a source of

* Warren E. Gauerke, "Is Centralization of School Support and Control a Threat to Democracy?" *Graduate Comment* (Wayne State University), IV, No. 5 (April, 1961). Reprinted by permission.

moral authority for the educator. A teacher whose views differ from local mores should not be bound by them since village lines mean little to a mobile population. Acceptance of the national community as the locus of moral authority would automatically rule out policies of communities which were inconsistent with national ideals, no matter how much support the ideas received from the locality.

Some Faults of the Local Unit

A great obstacle to the attainment of quality education is the pattern of organization in which small districts are the dominant feature. School boards, types of district organization, and various patterns of grade organization are parts of a crazy quilt that badly serve as vehicles for learning. The local school district—some 42,000—can no longer serve as the basic unit of public education. School board members in Middletown, U.S.A., are usually selected from among the most prominent and busiest citizens of the community. The complexity of life and business tends to cut down the time they are free to devote to school matters. The local school district was at one time THE hope of public education. Now it is the despair of thoughtful persons.

To even the most casual observer it must be apparent that widely divergent standards of pupil ability exist in different sections of our country. After World War II, data showed that more men from economically privileged sections had died in battle because quotas could not be met from those states where educational achievements were low. Often the less privileged child is burdened with weaker teachers and leftover textbooks. Salaries are matters for competition among school districts.

Besides unequal chance for schooling, there is a more underlying fault of localism. American public education lacks any system. Schools ought to belong to national governments, administered by governmental bureaus and professional workers. Look at current practices in teacher certification—a frightening picture of confusion. The preservice preparation of teachers varies so greatly that teacher means "salad-fixer" and theorist alike. The recruitment of new administrators is left to chance. The route often sought is through elementary school teaching. Here the young man can get his "sea legs" and then aspires upward. Tenure, leaves of absence, and work load vary so

371

greatly among school districts that comparisons are without meaning.

Related to the basic lack of system in American public education is the faulty tax base. There are contrasting abilities to pay for adequate programs because the federal government continues to preempt the major sources of revenue. Tax structures of both local and state governments are much less flexible than those of the federal government. Let's compare school district X with Y. District X has a total school membership of 5,000 children. The assessed valuation of property behind each child is $30,000. The local tax rate in mills is thirteen. The cost per pupil here for school operation is above $650 for the ten-month term. School district Y has about the same number of children to educate. The assessed valuation behind each child is $6,000. Yet the local tax rate in mills (which represents the effort of the people—their commitment to education) is twenty-five mills. With almost double the effort expended there, only $250 is available to educate each child for the school year.

Advantages of Centralized Control

American public education is big business. A national system would enable school systems to operate independently of local whims and pressures. A result would be maximum of uniformity in records and housekeeping chores. Data would be readily usable for study because the bases would be comparable. Central data-processing is possible when uniform controls are exercised. No longer would state departments and the Commissioner have to beg, cajole, request, and hint broadly that complete records should be forwarded.

The use of bookkeeping machines, punched-card tabulators and auxiliary equipment would be mandatory. The pencil-in-hand performance—which is still believed by many to possess inherent qualities of honesty and accuracy—would be relegated to the streetcar barn. Machine accounting would increase accuracy. Tax dollars would be saved. Machine tabulation would give facts that could not be obtained otherwise. Such equipment would conserve valuable floor space. Accounting would be uniform, based upon acceptable business procedures. Physical and mental effort would be reduced and hours saved. Good employee relations would surely result. Machine accounting and related services for school administration are practical cost items for the federal government.

National guidelines, once established, would help local administrators to facilitate instruction through better personnel, business, and public relations practices. Employment and budgeting would still require local concern. Curriculum planning, public relations, guidance programs, and a number of other diversified school functions demand the top priority of recognized national education thinkers and doers.

When the proposition of federal aid for education is made, a number of objections arise at once. The first one is the bugaboo of federal control. We hear: "The local governments, or at least the local governments with state aid, can do it." "Do you realize how much federal aid would cost? We could never balance the budget." "The truth is, the teachers are doing very well. So what are they beefing about?" "The entrance of the government (federal, of course) would make education very inefficient. Heaven knows it's bad enough now." One of the most succinct and authoritative answers to questions which really purvey objections is given in the following NEA pamphlet by Sam M. Lambert.

QUESTIONS ON FEDERAL SUPPORT FOR PUBLIC SCHOOLS
*Sam M. Lambert**

How can the national government spend $1 to $4 billion on education when the federal debt is already so high?

The federal debt is a little like the old gray mare: She ain't what she used to be.

Debt, either personal or public, is important only in relation to assets. Our national debt is high, but it has decreased sharply in relation to our national assets.

In 1949, the federal debt was 93 percent of our gross national product, but in 1959, it was only 62 percent. In 1949, the national debt was equal to 115 percent of our national income; in 1959, it was only 71 percent.

This is an even more striking picture: In 1948, the federal debt

---

* Sam M. Lambert, "Nine Questions on Federal Support for Public Schools," *NEA Journal*, XLIX (February, 1960). Reprinted by permission.

was seven times the revenue of the federal government; in 1958, it was only four times the revenue.

Of course, the national debt is a serious problem to the federal government, but we should not overlook the fact that the growing debts of school districts are also serious to local and state school authorities. Let me give you some rather surprising figures: Between 1949-50 and 1959-60, current expense for education increased 154 percent, but during the same period, interest payments increased 275 percent and payments for capital outlay increased 221 percent.

The normal prewar outlay for capital outlay and interest for public education was about eight cents of each school dollar. At present, it is about 25 cents.

Why send a tax dollar to Washington when, by the time it gets back to state and local governments, it will have shrunk to 60 cents?

This frequently voiced objection is a myth. Here are the facts: The cost of collecting federal taxes is approximately 44 cents per $100. There have been several studies of the costs of collecting state taxes, and they show that costs range from 95 cents to $2.34 per $100 collected. The cost of *collecting and administering* local revenue has run as high as $5 to $10 per $100, according to experts who have studied the problem.

You will note that I have omitted administration of state and federal taxes, whereas I have included administration of local taxes. We have no figures on the costs of administration at the state level, but the cost of administering 10 grant programs of the federal government averaged 1.2 percent of the amounts distributed.

This means the cost of collecting the federal tax dollar and the administration of federal grant programs totals about 1.6 percent. The NEA Research Division estimates that administering Murray-Metcalf allocations would total less than one half of one percent.

Would such a bill be inflationary and would it unbalance the President's budget?

This is the theme song of the Administration and the Chamber of Commerce of the United States. When revenue is short, these groups always concentrate on a balanced budget and the national debt. On the other hand, when it looks as though revenues will exceed budget commitments, these same groups always shift their attention away from the national debt to the possibility of a tax cut.

The U.S. Chamber and prominent spokesmen for the Administration are already talking about a tax cut of $3.5 billion in 1961. In fact, both groups appear to be pushing hard for the Baker-Herlong bill, which calls for income-tax cuts in the top bracket from 91 percent to 47 percent and in the lowest bracket from 20 percent to 15 percent. Under the same bill, corporation taxes would be reduced from 52 percent to 47 percent. To replace a temporary loss of revenue receipts, a national sales tax would be adopted.

Congress has liberalized social-security benefits in every election year since 1950. From all appearances, 1960 is not going to be an exception. Inflation, the national debt, and the President's budget will take a back seat when the liberalization of social-security benefits is considered.

Aren't we doing pretty well as it is? Why get so excited?

All of us know that we have made some significant gains in recent years. For instance, teachers' salaries have been going up an average annual rate of about 5.6 percent since 1950. Also, a larger proportion of teachers now have college degrees, and we have a few more guidance counselors, a few more textbooks that are available without cost to boys and girls, and more adequate administrative and supervisory services.

On the other hand, whatever optimism we may have about the status of public education in America is tempered by these facts: (a) Of every 10 boys and girls in the fifth grade, only six stay through the twelfth; (b) of every three entering high school (ninth grade), one fails to get his diploma.

Things certainly are not as good as they should be. Education still has a long way to go in meeting the needs of all American youth.

Why include teachers' salaries? We could get the building funds through, but teachers' salaries are going to make things difficult.

In my opinion, the salary problem is more serious than the building problem.

Everyone is now talking about quality education, and certainly we need to strive for quality education in every school in this country. On the other hand, all of us know that about 95 percent of whatever quality we have, or ever will have depends on quality teaching that can be done only by quality teachers.

The low birth rates of the 1930's and the big increases in the late 1940's and 1950's have provided a peculiar configuration to our population. During the 1960's, we will have big increases at the top and bottom of the age ladder and a constriction in the middle.

According to Secretary of Labor James P. Mitchell, of the expected increase in the labor force in the 1960's, 47 percent will be workers under 24 years of age; 41 percent will be over 45; but only 13 percent will be 25 to 34. The number of workers in the age group 35 to 44 years will actually decrease.

With business and industry becoming increasingly interested in college graduates, we are going to have a difficult time recruiting talent.

Actually, we will have a difficult time recruiting any type of college graduate during the next decade. Unless we can get the average salary up to about $7500 by the mid-1960's, we are going to have a difficult time in education. The only possibility that I see of reaching this average is through some substantial federal support of education with funds available for salaries.

The average salary of teachers during the current year is just a little over $5000. We still have six states where the average salary is $3600 or less per year.

How can we answer the charge that some states will not get back as much as they put in? (Our proportioned share of Murray-Metcalf funds will be less than our share of all federal taxes paid.)

In connection with this question, I wonder how Rhode Island compares with Iowa in the soil-bank program and in crop-support funds. I also wonder how Delaware compares with Texas in federal funds for highways.

There is another way to approach the problem. By the time the children in your state are adults, a large percent of them will be living in another state, and a large percent of the adult population of your state will have been educated in other states.

376

I sometimes wonder why there are so many objections to federal funds for education when we use federal money for practically everything else. Nearly anyone in any state would be surprised if he knew how much federal money is now going to state and local governments and to individuals.

For instance, federal aid of various types to state and local governments and to individuals totaled $143 million in Minnesota in 1958. This amount in Minnesota was equal to 45 percent of the total state tax revenues collected. It was also equal to 47 percent of all taxes on property. Nearly all states lean heavily on federal funds.

Actually, we could not operate state and local governments without federal assistance of many kinds. If all such aid were suddenly withdrawn, our state and local governments would find it extremely difficult to operate at all.

Since all the wealth is located in the states and localities, why not raise school money there rather than go to the federal government?

All of us know that we will have to continue raising more money at the state and local levels every year to meet the tremendous problems in education that lie ahead. Every level of government must do much more.

On the other hand, state and local taxes have increased to a point that they may be having a serious effect on the location of business and industry. The states are becoming increasingly cautious about raising taxes for fear of discouraging business and industry.

A recent study of a hypothetical corporation with assets of $3 million located in 18 urban and suburban places in the Central and Northern industrial states indicated that local tax bills varied from $17,000 to $66,000. State tax bills varied from $4,000 to $28,000. The total of all local and state taxes in these 18 different locations varied from $23,000 to $76,000.

But this is the most important point of all: As a percent of net income, state and local taxes varied from 8 percent to 26 percent. If this study is representative, there is no question in my mind but that the level of state and local taxes can affect the location of business and industry.

The only effective way we have to avoid tax competition between states is through the federal tax system.

Local and state governments have done the job over these many years; isn't it possible that they could continue doing it?

Let's look at what is going to happen in the next 10 years. According to the estimates of the NEA Research Division, school costs are going to increase from the present $15.5 billion to at least $31 billion. This estimate is based on the current rate of growth and development of our public schools, and it is backed by similar estimates from independent groups.

In 1955, the White House Conference on Education reported that school costs would double in the coming decade. In fact, costs are rising even faster than estimated. Based on the WHC prediction, school costs would have been up 40 percent four years later. Actually, they were up 50 percent.

The important question is this: Can we raise, through state and local sources alone, another $15.5 billion for education? In seeking an answer to this question, we must remember that the total is going to $31 billion. This is two thirds of the present cost of national defense. It is also approximately equal to the present total of all state and local tax collections for all purposes. This means that public education 10 years from now must get as much money as is now being raised by state and local governments for everything.

Can we squeeze approximately half of this money from the property tax? In my opinion, you're not going to be able to do it in many states. . . . In North Dakota, property taxes now amount to $6.10 of each $100 of personal income. The national average is $3.70.

Can we squeeze another $5.4 billion of this $15.5 billion needed out of the variety of state taxes? I think we should take a long hard look at the present level of state taxes in several states. . . .

The only realistic way to look at the tax load is to consider state and local taxes together as a percent of personal income. Where local taxes are low, state taxes are usually high. The over-all state-local load provides a rather interesting picture:

In North Dakota, state and local taxes for all purposes take $11.70 of each $100 of personal income. This sounds more like the federal income tax than the load of state and local taxes. In Mississippi, which is second among the states, the corresponding figure is $11.20. In South Dakota, it is $10.50; in Vermont, $10.40; in Louisiana, $10.40; and the national average is $8.30.

Again, I think we should note the Southern states. When we put state and local taxes together as a percent of income payments, we find several of the Southern states near the top. Our research into the tax load carried by the states of various geographic regions of the country indicates that serious trouble lies ahead in the South, Middle West, and New England.

This brings up the question of what is to be done, provided the federal government does not help support the cost of public education. Is West Virginia going to get an income-tax law? Are the citizens of Michigan going to approve a constitutional amendment to increase their sales tax from 3 percent to 4 percent?

These are decisions which are being faced all over the country, and the needs are not limited to those of elementary and secondary schools. . . .

Editors' Summary

In all the articles we have presented, we believe that the authorities agree that we must have higher quality education, and we must be prepared to pay for it. The different opinions revolve around the question of the means of getting the money. The main argument against federal aid is that it will lead to federal control. A vague but horrifying picture of frozen-faced, inept bureaucrats in Washington, supervising the geography lesson of Willie Beditts in Hopkin's Center is painted, and this is supposed to be a sufficient scarecrow to deter any of the mercenary souls searching for federal funds. It is useless to argue that the states or the local bodies will have "real" or "ultimate" control over education if the federal government is footing the tab. If large amounts of money are forthcoming from the federal government, the method of distribution, the criteria and standards should come under centralized control.

The crux of the argument against federal control is that the quality of education would deteriorate if bureaucrats have the higher echelon positions of administration. Essentially, the fear is that education would be controlled by outsiders, or people unsympathetic to education. (The wry argument to uphold localism is that 46,000 groups of outsiders—the boards of education—are bad enough; the co-ordination of the outsiders would be much worse.)

Enough truth is inherent in this argument to give teachers pause. Outsiders can take over education. But they can do so only by default of leadership of the educators. Educators are qualified to run the schools and apportion the uses of the funds. If they supinely accept others doing their jobs, they will gradually be pushed into the roles of puppets which their posture invites. Generals run armies, managers run industry, and experts perform their appropriate acts in the professions. The public which raises the funds for these activities are, of course, interested in getting their money's worth, but this is no license for them to place commissions in the army and spies in the classroom. However, if teachers become so overjoyed with a few crumbs from the master's table that they fawn on him and ask for directives, they will get directives.

When the argument is made that education will become a big political football, the arguers are right for the wrong reason. Education, and any other important issue, has political ramifications. If teachers are seeking a system which is sterile and untouched by politics, and one in which they will accrue their just deserts by playing the role of genteel poverty, they are unequipped as teachers because they have a fantastic, unscientific view of the human race.

The notion that simply being genteel and deserving will bring them professional status is unrealistic. The power and prestige teachers seek will come through practical politics played with real people. The way for teachers to acquire leadership in our society is mainly through hard-slugging, everyday work. Most teachers quail at the thought of any violent opposition. Unfortunately, such opposition cannot be guaranteed against. If there are cases of "dirty politics" against education, teachers must be prepared to fight back. Yet it is more likely that the drama of the establishment of the profession will be one in which exhaustion and apathy of themselves and the public will be the major handicaps. In any event, through it all, an unrelenting pressure will have to be maintained to see that education is controlled by educators.

The many problems of standardization, purpose, leadership, and

380

synthesis-in-variety that go along with nationwide or world-wide education will have to be matched by the professional ethic and competencies of the teacher. The aim of teachers should be to turn the light of intelligence on the clichés and slogans whipped up by anti-educational forces. "Federal domination" is a bogeyman which an understanding of the meaning of standards and the reasonable sureties of good use of federal tax money would dispel. The GI Bill, in which 17 billion dollars of federal money was well spent by all reasonable standards, is a case in point proving that corruption is not inevitable with federal expenditure in education. As to governing bodies being remote from teachers, the teachers know that state boards are more remote from them, if anything, than a federal board would be. And if equalization is a good principle, it had better be applied at the national level, rather than merely the state level.

RELATED READINGS

Bailey, Stephen K., Robert C. Wood, Richard Frost, and Paul E. Marsh. (Orig.) *Economics and Politics of Public Education, No. 1: Schoolmen and Politics; A Study of State Aid to Education in the Northeast.* Syracuse, N.Y.: Syracuse University Press.

Brookover, Wilbur B., and David Gottlieb. *A Sociology of Education,* Second Edition. New York: American Book Co., 1964.

Burkhart, J. "The Dangers of Federal Aid to Education," *School and Society,* LXXXII (September 17, 1955), 83-84.

Burkhead, Jesse. (Orig.) *Economics and Politics of Public Education, No. 7: State and Local Taxes for Public Education.* Syracuse, N.Y.: Syracuse University Press.

Burkhead, Jesse. *Public School Finance, Economics and Policies.* Syracuse, N.Y.: Syracuse University Press, 1964.

Butts, R. Freeman. "States' Rights and Education," *Teachers College Record,* LVIII (January, 1957), 189-87.

Campbell, Ronald F., and John A. Ramseyer. *School-Community Relations.* Boston: Allyn and Bacon, 1955.

Clark, Harold F. (Orig.) *Economics and Politics of Public Education, No. 5: Cost and Quality in Public Education.* Syracuse, N.Y.: Syracuse University Press.

Conant, James B. *American High School Today.* (Orig.) (12390) New York: McGraw-Hill Paperback Series, McGraw-Hill Book Co.

Corey, Arthur F. "Federal Aid Without Federal Control," *School and Society,* XXCIII (March 17, 1956), 104.

Freeman, Roger A. *Federal Aid to Education—Boon or Bane?* Washington, D.C.: American Enterprise Association, 1955.

————. "A New Look at Federal Aid to Education," *School and Society*, XXCIII (March 17, 1956), 90-96.

Kerr, Norman D. "The School Board as an Agency of Legitimation," *Sociology of Education*, Vol. 38, No. 1, Fall, 1964.

Marsh, Paul E., and Ross A. Gortner. (Orig.) *Economics and Politics of Public Education, No. 6: Federal Aid to Science Education; Two Programs.* Syracuse, N.Y.: Syracuse University Press.

Martin, Roscoe C. (Orig.) *Economics and Politics of Public Education, No. 2: Government and the Suburban School.* Syracuse, N.Y.: Syracuse University Press.

Martin, Roscoe C. *Government and the Suburban School.* Syracuse, N.Y.: Syracuse University Press, 1962.

Morris, V. "Grass-roots-ism and the Public Schools," *School and Society*, XXCV (June 22, 1957), 217-19.

Munger, Frank J., and Richard Fenno. (Orig.) *Economics and Politics of Public Education, No. 3: National Politics in Federal Aid to Education,* Syracuse, N.Y.: Syracuse University Press.

Sufrin, Sidney C. (Orig.) *Economics and Politics of Public Education, No. 4: Issues in Federal Aid to Education.* Syracuse, N.Y.: Syracuse University Press.

382

PART VI
THE ASSESSMENT OF SCHOOLS

XV

An Evaluation of
American and Russian Education

Editors' Comment

*Though some of the discussion of schools today is favorable and
constructive, there is no doubt that much is negative and heavily critical. Even if most reports were favorable, it would still be significant
that so much discussion is felt to be needed. The feeling is hard to
overcome that professional educators in their journals, newspapers, and
public appearances protest too much about the goodness of the schools.*

*It is very easy to build a case for either side. We can urge that all of
the present delinquency and low achievement of our youth is caused
by the sins of the schools. On the other hand, we can whitewash the
schools and toss the blame right back on society by saying that if the
schools and the teachers were perfectly efficient, the youth would still
be victims of poverty, delinquency, and frustration.*

*At the level of destructive criticism, it is much like a contest of two
equal-sized serpents endeavoring to swallow each other by the tails.
No matter how the contest turns out, neither can win. We all realize
that teachers are required to do too much when they stand against a
brick wall and try to socialize forty youngsters with the gun, whip,
and chair of psychology and common sense. Yet it is quite easy for
teachers to rationalize that others, or society in general, will teach items*

that they failed to teach. Because they are unable to reach forty children in an hour, they convince themselves that it is useless to attempt to reach every one. And they feel, as many realize, that though a lawyer or a surgeon is shown his mistakes immediately, the mistakes of the teacher may walk abroad in the land for sixty or more years.

Even the best intentioned and scientifically devised research to determine the truth of the situation is fraught with tremendous difficulties. The chain of cause and effect, from poor teaching to juvenile delinquency for example, is chock-full of gratuitous assumptions. On the other hand, proving that the school has a beneficent effect on the community is no easier. The multiplicity of factors involved in showing the effects of the school, good or bad, on the community is so great that any limited study needs much qualification.

With such cautions in mind, it is possible to evade issues and problems directed from either side—from those who make the schools scapegoats for our ills, and those who whitewash it. This is the greatest danger of all, of becoming indifferent or hypocritical in these days when constructive changes are so vital. We argue for free inquiry, the willingness to accept the best evidence we can attain, and accepting the moral responsibility to work for betterment.

We should therefore look at our ills unblinkingly and consider not only the numbers who can't read or have had dealings with the police, but the whole structure and purpose of the school and the society from which it cannot be separated. If we achieve the understanding that the boy who gets up, yells at the teacher, and runs out of the classroom is everyone's problem and not a matter for a picayunish assessment of blame to a single teacher or parent, we shall be on the right foot to solving our problems.

We therefore want to know how badly off our whole society is, especially our youth, and what can be done about the ills of the society through the educational institution.

In some ways we are better off than we think. The kind of teaching and learning done in our schools is of a generally higher standard and efficiency than obtained a few years ago. We can argue against those who want to radically revamp a system which we have built for the purpose of educating all and not just those selected after various traditional or constructed criteria. We need not take direction from the Rus-

sians, nor should we disdain to look at any facet of what amounts to a gigantic learning experiment in their country. We have to assess the effectiveness of our schools by looking at the best primary evidence—the youth turned out, ready to take their places as mature adults. In all this, we must avoid being rashly judgmental. The quick scanning of a scene like American education is comparable to reconnoitering a continent from a flying saucer. We would unavoidably miss much detail as well as over-all consciousness of the general situation. Yet we shall find much we can change by new experiments in human creativity.

When we look over some of the literature and listen to the criticism of the American schools, we sometimes wonder how this great institution manages to keep going and fulfill its functions. The teacher is hedged about with all kinds of "do's" and "don't's," many of them opposing, so that he is bound to land in trouble whatever he does. The administrators are subjected to a variety of community pressures that ask variously for more religion in school, less athletics, or higher or lower standards. All their expected activities are inhibited by interruptions and investigations by public-spirited citizens. The public school is exhorted, cajoled, and pleaded with to do better and fulfill many divergent, inconsistent, and unrealistic goals. Failing to perform, voluminous abuse is heaped upon it, and it is held at bay by the fact that the public always holds the purse strings.

If we were to imagine the system as a personalization, we would find an old man with a heavy load, suffering and creaking at the joints, harassed by spectators and even well-wishers at all sides, and confused by opposing bits of advice. This, of course, is an oversimplification. Yet even the ideal school system in our society is filled with all kinds of problems. The strange fact is that education manages to keep going.

Some critics say that standards are not high enough, that our boys and girls are not really challenged. Others charge that we go in for "frills" and social passing, and we do not educate the students in the real subjects, such as mathematics, physics, and foreign language.

Many charge that education is too permissive and luxurious, that lack of discipline has disorganized the youth and turned them toward delinquency. Passing is easy, work is minimal, and nobody in the modern school really seems to care.

In this chapter, differing assessments of various kinds make the *problem more complex than just a pro and con. There is no conclusive answer; we leave the final judgment to the reader.*

As Santayana observed, people who do not read history are doomed to repeat its errors. Unfortunately, history is like the Oracle at Delphi which "neither reveals nor conceals, but merely indicates." We are never able to observe the same identical situation and make another decision in the crystal clear imagery of hindsight. Yet, though we see the future "as through a glass darkly" this is better than no vision at all. We see something because the past wells up before us in our hour of decision. We are presently engaged in a cold war with Russia, in which everything the Soviets do, and everything we do, assumes a competitive posture. An historical parallel that comes to mind is the rivalry between Sparta and Athens. Sparta became a great military camp, in contrast to Athens which was a democratic state in many ways. Sparta dedicated itself to building physical might. Athenian education sought to build the "whole man." In a war between the two, Sparta won, and Athens vainly attempted to regain her lost power by conquest and coercion. (Sparta fell to Thebes, who eventually met her master, too.)

In war, the "ultimate extension of politics," the one with the greatest power wins. War is a simplification and degradation of human ends. All truly creative thought, all decisions on the nature of society itself are held in abeyance, submerged to the end of winning. Unfortunately, the side which is most debased and most determined will probably be the victor.

Soviet education is modeled on a bleak, Spartan plan that makes for admirable economy of effort and productivity. The planners know exactly where they are going and how to get there. The underlying motivation is a war psychology: Beat the capitalists in every possible department—in production, in domination of world population, in educational effort. In education, hours are long, the testing brutal and unrelenting. The marchers never halt to aid their fallen comrades. Every new school is a skirmish lost or won; every graduating class joins the ranks of militia that desperately need them.

We would do ourselves a disservice to underestimate the Russian educational plant. However, although numbers given us may be accurate, they may also be misleading, since the conditions of the two countries are so dissimilar. For example, it is said that Russia turns out three or four times more engineers than we. Others argue that Russian engineers in general do not deserve the name. The numbers and quantities are relatively meaningless, and we think should not greatly concern us.

The important question is how much is concern for Russian education affecting us? It can affect us positively or negatively, and the evidence is that it has largely had a negative effect. We are exhorted to be like the Russians with their emphasis on tough classes and high standards, and our crop of gutless, social passing nincompoops are held up as the horrible example of our education. We are reminded that we cannot expect to fill our reserves on the eve of Armageddon by our means of recruiting and training. Outside of the enjoinder to "be like the Russians," our critics have merely contributed a flood of invectives.

If we allow ourselves to be governed by a war psychology, Russia will have, in a sense, won the battle; we would be meeting the devil on his own terms. Education would become an institution of military barracks, with each student going through in lock step, learning specified materials as fast as he could, but not learning to think. Little choice would be open to him; a test failure would be fatal. Worst of all, the society would lose its objectivity, its sense of self-criticism, its creativity. The wheel would have turned full circle, taking us back into an authoritarian, tyrannical state and a rigid social hierarchy.

The several articles that follow are aimed at an assessment of Soviet education in comparison with our own. Ever since Sputnik knocked America's provincialism into a cocked hat, we have been making a reappraisal of our educational system. More than ever, people are aware that the greatest battle in the ideological war is being conducted in the field of education. Now that the initial clamor has died down, we are able to distinguish some of the salient similarities and differences between our and Soviet education.

1) Soviet education is not something new. It is based on the continental model, emphasizing academic excellence.

2) Soviet and American education are not directly comparable, as they are institutions inextricably interwoven with their respective cultures. Thus many parallels made out of context are largely meaningless.

3) Soviet education is more democratic than ours in the sense that those who have ability are given every opportunity for advancement.

It is not as democratic in that those who fail never get another chance, and the whole Soviet society is more rigid, more closed to mobility than ours is.

4) Education has become more extensive in its operations and implications than mere classroom teaching. The ground swell of change has made every tool and every symbol a matter of learning. Education has become a cosmic race for survival.

In a masterful address to the American Association of Colleges for Teacher Education, Sidney Hook identifies the core elements of attack on education in the arguments of Albert Lynd, Robert Hutchins, and Arthur Bestor and makes a trenchant, logical refutation of their positions. We present only salient parts, but the reader should study the entire address.

MODERN EDUCATION AND ITS CRITICS
Sidney Hook*

. . . I propose tonight to consider some general criticisms of modern education and the assumptions behind them. And for occasions of this sort I shall proceed in an unprecedented way but one consistent with the principles of modern education. I shall take as points of concrete departure the recent writings of three widely-heralded critics—Mr. Albert Lynd, Mr. Robert Hutchins and Mr. Arthur Bestor—examining in each case some central points in their animadversions against modern education. After assessing the validity of their charges and the worth of their major recommendations—I shall conclude with some critical observations of my own.

To begin with we must distinguish between the substance and the manner of these criticisms. The manner is almost invariably rude and contemptuous. The title of Mr. Lynd's book is *Quackery in the Public Schools*. Professional educators, especially professors of education, are the quacks, and the teachers, with some exceptions, their unwilling or willing victims. . . .

* Sidney Hook, "Modern Education and Its Critics," *Seventh Yearbook*, The American Association of Colleges for Teacher Education (Washington, 1954), 141-43, 148-50, 151, 152. Reprinted by permission.

Let us state his argument for him. His charge is that modern schools have by and large failed to fulfill their proper function. Their proper function is to teach students how to think, to develop their powers of observation, to make them aware of their cultural origins and continuity with the past, and to instill in them a devotion to the heritage of freedom. In the past these ends were achieved by "formal study in skills and abstract principles": in the elementary schools, through conscientious application to the three R's; in the high schools, through the conventional curriculum of mathematics, foreign languages, grammar, Latin, systematic history, and some sciences; in the colleges, through more of the same. The products of our schools today cannot think or observe properly. They are ignorant of history, and impatient of the intellectual and moral discipline necessary to freedom. All this is a consequence of the abandonment of the conventional curriculum. But the cause of the abandonment is the acceptance of the ideas of the new education whose fountainhead is Dewey. Therefore, to the extent that professional educators and teachers profess allegiance to these principles, they are opposed to "true" education; to the extent that our schools are operated on these principles, they cannot impart "true" education.

Nowhere does Lynd consider whether the ends of a proper education—which he fails to see are among the ends of modern education, too—were *in fact* realized by the traditional curriculum, or whether they were more *completely* realized by the traditional curriculum than by current curricula. He simply ignores all the failures of the past and all the successes of the present. By Mr. Lynd's anecdotal method one could make out a very damaging case of widespread failure in the past. But such a method establishes nothing.

Nor do his historical references establish much more. Examine—in the light of historical evidence—the typical, exaggerated claims by critics of this school that the classical curriculum has been the chief and continuing support of freedom in the Western world. After all, the European countries in which the educational curriculum was and still is the most conventional, in which the secondary schools give *all* students instruction in the classical disciplines, so dearly beloved by Mr. Lynd, were the countries which produced, often with the direct connivance or benevolent neutrality of their classically-educated elite —Fascism, Vichyism, Nazism, and Bolshevism. . . .

A second type of criticism goes further than that so far considered.

It underlines current strictures against modern education but is not content with a return merely to the conventional models. It substitutes a comprehensive conception of education—new in form but perennial in essence—to guide the remolding of our educational institutions. This conception, whose banner bearer is Mr. Hutchins, has been worked out in detail for liberal education of a specific kind—the only kind there is, we are assured—on the college level. The curriculum of the elementary and high schools is to be reorganized in such a way as to make this kind of liberal education possible for all students.

This view, whose most recent expression is found in *Conflicts in Education* (N.Y., 1953), is frankly and proudly nonempirical. It makes great play with deductions from axiomatic first principles and proposes to do what I have tried to show cannot be done, viz., validly to derive a desirable educational program from metaphysical premises.

Here I wish only to analyze some of the leading assumptions behind his position. The first assumption concerns the ends of education and how they are derived. The second concerns the curricular means by which these ends are to be achieved. The third, and most important, concerns the claim that to deny the adequacy of Mr. Hutchins' curricular means involves a denial of the democratic philosophy itself.

That the *central* aim of education should be the development of man's power of thought is, so far as I know, denied by nobody—provided we do not identify power of thought with a specific intellectual skill. But, whereas most educators justify the emphasis on thought because of its key role in the organization of impulse and feeling, the control of action, and the enrichment of the meanings of experience even when we cannot act, Mr. Hutchins derives it from a definition of man's fixed and essential nature.

Man is a rational animal. He is uniquely different from other animals by virtue of his power to think. Therefore, education must be directed exclusively to the cultivation of his intellect.

Now there are several things wrong with the deduction. First, even if we deny that other animals can think—and not all psychologists agree with this—the power to think is not the only differentiating feature of the human animal. There are others. Man is the only animal who makes his tools. Man is the only animal with a sense of humor. If we were to derive our educational aims from these differentia, we

392

should have to say that man's education must primarily be vocational or technological or that it must develop his power to crack jokes.

Second, the nature of a thing is not completely given by what differentiates it. It includes what it has in common with other species in its genus. Man is a creature of emotion, an organism which adapts to and modifies its environment. An education appropriate to the nature of man must be appropriate to the *whole* of man's nature. This would include some things which Mr. Hutchins excludes. The Greeks, whom Mr. Hutchins takes as his model, regarded as the end of education, not exclusively intellectual development, but the harmonious development of all human faculties. For them a life of reason was no more identical with a reasoning life than a joy of life is identical with a life of joy.

Third, what do we mean by thought? Modern education, to the extent that it is inspired by Dewey, interprets it broadly as creative intelligence in the solution of problems which arise in *all* fields of human experience. But Mr. Hutchins seems to identify thought or reason with academic intellectuality, with verbal skills in the interpretation of texts.

This deductive approach from fallible first principles is carried over into discussion of the curriculum of education. Since by definition all men have a common nature, the education appropriate to that nature must be common, and the means of achieving it—the educational curriculum—must be common. Therefore education everywhere, at all times, and for all men (and women), must be the same. Contrast this with modern education which, not by deduction but by inquiry, discovers that men have a great many needs in common and yet vary greatly, that their differences in culture and time reflect themselves in the way their common needs are fulfilled, and that even in the same culture variations among them are appreciable. It therefore stresses the fact that their indisputable common need—the development of intelligence—may be achieved in different ways.

An analogy might make the point clearer. Everyone needs to be healthy. What it means to be healthy, i.e., the *definition* of health, is the same for all men. We might even concede that the *formal* requirements of a well-balanced diet necessary for health are the same for all men. But who will therefore deduce that all men must eat the same things at the same time, or exercise in the same way, in order to be

393

healthy? If there are differences among men, if they live in different climates and must perform different tasks, to prescribe a *common* dietary regimen is to guarantee that not all of them will be healthy. Just as there are different dietary roads to health, so there are different curricular roads to educational maturity. Great segments of these roads, of course, will be common. . . .

Accused in the past of advocating an education irrelevant, if not hostile, to the needs of men in a democratic society, Mr. Hutchins is now contending that only those who agree with his conception of the best education can be considered consistent democrats. To have "strong faith in the political judgment of the masses with strong doubts of their intellectual capacities," i.e., of their intellectual capacities to acquire the best education, writes Mr. Hutchins, is a paradox. And in criticism of those who penned the report of the President's Commission on Education he says, "They most undemocratically assume that the mass of people are incapable of achieving such an education. . . ."

What Mr. Hutchins is really saying is this: either accept the rule of an élite or of intellectual experts and give up democracy or admit that the masses are all potential intellectual experts in a democracy and educate them to be experts. But it is not necessary to be an expert to judge the basic policies proposed by experts. One can choose his doctor wisely without a medical education. It is Mr. Hutchins who is inconsistent here. For, in addressing his appeal for the reform of education to the community, he himself admits that wise educational decisions may be made by those who are not educational experts or who have not been nurtured on the great books. If there are any experts in the wisdom of life, they cannot be mass produced by the same education. It is one thing to say that a healthy democracy rests upon some kind of common education. It is quite another to say that *all* education in a democracy must be common. And it is still something else again to assert that the content of a common education must be unchanging and identical in every respect. . . .

In discussing Mr. Bestor's *Educational Wastelands* (Urbana, 1953) we are moving to another plane of criticism—one which is frankly empirical. Although Messrs. Hutchins and Lynd fortify their indictment of modern education by citing some unhappy experiences, they rest their case on other considerations. We have seen that Mr. Hutchins minces no words about it. Since the metaphysics of modern education is bad, its results must be bad.

Mr. Bestor, however, speaks for a large and ever-growing number of individuals who profess to judge modern education by its results. And he is profoundly convinced that the results of our schools, especially of our elementary and secondary schools, are turning out young men and women not only unwilling to think in a disciplined way but unable to do so; not only ignorant about what they should know but, even worse, ignorant of what to do and where to go to repair the deficiencies of their knowledge when they become aware of them. They simply lack the habits of inquiry. "Intellectual training," he says, ". . . has been pushed out to the periphery of the public school program." (p. 44.) "Public school educationists have severed all real connection with the great world of science and learning" (p. 47).

The evidence? Some startling quotations from the writings of a school principal or a professor of education, with no confirming evidence that it represents the dominant sentiment among modern teachers or that the results of modern instruction verify it. For example, Mr. Bestor quotes a sentence which, although he characterizes it as extreme, he nonetheless takes as representative of the current mood in American schools. It is a sentence which has been picked up by popular magazines in what seems to be a campaign to scare the parents of the country.

"We shall some day accept the thought that it is just as illogical to assume that every boy must be able to read as it is that each one must be able to perform on a violin, that it is no more reasonable to require that each girl shall spell well than it is that each one shall bake a good cherry pie."

The implication is that this truly horrifying thought is guiding current practices in teaching the fundamental skills in our elementary schools. But what of the studies which show that modern schools do better in this respect than those of the past? All that shows, according to Mr. Bestor, is that, making allowance for improvement in physical conditions and for the increase of the school year, the improvement is not good *enough*. The results of the *Eight-Year Study*? All that shows is that the colleges in which the products of progressive high schools did well were not very good to begin with.

.   .   .   .

But there is another device which modern educators sometimes use which is not more widely used because it is feared that it has undemocratic implications. This is the differentiation of students on the basis of their native capacities and achievements in order to prevent the more gifted from being bored by teaching approaches necessary to motivate the less gifted, and in order to prevent the latter from falling behind when the former are given their head. I do not see how this breaches the democratic commitment of modern education in any way. That individuals vary in their musical or athletic prowess is accepted as a matter of course. It is not unfair discrimination to give to those who vary in their learning power different tasks or the same tasks to complete in different times. In many schools this device is widely used. Some high school students cover the course in intermediate algebra in six months; others take a year; a few are encouraged to master the material by self-study. In some English classes four books are intensively studied, in others three. There seems to be no resentment among student who travel at a slower pace, and there is less educational dissatisfaction than there probably would be if they found themselves in the same classes.

This principle can be generalized and applied to colleges, too. In each case, the end of education will be the same—the development of habits of intelligent inquiry. But the curriculum and methods by which the end is achieved do not have to be the same even when certain disciplines are required for all. Some critics of modern education do not object to this so long as institutions which depart from standard curricula are not *called* colleges. But it is unimportant what educational institutions are called. What is important is that genuine learning goes on in them, even if they are not degree granting, and that teachers do not settle for less if better training can achieve more.

The best adult education gives us a parallel and many helpful clues. Subjects, methods and levels of instruction vary. But they all justify themselves to the extent that they contribute to individual growth.

One final word. Modern education will always be on the defensive if it waits for criticisms from those who are hostile to its philosophy before facing its problems and correcting its defects. It is the modern educators themselves who should be the foremost critics of modern education.

Since many of the attacks on education are made on empirical grounds, "Johnny can't read" and "they don't teach the kids any more," are the substantial charges. A large body of evidence definitely disproves this. We append some facts from a typical study comparing modern and older education, which attests to the superior job that most of our schools are doing as compared with "the good old days."

THE TRUTH ABOUT OUR PUBLIC SCHOOLS *

. . . The truth is that your youngster, unless he's the victim of some unfortunate exception, probably is getting a better education today than he ever could have got in the public schools before. That means in both grade school and high school. Modern schools and modern methods are, by and large, turning out a superior product despite enormously increased enrollments.

The point is to prove it.

Professional educators insist that it's ridiculous to hold that science, medicine and other fields have made great strides through research and new practices in the past 25 to 30 years and that education alone has not.

They add that parents who hark back to "the good old days" are really comparing a nostalgically ideal situation they *think* they remember with isolated horrible examples they hear about at second and third hand.

These two views probably make sense, but how can we know for sure?

More than a century ago, in 1848, the 40 best pupils in Cleveland —10 from each of four public schools—took a special test.

* "The Truth About Our Public Schools," *Changing Times: The Kiplinger Magazine*, VIII, No. 6 (June, 1954), 9-10. Reprinted by permission.

In 1947, the 40 brightest youngsters from four Cleveland junior high schools took the same test.

The 1848 children ranged from age 10 to 19, nine of them being 15 or over. The 1947 students were 12 to 14 and were in the eighth grade—a placement deemed comparable to that of the earlier group.

The examination included ten questions each on definitions of words, mental arithmetic, written arithmetic, American history, grammar and geography.

The 1947 youngsters heavily outscored those of 1848 in definitions, beat them in mental arithmetic, and nosed them out in written arithmetic. They barely lost to the 1848 kids in American history, despite the handicap of having nearly 100 years more of it to study.

The 1848 pupils won handily in grammar and geography, but over all, the 1947 boys and girls outscored those of a century before by compiling a total of 955 correct answers to 924. It was a clean-cut victory for the modern-day student.

In Indiana, someone dug up a test that had been given in 1919 to 5,748 seniors from 320 of the state's high schools.

Some 2,609 seniors in Indianapolis high schools were asked to take the same examination in 1941. The ten subjects ranged from rote memory to arithmetic to practical information.

Of a possible 190 points, the 1919 girls scored an average of 136 points; the boys, 139.

The 1941 girls averaged 151 points; the boys, 153.

In 1921, 5,690 children in the third through the eighth grade in Lincoln, Neb., were given a reading test. In 1947, some 5,100 Lincoln kids took the same test.

Here are the average scores, grade by grade, with the 1947 scores [italicized].

Grade 3: 44.34%—*57.69%;* Grade 4: 65.29%—*73.28%;* Grade 5: 76.47%—*90.13%;* Grade 6: 79.69%—*91.96%;* Grade 7: 89.50%—*94.01%;* Grade 8: 89.19%—*92.92%.*

A score or more of such instances rest in the files of educational offices throughout the country—most of them unpublished except in professional and related journals and unknown to the public at large.

Chicago, in 1950, for example, tested 10,000 of its public school pupils in arithmetic, scoring them against the national norm or average for their particular age group. The youngsters, all sixth graders, showed an arithmetical ability equal to that of seventh graders.

Austin, Minn., selected two of its schools in 1951 to repeat tests given children in the third through the sixth grade in the very same schools 30 years before. One test was in reading; another was in spelling.

In reading, the 1951 pupils were anywhere from a full year ahead of their 1921 counterparts at the third-grade level to a half year ahead at the sixth grade.

But in spelling the 1921 kids won.

In Dearborn, Mich., five public schools compared pupils in the fourth through the sixth grade in 1926 and 1951.

The 1951 youngsters showed themselves as much as a year and a half ahead of the 1926 boys and girls in reading and at least one semester ahead of them in arithmetic. In written and oral English the difference was even greater—the 1951 kids registering as much as a two-year lead over the corresponding 1926 class.

Only in spelling did Dearborn's 1951 crop of pupils fail to beat students of the previous generation.

One more instance. Fifty-seven fourth graders were chosen in Evanston, Ill., in 1952 to match in age, intelligence and family background a group of 57 children who in 1932 had taken reading, vocabulary, arithmetic and spelling tests.

The Evanston children of 1952 showed six to eight months' advancement over the 1932 group in reading comprehension, vocabulary and arithmetic.

But guess what.

In spelling, the earlier kids triumphed again. . . .

The tragedy of our schools is not found in objective tests, but in the quality of our education as received and used by the people. The totality adds up to a great under-utilization of potential.

THE UNDER-EDUCATION OF AMERICANS
*Wilfred R. Smith and August Kerber**

Two opposing arguments about the nature of American education are loudly proclaimed in the land. One side says that we are "too easy" on the children; we teach the stuffing of bunnies and home and family living from kindergarten through twelfth grade. We teach the children to relax, "get along," and become "good citizens"—back slapping conformists with empty heads. Bestor and Rickover bewail the miserable academic showing of students on hard subjects—mathematics, natural sciences, language, and history. They twit us with the statement that continental schools are better than ours. We are wasting our talented students, our teachers teach "the normal curve" and "students rather than subjects," and the whole fiber of our schools has deteriorated, they say.

The other side argues that our schools have been steadily getting better. In every area (except spelling in some cases) American children have been doing better in tests of subject mastery. A number of large cities have carried out systematic tests, and the well-documented results favor the modern students. We can hardly compare American students with those of Russia, because the systems are so different, but there is much room for challenging the Russian claim for superiority. Reports on the education of children of Great Britain are much more comparable to ours, and here again American children stand out well. One report revealed that British children were below a comparable group of ours in reading ability.[1] A study made by a Scot in the uncompromising atmosphere of his own schools showed that about half the time was spent on reading in their schools, compared with equivalent groups of Americans.[2]

* Wilfred R. Smith and August Kerber, "The Under-Education of Americans." Unpublished monograph, Wayne State University Press (Detroit, 1961).

[1] C. D. Taylor, "The Effect of Training on Reading Readiness," *Studies in Reading*, Vol. II (University of London Press, 1950), 63-80.

[2] W. W. Inglis, "The Early Stages of Reading: A Review of Recent Investigations," *Studies in Reading*, Vol. I (University of London Press, 1948), 1-92.

How about comic book reading? This proved to be indulged in twice as much by the English 11 to 15 year old as compared with their American cousins.[3]

Strangely, both viewpoints are right and equally wrong at the same time. If we tried to educate our children with a steady blast of core learning, the result would be disastrous. The children would stage a gigantic sit-down strike. On the other hand, the amount of under-education in the United States is cataclysmic. The difference, of course, is the gap between the actual and potential.

The whole school system of the United States is replete with tests to prove this under use of potential. We are talking of valid, reliable tests, not the *ad hoc* results obtained from studying an assigned chapter the night before. College entrance exams, Iowa Achievement Tests, civil service exams, placement tests of the military services, and many tests developed in schools and research institutions attest to the under-education of Americans.

Let us clarify that we mean all Americans, including the adults. In Flint, Michigan, a group of businessmen failed on a standard test that most sixth graders could pass. On a television program, "Candid Camera," the only person who could perform the particular mathe-matical problem presented was a junior high school boy—the only non-adult of the group. We are all familiar with the abysmal ignorance of world affairs of the man on the street as discovered by popular polls.

The argument is made that over 90 percent of history, chemistry, language, and mathematics is expected to be lost. What is important is transfer learning. Yet many tests show that Americans accrue very little transfer learning. In one investigation, when the ones tested dealt with certain operations of mathematics, like factorization, 1,000 of 1,200 succeeded. When these same operations were sufficient to solve simple problems, only 300 succeeded. If the children are asked to prove that the square of the hypotenuse is equal to the sum of the squares of the opposite two sides or right triangle ABC, most of them of the appropriate level succeed. Ask them to prove it for triangle PQR, and a surprising percentage of failure occurs!

We can also point out that the busses run, the utilities are main-tained, and the picture of Americans on the downtown streets is one

[3] A. R. Williams, "The Magazine Reading of Secondary School Children," *British Journal of Educational Sociology,* XXI (November, 1951), 186-198.

of happy, well-clothed, well-fed people. If they want to find out facts, there are almanacs, and there are experts to fix the leaks in the pipes, or frame the note to the Kremlin. This is a gratuitous assumption. We may take any kind of attitude toward a fact we want, is the general attitude. School will keep and chanticleer will call cheerily to greet the morn.

The tragedy of American education lies not in the objective and pragmatic results of the total society: Admittedly the achievement of producing 425 billion dollars of gross national product per year is not to be sneezed at. The statistics of size, of performance, of numbers in any given field, including education, are impressive. The tragedy is the smug and complacent attitude of the average American, who has only the most superficial and distorted awareness of learning which any reasonable person would expect him to master. So many Americans do not have a fundamental knowledge of arithmetic, geography, physical science, and social studies.

The danger is that the machine we have made, our culture, will outstrip the ability of average Americans to understand it. We already have to depend too much on experts and elites in "think tanks" to tell us how much we need of what, when, where, and how. Large blocks of areas are already declared secret, "vital to national defense." An ancient rule of expediency hallows much of this. But where will it end? The crisis is qualitative, not quantitative. The determination of one's fate in a democracy depends on knowing foreign languages, the life cycle of tadpoles, heat of fusion, quadratic equations, and constitutional law. The muttering apology of "Let George do it," is the creaking of the imminent avalanche for a civilization of conformists and carriers.

Anthropologists point out that the institutions of man are impli-cated in the whole culture, and the doctrine of the "strain toward con-sistency" prevails. Soviet education, like ours, must conform to the prevailing cultural patterns. The following article by Brubacher is an insightful and comprehensive resumé of USSR education frankly pre-sented to a "bourgeois" audience. Naturally, such an article reveals biases on both side. Our question would be to both sides—"Wherein lies freedom?"

NOTES ON EDUCATION BEHIND THE IRON CURTAIN
John S. Brubacher

The following notes are the result of an Eastern European seminar conducted in the summer of 1964 by the Comparative Education Society. The seminar held sessions for six weeks, spending a week each in Warsaw, Moscow, Bucharest, Belgrade, Budapest, and Prague. In each capital members of the local Trade Union of Teachers arranged lectures, symposia, and open forums in which we discussed educational problems of mutual concern. As you might expect, pedagogical issues constantly involved broader political and economic ones. Discussions at all times were amazingly frank. We pulled no intellectual punches and they countered, I have no doubt, with the party line. The thrust and parry on both sides was continually challenging. The men and women who met with us were uniformly from the upper echelons of educational and party leadership. On at least two occasions we met with vice-ministers of education and on at least two others with vice-rectors of universities. Besides meeting in seminar we also visited school plants. No classes were being held during the summer vacation, of course; however, on several of our field trips out into the countryside we saw children in summer camps.

In the following remarks I have tried to digest the lectures and dialogue of the summer. I have not consulted treatises. My effort rather is to tell what our informants thought important to tell us both in their prepared remarks and in their responses to our questions. In reporting my reactions my principal anxiety is that I will over-gen-eralize. There is much about Communist education that is uniform in all the countries we visited, but there was disavowal that Moscow insisted it be so. Moreover, there is increasing diversity in the satellite countries. Our newspapers have confirmed this diversity since the fall of Khrushchev, but we were aware of it that summer even before the event.

It will come as no surprise and certainly as no over-generalization at the outset when I say that education in the iron curtain countries is predicated on Marxist-Leninist principles. This is basic. Repeatedly, when sharp differences of opinion on educational policy arose in our discussions our Communist hosts would remind us that we and they started from basically different assumptions. But that is to be expected. Aristotle made this point clear centuries ago in his *Politics*. There he says that an educational system should be in harmony with whatever form the constitution takes. Let me first, therefore, report these Marxist-Leninist principles as our informants expounded them. After that we can note how Communist education is in harmony with them.

I

Perhaps the appeal of Marxist-Leninist principles can best be gathered from the remarks of a member of the government in Belgrade. He recalled for us that before World War II Yugoslavia had been under the rule of King Peter, a Serbian, and a landed aristocracy who were often absentee landlords. After the Germans overran Yugoslavia, Mihailovitch organized a resistance movement, expecting to pick up the pieces after the Germans had been driven out. But for whom? Obviously, to return them to Peter and his nobility. Here is where Tito entered the picture. He too organized a resistance to pick up the pieces, but for the people themselves. Confronted with a choice between the two leaders, it is easy to see why the people preferred the Communist, Tito. The birth and *raison d'etre* of communism in Yugoslavia was as simple as that.

Perhaps elsewhere behind the iron curtain the transition to communism was not so simple, but there can be no doubt that the Marxist-Leninist notion that the land and instruments of production should belong to the people, i.e., be publicly owned, makes a strong appeal. Instead of being exploited, the Yugoslav people now work for themselves, we were told, and as a result economic productivity has jumped twofold. Like all iron-curtain countries, the Yugoslavs have a people's democracy. Once we asked what other kind of democracy there could be than a people's democracy, seeing that the Greek origin of the word means "rule by the people." Our respondents said that Western democracy is "bourgeois democracy." In other words, they want all to wield the power so far wielded only by the few, even in our democracy.

Inasmuch as the people in Communist countries own their resources, they must decide how to spend their public income. In any economic society, capitalist or Communist, perhaps the single most important decision is to determine how much of the public income shall go into wages and how much into reinvestment. In capitalist economies private entrepreneurs may decide that times are inopportune for investment. If they do, opportunities for employment may correspondingly decline. The working force is at the mercy of private owners. This situation is unlikely to occur in a Communist economy because the people will insure continuous investment and thus insure continuous employment. Indeed, Communists pride themselves on the fact that they do not suffer from periodic unemployment. If anything they suffer from overemployment. Yet when we asked whether it isn't inefficient to have what we would call "featherbedding," they immediately asked whether efficiency and unemployment were to be preferred to inefficiency and full employment.

The Communists are, however, not unmindful of efficiency. Collectivised farming, of which we hear so much in the press, is a good instance. When we flew into Warsaw we noticed how the landscape was shredded into narrow ribbons of crops. These narrow ribbons have resulted from the laws of inheritance and the successive divisions of the patrimony among sons. As a result, most of the farms today are far too small to afford labor-saving machinery. No wonder the state tries to encourage these farmers to consolidate their holdings in collectivized farms. But even where this occurs through assent or force, the same problem bobs up of how much of farm income to allot to wages and how much to machines, fertilizer, and the like. This critical decision is a people's decision.

Obviously, the apportioning of income involves planning. What portions are to be set aside and for what activities is not left to chance as in the free market of capitalism. The Communist tries intelligently to foresee events and plan for them. This is more necessary in underdeveloped economies—and all the iron-curtain country economies are underdeveloped—than in the more fully developed ones of the West. The Eastern Europe economies are striving mightily to lift themselves by their economic bootstraps. The only way to get relatively large amounts of capital for this purpose quickly is through state effort and planning.

The role of public ownership and public planning is so important that one can't help but ask the question, How can one ever expect the state to "wither away," as in traditional Marxist-Leninist ideology? To this question we got several answers. In the first place there is no intent that it should wither away so long as there is danger of war between capitalist and Communist countries. A strong state is indispensable to waging war successfully. Moreover, one should remember that eliminating the threat of war is more than a matter of controlling nuclear explosions or reducing armaments. Communists do not think peace can be assured till everywhere man is free from the threat of economic exploitation by his fellow man. In the second place, on the assumption that peace is assured, the withering away of the state is not supposed to leave a condition of anarchy. On the contrary, political units will be replaced by economic ones, notably trade unions. But more of that shortly. In the third place, we must remember that none of the iron-curtain countries thinks it has achieved communism as yet. All are still in a state of socialism. Communism still lies ahead. Upon asking what the difference between the two is, we got the following answer: In a socialist economy a worker's pay is roughly apportioned to his production. In a communistic economy he will produce according to his ability but receive according to his need.

II

Now, what are some of the ways in which educational practice is predicated on the foregoing principles? Let us start out with the point left hanging a moment ago, the development of trade unions which presumably will some day replace state authority. This goal for the development of trade unions will indicate at once the importance of the Trade Union of Teachers which was our constant host in each of the countries we visited. The union enrolls 90 percent and more of all the teachers and is organized in the form of a pyramid. The top officials of the Trade Union of Teachers meet with the top officials of other trade unions to plan economic policies such as the division of the national income. The Central Council of Trade Unions will, of course, be represented in the Central Committee of the Communist Party and ultimately in the Presidium.

You might think that the interests of education could easily get lost as they wend their way up such a power structure. But not so, we were told in Moscow. For illustration, trade-union officials took the national salary hike for teachers which was announced that summer. In the preliminary deliberations considerable dissatisfaction was expressed about the proportionate slice of the national income to be awarded teachers.

Through thorough discussion of the issue from top to bottom of the Trade Union of Teachers pyramid, it was possible for the union to prove itself deserving of a larger slice than originally apportioned.

The importance of the trade union can also be seen in the direction of what we would call fringe benefits. The union is the agency through which the teacher arranges his summer vacation and also the placement of his child in a summer camp. (Incidentally, we could not help but note a certain élitism in the pioneer camp we visited outside of Moscow: It was limited to the children of members of the trade unions of teachers and scientific workers.) Similarly, one's union is the agency through which to arrange for hospitalization if one needs it. Indeed, if the teacher just wants to change his apartment, his union must say whether he deserves it.

Similarly, if the administration wants to change a teacher's assignment it cannot be done without the teacher's consent. If negotiations are necessary the union must be consulted. Again, if the teacher must defend himself against complaints as to his work the union will be involved. No wonder 90 percent of the teachers belong to the union!

On one occasion we asked whether the theory of collectivism underlying the trade union had any impact on classroom instruction. In asking the question, of course, we were wondering whether teachers share with children the planning of the curriculum. But no, Communist theory does not call for this. To them collectivism in the classroom means only that the children have a right to complain about the amount of work assigned and the quality of the instruction—a typical trade-union point of view, one might say.

It would be a mistake to think that the only significance of the

Trade Union of Teachers is economic. The union is also interested in upgrading its members professionally. To this end it arranges for the in-service training of its members through courses of one sort or another.

Not only do the interests of education not suffer from being caught up in a power structure like the one of which the Trade Union of Teachers is a part, they actually seem to benefit from it. No doubt this is one of the advantages of planning. Behind the iron curtain teachers do not have to wage an uphill battle to gain national recognition of their contribution to the national welfare. On the contrary, it is seen by the Presidium and Central Committee of the Communist Party that the fulfillment of the goals of socialism and communism cannot be had without an important reliance on education. A prestigious educational system, therefore, is not the random result of a free competitive system but of a deliberate national plan.

As a result, interestingly enough, the iron-curtain countries have no problem in recruiting teachers. Neither, at the same time, do they have overproduction of teachers or other learned professionals. In a planned society they know in advance how many highly trained personnel they will need in the period ahead in various categories and so admit only that many to places in their institutions of higher education. Selection thus takes place before students enter these institutions, not after they leave and seek jobs.

If it is possible to upgrade the prestige of education by national planning, so too Communists believe that national taste in the arts can be similarly upgraded. On the outskirts of Moscow we visited a vast industrial and agricultural exhibit. The music wafted from loudspeakers on the grounds was uniformly of classical quality. Again, in Hungary we talked with the minister in charge of radio and television programs. The government, he told us, put the choice of programs in the hands of a committee of artists. They, better than private entrepreneurs wanting to advertise their goods, can be the arbiters of what the public should enjoy. And what a joy to have television without commercials!

Not only does the planned society upgrade the standards of public taste, it does another very important thing. It brings them within the range of the humblest purse. In Warsaw we attended an operetta rendered with excellent voices amidst excellent stage trappings. The tickets

408

were so cheap, however, that I opined to our host that the evening's "take" wouldn't even pay for the costumes. He replied that it was the policy of the state to subsidize the performance so all could attend. Judging from the people we saw at the ballet in Moscow, I am sure the state was also subsidizing their presence.

However successful or well-intentioned this planning, the question leaps almost at once to Western lips, "Is there not danger of abuse in this control of the public mind?" Take newspapers as an instance. In the hotels where we stopped about the only papers it was possible to buy were Communist. Only on rare occasions could we obtain even a Paris edition of the *New York Times* or *Herald-Tribune*. But then, in how many leading American hotels could you buy a copy of *Pravda* or *Izvestia*? Although I lacked the foreign-language facility to read the local press, I was assured that there was a continual lively discussion about Marxist-Leninist principles. In Hungary even a Catholic press was tolerated.

In Moscow we spent a morning with the editor of the *Pedagogical Gazette*, which has a national circulation. The editor, who had had wide experience in the public schools both as teacher and administrator, assured us that she admitted to the columns of the *Gazette* a wide diversity of viewpoints. She was aware of no one, she vigorously claimed, who was looking over her shoulder to censor her judgment.

But the most dramatic incident on the point of freedom arose in Yugoslavia. After one of our very able informants had made a broad claim for the existence of intellectual freedom in his country, one of our number parried with, "What about Djilas?" Djilas, it will be remembered, was one of Tito's closest intimates in the resistance against the Germans. Yet, because he differed sharply with Tito on the reconstruction of Yugoslavia after peace came, Tito threw him in jail. Subsequently, Tito relented and released him, but Djilas persisted in criticizing the regime to a point where Tito felt he had to rearrest him. Of Djilas' patriotism, as anyone can see, there can be no doubt. So it was a very pointed question to inquire why Djilas was still languishing in prison.

Our informant fielded the question with unusual candor and frankness. In the first place, he said, in the early days after the war Yugoslavia's new regime was not stable enough to withstand such penetrating criticism as Djilas offered. In the second place, now that stability had been achieved it was too late to reconstruct society along fundamentally different lines such as Djilas had in mind. Besides, in the third place, our informant said, Djilas had no following. Well, if he had no following, why was Tito afraid of him? Presumably because stability of the present regime is to be preferred to some unknown instability. These answers may not seem irrefutable, but one must admit they are straightforward.

The identification of freedom with security has one further dimension in which Communists take pride. If you say you think they sacrifice freedom to security, likely as not they will say, "Is it nothing that we have free higher education, free medical service, and are looking forward to the day when we will have rent-free apartments?" No people in capitalistic countries are free from anxieties on any of these points. To be sure, this is a different kind of freedom from what we have been discussing, but it should not be overlooked.

There is now one final critical point at which the Communist system demands, as Aristotle put it, an educational system in harmony with it. This point concerns the spirit of motivation. In a planned society like that behind the iron curtain, how can the people assure themselves that the planning is done in their interest? One answer, of course, is to join one's trade union and thus have a voice, however small, in the planning, as did the teachers in their pay raise. Another answer is to join the party and have a part in its activities. In a way, however, this answer begs the question. As everyone knows, the party is only a small minority of the total citizenry. It is, as one might say, an élite citizenry. Consequently the question still arises, How can the mass of citizens be assured that this élite group will not plan and manage in their own interest?

The real answer to the question of motivation is education. In Russia, particularly, they talk of educating the "new Soviet man." Who is this *new* Soviet man? Primarily, he is a man whom the schools have taught not only to work but to *esteem* work. Indeed, when communism succeeds socialism, as indicated earlier, the *new* Soviet man will have learned to produce according to his ability and receive according to his need. Most capitalist-minded people believe that communism will inevitably fail in this attempt because it runs counter to human nature.

410

Man, they believe, is biologically a self-seeking creature and there is no known way to change heredity. The Russians, on the contrary, believe that man's motives are socially conditioned and that it is, therefore, quite possible to educate a *new* man, one who is socially rather than selfishly oriented.

This kind of education continues out of school as well as in. Outside, one is taught to give as much of his unpaid time as possible to the party. Work for the benefit of society is the unqualified duty of all. Moreover, any work, whether mental or physical, commands respect. On at least two occasions we saw teen-agers engaged in just such social service. In Yugoslavia we saw youths working with road crews to build a new highway along the Dalmatian coast. And later in Czechoslovakia we saw rural villages overrun by teen-age boys and girls who had come out to help harvest hops for the famous Pilzner beer. Experiences such as these give the young the feeling of having a real stake in the economy.

Just as the Christian is taught to lay up treasure in heaven, so iron curtain youth are taught to lay up treasure with the party. Indeed, iron curtain countries make a moral issue of Communist motivation. In the vestibule of an elementary school we visited in Moscow we saw the following Communist decalogue, or rather duo-decalogue, painted on the wall and enjoining:

1. Devotion to the Communist cause; love of the socialist motherland and of the other socialist countries.

2. Conscientious labor for the good of society—he who does not work, neither shall he eat.

3. Concern on the part of everyone for the preservation and the growth of public wealth.

4. A high sense of public duty; intolerance of actions harmful to the public interest.

5. Collectivism and comradely mutual assistance; one for all and all for one.

6. Humane relations and mutual respect between individuals—man is to man a friend, comrade, and brother.

7. Honesty and truthfulness, moral purity, modesty, and unpretentiousness in social and private life.

8. Mutual respect in the family, and concern for the upbringing of children.

9. An uncompromising attitude toward injustice, parasitism, dishonesty, careerism, and money-grubbing.

10. Friendship and brotherhood among all peoples of the USSR; intolerance of national and racial hatred.

11. An uncompromising attitude toward the enemies of communism, peace, and the freedom of nations.

12. Fraternal solidarity with the working people of all countries, and with all peoples.

How successfully is the iron curtain system of education aiding Communist principles of politics and economics? There is no telling from a short six-weeks trip such as ours. We had reason to believe that there are some behind the iron curtain who have genuine misgivings about the outcome. But we have no doubt, too, that most of those in charge are dedicated to the future and have high hopes for its outcome. It will be a grave mistake for us in the West to fail to assess accurately the driving force of Communist utopianism.

The doctrine of cultural relativism is that finally, in human understanding, a culture can only be understood on its own terms. We cannot say whether we are better, or worse, than another people. Education is so inextricably interwoven with all of culture that we cannot meaningfully compare two educational systems like that of the United States and that of Russia; it would be like comparing two utterly different satellites of two utterly different worlds. George Counts makes his point well in the next excerpt.

THE REAL CHALLENGE OF SOVIET EDUCATION
George S. Counts*

. . . The question is often asked: "Is the Soviet system of education better than ours?" Put in this form the question makes very little sense. Since education is always a most intimate expression of the

* George S. Counts, "The Real Challenge of Soviet Education," *Education Digest*, XXV, No. 1 (September, 1959), 5-8. Reprinted by permission.

life and institutions of a given society, unless it is imposed from without by armed force, comparison of different systems is extremely difficult and hazardous. The ancient philosophers knew this very well. But let us turn to one of the most thoughtful students of the modern age, to a man whose writings influenced the founders of our republic—Montesquieu. Over two centuries ago in his *Spirit of the Laws*, he observed that "the laws of education ought to be in relation to the principles of government." One should add: to the whole system of society with its social heritage, its institutions, its body of values, and its power structure. This means that a program of education entirely suited to one society might destroy another.

The educational implications of the Soviet political system are plain. At the polls in the Soviet Union the ordinary citizen is not expected to pass judgment on issues of policy or of personality. At the election of delegates to the Supreme Soviet last March—the institution corresponding to our Congress—99.97 percent of the eligible voters went to the polls. But of these less than one half of one percent entered the voting booths. All the rest merely picked up a ballot over here and put it into a box over there—an act that one of Pavlov's dogs could have learned to perform in a few hours.

The preparation for citizenship of the citizen of the Soviet Union must take the form of inculcating in him unquestioning loyalty to the regime. The central ingredient in education in Communist morality, a subject which receives more attention in Soviet pedagogies than instruction in natural sciences, is the development in the young of "love of the Motherland and the Communist Party." Children are told over and over again that the two loves are identical. After the downgrading of Stalin at the Twentieth Congress of the Party in February, 1956, apparently some Soviet citizens got the idea that the system would be fundamentally changed in the direction of political liberty. Such heresies were quickly nipped in the bud by a powerful and unequivocal editorial in the July 6, 1956, issue of *Pravda*, the organ of the Central Committee, entitled, "The Communist Party—the Inspirer and Leader of the Soviet People." The key sentence in the long editorial reads as follows: "As for our country, the Communist Party has been, is, and will be the sole master of the minds, the voice of the thought and hopes, the leader and the organizer of the people in their entire struggle for Communism. . . ."

413

We are impressed with the discipline, the long hours, and the academic results of the Russian system. We also notice that the teachers (according to their literature) command not by terror, but by understanding and example. However, when we examine what is being taught (history à la Marx, the genius of Russian "inventors," John Dewey depicted as a capitalist stooge); the social context of education (night arrests by the MVD, ten million prisoners in concentration camps); and the motivation of the students (failing the seven-year tests means manual labor for life), we do not want classroom discipline at that price. Furthermore, the achievement levels of the students come into question. After so many hours in a classroom chair, Russian children, who are still human, have a fatigue and ennui factor working against them. Some of the Russians themselves dare to complain about this.

The truth is probably somewhere in between the picture of the police-state system, with superiors ruling inferiors by terror, and the very happy and compatible group who universally love learning and are taught by teachers who rule by moral example and superior knowledge.

The type of Russian thinking pervading their educational enterprise and whole society is suggested by the following emendation, symptomatic of their ideological propaganda line.

THE COMMUNISTS AND JOHN DEWEY*

John Dewey (born 1859)—a reactionary bourgeois philosopher and sociologist, a subjective idealist, leader of contemporary American pragmatism, professor at Columbia University. While ideologically serving the interests of aggressive American imperialism, Dewey worked out a variation of pragmatism called instrumentalism. Dewey, answering the basic problem of philosophy as an idealist, agnostically asserts that man in the knowledge process does not deal with objective reality but with his own conceptions, which are arbitrary "working hypotheses," "tools," "instruments," for solving practical difficulties. Treating experience in the spirit of subjective idealism, Dewey denies objective truth and asserts that any "conceptual instrument" which

* *Large Soviet Encyclopedia*, 2nd ed., Vol. XV, 343-344.

assures "the success of my undertaking" is true. Any view or fanciful notion which profits and pleases American imperialists can be proclaimed "scientific" and "true" with the help of this "philosophy." Religion, says Dewey, is "in harmony with the accepted scientific convictions of people." Dewey attempts to disguise the reactionary character of his sociology and his intentional defense of the piratical imperialistic state by the hypocritical use of the phraseology of liberalism and by a deceitful "criticism" of the most obvious vices of capitalism. In the interests of the aggressive policy of the government of the USA, Dewey fights with all his resources against the principle of national sovereignty, and actively preaches the cooperation of the classes and the rejection of what he calls an "irrational" class struggle. Dewey counsels the workers that for the "good" of their families they should not participate in strikes, that they should submit to the capitalists. Propagating racial prejudice, amoralism, unscrupulousness, Dewey cynically proposes that moral norms be replaced by "working plans of action" adapted to situations that arise. For the bourgeoisie and their governmental workers, according to Dewey, any means are good which fortify the position of capitalism and prevent social revolution. In education, Dewey is a supporter of those methods of instruction which contribute to the rearing of energetic and enterprising defenders of capitalism who are permeated with a spirit of worship of capital and hatred toward communism.

The philosophy of Dewey is a philosophy of war and fascism. Dewey is the mouthpiece of modern imperialistic reaction, the ideologist of American imperialism, a violent enemy of the USSR, the countries of the People's Democracy, and the revolutionary theory of Marxism-Leninism.

Editors' Summary

We have seen that some consider Soviet education to be very good in terms of numbers and product, but others question even this. There are those who assert that the Russians are 70 percent ahead of us in the number of persons in higher education, while Havighurst argues that in meaningful numbers we are ahead of them.

What can we learn from Soviet education? We can learn that education is the best possible investment. In a felicitous phrase, former Premier Nikolai Bulganin spoke of the "gold reserve" of Russia, meaning the new generation with advanced skills. The Russians know that the world belongs to the most educated, and they are not sparing their resources to attain the educational forefront.

We can learn from the Russians in all their educational, scientific, and cultural apparatus. Their learning, programs, and experiments are a vast resource to us. The idea of secrecy, of provincial spite, is too expensive to be afforded in the world of atomic power and banks of thinking brains. We cannot do enough to communicate with the Russians. At the grass roots level of communication between persons we do more to establish peace than scores of summit conferences among the puppet statesmen. An undercurrent of forces circulates to the top in more ways than even the Politburo consciously surmises, or the Pentagon can graph.

We have presented some of the most prevalent negative feelings about the schools, and the stoutest defenses. The administrator, teacher, parent, or community leader cannot place these writings as templates over their particular situations and do the proper cutting and fitting to make all necessary comparisons. Alfred North Whitehead, the great "synthetic philosopher," had the belief that every man had some of the truth in him, and therefore nobody was ever entirely wrong. What is needed, he generally believed, is clarification, *or as we would call it,* understanding. *We need to know our real situation, our real problems, our real aims and goals. Immense difficulties attend the achievement of this understanding, because such understanding requires that we be able to communicate about the empirical reality and the value systems with which we wish to attack that empirical reality. We know that these two go together—that what we see depends on what we believe. You and I differ on our view of reality, our ideals, and the methods by which we operate. Crucial in the setting by which the communication, contention, and programming may be carried on is the public school.*

Perhaps all we have left after this discussion is a set of diverse images of better education. Yet we would say that if these images call for great effort, and the people believe that the images are formed from demo-

cratic concepts, the result is still better than vacuous skepticism, indifference, or despair.

We should know, most of all, that our education must be improved in its own kind and after its own way. This means an apparent loss of efficiency, because we lack a blueprint of our future progress. If we did we would be marching, not observing, weighing, and considering. In being true to ourselves, we shall in the end be doing the greatest service for ourselves, for the uncommitted millions, and for our neighbors of times to come.

RELATED READINGS

Adler, Mortimer J., and Milton Mayer. *The Revolution in Education*. Chicago: University of Chicago Press, 1958.

Bauer, R. A. *The New Man in Soviet Psychology*. Cambridge: Harvard University Press, 1952.

Berkson, I. L. *The Ideal and the Community*. New York: Harper & Brothers, 1958.

Bestor, Arthur E. "We Are Less Educated than Fifty Years Ago," *U.S. News and World Report*, XLI (November 30, 1956), 68-72.

Brown, Herbert L., Jr. "Are the Public Schools Doing Their Job? Yes," *The Saturday Evening Post*, CXXX (September 21, 1957), 39ff.

Chapline, Allen W. "Soviet Education: What Do They Want to Know About American Education?" *The Clearing House*, XXXIV (September, 1959), 33-35.

Conant, James B. *The Citadel of Learning*. New Haven: Yale University Press, 1956.

Counts, George S. *The Challenge of Soviet Education*. New York: McGraw-Hill Book Co., 1957.

Derthick, Lawrence G. "The Frightening Challenge of Russia's Schools," *Look*, XXII (October 14, 1958), 38-40.

DeWitt, Nicholas. *Soviet Professional Manpower: Its Education, Training, and Supply*. Washington, D.C.: National Science Foundation, 1955.

Ebel, Robert L. "The Social Consequences of Educational Testing," *School and Society*, Vol. 92, No. 2249, November 14, 1964.

Education and the Cult of Efficiency: A Study of the Social Forces that Have Shaped the Administration of the Public School. Raymond E. Callahan (P149) Phoenix Books, University of Chicago Press, 5750 Ellis Ave., Chicago, Ill.

Havighurst, Robert J. *The Public Schools of Chicago*. Chicago: The Board of Education, 1964. Chapter 20 presents a discussion on the administration and organization of the Chicago schools.

Hechinger, Fred M. *The Big Red School House*. Garden City, N.Y.: Doubleday & Company, Inc., 1959.

————. "The Fate of Pedagoguese," *Saturday Review*, XXXVI (December 12, 1953), 18-20.

Hutchins, Robert M. *The University of Utopia*. Chicago: University of Chicago Press, 1953.

Khrushchev, N. S. "Proposals to Reform Soviet Education," *Soviet Bulletin #42*. New York: Universal Distributors Co., 1958.

Kline, George L., *et al. Soviet Education*. New York: Columbia University Press, 1957.

Korol, A. G. *Soviet Education for Science and Technology*. Cambridge, Mass.: Technology Press of Massachusetts Institute of Technology, 1957.

Moehlman, Arthur Henry. "The Education of Youth in the U.S.A. and the U.S.S.R.," *Phi Delta Kappan*, XL (November, 1958), 78-87.

Moos, Elizabeth. *Soviet Education Today and Tomorrow*. New York: National Council of American-Soviet Friendship, 1960.

Neff, Frederick. "John Dewey and the Luce Ends of Education," *Phi Delta Kappan*, XL (December, 1958), 130-131.

Read, Gerald. "Soviet Educators Have Their Problems Too," *Phi Delta Kappan*, XXXIX (June, 1958), 386-393.

Rickover, Hyman G. *Education and Freedom*. New York: E. P. Dutton & Co., Inc., 1959.

————, and others. "European vs. American Secondary Schools," *Phi Delta Kappan*, XL (November, 1958).

Tannenbaum, Abraham J. *Adolescent Attitudes Toward Academic Brilliance*. New York: Teachers College Bureau of Publications, Columbia University, 1962.

Tyler, Louis L. "The Concept of an Ideal Teacher-Student Relationship," *The Journal of Educational Research*, Vol. 58, No. 3, November 1964.

PART VII

THE TEACHING PROFESSION

The importance of this section depends upon what the reader believes to be the importance of the teacher in our society. Some have the regard for teachers evinced by a New England society matron, when advised by the school her son attended, that he was having trouble getting along with one of the men teachers: "That's strange, Rudolph gets along well with all the other servants!"

In the professional training and certification of teachers we make some assumptions about the desirability of certain kinds of training and standards. We assume that teachers will be *better* with certain kinds of experience and university courses, and that the profession will be *better* with the setting up of and adherence to standards. At this point, many disagree—including teachers!—saying that teachers are born, and no course in education will help to attain the desired goal of improving the teacher.

Assuming, however, and we hope not rashly, that some preparation and minimal standards are necessary to have good teachers, we again run into many difficulties and differences of opinion. Certainly no one argues that an indiscriminate addition of education courses and an arbitrary raising of years and credits required for certificates are the answers to securing better prepared teachers.

As we see it, the problems of the worth and making of teachers are divided into two main areas. First, is teaching a profession? The answer to this revolves around definitions and depends on what one calls a profession. The fact that doctors are considered members of a profession, while there is some question about teachers, is quite significant. No matter whether they are considered a profession or not, all teachers should be interested in improvements of their role. This of course leads us into many considerations about the political posture of teachers, the goals of associations and unions, the educational background requirements, merit pay and pay scales, and many other acrimonious debate topics. We have tried to present the issue fairly and pertinently in the first chapter of this section.

The second area is centered around the means by which we may improve, standardize, clarify, and make intelligible and inspiring to the public the general education requirements and certification standards of teachers. Our own answer is clearly given—to leave the making of standards to a process controlled by the profession but subject to legitimate checks by the general public.

The importance of education to the United States and to the world has become so obvious and vital in the last few years that those who take up the profession, art, science, or practice of education have become correspondingly more important. If we address ourselves to the larger task of bringing education up to date in light of the last third of the twentieth-century needs, the teaching-preparation problem will be put into proper perspective and solutions will become more clearly manifest.

XVI

The Changing Teaching Profession

"A teacher affects eternity; he can never tell where his influence stops."

—HENRY BROOKS ADAMS

Editors' Comment

The teacher has changed as a professional person simply because teaching has changed. The addition of more specialties; the development of more kinds of schools and colleges; and adult, industrial, government-supervised, and in-service training have marked the increasing complexity of the educational institution. The people who teach, though they have certain similarities, are of course seen in somewhat different light in all the new and variegated situations that our modern civilization requires. This of course means a breakdown of old stereotypes of the teacher. It means that teachers are as different among themselves as any cross section of the population.

Teachers have increasingly gained social freedom and the right to militantly and politically press their demands in an organized way that squares with the evolution of the complex groups, structured operations of such groups, and specialization. This has been a positive movement of the profession. As to whether teaching is a profession, an

421

issue of paramount importance remains. Some think teaching is not a profession. Others think it is a hierarchy of professions. Teachers' organizations generally crusade to get teachers recognized as a fairly homogeneous profession.

We are aware that a great amount of indigenous literature on teacher stereotypes would have been interesting in this connection (like Ichabod Crane, the schoolmaster of Tom Sawyer, and "Our Miss Brooks" of TV fame), but we have concentrated on current issues of professionalism and standards, and common attacks on teachers.

The certification of teachers might seem a dry, technical subject, and it is in many aspects. The average person soon finds it boring to follow the argument on whether we should have more or less child psychology, practice teaching, or courses in the teacher's major field.

Nevertheless modern conditions make certification a matter of hot debate. Almost no one advocates we do away with teacher certification—although some articles and editorials sound like this. In all modern states, licensure of professions and activities of various kinds has been found necessary for public welfare. But the certification of teachers immediately plunges us into whole areas of contention.

1) The differing philosophies of education, through their proponents, clash on the requisite type of teacher preparation.

2) A matrix of forces of the people directly concerned with teacher preparation—teachers colleges, administrators, old teachers, young teachers, teachers with educational vs. liberal arts backgrounds, school boards, private schools, higher educational institutions, junior colleges, and many more want more or less hours of certain kinds in varying fields.

3) The demographic and political scene is one of tremendous pushes and pulls. The general public wants the best qualified teachers, and certification is the best over-all answer for attesting to qualifications. Yet the numbers of children who are flooding the schools create a crying need for teachers now. The only immediate answer is to accept teachers with lower qualifications.

4) Certification is an obvious focal point in the grand strategy of the battle of teachers attempting to elevate and strengthen the profession. The militancy and effectiveness of teacher organizations can be generally judged by their success—or failure—in establishing a good certification program.

Certification, then, is important because of its implications. In general, the detractors of education will want lower standards, elastic to the demands of those in power, and responsive to local control. Those who wish to elevate education will want higher standards, rationally and objectively arrived at, and as free as possible from the exigencies and current inanities of local demands.

An interesting study of the teaching profession, as portrayed in motion pictures, was done by Jack Schwartz.

Schwartz found that 63 percent of the educators were portrayed as male, and 37 percent female. In 64 percent of the cases, the males were portrayed as unmarried. In only 50 percent of the relationships with the opposite sex was there a successful romantic outcome. (Successful is defined as an instance in which both partners are optimistic about the outcome of the film's end.) Examination of "happy endings" reveal that an educator is seldom expected to sustain a romantic involvement and 1) remain in teaching, or 2) have a partner of the same or more education. In interpersonal relationships with students, males were more likely to be domineering and aggressive, while females were considered more likely to be congenial. This image of the teacher largely supports the stereotype of the middle-aged, unmarriageable woman, and education as a refuge for the unsexy and unsalable.*

* Jack Schwartz, "The Portrayal of Educators in Motion Pictures," *American Journal of Sociology* (October, 1960).

In the spring of 1958, Life *presented a series on American education which held up some of the negative images with which we are familiar. Dr. Paul Woodring, at the time a consultant of the Ford Foundation's Fund for the Advancement of Education, wrote the following letter blaming the educators for their plight because of lack of leadership.*

AN EDUCATOR'S MESSAGE TO U.S. EDUCATORS
*Paul Woodring**

The leadership of American education is rapidly passing out of the hands of professional educators. The crescendo of criticism that has assailed the schools for the past 10 years has, since the launching of Sputnik, become a deafening roar. It is obvious that our schools from kindergarten through college must make dramatic changes and equally obvious that the present tremendous public interest in education offers an unparalleled opportunity for us to make some long-overdue improvements.

But instead of leading the way, instead of planning new programs to meet the exciting demands of the last half of the 20th Century, most of us are fighting a futile delaying action. We are resisting the attacks, fending off the flying brickbats, offering evidence that our schools are just as good as they were in 1900, denying charges, and advising our cohorts to cancel subscriptions to any magazine that dares to challenge current practices.

This is not leadership—leadership is not possible from a defensive position. If the control of the schools is not to pass entirely out of our hands we must again take the offensive. We must ourselves identify the weakness and shortcomings of our schools and offer bold and imaginative solutions.

It is futile to waste our time pointing out that much of the criticism misses its proper target and that some of the critics are confused by the enormous complexity of American education. The important fact is that, while educational spokesmen resist change and feebly defend the status quo, the critics offer strong and positive suggestions for the im-

* Paul Woodring, *A Fourth of a Nation* (New York, 1957). Copyright © 1957 by the McGraw-Hill Book Co., Inc. Reprinted with permission of the publishers.

provement of our schools. They are urging that we raise our sights, that we establish priorities based on a clear sense of purpose, that we resist, instead of going along with, the anti-intellectual trends of our culture, that we find ways of challenging the greatest potential efforts of bright and gifted students without neglecting the less able, and that we find better ways of educating teachers and of making their job more attractive to men and women of high intelligence.

There is growing evidence that this is what a great many of the American people want. There is evidence, too, that many educators want the same things. A recent Gallup Poll found that 79% of high-school principals think the schools demand too little work of their students, 63% are convinced that students do not read enough books, and 61% think athletics is overemphasized. But the voices that speak for professional educators have failed to make this plain, have failed to offer solutions, have failed to lead the way or even to point out the weaknesses.

The critics themselves—those outside the schools—cannot rebuild the American educational system. All they can do is illuminate the errors. The rebuilding must be done by professional educators working along with the support of lay groups.

The American people are ready to move. If we will show the needed courage, enthusiasm, perception and intellectual vigor, we can now build a system of education far superior to any that our nation or any other nation has ever had. But first we must get out of this ridiculous defensive position and start acting like leaders again.

Is teaching a profession? This question is heretical to many who want a raising and a homogenization of all personnel in teaching. That is, to lay public the credo goes, a teacher should be a teacher. One person may be in three specialized fields in school work, while another is a borderline functionary with the barest minimum of credentials. Still, to the public, the two are to be given equal respect as professionals. Counter to this is the divisive force of specialization which makes or should make the educational enterprise contain a "hierarchy of professions" according to Myron Lieberman. The general principle is stated by Dael Wolfle: "A trained expert seldom works alone. A lawyer has his clerks, an engineer his draftsmen, a doctor his nurses and technicians, a research scholar his assistants. How much the expert accomplishes is determined partly by his own ability, but partly by the number and skill of his assistants and by the effectiveness with which he uses them."

The standpoint of the average teacher toward professional levels is across-the-board single level for classroom teachers, and some multiple levels among specialists and administrators. The inexorable move toward complexity and specialization has been going on despite the views and goals of teachers. The advantages of specialization are a fact of life. It is more efficient for each person to do that which he can do best.

In the case of classroom teachers, it has long been noticed that much of what they do is non-specialized. If this menial and custodial work were done by others, the teacher could put 100 percent of her time into truly professional work, and the total productivity would go up. The para- or sub-professional work could be done by aids, or such a name. The Detroit Board of Education employs six levels of sub-professionals, each with a civil-service rating.

The implications of this para-professionalization are of vital import to the classroom teachers, to the multiple higher strata, to all education, and to our society. Two great issues are involved: Should classroom teachers uphold a uni-level professionalism, or move toward creative leadership in maintaining and designing specialization? Should we accept subsidies—chiefly federal—in implementing this multi-storied professionalization?

Practical problems are here, too, which teachers and educators must wrestle with. Teacher aids are already a fact. Therefore, how should we train them, and the teachers who relate with them? What changes are necessary in institutions of teacher preparation, in curriculum, and in the organization of our schools?

Myron Lieberman has a different criticism concerning present practices of teacher preparation. He sees a distressing lack of professionalism among teachers, and one of the great faults stemming from this or, if you like, causing it, is the lack of uniformity in standards of administrative boards, curricular requirements in higher institutions, and levels of title and specialization, as evidenced in a confused tangle of *programs run by outsiders. In the following excerpt from Lieberman's book,* The Future of Public Education, *he states his main argument, and outlines the objectives which he conceives as worthy of professional support.*

TEACHER EDUCATION AND CERTIFICATION
Myron Lieberman*

1. There must be national standards for teacher certification; the legal form of their implementation is important but not necessarily decisive.

2. Teacher education must be confined to institutions of higher education which are centers of research.

3. There must be day-to-day articulation of theoretical and practical training in teacher-education programs.

4. There must be unified control of teacher education and of the schools in which prospective teachers receive their practical training.

5. The academic course structure must recognize that not all education courses are professional and that some of the courses in the teaching field of specialization are of this nonprofessional nature.

6. There must be an examination system interposed between graduation from accredited teacher-preparing institutions and actual entry to teaching. This can be initiated with examinations in the teaching field of specialization, prepared by specialists in each field. All states should be encouraged to use the same examination, prepared and evaluated on a national basis.

7. Requirements for a teaching certificate must not be enacted into law by state legislatures but should be delegated to an agency responsible to organized professional opinion; the requirements of this agency should have the force of law.

8. The number of teacher-training institutions should be drastically reduced. This should be the natural consequence of raising the

* Myron Lieberman, *The Future of Public Education* (Chicago, 1960), 277-78. Reprinted by permission of The University of Chicago Press. Copyright, 1960.

standards for admission, retention, and graduation along with a system of state board examinations for entry.

9. Certification requirements should be highly prescriptive and allow relatively little room for electives in a total program of teacher education.

10. Teachers must learn to see their stake in high standards of entry and why this requires them to assume the control over teacher education which has passed by default to the colleges and universities.

11. The persons who teach methods courses and supervise the practical training of teachers of academic subjects should be members of the appropriate academic departments in their subject fields.

12. The practice of spelling out the requirements for a teaching certificate in terms of a given number of course credits must be replaced by a system which indicates the specific content which must be mastered, regardless of courses taken.

13. The most constructive step that liberal arts colleges can take for public education is to put their own house in order. This means eliminating course proliferation, curtailing emphasis upon non-educational activities, setting up a new framework of employer-employee relations, insisting upon high standards for admission, promotion, and graduation, stopping the intensive recruitment of high school athletes, and otherwise setting a better example for education at lower levels.

14. The study of education as a social institution must be included in the general education program for all students.

A legal relationship between two persons, of great importance in Western civilization is the contract. In contradiction to traditional, verbal, or ad hoc arrangements, it promotes stability, and is rational and efficient. The conditions and description of the contractors change with time. The person, for example, as a legal entity, could be the A.T. and T. corporation, or a local teachers' association. What has made the contract a cutting issue now in education is that teachers' associations have entered into the power sphere of social relations as never before, and negotiate as a body. Also, the points of contention become in toto

428

the definition of professionalism of teachers in fact. Ronald Daly's remarks get at the heart of the matter in the following excerpts.

NEW DIRECTIONS FOR
PROFESSIONAL NEGOTIATIONS
Ronald O. Daly*

A new development in the negotiation field is the type of agreement which is substantive as well as procedural. As in group contracts, such agreements specify conditions of professional service in a series of articles. The procedural-substantive agreements have the following advantages over strictly procedural agreements: They establish a basis for future negotiations; provide concrete evidence of association effectiveness; enable each teacher to have a copy for reference.

State legislation has clearly provided the precedent for an increasing number of written substantive agreements. The statues in Connecticut, Rhode Island, Massachusetts, Michigan, and Wisconsin provide for reducing the results of negotiation to writing and entering into a contractual agreement. This substantive contract enumerates the many conditions and policies which affect the individual teacher but in no way replaces the individual contracts. Substantive agreements serve as another means of communication between the professional staff and the board of education.

The following subjects might be found in the articles of a substantive agreement: grievance policy; class size; teaching hours and load; work year; holidays; storm days; after-school meetings; nonteaching duties; specialists; teaching assignment; transfers; promotions; teacher facilities; textbooks; salaries; substitute teachers; summer school program; protection; personal injury benefits; sick leave; leaves of absence; professional development and educational improvement; fringe benefits; annuity plans; duration; dues deduction; salary schedules for various assignments of certificated employees.

Another new direction comes from the need for a responsible negotiating association which can act rationally and participate in some long-range planning. Exclusive recognition requires a feasible method of determining the majority organization. Experience is pinpointing the

* Reprinted by permission from NEA Journal, October, 1966.

problems that need attention when competing organizations vie for this recognition. The need for granting the recognized association such privileges as payroll deduction for dues and use of school bulletin boards and the intra-school communication system is now receiving greater consideration.

A new approach is also evolving in the area of presentation and negotiating rights. The vast majority of the voluntary agreements written between 1962 and 1965 make provision for individuals or members of minority organizations to make presentations, independent of the recognized responsible association, to the board of education. A presentation, unlike negotiation, may be acknowledged or ignored. An example of this direction is the agreement recently entered into by the Columbus (Ohio) Education Association and the Board of Education which provides suggested channels regarding presentation and provides an opportunity for the recognized association to be present and enter into any discussion on the issue presented.

. . . Any certificated employee or group of employees may present a proposal to the Columbus Education Association for the consideration of the Professional Agreements Committee. If the Columbus Education Association does not choose to present the proposal, such requests by said individuals or groups may then be presented in writing to the Superintendent. If a hearing is granted, members of the Professional Agreements Committee will be given opportunity to be present and to participate in the hearing.

Normal turnover and expansion of school staff and consolidation of our school systems have caused the local associations to build security measures into their professional negotiation agreements. The multiyear contracts which expire in the middle of the school term provide more time to educate the new staff members about the value and purpose of a responsible negotiating association.

No state law precludes the negotiation of a multiyear contract and some laws provide the advantage of continuous recognition during the duration of these contracts. In states without mandatory professional negotiation laws, more than 88 percent of all the professional negotiation agreements provide for recognition of the association for more than one year.

Many state associations hope to pass legislation for professional negotiation during the 1967 session of their legislature. The degree of success of these states and the ever growing desire of professionals to participate in policy development will determine the new directions for years to come.

Editors' Summary

The letter by Woodring, we believe, strikes the keynote of the challenge of education to the teachers. They have been apologetic in the face of many well-planned attacks, and though they have retreated without a disastrous rout, they have left the impression they can be attacked with impunity. The worst that can happen to an attacker is that he be fixed with a glare of genteel hauteur that he can be so ignorant or oafish.

The reason teaching is not a strong profession is that teachers do not or cannot sufficiently maintain professional standards under their own power as an organized group. The reason stems from a complicated set of factors. It is useless to blame the teachers entirely for not raising wages of their group, and the public could save their breath in appealing to the teachers to "dedicate" themselves for low salaries when agents of industry flash contracts offering several thousand dollars more under their noses. As long as the government guarantees education to each child, the government can offer contracts to individuals who are pledged not to strike for higher wages. If the government is willing to hire substandard teachers, there would seem to be no hope for the raising of standards, nor for the establishment of the professionalism of teachers.

The government, of course, is the people. If the general body of people is apathetic or satisfied with poorly trained, incompetent teachers, that is what they will get. This is a common argument that explains away the low position of teachers on the occupational totem pole. The argument is a dangerous oversimplification, and the teachers are much to blame for its prevalence. What the public wants is not a simple projection of their values, but a complicated set of priorities which shifts and changes as their knowledge of the relevant situation changes. If teachers really undertook to inform the parents of what is going on

—how destructive some classrooms are, how certification is being flouted, the flimsiness of school buildings, and the dearth of materials —the effect would be one of a great demand for higher standards. Notice that the teachers do not have to become crusaders. They merely need to illuminate the realities and remind people of the laws.

Again, this is too simple. Of course the teachers must have overall planning and purpose. There must be follow-through. One barrage of truth might be cataclysmically destructive. To tell the people that the average of teaching in the U.S. today is substandard and leave it to the public devices to change it would invite a holocaust. Information about ills must be followed by prescriptions. The public also wants responsible leadership.

Teachers do not have to wait to be accepted by their communities, as has been implied. Nor do teachers have to become strong-arm men to enforce their demands. The public, we have seen, has a high respect for teachers and certainly a very high regard for education for their children. Enough of a potential of good feeling and idealism exists so that teachers could very easily become leaders.

Most authorities seem to agree that teachers do not appear as a strong profession. Yet the general public can be led in various ways so that teachers can acquire the professional mantle. Without any danger of destruction to life and reputation, job security, or administrative slaps on the wrist, they can aggressively build a profession, improve standards, inform the public of their best interests, and make a better educational institution—all at the same time. The present teacher militancy has a potential for going on to a secure growing professionalization, or it could deteriorate into internecine hassles.

Two divergent approaches characterize teacher preparation. One view is that the educationists have thoroughly stultified the preparation with an impractical, self-centered trade-union approach which is in itself one of the great sources of damage in education today. The other point of view is that teacher preparation is as good as can be devised in the present imperfect state of affairs.

What is the truth? There is no one truth, and any estimation would depend on the reader's values of certain goals. We can make teacher preparation cheap or dear, long or short, intensive or extensive. Very likely the answer to certification problems does not lie in any of these continua.

We believe that certification is primarily a professional problem. Only a professional body with requisite background and knowledge can lay out the courses; pass on the merits of the candidates; determine the levels of preparation for the various courses and areas; and evaluate the need for refresher courses, additional preparation, or the setting up of competitive examinations for positions. Only a professional group is qualified to pass on the competence and qualitative merits of teachers. The lay public is interested in results. The public is qualified to judge the facts of growth, or curricula from the standpoint of performance or nonperformance, but the public is not qualified to judge whether a given teacher's methods require'too much or too little of the students, or whether most of the students in the room are in need of remedial reading. However, as long as the teachers are willing to let laymen hash over the professional requirements and performance for teachers, and abide by the decisions of these laymen in the name of democracy, schoolmen have none to blame but themselves if professional licensure is a Joseph's coat, changing in motley array with the political winds, but always low in standards, confused, and unsatisfactory to all.

RELATED READINGS

Adler, Irving. "Teaching Shortage: Cause and Cure," *The Nation*, CLXXXVI (May 10, 1958), 407-09.

Bailey, Stephen K. "Education Is a Political Enterprise," *NEA Journal*, Vol. LIII, No. 8, November, 1964.

Bestor, Arthur E., and Karl W. Bigelow. "How Should America's Teachers Be Educated?," *Teachers College Record*, LVI (October, 1954), 16-24.

Briggs, Francis M. "As Five Teachers See Themselves," *The Educational Forum*, Vol. XXVII, No. 4, May, 1964.

Cartwright, William H. "The Teacher in 2065," *Teacher's College Record*, LXVI, No. 4, January, 1965.

Cottrell, Donald P. (ed.). *Teacher Education for a Free People.* Oneonta, N.Y.: American Association of Colleges for Teacher Education, 1956.

Crow, Lester D., and Alice Crow. *Mental Hygiene for Teachers: A Book of Readings.* New York: Macmillan Co., 1963.

433

Eby, Kermit, *versus* William Heard Kilpatrick. "Teachers' Unions? Yes! No!" *Progressive Education*, XX (October, 1943), 260-63ff.

Foster, Richard L. "Poise Under Pressure," *Educational Leadership*, Vol. 22, No. 3, December 1964.

Future of Public Education. Myron Lieberman. (P94) Phoenix Books, University of Chicago Press, 5750 Ellis Ave., Chicago, Ill.

Givens, Willard E. and others. "Growth of the Association Idea," *Phi Delta Kappan*, XXXVII (1956), 129-93.

Gross, Ronald, and Judith Murphy. *The Revolution in the Schools*. New York: Harcourt, Brace and World, 1964.

Gusfield, Joseph R. "The Meaning of Occupational Prestige: Reconsideration of the NORC Scale," *American Sociological Review*, XXVIII, No. 2, April 1963.

Jersild, Arthur T. *When Teachers Face Themselves*. New York: Bureau of Publications, Teachers College, Columbia University, 1955.

Kennedy, Millard Filmore, and Elvin F. Harlow. *Schoolmaster of Yesterday*. New York: The Philosophical Library, 1946.

Leighbody, G. G. "What Makes a Professional, Professional?" *Phi Delta Kappan*, XXXIV (1953), 295.

Lieberman, Myron. *Education as a Profession*. Englewood Cliffs, N.J.: Prentice-Hall, Inc., 1956.

———. *Teaching as a Profession*. Englewood Cliffs, N.J.: Prentice-Hall, Inc., 1957.

———. and others, "NEA Centennial Issue," *Progressive Education*, XXXIV (July, 1957), 97-120.

Lowe, William T. "Who Joins Which Teachers' Group?," *Teachers College Record*, LXVI, No. 7, April 1965.

Marshall, Sybil, *An Experiment in Education*. New York: Cambridge University Press, 1963.

Maul, Ray C. *Teacher Demand and Supply in the United States*. Washington, D.C.: National Education Association, 1952.

National Education Association. "NEA Reply to AFL-CIO Charge," *School and Society*, XXCVI (March 29, 1958), 146f.

Nelson, Robert H., and Michael L. Thompson. "Why Teachers Quit," *The Clearing House*, XXXVII, No. 8, April 1963.

Perry, Bliss. *And Gladly Teach*. Boston: Houghton Mifflin Co., 1935.

Rasmussen, Glen R. "Perceived Value Discrepancies of Teachers and Principals— A Threat to Creative Teaching," in *Society and Education*, James D. Raths and J. D. Grambs, Editors. Englewood Cliffs, N.J.: Prentice-Hall, 1965.

Reinhardt, Emma. "The Teacher Who Helped Me Most," *The Clearing House*, XXXVIII, No. 4, December 1963, pp. 224-226.

Russell, William F. "Unity in the Teaching Profession," *Phi Delta Kappan*, XXXI (March, 1950), 341-52.

Sayre, Wallace S. "The Politics of Education," *Teachers College Record*, LXV, No. 2, November 1963.

Scanlon, John. "Strikes, Sanctions and the Schools," *Saturday Review*, Vol. 46, No. 42, October 19, 1963.

Shaplin, Judson T. "Team Teaching," in *American Education Today*, Paul Woodring and John Scanlon, Editors. New York: McGraw-Hill Book Co., 1963.

Unruh, Adolph. "Can Men Afford to Teach?", *Phi Delta Kappan*, XXXIII (November, 1951), 138-39, 141.

Waller, Willard. *The Sociology of Teaching*. New York: John Wiley and Sons, 1965.

Winick, Charles. "When Teachers Strike," in *Society and Education*, James D. Raths and J. D. Grambs, Editors. Englewood Cliffs, N.J.: Prentice-Hall, 1964.

Woodring, Paul. *New Directions in Teacher Education*. New York: The Fund for the Advancement of Education, 1957.

PART VIII
ORGANIZING FOR BETTER SCHOOLS

The issues of the school are on display so to speak, and in this book we have aimed to report as faithfully as possible what those issues are. However, it has occurred to us that nowhere does the institution of education raise its voice on its own behalf in the proclamation of ideals now and for the future, undetermined by charges of the anti-educationists and untinged by the tone of apologetics. The reader may not think this an issue— but neither was morality before the advent of the great religions, nor world law before the League of Nations. We think education deserves a voice in saying what its mission can be for society, and what it can do for the future of mankind.

Our last chapter deals with prescriptions for the future. It is strange that the spirit of the educational community is so anemic and lacking in imagination in this perspective. Instead of the zealous ecstasy of explorers given new worlds to embrace, the group is led like a child to nursery school, squalling and kicking into the age of modern miracles. To be sure, unless culture is going to be overcome by a general and pervasive phobia about innovations, some people will make the laws and manage the space ships. But the opportunity of education to take an overseeing and synthesizing view of the values that determine the directions of change will be lost—and it could be lost to selfish power groups that manage a neo-fascistic coalition.

We therefore suggest in general ways, perhaps too general for implementation in programs presently under discussion, what we believe to be some major goals that must be achieved for the educational institution to acquire leadership in the future. Some of this achievement must come from sheer force and courage, and teachers should know there is no royal way to this. A great part of the achievement will come from the requisite knowledge and techniques, and plain hard work. It is in this area of knowledge and work that we offer information about teaching machines and audio-visual methods.

The future of education, we are saying, must not be determined by the examination of the entrails of roosters, but conceived in the intelligent contemplation of the products of men—the ideas, cultural forms, political structures, and whirr of electronic brains.

XVII

Design for the Future in Education

"Everything in the past died yesterday; everything in the future was born today. The future so terribly real waits where it cannot be seen and comes rushing at us like the wind. What does history say of tomorrow? History says tomorrow waits with a big broom. Lincoln said the dogmas of the quiet past are indequate for the stormy present. We must think anew; we must act anew, 'we must disenthrall ourselves.' When you disenthrall yourself you break from the bonds that hold you. You cut loose from old traditions and begin to make new ones."*

The one great task each man has is that of learning his own culture. Among some primitive groups, every adult can perform all the roles of the culture. If a large fraction of the adults of these primitive societies died, the culture would remain intact because the survivors would know as much as the deceased. They would not know the idiosyncratic memories, but they would speak as well, be able to tan skins, avoid poisonous plants, sacrifice to the rain gods, and, in general, carry

* Carl Sandburg as quoted in Charles A. Blessing, "Two Cities Designs for Life in Milan and Detroit," *Graduate Comment* (Wayne State University), IV (October, 1960), 6.

on all the activities which the people of that society would consider essential for survival.

More advanced cultures have more roles, more traits, and more specialized knowledge. In this case if certain people died there might be an irreparable loss of certain arts and lore. To keep the culture intact, to say nothing of promoting its development, a special activity called education must be brought in.

To the individual human being, the cultural process is understandable only in part, and in terms of the values he has learned. No man ever "sees" synoptically a civilization. He merely accepts his civilization as a good and is willing to lend himself as a cog in a great machine. If enough men agree, and co-ordinate their efforts, the result is as if a super brain were ordering the activities of men. The means by which each man learns to become a part of such a complicated whole is most critical. This means is education in its broadest sense.

At a certain stage of civilization, the educational institution can be a relatively limited, loosely integrated affair. The children learn reading and writing and basic subjects upon which they can build further knowledge. As adults, it is assumed that they can pursue their lives by habit, if by habit we mean the following of patterns which have been laid down by society. Women can do housework, men can work in factories, and both can follow the mores of socializing, consuming economic goods, and reproducing themselves.

To break the cake of custom and to make genuine changes, a more deliberate intellection of means and ends must be made. The whole of reality as man knows it must be subjected to inspection and utilized in planning. In the execution, man learns new facts about reality, relative to solving the problems his novel departures require. The whole process of thinking and acting becomes more organized. The scientific method, the sciences, and schools of philosophy are the most general ordered ways by which any kind of purposive action envisaging desired ends by man can be organized.

Our modern world is not only extremely complicated, requiring a large apparatus of education to subtend it, but it is changing. This change is proceeding at a miraculous and explosive rate. It is the greatest story in the history of man. But it is just beginning. It can lead to happiness or tragedy.

440

The Inadequacy of Traditional Education

We have up till now been making do with an institution designed for a static world. Since the world has not been static it might be argued that this is proof positive that our educational plant is sufficient after all. It appears to us that the general culture has been most dynamic *despite* the horse and buggy education we have. There has been education, but it has come under many independent programs, not well integrated with society. At times education has conflicted with other institutions or even with society in general. Sometimes it has been casual or furtive, even at times bootlegged under stairs and in dim ateliers. The general result is a failure of direction and a high internal friction. To the man on the street, it has meant a world which he assays by fits and starts; to him the whole appears to be a tower of Babel.

We have a frenzied productivity of parts, and in themselves these parts are marvels of scientific and technological development. Complex electronic computers with feedback controls, fast flying jets, miniaturized devices of unprecedented power and accuracy, machines that tend machines, machines to tend the machines tending the machines, sleep learning, brain mapping and induced hallucinations, preset automatic weapons guaranteeing total destruction, factories in the field and farms in the factories, nuclear powered cities in the sea are here now, soon will be, or will be superseded by other things equally ingenious. *Men* devise these things and use them and in the end the big question is, how will they be used to improve human life? Will hate, war, suffering, filth, disease, frustration, hunger, ignorance, insanity, boredom and despair be conquered by these things?

We find that young men are busy penciling vapor trails at 50,000 or 60,000 feet at about 20 miles a minute. They interweave their arabesques, return to earth, and rise again to repeat the process. Millions talk about the fleetingest fancies on the phone every day. Nearly half of the nation watch animated cartoons on TV, or the "Duel at Dead Men's Gulch." Soldiers guard secret war machine dumps, and are more aware of their cigarets or their evening dates than of the import of the suggested hulks under canvas. Univacs process the data from astronomers or from nose counters using telephone books. The president talks using a prepared speech coached by specialized admen. Universities offer courses in hotel management, dancing, and field trips through nature trails. In all this there is a lack of over-all purpose, and an astounding ability to be busy without knowing why.

Social scientists might say that we have selective values that enable us to go on treadmills and turn out bolts of cotton in highly mechanized factories, without having the corresponding values of human relationship developed to encompass the need of a unified, purposeful culture. But how do men get this purpose, this sense of unification? They can only achieve it through a means which will make it possible to know that they are engaged mutually with their fellows in purposive activity.

We said that an unspecialized and loosely integrated educational institution was sufficient to maintain a civilization of a rather low level, which was not changing very fast. It should appear, too, that our statements imply that an educational means must always accompany an advance in culture. This is not to say that any civilization, becoming more complex, can be expected to develop the most efficient educational system to get the job of transmitting the culture done. There may be many lags or inefficiencies in the educational institution which have to be modified or eliminated. Our culture, as we have said, advances despite its educational system. It is possible, we believe, to so organize education that change of the modern intensity of dynamism can be made productive of qualitative as well as quantitative changes.

The size, structure, effort, and time demands of the educational institution are determined by the goals in an existing culture. The criteria of the success of the institution in functioning well for the culture can be set up in terms of fulfilling these goals. Although this may seem to be evasive and meaningless, this level of generalization is required. The principle to be observed is that the culture determines the educational effort. Education, it is true, reacts with the culture and helps to make it, but the culture is the greater entity and includes education. Education is not to be judged or formulated in and of itself. It is judged as it functions, in its totality of internal relations with the culture.

These statements have more significance when we observe the actual situation of education. It is following a traditional pattern with only a relatively small amount of modification in response to the local community pressures. This modification has been determined by lay people in localized sectors of our general society. The result is an institution which strives to reflect the desires of the local community. We are teaching a saber-toothed curriculum in a jet age, and we are looking for advice on jets from village elders whose knowledge never reached the internal combustion engines.

Paraphrasing John Dewey, we could say that the educational institution can take one of three choices in its response to the needs of the institution. (1) It can attempt to reflect the culture, giving to the society (local or general) what that society currently wants, or appears to want. (2) It can preserve the cultural heritage as well as it understands that heritage, and transmit it as nearly intact as possible to the coming generation. (3) It can be creative and help to shape the culture in a better form, using science and knowledge in a constantly earnest and critical fashion. It can take the position of leadership among the institutions and become the fountainhead, the store, the standard, and the reparations of the values of our society. At some unknown point in future time, we hope, every volitional act will be ushered in against a backdrop emblazoned with the inscription, "Does this have educational value?"

The Modern Challenge to Education

Any way you look at it, the next 20 years are sure to be a strain.

—The population will continue to increase, at a rate of perhaps 3,000,000 per year. By 1970 we shall have a population of around 200,000,000. About 60,000,000 may be in schools or college, because more are attending school longer.

—The technological buildup which has changed the face of the earth and plumbed deeply into the microcosm and macrocosm will continue to explode. Though machines are building machines rapidly, the frontier of expansion depends on adequate recruitment and steady employment of skilled workers. The skills will appear suddenly with the advent of the innovations.

—Cultural pluralism will continue in America, making all "ologies" and "isms" rendered suspect. The human advancement will be one of exuberance, not parsimony. Man will be more interesting, but more problematical. To understand the human problem of the new age, education will have to develop sufficiently to match the cultural changes.

—The ideological struggle in the world, continuing population pressures, and the rise of new nations with varied aims and directions will require sapient guidance of relationships. The orientation of the rank and file to world problems, to make them effective world citizens, will require heavy educational commitments in relevant areas.

—The desegregation issue will continue as the number one social problem for some time. Education will be heavily involved though not solely responsible. Desegregation, or integration, will affect all areas of human life in some way or other. The previously stated trends, for example, are encoiled with this problem. Selecting technological expansion as a least likely example, we would say that the entrance—or not—of Negroes in universities, factories, research foundations, government posts, and in the various niches of production and consumption of our economy will have pronounced results on the general trends.

—Education, whether pushed or guiding itself, will have to become much more complex to service the other institutions and the general society. Education will take place in its most essential forms for the development of civilization under an official educational bureaucracy. If that bureaucracy is not given the fullest support and implementation, the needs of the age will enforce a less efficient bureaucracy, and education will be partly or imperfectly handled in that bureaucracy. Some essential tasks of education would then be farmed out, or done under the aegis of many diverse, improvised agencies haphazardly set up to respond to the needs.

The Preservation of the Basic Values of Our Democracy

The lack of integration of our culture and the underdevelopment of the educational plant are conditions for which we as a general group pay dearly. Any selfish advantage on the part of sections of our society in the existing state of affairs can be shown, in almost all instances, to be based on narrow short-term interests. In the long run, virtually everybody would profit by an expansion and equalization of education, at least in absolute terms. Some might lose some of their relative positions on the social heap. We will have to admit that if such relatively high positions are the greatest good, some people would suffer by the kinds of big changes we would suggest.

Consider the inequities that the political and financial localization of education brings. Certain sections of the country, notably the South and the rural sections, rear children and educate them, only to have these children move on, when adults, to the North and to cities. The economic and political institutions, most notably in the areas of immigration, profit by the influx of manpower. The general society receives people who are undereducated as compared with the national average. The places from which the people come are not apt to complain even though a relatively high share of their income goes into schooling. Few people seem to think of charging a bill for educational expenses to those communities who receive the educated adults. Industries in the receiving area are apt to be cordial on hiring the men, especially during good times.

Considering society as consisting only of employers and employees, the former profit disproportionately from the amount they contribute to the education of those who work for them. We would not suggest that they be made to pay. If education depended only on the economic institution, we can imagine it would quickly deteriorate. Because the business community exerts such disproportionate pressures on education, the curriculum becomes unbalanced in favor of the things business wants. What is more seriously damaging, the educators stand immobilized, bankrupt of all creative direction until they get the signals from the "important" people. These are not the officials of the bureaucracy of education, not the teachers colleges, but the most organized part of the community, the business leaders. The result is inequities of educational program among the students in terms of need.

The democratic ethic of the United States depends upon a "perpetual revolution" of social classes, so that the individuals of society will be able to assert themselves on their merits. Any rigidifying of structure, or persistence of privilege through inertia, will threaten the democratic spirit of the society. The lower class, or the underprivileged groups in general, have not the means to improve their lot. We recognize that education is one main way by which the underprivileged can rise in their station. Unfortunately, because of the "middle class press" of the school, the lower class children compared with middle and upper class children do not have an equitable opportunity to get as much education, or of as good quality. This applies to the whole educational experience as a broad spectrum of success experiences in social recognition, group participation, extracurricular activities, teacher help, marks, and distinctions. This is an area of broad and persisting inequity in education, almost calculated to reinforce the existing stratification.

The great changes we have previously mentioned will bring with them inequities, because the needs of the new generation will be imperfectly serviced. This will mean added expense for private instruction, lower wages for workers getting instruction, poor teaching and a snarl of problems in standards, evaluation, and accreditation. It will mean premiums paid to the few who are capable of developing the new specialized services, and a wasting of talent and underemployment among those who would like to serve but can't.

Making Education an Institution of Leadership in a Changing World

To solve the problems of the coming changes, and to overcome the existing and incipient inequities, we would suggest some radical changes in the educational institution.

A break in the traditional lock step of grades, all the way from nursery school through college is necessary, to free the individuals of all ranges of learning ability from the cramping efforts of the institution. The students would learn subjects, skills, and programs at the rate of which they were capable. The total area of learning, or generally speaking, the curriculum, would be organized to be functional in the modern world, considering the necessity for core learning, social adaptation, and citizenship in the dynamic and multicultural society of which we are a part. The criticism that this would all be a hopeless eclecticism must be met by prodigious effort to fulfill the general needs of the student and of society.

The educational institution should be made an efficient bureaucracy, large enough to do its main, common tasks, and specialized and adaptive in its parts to service the magnitude, dynamism, and variety of our modern multicultural society. The current setup is one of undersized, relatively inflexible, tradition bound units without the means for change. If the future society is to fulfill its tasks, its promise, education must come under a country-wide system. In this integration, the advantages of national co-ordination and the flexibility of local control must be maintained. A reasonable proposal is to make it the fourth branch of the federal government. Only the federal government is big enough to provide funds and furnish the necessary degree of control.

To overcome the argument that such control is inherently bad, the personnel who work in the government positions of the educational bureaucracy must be professionals. One of the hallmarks of professionalism is concern for the quality of education. While having all the capital and authority of government administration, the profession should exert its influence to get the right persons in the right positions and properly evaluate their jobs. For example, the person who handles a state program for the handicapped should be recognized as a capable professional, and should perform his work like one. If not, the profession utilizing government services in commissions and tenure boards should have him corrected or replaced.

The idea that education should be accomplished in a few immature years and then never adverted to should be replaced by the notion that it is a constant, ongoing activity, an inescapable aspect of modern life—if we want to have modern life. Everybody should understand that his social responsibility is to dedicate himself to a lifetime of education. This means, at the very least, refresher courses in significant changes in the world for everyone, so that each man may have intelligent consciousness of the world in which he is a part, and judge and vote wisely.

The tactical questions of how many hours and how many days this would require in each person's life cannot now be gauged. These depend on the sweep and complexity of future events, with which education—the intelligent formulation of purpose in this context—must be matched.

Modern life is one of interdependence, and education cannot be an autonomy by an elite of professionals. There must be ordered ways for the educational institution to know of the demands of the culture. To this end we would suggest setting up a national body, co-operating with an international one with which the educational institution would confer and co-ordinate. The general purpose of this commission or bureau would be to determine the learning needs of the society. To be functional, it should be one in which the lay public is heavily involved in an intelligent, concentrated way in analyzing, reflecting, and creating the goals and types of knowledge which the schools would undertake to supply. The success of this body would depend upon the extensiveness and intensity of its work. The need, rising from the growing complexity and innovations of the culture, would stimulate the development of the work undertaken. It would be hoped that by some involvement in an organized activity relating to assessments of needs in education, that the average citizen of the future would become culturally literate, and competent to pass judgment on the product of effort in the school.

The whole teacher training program must undergo extensive modifications and improvements. Much of the inferior quality of teaching comes from low standards and salaries, and cannot be avoided in large measure at present. In the future, however, we would look to see these important changes:

—More careful selection of teachers, for the profession in general, and selected positions in particular. Screening would aim at procuring high-level people of good general ability and specialized talents.

—A more extensive, relevant and rigorous program for learning, with great improvement in both the core learnings ("subject matter") and applied skills ("practice teaching"). A person would be able to try himself in many more areas of teaching before he made up his mind. But if he were not able to perform up to standard on the basis of understandable expert criteria, he would be persuaded to try something else.

—A more careful and variegated processing of the learner to be able to develop a self-image and a greater knowledge of his performance and potentialities. A dozen or more specialists might confer with, advise, teacher, and evaluate him, in groups and/or in closed, confidential sessions.

—The teacher would be expected to continue in-service training which has some muscle in it—to improve himself, and to return his learning to the benefit of his colleagues.

—The over-all investment of effort (but not necessarily time) would be greater, but financial aids by scholarship and working in training on part pay would be examples of financial help. Of course, recruitment and holding would be improved by giving a professional salary.

—A great deal more specialization of teaching is to be expected, and because of this, the goal of lumping all educational personnel into one profession may become impractical. It would then become a professional decision to regard the educational enterprise as serviced by a hierarchy of professions. With this realism, professions of education would work more efficiently, separately and in concert.

The Emerging Technology of Teaching

A whole body of educational services such as audio-visual aids, machine teaching, field trips, on-the-job training, teaching aides, and student exchange could be promoted under a special head of the Branch of Education. A small percentage of all funds allotted for education—say 3 percent—would, when concentrated in development, improvement, and adoption of proven means and techniques, make enormous differences in the type and quality of experimentation. This experimental division could be just as broad and elastic as the general educational venture.

The role of teaching machines in the education of the future is worthy of special mention. Like automobiles, the telephone, and other inventions, teaching machines bid fair to develop into massive significance in many ways both large and small that cannot be foreseen. Teachers should by all means accept these machines as ways to make their work easier and more effectitve.

The critical feature of teaching machines is the programming of learning. The student learns progressively by the mistakes he makes; thus the sequence of questions must be expertly designed to be effective. The amount and kinds of knowledge which can be subjected to programming, so that the students can learn by machine, is not known. But it is apparently much wider than had been thought, as several undergraduate college courses have already been successfully programmed. Then too, there are machines or batteries of machines which administer tests, allow students to train systematically for motor skills (typing, etc.), or appear in situations which simulated "natural" situations, as in airplane flying, for example. The teachers of the future may be used chiefly in guiding the students in using machines, or in setting up new learning programs.

Operations Research and Systems Analysis

It should not be hard to convince people of the need for making education more extensive and intensive in both quality and quantity in the lives of everybody. The average person sees quite clearly a world of great complexity, and he is willing to accept education as the means to keep up with this world. He is unfortunately painfully aware that much of what goes on in schools is not functional for the education required. He cannot himself answer the questions asking what specific improvements are needed, but he is quite capable rejecting the proposals of many professional educators for these improvements.

More courses, bigger rooms, laboratories, audio-visual, and extra-curricular activities often fall short of the avowed goals. Those who want to teach students to *think*, those who want them to get along with each other, and those who want the students to be able to get out and *do* something to make a living all seem to bungle the job even when they have fairly good conditions to implement their philosophies. The basic fact is, American education is woefully inefficient as an enterprise, and any system which takes over its traditional trappings and workings gets mired in the slough of ages.

This is not to say that all other human enterprises are efficient, but the school has been peculiarly refractory to improvements of productivity. We shall not say that modern techniques can entirely overcome this inefficiency, yet we are convinced that demonstrable gains could be had immediately in innumerable areas of all kinds, and a breakthrough of radical proportions is about to begin. We must be rationally convinced of the need, however, before this revolution can take place.

Research techniques using team approaches, more sophisticated models and procedures, and "thinking brain" computers have made possible designs to maximize human effort in ways hitherto undreamed of. The means are not radically new (automation, for example, is not strictly speaking a new innovation), but the effects could be complete reconstruction of the school.

The approaches of operations research and systems analysis are a combination of the scientific method, a team of experts, and technological apparatus with which to carry on the research.

Typically, the solution of problems by OR (as it is called, and we shall lump systems analysis with it) consists of:

1) Setting up the problem or problems. Desire to maximize human effort must be present, and the program must be feasible.

2) Determining objectives. These objectives must be formulated so that the marshalling of data, environmental factors, and calculations of means can be performed.

3) A hypothesis of the needed solution to the problem must be tested by models of the problematic situation.

4) Having *verified* a theory, the analysts (those using OR to improve a system) recommend action for the decision-makers or policy-makers (those actually working in a system which to them is dissatisfying).

The formation of models in OR is crucial. Models, of course, are as old as science, but they are used with an extensiveness in this type of research as to constitute the key to the breakthrough. For a small example, consider the water system of a small town. If the lines are laid out inefficiently, the greatest number of customers cannot be reached and maintenance, costs, etc., are excessive. It is impractical to dig up the lines to look at them and consider improvements. A model of the layout of the water lines helps to suggest improvements (hypotheses) and what is more, enables a pretesting of these to a very significant degree. Models can be either iconic, which visually present some aspects of a system, as a map; analogic, in which one set of properties is translated into a similar set of properties, as a flow chart; or symbolic, designating properties of a system by symbols, for example, electricity represented by $+$ and $-$ signs.

Operations Research and Education

In many ways, as we have said, education is beyond scientific measurement. Even if the schools were run by systems analysts, any particular boy might not be up to the task of becoming a good man. But if we can show that many of the situations, means, structures, and content are inefficient in the school, we can point to some kinds of immediate maximization. As improvements are made, greater, more specialized and integrated improvements may be instituted tomorrow.

Research can begin anywhere, and at any level. The teaching of fractions in arithmetic may be studied. Having analyzed the present methods and situations, hypotheses suggested by appropriate models—of psychological, social, physical, or other designs—are tested. The general formula is: $E = f (Xi\ Yi)$ where E is effectiveness of the system; f is function; Xi is a variable(s) subject to control; and Yi is a variable(s) not subject to control. From this research the sequence of teaching fractions is altered, because more children can learn fractions more quickly and understandably in a new presentation.

451

This, of course, creates new problems. All areas of mathematics, and English, social studies, and science are brought into study as new solutions are recommended. The effectiveness of the whole program of studies becomes a research project. Operations research tells us that our curriculum is repetitive, irrelevant, and costly, and suggests streamlining and synthesizing the whole program.

Suppose that an elementary school has twenty teachers, each of whom teaches six subjects to twenty-five children in twenty different rooms. Operations research might suggest a program in which as many as 150 might be in a room at the same time, getting a social studies program on TV. Seventy-five might be taught fractions in one class by two teachers, one demonstrating and lecturing on a large board using a number of audio-visual aids. In a part of each teacher's day, she might be tutoring children singly or in classes according to her specialty.

Consider the paper work of a large university. Studying one of several hundred forms, it might be found that students spend twenty minutes trying to understand it, and in 90 percent of the cases they fail to do so. The questions on the form might never be used in the university again. Subjecting the whole system to research, OR might suggest ways to eliminate most of the present work, and make the whole system more convenient, understandable, and available at enormously less cost.

Joseph E. Hill warns that the present spate of instructional aids can lead to a grab-bag eclecticism which adds up to meaninglessness. Give a boy a bright new hammer, it has been observed, and he will find things to hit as he moves around. Give our educators clever gadgets and shiny computers and they will run these things. To make the activity with the new innovations add up to education, Hill envisions a four pronged thrust: (1) students needs a new ethic to transvaluate the old; (2) a seven-strata "educational science" curricula and research area from the physical DNA molecule to the most sophisticated cultural motif must be developed for educators; (3) the action phase implied in (2) must be implemented in the various educational areas; (4) education, government, and industry must be integrated into an ongoing development of man and his works.

EDUCATION IN AN AGE OF AUTOMATION AND CYBERNETICS*
Joseph E. Hill

Each age of significant innovation is, in essence, an age of revolution. The invention and extensive application of the machine wrought the industrial revolution. Similarly, the invention, development, and expanded use of automated and cybernetic devices will produce the revolution (and the age) of automation and cybernetics. Paradoxically, the agents that foment this revolution, properly employed, will control it for man.

Before proceeding further with the discussion of this new revolution, however, it might be wise to define the principal terms of the topic under consideration.

First, the term automation was coined circa 1949 and denotes the automatic handling, processing, controlling, and delivery of manufactured materials in industry.

Second, cybernetics is the term that denotes the science that studies the transmission and processing of information, and the control devices, in automata and organisms.

With these terms defined it should now be noted that educators,

---

* The following address was delivered at the Michigan Education Association Region VIII conference held at East Lansing, Michigan on October 7, 1966.

either as willing or unwilling participants, are embroiled in the revolution of this rapidly developing new age. And as highly important participants, it is essential that educators realize that man controls the device of automation and cybernetics, and through proper employment of these devices is capable of controlling the revolution.

To bring about this control, however, it is necessary for educators to adopt a philosophy of education that: (1) allows the establishment of a *self-adjusting system* of education that is compatible with the needs of contemporary society; and (2) avoids the pitfalls of educators being engulfed and swept along by the pervasive current of the false dynamism which is created by the employment of the artifacts and operations of automation and cybernetics without regard for long-range objectives. For example, certain educators, at the present time, are busily engaged in the extensive use of computers, not only in connection with "computer-assisted instruction," but in "computer-controlled management" as well. In most cases, those innovations are, at best, in the exploratory stages of development. But many of the poor, unfortunate innovators, hopelessly caught in the whirlpool of the false dynamism, staunchly defend their actions, and would have other educators believe that these activities are highly successful and well beyond the stage of hypothesis testing.

These observations are not made carelessly, nor are they without foundation. Witness the willingness of certain governmental agencies to approve for financial support these proposals that call for extensive use of the artifacts and operations of automation and cybernetics, with little treatment of the topic of long-range objectives.

For example, with financial encouragement from these governmental agencies, a certain institution of higher education has installed elaborate hardware. Now after approximately two years of operation, administrators are beginning to feel the real impact of their earlier decisions and actions. With a cadre of officials that had been impressed with the "need to do something, and do it now," the institution was plunged into the dangerous rapids of the false dynamism, by employing extensively the artifacts and operations of automation and cybernetics without regard for long-range objectives. Although these officials have been encouraged to continue the false dynamism, by additional financial grants, they are slowly becoming aware of the fact that their hasty actions, based upon short-range objectives, have had serious effects upon the lives and future of not only the students and faculty members of the institution, but also upon persons in many different segments of the local community.

The false dynamism is admittedly a serious problem, but one that does *not* defy solution. The problem of developing a self-adjusting system of education compatible with the needs of contemporary society, however, is almost an overwhelming one. Basically, the development of such a system depends on considerations involving the use of human resources in this new age of revolution. The problems involved in these considerations are of titanic dimension, and educators must give serious thought to the course they chart for navigating these danger-filled waters. Although we know that many different types of jobs, including the service occupations, will be available in this new age, we also know that persons of relatively low intelligence will not be employable in the intellectually demanding work programs that are developing with the expanded use of the devices of automation and cybernetics throughout society.

The shorter work day, work week, work year and, finally, working life of man coupled with longer vacation periods, an earlier retirement age, and more leisure time are all problematic matters of reality that require optimal solutions expressed in large-scale dimensions. It will not be enough to turn to art, music, and recreation for the best use of this leisure time that, incidentally, is creeping into modern man's life space at an insidiously rapid pace.

Are there solutions to these types of problems? Are there models that can be constructed, altered, and reconstructed on the basis of the needs of contemporary society, so that they may be employed to derive solutions to these enigmas? Are educators the individuals in our society who should assume leadership in this domain? Or is it the responsibility of political leaders? Or leaders in industry? What to do?

All is not gloom. There are courses of action to be pursued. One of them that appears to be feasible involves the following actions:

First, contemporary society must be made aware of, and ultimately inculcated with, ethics other than the work ethic. What commitment does this action imply for educators?

It is time that we as educators realize the necessity for de-emphasizing the work ethic in school curricula. Note well, please, the call is for *de-emphasis, not* elimination of the work ethic. If we do de-emphasize the work ethic in school curricula, what content do we insert to replace that which might be removed? Actually, there are four ethics that should be included in school curricula, and should be *inculcated* in the students. Yes, I used the word inculcated, instead of educated, for reasons that I hope will become obvious. The four ethics referred to are those of: (1) health; (2) education; (3) law; and (4) politics. The acronym for these four ethics, according to the order in which they were presented, is HELP. And their inclusion in school curricula continuously from early levels of education through the fourteenth year will provide the *help* that contemporary society needs to solve some of its most pressing problems. Please note that the action being called for here need not lead to a new form of government. Nor would this de-emphasis of the work ethic encourage communism or socialism. On the contrary. Communism, seeking a source of energy, calls upon manpower, e.g., the proletariat, and as such holds the work ethic in higher esteem than any other form of government known to modern man. Socialism also holds the work ethic in high esteem (witness the Kibutz in Israel). But a democratic free enterprise system, a modification of which we live under, shackled with manifestos, thus can call upon machines and the atom as sources of energy instead of manpower, and therefore need not emphasize the work ethic to the extent that it currently does.

In fact, if our society continues to emphasize the work ethic with groups of people that we know will not be employable in an age of automation and cybernetics, we are brewing the most powerful and dangerous type of social dynamite that can be developed. For example, we know that thirty percent of the school dropouts, ages 16-21, show I.Q.'s of less than 80, with the main cluster of the distribution located around an I.Q. of 70 (moron stage). Knowing this fact, we still insist upon bringing these young people into *Job Corps Centers*, so that they may (according to the OEO slogan) "Learn to earn."

The Economic Opportunity Act of 1964 provides for three opportunities. Paraphrased, these opportunities are: (1) the opportunity for education; (2) the opportunity for employment; and (3) the opportunity for the individual to live in decency and dignity in society.

Of the three opportunities cited, the one being given the most emphasis (almost to the neglect of the other two) is the opportunity for employment. The primary objective of the Job Corps Center is to *train* the enrollee (note the word "train") as fast as possible for a job, or occupation. When many of the trainees graduate from these centers, after a relatively short, intensive training program, they get jobs. Although most of them are capable of performing the tasks demanded by their jobs, many of them are dismissed, either because they do not possess an adequate basic education, or because they do not know how to live in decency and dignity in society. Poverty has a value structure of its own. It is *not* a condition of low income associated with a set of middle-class values. Here is the cauldron in which the social dynamite is brewed. These trainees have worked hard, and know how to perform the work tasks demanded by their jobs. As far as many of them are concerned (because time has not been taken to educate them otherwise) they have been dismissed from their jobs without reason. These persons become more disgruntled after they share their grievances with others who are unemployed, and therefore in our work ethic-oriented society these persons are not *allowed* to live in decency and dignity and, in combination, a considerable force of rebellion is generated. This force is augmented during economic recessions because there are more persons unemployed, and therefore more persons feeling guilty, because it is immoral not to work in our society regardless of the economic conditions.

It is in this context that the value of inculcating the health, education, legal, and political ethics becomes apparent. Under such circumstances the individual will derive *worth* not by *work alone*, and *first* by merely being *healthy* and perhaps contributing to the betterment of the health conditions of his community; *secondly*, by being *educated*, and for no other reason than the mere sake of being educated; *third*, by understanding his *legal rights* and *responsibilities;* and *fourth*, by participating regularly, in some fashion, in the *political* arenas of society.

A bold stride into the age of automation and cybernetics can be taken by educators, if those four ethics are included throughout the curricula of the school and, at the same time, a little less concern is shown for preparing students for "the world of work." Carrying out this curricular commitment will lead to the *second* phase of the proposed course of action.

If the educator plans to inculcate the education ethic, he must be prepared to educate the student in a fashion different from that which is currently in force. For example, schools are overcrowded under present circumstances. With the possibility of human worth being derived merely from the fact that one is educated there will be a greater demand for education than that which currently exists. How can additional numbers of students, of various age ranges, be served under conditions of limited human, financial, and facilities resources? The answer to this question, at the present time, is that they cannot be served. Thus, there is need for a new approach to education: an approach that makes possible individualized programs of instruction, while at the same time not overtaxing the financial, human, and facilities resources of the school. Is there such an approach? The *second* aspect of the proposed course of action is mainly concerned with answers to this question.

Certain educators have been engaged in the development of an architectonic schema called the "educational schemas," which provides solutions to some of the problems and explains certain phenomena in the educational establishment of the nation, and these explanations, in turn, contribute to the development of the approach in question.

At the present time the educational sciences are composed of the following seven strata: (1) the symbol and its meaning; (2) perception, i.e., cultural effects on the meanings of symbols; (3) modalities of inference; (4) neurological, electrochemical and biochemical aspects of the brain; (5) cognitive styles of students in certain educational settings; (6) teaching styles in certain educational settings; and (7) systems analysis and decision theory in educational administration and management. The development of this architectonic schema permits extensive use of the devices of automation and cybernetics, and insures the consideration of long-range objectives in determining how, when, and where these devices are to be employed in the educational establishment of the nation. The schema also contributes to the differentiation between content that rightfully belongs to, say, the behavioral sciences, and that which should be the concern of education.

The *third* step of the proposed course of action calls for the imple-

458

mentation of the educational sciences in such broad areas as: (a) teacher preparation; (b) curriculum development; (c) educational administration and management; and (d) the "support services" (e.g., counselling and guidance). The *third* phase of the action cannot be effected until educators accept the fact that, *at the present time, as professional persons, they do not have a universe of discourse to profess!* Once this fact is accepted the need for the educational sciences will become more apparent, and with the press for this approach made more evident by the continued expansion and use of automation and cybernetics in our society, educators will endeavor, to understand, develop, and then refine this much-needed professional content.

The *fourth*, and final, *step* of the proposed course of action calls for the establishment and development of a triumvirate composed of industry, i.e., labor and management, government, and education. This triumvirate will be charged with the responsibility of providing the financial and human resources necessary to implement the recommendations of educational scientists, and further develop and refine these recommendations on a broader scale than otherwise would be possible. The fact that such an organization is almost a reality at the present time, because of efforts currently being exerted in each of the sectors involved, augurs well for its future.

In closing it should be noted that the educational sciences proposed here are not envisioned as a *theory* of education. They merely form an architectonic schema that hopefully can lead to a theory of education that will be compatible with the needs and demands of society embroiled in the revolution of the age of automation and cybernetics.

The authors of the following state that we may not perhaps be able to suggest the subject matter of the curriculum of the school in 2066, but we can pose the major problems that education and man will face because of our astronomically increased technology: increased productivity in all known and many unforeseeable dimensions; increased power over the environment, including capacity to annihilate man; increased complexity of the environment with the problem of making intelligent reactions therein; and the increased leisure of man, with the need to achieve purpose and meaning in this free time.

CHALLENGES TO THE FUTURE CURRICULUM
Wilfred Smith and Sharon MacLaren

The problem of curriculum in the future might be negatively stated: no longer is there a problem of curriculum. The term has to do with learning in a relatively static environment, in which scholars in ivory towers pick and choose the tidbits of knowledge. Now, the great problems of man subsume education and curriculum; only insofar as these contribute toward the betterment of man in the new age is consideration of curriculum meaningful, rather than an exercise of mental gymnastics.

The cause is modern technology. During the past decade or so the development which has proceeded in the areas of technology and science has steadily increased until it has culminated, according to the contemporary social economist, Robert Theobald, in man's being capable of effectively controlling his environment. The implications of this concept of man's relationships to the effectiveness in his environment are complex and not altogether clear. However, these implications are likewise deserving of our acute awareness and our extensive probings. The fact is that many new needs—multiplying almost overnight—have arisen within human society which must be brought into full scope of awareness and taken in stride if they are not to create an overpowering and irreversible force directing human society to inevitable disaster or chaos.

Increased technology produces the tools; the tools are the problem. The problem cannot be dismissed by saying tools are merely means or agents of man. The structures and energy usages around us are of such great quantitative increase that a qualitative change in human environment is caused. If the tools are effectively constructed with purpose, order and control taken into consideration, the problem is in large part resolved. There will be more tools; there will be more problems. Man can play a large part in the direction in which construction proceeds only if he assumes the responsibility of awareness and control.

The overwhelming acceleration in the areas of science and technology allows no time for evolution to take place. The pressures which are brought to bear compel us to re-evaluate and deliberately revise the values and institutions which we find in our social setting. Evolutionary gradualism proceeds at too slow a pace to keep abreast of the changes of the time, and a transcendental something will not assure progress. The potential of progress is here, but it can be achieved only by actions of our wills and minds, following methods of intelligence.

It is evident that institutions of higher education now face their greatest challenge. They are now confronted with a dilemma of new dimensions. In our future society we expect to see wiser use of our capacity to generate abundance, an enlarged capacity for cherishing and developing our natural resources, attainment of happier accommodation of humans to their environment and to the fulfillment of individual human endowments. The institutions of higher education are charged with the task of initiating a curriculum to cope with the problems of this future society and to fulfill the needs of that society.

The dynamism of the age insures change, but it appears quite possible that these changes may take many directions that will not in general make sense or bring joy to the average man. Worse yet, man could become the victim of the genie he has let loose.

Man has available to him now the destructive power of approximately 650 overkill. We have recognized recently that the great weapons which have been constructed in our technological rush have eliminated war as a method of resolving international conflicts since they can culminate in the obliteration of civilization. Even the clinically psychotic recognize that annihilation is no resolution to conflict. We assume, possibly with naivete, that man will not persist in jeopardizing his species by perpetuation of the constant threat of an unthinkable war. We shall therefore have to develop social means which obviate annihilation by submitting our disputes for arbitration to universal structures and functions implementing the moral order. By opposing the powers or drives of technology unselectively man will not retain enough social energy determining how to use technology to advance human ends. Let us hope that with the vast increase in production, however, there will be a concomitant increase in control and understanding and that society, with direction from educational institutions, will initiate the values and structures which insure that technological and scientific advancement converge upon the advancement of humanity.

Education must meet the challenge of the age. We cannot go back, and we cannot remain as we are. We cannot preserve our present industrial-age values nor return to the simple values of the agricultural era. The values of this new era, the Cybernetic Era, are unique. In the future we are going to value those who can think in all fields, who can function as specialists and react to all that society means at the same time. The concept of the liberally educated man will be of one who positively contributes to a very complex and dynamic society.

If the anticipated end in the educational system is to turn out those individuals who can think and function in a wide area of circumstances the curriculum will have to be designed to accomplish such ends and the subject areas will be established with this purpose in mind, since curriculum is ultimately determined by the values which society feels necessary and acceptable for transmission. It has been stated, and there is a great deal of evidence to support it, that revising a curriculum is like moving a cemetery. A paradox is in evidence. In the United States, land of plenty, about a third of the population live in cyclic poverty. Why should not consumer goods be available to all in need, and who should determine which individuals should receive which goods?

The combination of increased number of academics and information made available by the computer insures that there is much more information available than any individual or human group can possibly absorb or even encounter through their sensitivities. The relative nature of facts implies the usefulness of preoccupation with them. Which of the facts available are those most valuable in the storehouse of an individual's knowledge?

Physiological and psychological manipulations have effectively altered human life expectancy and have introduced a new prospectus for life, based on vastly increased organic controls and functions. The implications of this obvious encounter for human society are extremely complicated and upsetting to the present social system.

The need is to constructively incorporate these problems, or powers, as you wish, into the future curriculum since these will undoubtedly have an effect on human values and therefore upon human culture. This is the task of education.

In the formation of the future curriculum most certainly the problems of concern to society and educators are those that arise from man's new relationships to his environment, namely: man's capacity to annihilate himself; man's virtually unlimited productive powers; man's unlimited information capacity; and man's leisure time, with the perennial challenge of building a purposive life of justice, efficiency and creativity, and beauty.

RELATED READINGS

Butler, J. Donald. *Four Philosophies and Their Practice in Education and Religion.* New York: Harper & Brothers, 1957.

Childs, John L. *American Pragmatism and Education.* New York: Henry Holt & Co., Inc., 1956.

Dawson, Howard A. "A Blueprint for Progress," *Phi Delta Kappan*, XXXVI (1955), 55-62.

Fitzpatrick, E. A. "American Education, 1891-1956," *American School Board Journal*, CXXXII (March, 1956), 46-54.

Gilchrist, Robert S. "Promising Practices in Education," *Phi Delta Kappan*, XLI (1960), 208-11, 269-74.

Hansen, Arnold S. "New Directions to American Education," *Phi Delta Kappan*, XXXVI (1955), 153-64.

Huxley, Aldous. *Brave New World.* New York: Harper & Brothers, 1932.

———. *Brave New World Revisited.* New York: Harper & Brothers, 1958.

Jacob, Philip E. *Changing Values in College.* New York: Harper & Brothers, 1957.

Meisel, James H. *The Myth of the Ruling Class.* Ann Arbor: The University of Michigan Press, 1958.

Kandel, I. L. *The New Era in Education: A Comparative View.* Boston: Houghton Mifflin Co., 1955.

Moehiman, Arthur H. "Fifty Years of Educational Thought," *Phi Delta Kappan*, XXXVII (1956), 131-40.

Murphy, Gardener. *Human Potentialities.* New York: Basic Books, Inc., 1958.

Orwell, George. *1984.* New York: Harcourt, Brace & Co., 1949.

Smith, Huston. *The Purposes of Higher Education*. New York: Harper & Brothers, 1955.

Ulich, Robert. "Some Recent Tendencies in Educational Philosophy," *School and Society*, XXCIII (January 21, 1956), 26-30.

Van Winkle, Harold. "Attitudes Toward Lay Participation," *Phi Delta Kappan*, XXXVIII (1957), 70-72.

———. "Lay Participation in School Affairs," *Phi Delta Kappan*, XXXVIII (1957), 110-11.

Woodring, Paul. *Let's Talk Sense About Our Schools*. New York: McGraw-Hill Book Co., 1953.

Index

465

International Geophysical Year, 45
IPAT, 173
I. Q., 173, 456
I. T. V. See Educational TV

Jencks, Christopher, 191
Job Corps, 222, 456
Jobs, 222
John, Vera, 105

Kennedy, Renwick C., 271
Kerber, August, 64, 127, 161, 212, 325, 365, 400
Kibbutz, education in, 200-5, 456
King, Edith, 104
Kornhauser, Arthur, 249

Lambert, Hazel M., 122
Language, the child's, 185
Learning explosion, 18
Leatherman, Roger L., 18
Lieberman, Myron, 312, 427
Library Resources, 363
Linton, Thomas, 170, 171-80
Localism, 357
Local school district, 371
Local Trade Union of Teachers, 403
Loebl, David H., 200
Loyalty Oaths, 235, 257, 277, *passim*
Lynd, Albert, 390

McAulay, J. D., 122
Mc Kee, John, 217
MacLaren, Sharon, 460

Marxist-Leninist principles, 404
Mass culture, 48-71, *passim*; functions of, 64
Mentally retarded, 212
Mill, John Stuart, 237
Miller, Herman, 153
Mobilization For Youth (MFY), 195-97
Modern education, 390
Moral and spiritual values in education, 76-102, *passim*
Mores, 64
Moynihan, Daniel P., 155, 152
Mumford, Lewis, 24

National Association of Education Broadcasters, 13, 115
National Citizens Committee for Educational TV, 56
National Compendium of Television, 63

National Council of Teachers of English, 187
National Education Association, 118, 194-95
Neff, Frederic C., 87
Negro, 141-68, 366
Negro schools, 141-50
Negro urban family, 150
Noar, Gertrude, 126
Northern schools, 141-50

Olszewski, Marie, 58
Operations research, 449, *passim*
Oral communication, 181
Organized interests and social power, 299
Overpopulation, 35

Parent Teacher Association, 312-15
Parochial schools, 282-95; and shared time, 282
Peabody Picture Vocabulary Test (PPVT), 105
Perry, Ralph Barton, 131
Pollock, Thomas, 181
Population explosion, 33-47, 357, 443
Poverty, 457
Preparation of Teachers, 417-35, *passim*
Private schools. See Parochial schools
Production, U. S. output of, 41
Professional negotiations, 429
Protestantism, 89
Public schools. See schools

Racial Gap, 141-68
Rafferty, Max, 315
Religion, Champaign Council, 87, 282-95
Reprint Revolution, 56
Retarded, 212
Ribicoff, Abraham, 285
Riesman, David, 119
Riot, 161-62; Detroit, 156; Newark, 155
Rosenberg, Bernard, 51
Russian education, 388, 403-18, *passim*
Ryan, William, 152

Sarnoff, Robert W., 60
School, curriculum, 127; district, 371; revenue sources, 338; neighborhood, 365
School to Aid Youth (STAY), 198
Schoolboards, 310
Schools, centralization, 370; financing, 333-54; assessment of, 383-418, *pas-*

The manuscript was prepared for publication by Ralph Busick. The book was designed by Richard Kinney and Richard Berube. The text type face is Linotype Granjon, designed in 1924 by George W. Jones, based on a face originally cut by Claude Garamond in the 16th century. The display face is Weiss Roman designed by E. R. Weiss and cut by Bauer in 1926.

This book was printed on Allied Paper Company's 50 lb. Paperback Book paper. The soft cover edition of this book was bound in Riegal Paper Company's Carolina Cover and the hard cover edition was bound in Joanna Mills Natullin over boards. This book was manufactured in the United States of America.